WILDLIFE WATCHING
In the Slow Lane

THE NATURE DIARY OF AN OCTOGENARIAN

Dr. Mary E Gillham, MBE

ryelands

First published in Great Britain in 2009

Copyright © Dr Mary E. Gilham 2009

Front Cover: *Black Bryony, Blue Tits and Rose Hips*
Back Cover: *Holly Blue, Orange Tip and Speckled Wood*

All rights reserved. No part of this publication may be reproduced, stored in a retrieval system, or transmitted in any form or by any means without the prior permission of the copyright holder.

British Library Cataloguing-in-Publication Data
A CIP record for this title is available from the British Library

ISBN 978 1 906551 18 6

RYELANDS
Halsgrove House,
Ryelands Industrial Estate,
Bagley Road, Wellington, Somerset TA21 9PZ
Tel: 01823 653777   Fax: 01823 216796
email: sales@halsgrove.com

Part of the Halsgrove group of companies
Information on all Halsgrove titles is available at: www.halsgrove.com

Printed and bound by Short Run Press, Exeter

Contents

	Prologue	6
	Introduction	8
1.	Moving Out and Moving In	10
2.	Letting Go the Old and Embracing the New	17
3.	The Insidious March of Urbanisation	22
4.	I Entertain. Barry and Forest Farm	28
5.	More Walks Abroad	35
6.	Lecturing at Cowbridge and Castle Viewing at Fonmon	40
7.	Garden Centres and Wild Daffodils	45
8.	The London Visit	50
9.	Easter 2008, Sully, Swanbridge and Merthyr Tydfil	58
10.	Gwaelod, the Wenallt and Radyr Golf Course	67
11.	Flatholm Society, Anomalous Spring and Riverside Walk	76
12.	Insole Court, Llanelli Waterfront and the Welsh Botanic Gardens	86
13.	Danescourt, Fox, Rabbits and the Taff at Radyr	93
14.	Local Ramblings, A squirrel Family and Cwm Nofydd	102
15.	Lamby lake, Cors Crychydd Canal and Floral Tributes	111
16.	Ledbury and Eastnor Castle, Roy Noble, Blackweir and the Old Cardiff Canal	119
17.	Afoot in the County Park and River Walk to Tongwynlais	126
18.	Tyntesfield near Bristol, Whitsun Weather and Picton Castle, Pembroke	135
19.	Picton Saltmarsh, Lockley Lodge, Monk Haven, Sandy Haven and Little Haven	143
20.	Brynberian, Whitesands Bay, St. Davids, Llanerchaeron and Newport	152
21.	Ty Canol Wood, Pembs., Pughs and other Local Gardens	164
22.	Radyr Woods in Summer, Coryton Roundabout and Wenvoe Limestone	172
23.	Brecon Mountain Railway, Midsummer Day and Dyffryn Gardens	182
24.	A "Townee" Guest, Lewis Merthyr Colliery, Penrhys, Rhondda and Cynheidre Railway Project, Llanelli	194

25. Rhymney Mouth, Cardiff Bay and Cosmeston 204
26. Cathedral Precincts, Llandaff Weir, Stream by Morganstown Motte and Gelynys Fruit Farm 213
27. Neath Valley, Blaengwrach Garden and Melincourt Falls, Bats, Coco-de-mer, Lily Pools and Bird Hides 222
28. Pembroke Waterfront, Stackpole National Nature Reserve & Bosherston Lakes 233
29. Cosmeston Tour with Warden and Pentyrch Treasures with CCW Personnel 241
30. The South Flank of the Little Garth and Home Territory 251
31. Aberthaw, Gileston and Llantwit 260
32. Radyr Farmland, Taffs Well Recreation Ground and Caerphilly Garden Centre 270
33. Pisgodlyn Mawr, the Big Fish Pond, and Brynteg Home Front 279
34. Porthkerry, Rhoose Point Quarries and Font-y-gary 288
35. Forest Farm Wetlands and Chestnut Coppice from Tree Planting to Fungal Decay 298
36. St. Fagan's Folk Museum, Tongwynlais, Fallen Tree and Himalayan Balsam 308
37. South Devon: Torquay, Paignton and Berry Head 319
38. Radyr Woods and Shunting Yards, Forest Farm Floods, Fruit and Fungi 328
39. The South Wales Coalfield, Forestry and Hill Farms 337
40. Ebbw Vale Owl Sanctuary and More Conker-eating Squirrels 347
41. Ogmore-by-Sea and Southerndown 355
42. From Weir to Canal, Gwaelod-y-Garth and Fforest Fawr 362
43. Cefn-On Gardens, Walterston, Font-y-Gary and Merthyr Mawr Dunes 371
44. Home Front, Radyr Farm, Pant-Tawel and Peterstone-super-Ely 382
45. The Salmon Run, Llandaff Weir, Roath Gardens and Lake 392
46. Lavernock Point Nature Reserve and Gun Emplacements 403
47. Boverton, Summerhouse Point Iron Age Fort, Limperts Bay and Sea Watch Centre 411
48. The Onset of Winter, Cold Front, Bewick Swans, Autumn Fungi and Howardian Dormice 420

List of illustrations 431

By The Same Author

Sea Bird Islands

Sea-Birds, Museum Press, London, 1963
A Naturalist in New Zealand, Museum Press London and Reeds, New Zealand, 1966
Sub-Antarctic Sanctuary, Summer on MacQuarie Island, Gollancz & Reeds, 1967
Islands of the Trade Winds, an Indian Ocean Odyssey, Minerva Press, London, 1999
Island Hopping in Tasmania's Roaring Forties, Stockwell, Devon, 2000
Memories of Welsh Islands, Dinefwr, Wales, 2004
Salt Wind from the Cape, South Africa, Lazy Cat, Cardiff, 2005
A Naturalist on Lundy, Halsgrove, Somerset, 2007
This Island Life, Halsgrove, Somerset. 2007
Exploring the Inner Hebrides, Halsgrove, Somerset, 2008

Welsh Countryside

The Natural History of Gower. Edns. 1 & 2, Browns, Wales, 1977 & 1979
Swansea Bay's Green Mantle, Browns, 1982
Glamorgan Heritage Coast, I. Sand Dunes, South Glamorgan Co. Ccl. 1987
II. Rivers, Glamorgan Wildlife Trust, 1989
III. Limestone Downs, Glam. Wildlife Trust, 1991
IV. Coastal Downs, Glam. Wildlife Trust, 1993
V. Cliffs and Beaches, Glam. Wildlife Trust, 1994
The Garth Countryside, Part of Cardiff's Green Mantle, Lazy Cat, Cardiff, 2001
A Natural History of Cardiff. Exploring Along the River Taff, Lazy Cat, 2002
A Natural History of Cardiff. Exploring Along the Rhymney and Roath, Dinefwr, 2006

Prologue

Accounts of the plant collectors and botanists of earlier centuries usually tell of a passion for plants developed during childhood. Like those pioneers, I started in a small way quite early, pressing specimens of plants gathered on 'Saturday rides' and camping holidays.

The first illustrated Nature Diary that I can find in my depleted archives dates from 1935. At the end of that year I attained the coveted age of fourteen - not too young to record unconsidered trifles, as so famously demonstrated by Ann Frank a decade later.

Adolescence, like retirement, allows time to browse, explore, make new discoveries and develop new interests. It became second nature to me to 'write things up' and make crude sketches when away from home.

Happily I was granted opportunity in middle life to pursue my interests as a professional. There were few new garden species left to discover for the Western World but plenty that was new and exciting to me. The question of "Why?" had superceded that of "What?"

I considered plants in context, bringing back colour slides rather than specimens to introduce my findings to others, the satisfaction of spreading the knowledge of these natural systems as satisfying as the initial discoveries. Field botanists of the twentieth century were learning how plants interracted with one another, the animals that depended on them and the geological and physical factors that determined their growth forms and very presence.

By good fortune I chose to study islands populated by colonial seabirds. Around Britain's coast I worked among thrift and sea campion grazed by rabbits, trampled and manured by puffins and battered by salt-laden gales.

In New Zealand and Australia, thousand-strong colonies of shearwaters excavated burrows, as in Britain, and there were penguins instead of auks. Cormorants, gannets, gulls and terns still made heavy inroads into the vegetation, Mesembryanthemums and salt-hardy shrubs in this terrain.

On Antarctic islands hosts of penguins augmented by albatrosses trampled such vegetation as could tolerate the climate and hordes of sea elephants wreaked havoc among the tussocks of Poa grass.

Indian ocean islands of Seychelles granite and coral atolls opened up different avenues. Boobies, frigate birds and noddies nested in trees above belligerent bosun birds and hundreds of lumbering giant tortoises.

South Africa and its offshore islands had provided many of Britain's best-loved garden and greenhouse plants, from red-hot pokers to bird of paradise flowers. Regal Arum lilies romped around sea-bird colonies there stimulated by guano and so common as to be referred to as 'pigweed'. Elsewhere the accumulated nutrients from gannets and cormorants were being harvested to boost domestic crops.

When the New World split away from the Old on its sliding continental plate it took many of our plant species and fashioned them to suit the new environment. Familiar genera of Arctic and Alpine plants that we admire in Europe turn up again in the Rockies and New England. "Adapt or Perish" has proved a good maxim to live by.

The nitty gritty of academic field recordings were followed by more readable accounts of my travels. Though so much more exciting than the familiar world of everyday, these were of little relevance or interest to the average reader. This present record of the small and local in the world on our doorstep may touch a more appropriate homely chord, bringing my browsings back full circle to those in the local parks and countryside of the Home Counties in my formative years.

Much of my later working life was spent in Cardiff, but I chose to live beyond the city's limits until the latter part of my eighties, when I compromised by moving in beside one of the capital's most versatile country parks on the coastal plain between two northern suburbs.

Here I could continue my local wanderings like anyone else with time on their hands in retirement. Features formerly ignored as commonplace, can yield unsuspected intricacies and adaptations with the help of hand lens and binoculars.

What a waste to ignore so much that can be enjoyed without climbing mountains or scrambling over cliffs. Perhaps this diffuse account of local peregrinations will help to stimulate others with enquiring minds to embellish their strolls.

Introduction

At my eightieth birthday party in 2001 my colleagues had presented me with a small commemorative tome entitled "The First Eighty Years". From nought to twenty years I had been "learning how", for the next twenty "doing", often in some of the world's remoter corners. From forty to sixty six I was "talking about it" as a lecturer in Cardiff University's Adult Education Department and from sixty six to eighty six "writing about it" in a series of natural history and travel books. So what then?

It was forty five years since I had bought my first permanent home in 1963, after a life lived largely 'in a suitcase'. My stone cottage, its deeds going back to 1837, clung to the lower slopes of the Great Garth Mountain at Gwaelod-y-Garth in South Wales and was becoming something of a liability. I feared I would have to move while I was still capable.

This achieved, I decided to keep a chatty day to day journal of my new, more restricted life style, which included visits to natural history sites, observing how much plant and animal life was still to be seen in the greener corners of our increasingly suburban world. The journal covers the move - from spacious cottage, outhouses and gardens to more restricted quarters closer to people, shops and other amenities.

With my sights trained on remote offshore islands, I had neglected the "here and now" in recent years. Since I first knew them, the local canal had been cleared out and reinstated to attain SSSI status, bald slag tips had greened over with heather, fescue and birch, old quarries had been re-invented as country parks and landfill sites as nature reserves. The River Taff, that formerly flowed black with coal dust, now supported salmon, trout, dippers and even the occasional otter.

There was, inevitably a downside in the inexorable spread of bricks, mortar and concrete, but the new housing estates with their neatly grassed 'play areas' are pleasanter to live in than the old miners' cottages with 'the mountain' at their back. Both aspects of change have been explored in everyday language as I mooch through out-of-the-way corners seeing what is still about. Consideration of living things in their diverse geological settings can afford food for thought, as well as enjoyment, and a welcome respite from the frenetic bustle of the computerised world.

I have my memories and photographic records of penguins and sea

INTRODUCTION

elephants, coral reefs and giant tortoises, kangaroos and kookaburras and flocks of sooty shearwaters many thousands strong rafting on turbulent seas.

There is a conspiracy of silence about age, arising from its negative aspects. It need not be so. Nature's edict "Adapt or perish" is as true for humans as for wildlife in this rapidly changing world. Our immediate environment affects our moods, wellbeing and stress levels most closely. It is pointless to retire enwrapped in a wet blanket of nostalgia and regret. We can still live enquiringly, with a lively curiosity and interest during our final years.

In lowering my sights to pay more attention to the everyday landscape within easy reach, I have been amply compensated. This is a book to be dipped into at random, locations indicated in chapter headings for ease of reference.

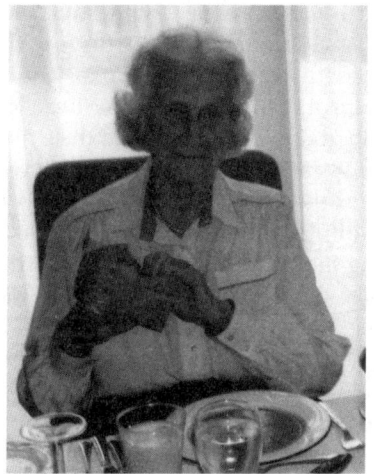

Mary E. Gillham
January 2009

CHAPTER 1

Moving Out And Moving In

The advancing years crept up insidiously, almost unnoticed, until I realised that the stone stairways in my terraced gardens had become more awkward when I was burdened with lawn mower or bags of wet compost. Ingress and egress from the garage drive to the steep, 'unadopted' mountain road seemed to wax more complex and the seventeen steps between kitchen and car more arduous when I was loaded with shopping or buckets of soil washed down the lane onto the drive during heavy rain.

The three village shops and the post office which were flourishing when I moved in to Gwaelod-y-Garth had all been closed long since. This was not the most suitable of places to live if I had to give up driving.

I had been watching the building of a new McCarthy and Stone "Retirement Home" on a leafy site at Radyr a few miles to the south - beyond the Taff Gorge through the Border Ridges which delimited the coastal plain. At the age of eighty six, I felt the time was ripe for a move.

The buying and selling of houses was at a low ebb in 2008, with mortgages hard to come by, but I had a buyer ready and able to move in when I moved out and as delighted to take over stewardship of the premises as I had been forty five years before. Much would have to be discarded in the move to smaller premises, but there was a communal garden and a fine view through the Taff Gorge to the mountains beyond. Squirrels and long-tailed tits shared the facilities of the lime tree opposite my window, on the brink where the lawn dropped away to the river far below and there were local walks in plenty.

As fit as anyone of my vintage can expect to be in December 2007, I felt that the trauma to be tackled during the necessary down-grading squeeze must be faced before the final rot set in. The problem was, how to sort the accoutrements acquired during forty five years of residence in six sizeable rooms plus kitchen, scullery, bathroom, cat annexe, outside loo, spacious garage and garden shed into two not particularly capacious rooms augmented only by kitchen, bathroom and two small annexes.

Instead of stepping out into floriferous gardens with crazy stone paths and rockeries, cherished over decades by my own muddy hands, I looked down from a balcony to a sloping flower bed shared with a score of others. The way between was along a carpeted corridor. Where does one wash the mud off one's boots with only a balcony, or feed the birds without being accused of attracting rats?

No matter. What is to be must be. My Christmas house guest was cancelled and I moved into a cluttered life style of general pandemonium, spiced by finds of objects I had not set eyes on for decades. The cliche, "If you havent used it during the past few years you don't need it" had never cut ice with me. "Things" have a way of becoming old and worthless and then antique and valuable.

Personal treasures were unearthed. A motley collection from my teens included life-saving medals and school magazine articles, Girl Guide proficiency badges and gold cords. These were interleaved with wartime identity card (BBAD 49 3) in its neat green case, and Women's Land Army insignia, along with highlights of days as a university student and junior lecturer. Passport photographs taken over three quarters of a century tell their own story of the passing of the years.

A minor leg injury acquired battling with trash bins and involving an ambulance trip to hospital a week before Christmas didn't help, but friends rallied round to fuel the treadmill of packing and stacking and of transport to other outlets. First and foremost, as always over recent years, was my printer and handyman friend Clive Thomas, helped now by his wife Lynne. They were there with moral and practical support at both the packing and the unpacking stages.

Robert Hubbard commuted from Monknash on the coast, bringing collapsible plastic book crates which proved invaluable. Naturalist friends Andy and Rhian Kendall carted away box after box of books, displaying prodigious physical strength in their transport from Cottage to Museum or appropriate storage and dispersal points.

The South Wales Archives Department made two journeys to salvage technical data encompassed in twenty or so Eastlight files and metal index card trays of coloured slides recording past natural communities. They conjured up a place to store them and a person to convert my old fashioned ramblings into the succinct computer data required by this modern age.

Madeline Beswick graduated from acquaintance to friend as she wrapped and packed, sieved and sorted and ferreted out the rear entrances to the Sally Army, Oxfam and other like emporia.

Monetary transactions proceeded apace, or as fast as can be expected where solicitors are involved. No estate agent was necessary, with buyers anxious to move in as soon as I moved out. These changed from little known neighbours to good friends during the course of the next few months.

As owners of the Inn, whose car park adjoined my lower garden, they helped in many different ways and were lavish with contributions of hot food, either carried up the lane under suitable cover or served by a cosy wood fire in the premises below. Victuals forthcoming included Christmas fare to save me from dining alone.

Their names, appropriately are Richard and Barbara or Ritchie and Babs Angell. After several years shacked up in a small annexe of the pub and a 'caravan' on Gower, they were anxious to move in to a more permanent home beyond the Escallonia, Hebe, Cistus and Hypericum bushes laced with everlasting pea that separated the two properties.

The actual move was deferred to the 25th January 2008 to accommodate a lecture I was giving in Cardiff on the 23rd, but my mover, Paul "Packer", who charged nigh on £700.00, only succeeded in packing the lorry on the first day. Moving in was delayed till the morrow.

This left me in limbo with nowhere to sleep. Three of my four beds, stripped to the mattress cover, were being left behind, so the incomers supplied me with bedding and tea making equipment, a few books to while away the evening hours - as if I had not seen enough books lately to last me a lifetime - and a hot meal before the 'troops' dispersed. I gazed my, almost, last on bare, cobwebby walls exposed by departed furnishings, with a salvaged vessel of water on the floor beside me to slake my thirst during the hours of darkness. A toasted cheese and cappuccino pub breakfast emphasised the feeling that I was on holiday, but, far from it.

It was the garden rather than the house that I was to miss most. As early as mid January, Robert and I had had difficulty walking on the upper lawn without trampling the masses of pale mauve, early flowering crocuses. A week later the hellebores were at prime, deep red ones and creamy white streaked with red, the circlet of green petals converted into nectaries offering nectar to an atmosphere devoid of pollenating insects - the clouds of winter gnats the only ones abroad so early in the year.

Backing out of the drive to get my M O T done (car licence and road tax, like so much else, cropping up in these busy days) I spotted a few crimson Kaffir lilies, offset by the contrasting blue of creeping Campanulas. My *Viburnum bodnantii*, although flowering all summer, continued to do so all winter and on into spring, vying with the winter jasmin and, of all the unexpecteds, purple star of the veldt from South Africa and perennial Erysimum wallflowers from the Canary Islands.

MOVING OUT AND MOVING IN

My last few weeks in this hill country of the South Wales Coalfield north of the Taff Gorge was punctuated by business trips to Cardiff. The solicitor overseeing the move on my behalf was based a fair step beyond Queen Street Station, with more steps to another solicitor "unknown to both parties" to "swear by repeating after me". I had to add "If this document is similar to the one I read earlier". (The only time that dour man managed to smile). The bank manager had his say, the auctioneer, my valuer and the buyer's surveyor - also those responsible for selling me my new apartment.

Clive and I, with the aid of a roll of graph paper passed on to his little daughter by my father in 1928, measured rooms and furniture, juggling a quart into a pint pot as my old mother used to say. (Who said such bric a brac would never be called into use?). I chose carpet, curtains and fire place and admired the view from my abode to be. This was not so very different from the one I had enjoyed through the years.

Formerly I had looked across the Taff Valley from west to east, spying Caerphilly Mountain between Graig-yr-allt to the north and Fforest Fawr with Castell Coch to the south. Now I looked up the valley through the gorge, to see the Graig framed by the Little Garth to the west and Fforest Fawr to the east, with the rounded bulk of Mynydd Meio and distant hilltop wind vanes beyond. The precipitous slopes were bathed in sunshine in the morning as well as the afternoon from this angle, but my northerly orientated balcony remained in shade. The lights which twinkled at night from the valley between were those of Whitchurch and Tongwynlais instead of Taffs Well and Glan-y-Llyn.

At last the gas, electricity and water metres were read, by buyer and seller together, keys changed hands and we took the cars south to await the moving van. Wait we did. Paul's mate had to do a paper round on his bike first and allow a spell for recuperation. Chaotic, yes, but as those encountered in my new premises pointed out "We've all been through it". Many were couples from family homes, their offspring flown, no doubt leaving most of their childhood paraphernalia behind. I hadn't a leg to stand on when it came to complaining.

Flat state of the art television and computer screens were bought in the new shopping complex at Talbot Green and substituted for the old bulky ones to save a modicum of space. Cosy niches were found for nests of tables and stools, slide projector and screen among larger items. At least half the residue of a lifetime's collection of colour slides were given sanctuary under the bed and weather-worthy items more suited to scullery or shed were banished to the balcony with the garden chair and tables. Problems such as where to dispose of mud from walking boots and spatter black polish during shoe cleaning operations remained temporarily unsolved.

My front door, through which the postman pushed his daily contribution, opened onto a carpeted corridor. Stepping from kitchen tiles to pennant sandstone path in my past life I had been wont to say "I can't imagine life without gumboots". Sadly gumboots were now relegated to the car boot with walking sticks and balaclavas.

I had a sneaking inner feeling that I came to be regarded as 'The new girl on the block who appears in slacks and hiking boots' by my elegant lady neighbours in their neatly pleated skirts, nylons and dainty footwear. Fortunately the men clung to more practical garb.

Although conceived since the start of the new millennium, the forecourt provided parking space for only eighteen cars and eighteen of the residents owned cars, although the building was only about two thirds full as yet. This meant that visitors and helpers had to park elsewhere - and not on the steep one way street that bounded the site- after dropping off timber and carpentry equipment to make the rooms habitable. The idea of even a single shelf, built-in cupboard or simple hook to hang a wet mac on had not penetrated the consciousness of the architects who designed these so-called 'luxury apartments', let alone the inclusion of a good old fashioned picture rail.

Nevertheless, under Clive's expert hands, wall cabinets and pictures were hung with the aid of various winged and flanged screws and rawplugs to hold onto the insubstantial wall linings. Stalwart shelves were erected and neat rows of books stacked jubilantly in size order were rearranged in far from neat rows, more usefully according to subject matter.

Painfully slowly spaces were found for clerical paraphernalia, staplers, punches, pens and pencils, paper clips and rubber bands, notepaper and envelopes, measuring tapes and sewing equipment, light bulbs and plugs and the wherewithal for an ultimate move to water colour painting. Remembering where everything had been put posed a long term problem.

No features of the bath pandered to the foibles of the elderly. It was up, over and in or not at all. At this stage most of the elderly resort to the shower, but nothing was gained by that here. That adequate piece of equipment was at the far end of the bath behind a half length glass screen swinging out on hinges, delicate manoeuvres necessary to ensure a waterproof joint.

It took several weeks to learn how to lower myself onto the child-sized lavatory pan - so much lower than the average chair and reminiscent of those 'knees full bend' and 'bunny jumping' days of our youth. Did the installers imagine us as dwarfs? The answer was 'No'.

The house manager, urging everyone at one of the weekly gatherings to "Enjoy the beautiful show of daffodils in the back garden", failed to realise that none but the taller of the men could reach over the top of the protective wooden gates to undo the bolts on the inside. His only reference to these was "Be sure to shoot the bolts when you come out, for security reasons." He dismissed the suggestion of a couple of rocks to stand on when reaching over. "What, help the vandals?" He ignored the athleticism of the average vandal. I, at least, could enjoy some of the flowers from my balcony. Fair, play, the gates were unlocked as the spring advanced, and, hopefully, for the summer.

In addition I was acquiring a pleasant collection nearer at hand, welcoming me into my new home or congratulating me on a recent award. There were presentation bouquets from the Cardiff and Merthyr Naturalists' Societies and from friends and callers, including the buyers of my old premises. Those offerings with their roots still in a little bit of the mother earth that I missed so sorely, were still blooming gaily a couple of months and more later - Cyclamen, Primulas, Kalanchoe and Begonia among them.

There was much, too, in Brynteg's front garden more accessible for February viewing. Blue Anemones, lesser periwinkles, Rosemary, multi-coloured crocuses, polyanthus, yellow spurge and exquisitely small tête-á-tête daffodils.

Shoots broken from potted mottle-leaved Begonia needed to be replanted. The question was, In what? Back doors to the garden were fitted with high security alarms, there was no sneaking out in private. I compromised by planting them in wet newspaper!

When I eventually gained access to the great out-of-doors, I wandered into the lowest, uncultivated corner where the ground was strewn with the cores of pine cones denuded of their scales by squirrels probing for the seeds. Among the wind severed twigs with bushy tufts of long needles was a single molehill. I returned with trowel and plant pot and scooped it up triumphantly. Another basic problem solved.

Indoor appliances such as washing machines and electric ovens were more difficult to come to terms with - mainly because the manufacturers concoct a range of obscure symbols instead of useful little words like 'on' and 'off'. The washing machines and tumble driers available for use in the laundry presented problems. There were dials here, none of those useful two lettered words. I learned the hard way to set a dial on the streak of lightning, then, when the noise stopped, half an hour or so later, to re-set it on the pattern of a univalve mollusc, to flip some of the water out before transferring to the drier.

The range of options offered did not help. What was the difference between "start pause" and "delayed start", neither mentioned in the file of instructions? Why would I want a "pre-wash" button and what did the flashing lights on the options button signify? Finally it usually rumbled into life, but even when the turmoil within ceased it was not possible to open the door while it took three minutes to recover from its exertions.

The kitchen sink was as meagre as the loo. My new rectangular washing up bowl fitted exactly - so exactly that there was not even a clear half inch to empty the teapot dregs alongside, and it needed a contortionist to extricate the bowl from under the over-arching tap or empty it of its contents. The smallest bowl obtainable was only just manipulable, but the cause of many spillages and much bad language. Oh for the lavish dimensions of that old cottage where the builders were not so cheese paring as the moderns!

I was two months into my tenure when the couple who had just moved in to number seven next door asked for help in getting a ready made quiche warmed up in the electric oven. Having removed something similar from my oven the day before, stone cold after a supposed half hour of fan assisted cooking, I was not much help. We did our best, manipulating all the dials and switches, but to no avail.

Rita was brought in from number fifteen across the corridor. She was a past mistress at producing casseroles and toasted cheese, the last on the grill that had blackened my last offering on top and left the rest soggily raw. No luck! We all longed for the sight of those lovely blue and yellow flames of North Sea gas, telling us not only that the oven was alight, but how much heat was being produced.

Gordon was brought in from along the corridor. After considering a number of possibilities, he wondered why there was no red light where it should be. He moved a remote wall switch to no effect, then moved it back again and the light popped on. "These electrical gadgets need a fillip like that sometimes." Maybe they'd get their quiche after all, even though they had to keep opening the oven door to see if any heat was being generated. No red signals here. The only sign of life was the noise of the revolving fan, which didn't help, as it was as likely to blow cold air around as hot.

Rita's and my combined efforts failed to infuse any life into my oven. Fortunately I was going to poach salmon and cook vegetables on the open hot plate, where the warmth could be detected by feel if not sight, as the initial red glow was transitory only. Gordon was called in again. He indicated the digital clock, which both of us had ignored tinkering with. It was telling the wrong time anyway. Apparently it was a vital part of the procedure. A button pressed changed the time to 00.00. Another pair of buttons pressed brought up a few figures. "It doesn't matter what the clock says, it just has to say something before the heat comes on." Maybe it was a timer. I resolved to put it on a time hours hence to stop it cutting off any heat obtained and leaving me with half cooked victuals.

CHAPTER 2

Letting Go The Old and Embracing The New

I missed my informal but carefully tended garden sorely. Terraced neatly into the eastern flank of the Garth Mountain, the various levels were linked by stone stairways, the bounding and dissecting walls draped with clipped ivy.

I had planted the gnarled Bramley in the upper lawn as an aspiring two-year-old forty four years before and had grown up with it. 2007's harvest had been prolific and was stored in the shed, most fruits individually wrapped in wooden boxes, while my new freezer was well stocked with the less viable windfalls, pushed off the tree by foraging jackdaws early in the season.

The skins were blemished, as always, making them quite unsalable, but, as I have always peeled apples, that worried me not at all. First class cookers, they were also as sweet as Coxes when the skins became flushed with pink. They formed the mainstay of my winter salads, as I am no fan of lettuce and the other green leaves that have swamped the market recently and usually occupy half the plate when one orders a hot meal in a cafe. I returned to Gwaelod at intervals until just after Easter to collect sufficient for 'the apple a day that kept the doctor away' - a tasty addition to my cornflakes and muesli.

My other, sparser legacies consisted of frozen damsons, gooseberries, black currants and raspberries - these more valuable since the elderly couple owning the only greengrocer's shop in Radyr had given up in the autumn, leaving empty premises. The grocers, not equipped to weigh individual items, could only sell fruit and vegetables pre-wrapped in large packs unsuitable for loners.

I welcomed the opportunity to roam in my old garden at will whenever I chose, but one of my purposes in so doing - to keep in touch with the three feral pussy cats who had accepted my hospitality throughout the last ten years, was not to be.

This tribe of undersized felines had been accepted as part of the establishment by the new owner and was being fed even more lavishly than before, but life had changed fundamentally for them. All were neutered soon after arrival and a fourth intruder was bullied until he made off so they were not troubled by Toms. But the two large, friendly dogs, which they had tolerated as near neighbours were now uncomfortably close.

Even with no open warfare, the canine rate of and capacity for demolishing food was vastly greater than the cat's. The latter were protected by a cat flap excluding dogs when they remained in their porch-cum-conservatory - until the door hinges loosened in a storm. Food bowls were transferred to their sleeping quarters in the garden shed - an alternative sanctuary.

Entry through the open, bench height windows defeated the dogs, but front paws could still support questing noses probing beyond the sill. Very off-putting! Cats became nocturnal and dogs diurnal and, after my first visit, I saw little more than stripy, disappearing rumps.

The average life span of a feral cat is said to be three years, so they had had three of the nine lives allotted to lap cats in full, a bit like me. They would find plenty of suitable cover in the half wild gardens and natural thickets clothing the bordering flanks of the mountain. The food continued to disappear under cover of darkness from the bench in the cluttered shed, where they could still find shelter from storms.

The shed had been their first home when they moved in - "Momma Puss" with two small kittens, which had to be pushed in under the foundations when their mother and the accompanying, presumed older sister, sprang aloft. One kitten died, the other grew to be the biggest and most pushy of the lot, having enjoyed regular victuals from kittenhood. Even "Momma" had to take second place. "Little-un" partook of what was left. Most of their days were spent in play, which they all joined in with equal enthusiasm, including the now ancient matriarch.

The only place I was allowed to handle them was when they came to the back door twice a day for food. Fondling was part of the feeding routine. When I sat and worked in the garden they often came to keep me company but I was allowed no closer than a couple of yards. After ten year's of delivering regular food! It apparently takes years to tame true ferals.

The little one often sneaked indoors for a sleep on the spare bed, but hid if she heard me coming and behaved like a fleeing fugitive when I opened doors to let her out. Sometimes she eluded me for hours and I might turn from my work downstairs to see her sitting quietly in the middle of the floor wondering why I didn't open a door for her to leave. She didn't ask. Seldom, in all those years did I hear any of them miaow, though they were capable of mighty shrieks when strange cats intruded on their territory. With Snowball they shrieked as they fled, hence my antagonism to that newcomer.

Knowing that my move was imminent, I had not been tempted to keep Snowball, the rather rotund white puss who had moved into their parlour and displaced them to the shed a few months before my move. He was determined to make this his home, scoffing the others' rations and yowling constantly whenever I was in sight, when I refused to take him in. He was pointing out in no uncertain terms that he was a house cat, not a yard cat, like those other inferior beings.

I finally let him indoors when he returned, bloody, from a fight with another Tom. A brief exploration of the downstairs rooms and he jumped onto my lap, rolled over on his back and curled little paws into the air, inviting me to tickle his soft white tum. He could not have won his case for staying more expertly. The submissive pose said it all, more plainly that the words "I am yours". There was no more hysterical yowling, just a gentle purring and triumphant, self satisfied, low key 'mews' which plainly said "There, I told you I'd be a good friend"

Only when a cat trap was acquired and baited to take him to the vet, did the distracted yowling start again, until light was excluded and he settled to his fate. The expert diagnosed him as undoctored and probably about three years old, remedying the first and patching up the scarred face but not the torn ears.

Back 'home' and released, he forgave me, but insisted on jumping onto my lap and rolling over to display that pristine white tummy and stop me reading or writing. But he was a quick learner. Only once did he try and jump up when there was a tray of food there. My shout sent him scuttling to the furthest recess of the cottage, to return cautiously after a suitable interval and stretch luxuriously at my feet. He enjoyed the same television programmes as I did, because that was when he was tolerated. Too young for an elderly mistress who he was likely to outlive, he nevertheless remained with me almost to the end of my residence, weaving between my feet as I moved around with my meal trays - an ever present menace to my stability.

He loved to come walking in the woods with me, trotting along beside or behind for as much as a mile along woodland paths, diving through bramble thickets and leaping puddles and streams. His blatantly white coat destroyed his chances of ever being a successful stalker - a skill which the ferals excelled at, though bringing back mostly shrews - twice a rare black and white water shrew. This did not stop him enjoying the wildwood, but not, the proximity of traffic. If we needed to return from our expeditions along the village road, he would dive into the wood leading steeply down to the Taff when he heard an approaching car. It seems he had had an argument with a vehicle in the past and was taking no chances.

Eventually, and sadly, I had to take him to the cats' rehabilitation home at Bryncethin near Bridgend, for a week in quarantine and a sojourn in one of the many apartments with adjoining pens until one of the potential cat owners took a fancy to him and became the doting patron he so obviously craved - even one such as myself, who had spent all our early acquaintance shouting at him and chasing him off my charges' food.

During the weeks after my move from Gwaelod, bushes were coming down and fences going up - to contain an adventurous three year old grandson from catapulting over the brink of an eighteen foot high retaining wall or the lesser one down to the pub yard. My visits became successively fewer as I shook off the ties of the old and settled down to find the assets of the new.

There were still happenings that I would have hated to miss, one such the burgeoning of flowers on my *Clematis montana* as it romped along the walls of the three ruined cottages with their blind, walled up doors and windows in sombre grey stone. The riot of blossom spread from the level of the old baker's oven in the former shop turned bonfire site and over the garage wall, to mingle with the darker pink of the *Cydonia japonica* or false quince.

Also not to be missed were the red flowering currant bushes, yellow Kerria and Forsythia and the long swathes of golden leopard's bane Doronicum whose big daisy heads followed the sun around through an angle of 180 degrees as that celestial body moved across the sky. Purple honesty would be joined by the multi-coloured columbines and blue spikes of monkshood. A garden is a lovesome thing!

* * *

The armchair in my new abode where I ate breakfast and lunch was as close to the glass doors onto the balcony as it could physically get. The garden rose steeply outside, through shrubs interspersed with a glory of golden daffodils and across a strip of greensward to the spreading branches of an ungainly tree on the brink. Beyond this the land fell steeply away through more trees to the station carpark by the Taff. The hilly panorama of the Border Ridges and Coalfield hills was visible through the ivy-clad bole with its five subsidiary trunks.

For two months the identity of this tree remained a mystery. My best guess from its general conformation was an elm, but elms should be peppered with brick red flowers by now. Not until I got beyond the garden gate did I appreciate the shining dark red of the ultimate twigs that I had interpreted as sun glint before, and the basal sprouts, constantly lopped, that labelled it as a lime tree.

CHAPTER 3

The Insidious March Of Urbanisation

In the early days, when shunting furniture about and humping books hither and yon got too tedious, I would sally forth to blow the cobwebs away. A brisk breeze blowing across the Taff footbridge could always be relied on as I watched the local pair of grey wagtails pottering on the shingle bank below. Fishermen stood, waist deep in mid river, one upstream and one down, making it seem positively cosy in that sometimes vicious air stream.

After a downpour in the Brecon Beacons or the Upper Coalfield the flow came rollicking down at speed, long trails of water crowfoot tugging at their moorings, as brilliant green in mid winter as at the height of summer and less burdened with encrusting algae.

Initially I headed downstream along the opposite, east bank - a firm gravelly surface with easily jumped puddles at first, giving opportunity to look out for mallard and moorhen being bowled along by the flood. Sadly, I spotted no goosanders this year, as in recent winters.

Further downstream, where a low stone wall precluded escape from the towpath to the lane alongside, stretches of path disappeared under mud and water, marginal brambles clawing at garments, as I tried to sidle past without carrying too great a burden of mud back to my so very indoor apartment.

The ornithological highlight of that first walk abroad was a great spotted woodpecker, hammering at the yielding bark of a mighty black poplar tree.

On drabber days I might stay suburban, peering over garden hedges to admire plants which were distinctly pre-vernal. Highlights here among the more-to-be-expected snowdrops, crocuses and hellebores, were summer snowflake, ill named seasonally, so as not to be confused with the much rarer true spring snowflakes, also the white christmas roses which flowered no nearer christmas than their more robust relatives in the hellebore fraternity.

Magnolias, primitive but flamboyant, were just unsheathing their stately flower buds, like melted down wax candles among the dried turrets of last season's seed crop. Prunus and related trees of the cherry family were just unsheathing pink and white petals, seemingly too delicate altogether for the environment into which they ventured.

There were mornings when I had to scrape a thick layer of frost from the car windscreen before heading out further afield, This clung only to sloping, not vertical windows and only on moist days when there was sufficient water vapour in the atmosphere to settle out as ice.

Apart from a few negligible flurries, snow, sleet and hail held off almost until the Easter weekend - of all unlikely times, Easter falling early in 2008. When I took the bus into Cardiff on 3rd March, however, I encountered two vicious hailstorms which failed to fall in Taffs Well, a few miles further up the valley, so these were quite local. I was waiting for the homeward bus outside the Millennium Rugby Stadium during the first. The second was as we drove into Llandaff. Outsize ice balls suddenly hit the bus roof with a tremendous clatter, making everybody jump, but stopped eventually as suddenly as they had started.

Walking west beyond the one shopping street into the residential part of Radyr, I was among big, upper crust houses with spacious gardens, many in a network of dead end roads. Where the shops ceased was the Daffodil Park, a sitting out place of grass and trees where jackdaws, busily probing the lawn with half open beaks ignored me, waddling up so close that I could see their pale yellow eyes. These were quite a surprise. Previous close views had revealed them as a pale blue, like those of a blind sheep dog.

Around Windsor Crescent on the other side of the main road, I was impressed by the swollen bases of the kerbside cherry trees - great mounds of solid timber engulfing the bases of their sturdy trunks, like tropical elephant's foot plants. Across the Heol Isaf highway from here and up an alleyway, I found myself on The Green, a sloping area of grass and trees, too steep for buildings but surrounded by an ellipse of elegant houses and gardens.

Up Windsor Road from the Daffodil sit-out and along a few dead end branches, another narrow walled alleyway led me into an extensive recreation ground, once again occupying gradients too steep for building. Parts of the curving walkway leading through were steep enough to consist of steps.

Some big trees had been saved from the original hedgerows in difficult hollows, one large oak supporting a squirrels' drey in an upper fork and with a carpet of greater periwinkles in full flower among the ground cover of ivy beneath.

Back towards the village was the new Medical Centre, built in the grounds of the old vicarage, behind the parish church and alongside the tennis courts. Towards the north was a children's play area with swings and slides. The see-saws of olden times seem to have gone out of fashion in these days of safety first. Too much jolting for the little darlings, perhaps. Below was a netball practising ground.

This was the area of open farmland that I had been asked to survey in 2001, before I dreamed of living so close. That exercise was a prelude to the threatened coming of the new houses, which now huddled close about the margins of this pleasant 'green lung'. I remember lavish hedgerows, with greenfinches, tits and willow warblers, these bordered with primroses and bluebells, an old parish road and tussocky meadowland.

Until the end of the twentieth century, stiles had led citizens over the hill, across verdantly clad undulating mounds of glacial till masking the St. Maugham's beds of the Old Red Sandstone bedrock below. Blackberries and crab apples could be gathered from the double hedgeline by the ancient track and the riparian strip of woodland along the trickling stream.

Some of the bordering trees had been coppiced at intervals, their rugged limbs rejuvenated by lopping. What tales they might have told of the woodsmen who had tended them, the folk who had ambled by or rested in their shade and the children who had played among the wood sorrel, violets and moschatel at their feet.

Dogs had run freely among the knapweed, yarrow, self heal and lesser stitchwort in the meadow, disturbing clouds of meadow brown and hedge brown butterflies, common blues and speckled woods. Ants supplied pickings for the green woodpecker, grass moths fell prey to the darting flights of a spotted flycatcher - an uncommon bird nowadays - and snails were having their armoury smashed on the stone anvil of the local song thrush. Tufted vetch, greater bird's-foot trefoil and lacy pignut wove tendrilar stems among marginal bracken.

The knowledge gained did not prevent the building of many more high class dwellings all around, but I like to think it may have directed the developers' thoughts to the concept of providing a green space on the steeper part for the new residents. Some, at least, appreciated it. Each time I passed during those early spring days there were mothers and toddlers and older children enjoying the facilities.

Following up a new road leading away from here across surviving farmland to the west, I emerged at the newest and more northerly of two roundabouts on the Llantrisant Road, an addition allowing the extra residents' cars to escape without emerging onto Radyr's one through road.

It was a somewhat similar story on a much larger scale on the old railway sidings in the valley bottom below Radyr village centre. My survey of this area was not by request of the locals to preserve traditional countryside but part of my comprehensive investigation of the Taff Valley, from the Border Ridges in the North, along the flood plain to the merged estuaries of the Taff and Ely, now swallowed up in the freshwater lake of Cardiff bay.

Known as the Radyr Shunting Yards, the many acres with parallel railway lines here had accommodated no more trains in recent decades than those now taking commuters on the two routes into Cardiff centre from their divergence at Radyr Junction.

Derelict for many years, since the great consignments of coal had come trundling out of the Valleys - the Rhymney, Cynon and the two Rhonddas, as well as the Taff, this was just wasteland to the average citizen.

To naturalists it was a wonderland of wild flowers and butterflies, rabbits and the foxes that hunted them, with the added bonus of exotic plants from the Mediterranean and more distant parts of the world.

Their disseminules had been dumped with ballast from ships coming into Cardiff Docks and transported hither with sand and rubble to heighten and level up the site for more rolling stock. Botanical members of the Cardiff Naturalists' Society in the late nineteenth century had had a ball identifying these and following their persistence. Some were with us still at the end of the twentieth century, but not any more.

Cutting into the steep Triassic scarp along which Radyr village is strung is the old Radyr Quarry that produced building stone for many of the city's buildings, walls and bridges.

During South Wales' industrial heyday the flat land of this part of the alluvial plain had been built up above the original level, leaving the adjoining edge of the Radyr Nature Reserve, including the Kingfisher Pool, at a lower elevation. This uplift made the land suitable for housing development, despite the modern agitation about building on flood plains in our increasingly temperamental climate.

No longer would we be able to spend happy hours botanising and birding over that much used but lately neglected tract that Mother Nature had reclaimed and clothed with a far greater variety of colour and form than on the rough tree dotted grazings of the river flats beyond.

By the dawn of the new millennium there were rumours of major developments on this land. This section of my trilogy of books on the Natural History of Cardiff seemed to be drifting into history even as I wrote it at the dawning of the twenty first century

At the proof reading phase I had encountered a surveyor gazing contemplatively at the ponies stepping lightly through the bluebells to reach into the willow spinney opposite Junction Terrace. There was a proud gleam in his eye as he turned to me, envisaging the future. "Hundreds of high value houses and flats."

He expressed no pity for the occupants of the attractive old houses with their much used front gardens on the other side of the road. As compensation for the loss of that idyllic view over the river to the wooded flank of the valley rising steeply to Whitchurch, they were to be given a new pavement and a layby for their cars, by a much broader road than the dead end that had served them over the years.

Rows of pink brick houses with a minimal strip of 'garden' mushroomed up opposite, onwards and ever upwards, to three storeys with lofty roofs above. Fortunately the old habitations backed onto a shaggy green slope too steep to build on without half burying or strutting any new erections. I and many another passer by frequently paused by the bounding fence there to fraternise with the friendly nanny goats and their winsome kids or offer handfuls of fresh grass to the ponies, which had included a couple of Shetlanders at one period.

Just downstream of Radyr Station the Taff loops away due east for about half a mile before turning sharply back at more than a right angle to resume its former direction. Eventually it comes up against the Radyr scarp near the old quarry and is deflected away at another right angle.

A goodly portion of the resulting half mile diameter embayment lies between the western railway line with its satellite sidings and the river. The eastern line, heading to between Whitchurch and Llandaff North cuts off another chunk of land from the curving river.

This, remaining at the original level, accommodates two sports fields and two to three times this area under rough pasture with encroaching shrubs. Its western boundary is marked by a railway embankment, the summit of which is at the same level as the new houses alongside. The mismatch ceases at the bridge where the railway crosses the Taff at the spot where the feeder canal powering the old Melin Griffith Tin Works empties its waters back into the river.

Dodging the heavy bulldozers on my first sortie from Brynteg in 2008 I spotted two surveyors with spread map pointing ominously out over the winter-sere flood plain. The answer to my query was. "No. The Earl of Plymouth owns that." It is marked as "Welsh Water Land" on local maps.

I drew their attention to the buzzard circling low over their heads, like an avenging angel. No. They hadn't noticed it during their lengthy discussion. Perhaps the land's proximity to river level will save it. In view of the inappropriate designations accorded the new developments, I was not convinced. The advertising sale boards and banners flapping in the wind sang the virtues of "Vale Meadows, The Grove, Wilde Court, Fisher Hill Way, the Gantry and Goetre Fawr" which latter translates as "The Big Woodland House". Sadly the trees had been chopped down long since.

I came again at the end of March. A soft rain was falling on a broad tract of churned up earth, levelled off and put down to grass, as a currently very muddy playing field. The solid newly built commuter bridge over the western railway line had to take all the road traffic from the houses on the other side out to Radyr as there was no way over the river to Whitchurch.

A little beyond it a rectangle of open ground had been furnished with gravel paths and a patterning of bare earth around plots of wispy grass, which must be the early phase of flower beds. - or more likely shrub beds, as in all the tiny garden plots round the buildings. There were garden designers about, however, to have made the attractive floral display around the sales centre, but not the plots that were for sale. It seemed the new residents were to enjoy the visual pleasures of this salvaged and rehabilitated green plot - so well hidden from the original inhabitants who were several streets away.

My current abode in Cwrt Brynteg, the "Fair Hill Court", was itself part of an adjacent new development - on the site of the old Radyr Inn, whose derelict garden I had been wont to explore occasionally in years gone by. Who was I to complain? I was part of the new invasion myself, one of those who chose to live alone and continue as a property owner beyond my allotted span. At least I and my only sibling had not added any offspring to the army of folk needing to be housed on our crowded little island.

CHAPTER 4
I Entertain

My first visitor, who dropped in 'out of the blue', once a year was Zoe Winter. She was a remarkable woman, a surgeon who devoted the greater part of her life to working in deprived areas of the Third World and spent the rest of the year as a roving vagabond in the U K.

She had no permanent residence, just a van and a motor cycle, which she manhandled into the back of the vehicle when she was not using it for lesser sorties. A knowledgeable biologist and a student of the Open University when in Britain, she had carried out a research project some years before on the lakes of MacQuarie Island in the Australian sector of the Antarctic.

She followed this up by reading a book written by Robin Burns dealing with pioneering women who had worked in such outlandish places in this. Its title was "Just Tell Them I Survived: Women in the Antarctic". Included was a colour photograph of myself and three companions, two Aussies and another Pommie, boarding the army DUKW that took us ashore through the moulting horde of elephant seals spread across the island's shores. The caption reads:- "Pioneering women in their Mae Wests about to go ashore on Macquarie Island for the first time, in December 1959."

Also therein was a reference to my book "SubAntarctic Sanctuary: Summertime on MacQuarie Island", dedicated to "Professor Lily Newton, who set my feet on the Naturalists' trail." She thought I was likely to be 'her sort of person' and got my address from Gollancz, the publisher.

So it was that she had been contacting me, usually unannounced, over a number of years, arriving in full motor cycling gear (essentially antarctic!) and hailing me through the window with a hearty, booming voice such I have never heard issuing from a female frame elsewhere.

This delightful, self sacrificing and competent middle aged lady was as tough as they come - necessarily when devoting herself to her patients in Africa, the Far East, South America or the Asian steppe, but voluntarily when touring Britain in her van, with no cooking facilities apart from a calor gas stove to heat water. A vegetarian, she preferred her vegetables raw, though demolishing some fried onions offered with alacrity.

Her last assignment had been in Ethiopia and the small matter of tracing me from Gwaelod to Radyr was no problem. She arrived here two days after I did, to pick her way through the stacks of books and cooking utensils. These occasional visits to settled citizens, were principally to make contact with an ample supply of water, preferably hot, and, in the old days before laptops, a source of power for her computer - whereon she recorded her remarkable itinerary.

Zoe's main need on this occasion was to establish herself in the kitchen to wash out her mainstay utensils and mix up a huge quantity of muesli to tide her over the next few weeks. She arrived with bags of oatmeal, sultanas, other dried fruit and I know not what, this her staple diet, moistened with water, not milk. Also there was a crate of raw eggs which she hard boiled in my two largest saucepans. I needed to be out most of that day but introduced her to the contents of the fridge, including a raw cauliflower, one of her favourites, an armchair by the fire and a regiment of books for when she finished her chores.

The van where she slept, in a hammock, with a canoe and paddles overhead, skis, snowshoes and other accoutrements of her tough, outdoor life underneath, carried all her worldly goods apart from a few stored temporarily in someone's barn. When she arrived she stripped off three anoraks, a jumper, head gear and a thick pair of trews. This was her sleeping attire. "I only put the heater on at night when it's freezing."

When she left it was to tour the rest of Wales, Cumbria, Scotland and much of England, calling on acquaintances scattered throughout for the occasional luxury of a hot bath and laundry facilities. A month later she sent me an exhaustive itinerary of her travels since she left me. It made me tired just reading it and picturing all the geological and nature trails that she had walked - more I imagine than any permanent resident. She thought nothing of hitch hiking with a punctured tyre to find a garage or changing a wheel on her motor bike after nightfall. Having seen life in the raw during her spells abroad, this was mere child's play. A remarkable woman indeed

* * *

On February 9th, only a fortnight after moving in, I was entertaining another guest, Irene Payne, as I had done in the few years since we had the good fortune to meet on Skokholm Island off the coast of Pembrokeshire. She was scheduled to stay in my four bed cottage on the Gwaelod mountain but the move forestalled us. No matter. There was a comfortable guest suite available for hire at Brynteg which no-one else needed just then.

My unpacking was a long way from complete but most of the crockery had been unwrapped and stowed away, the only breakage three large dinner plates. We made a joke of emptying the marmalade into one of my mother's elegant cut glass jam dishes, the lid pierced to accommodate the spoon handle. This was an attempt to negate the sound advice given by my mentors at Gwaelod. "You never use those, what's point of taking them?"

Quite true, I could not recall having done so during the last forty three years, but I had often admired them on the shelf and I well remembered them adorning the breakfast table before cycling off to school three quarters of a century earlier. No way would my mother have tolerated a labelled jam pot on the damask tablecloth and more than just the jam dishes appeared when visitors came to tea. How could I in all conscience abandon such memories?

Everybody was very much poorer in those days, but we seemed to live more graciously . Walking round the kitchen, toast in hand, would certainly not have been tolerated and we did not rise from the table until excused. Have we lost something important in this frenetically hurried age, or are we getting all our visual satisfaction of beautiful things from television or visits to great houses? Irene and I were not over concerned, but conforming now to the expected etiquette of childhood days was good for a laugh.

Although domiciled in the Prescelly Mountains in the heart of Pembrokeshire Irene had, in fact, popped up unexpectedly out of the gathering darkness of the Garth Mountain road on the evening of the house move. It was Friday 25th January and she was driving back to West Wales after looking after an invalid aunt in the Home Counties. Not knowing where I might be or where I was headed, she came chugging up the mountain road in low gear to find out just as my little band of helpers was dispersing. The removal van, parked by day in the pub yard, had been driven off to a vacant lot in Danesfield. Robert and I were walking down to the pub for our evening meal and Clive stowing my computer into his car for safe keeping when she came running down the hill clutching a pot of Cyclamen - a stranger in the night until I recognised her voice.

A few minutes later and the Cottage would have been deserted, the lane empty of people. Greetings were brief, our Welsh cawl awaited us and she had 130 or so miles yet to drive. We caught up with the news a fortnight later over steak casserole and Bramley crumble.

This early February rendezvous had become an annual occurrence during the past few years, the date set by that of the assembling of the "Friends of Skokholm and Skomer". The Saturday conference of a hundred or so people took place in the Old Tithe Barn at Cheltenham, a delightful edifice of yellow Cotswold stone set among tall trees.

Many of the island-goers attending came from London and the Home Counties to savour the delights of Wildest Wales in summer and this was a convenient half way point for us to meet when winter gales made the islands unwelcoming and often inaccessible.

This year there had been a double booking and we were relegated to the spacious village hall at Uckington nearby. A superb sunny day, with green fields and leafy lanes beckoning, we were loath to go indoors, old acquaintances gossiping in the car park, balancing coffee cups and biscuits.

The 2008 theme was island history - a particularly interesting one for me as I was one of the oldest inhabitants present. I had started my studies on Skokholm more than sixty years before, in 1946. In fact most of the illustrated talks presented referred to the period from the 1960s to the 1990s when I was away elsewhere, so these filled a gap for me. The reminiscences of others brought me up to date.

Some of the most exciting revelations, however were quite modern. Most intriguing was newly gained knowledge of where representatives of the forty thousand pairs of Manx shearwaters go when the nesting season on the islands ends.

Miniature electronic recording gadgets attached to birds in their nesting burrows in autumn showed that, not only did they spend our northern winter in the southern summer in the South Atlantic, off Argentine and Patagonia, as was already known from ringing recoveries, but also in the north and west. The complicated spider web maps of their ocean wanderings were also aggregated off the coast of New England to the west of their nesting territory and of Norway to the north.

Professor Christopher Perrins of the Edward Grey Ornithological Institute in Oxford University who was instrumental in making these discoveries, had been a contemporary of mine during those summers on Skokholm in the forties and fifties. We were students then, myself his senior in years after war service and so retiring from active service ahead of him. He was a regular at these reunions. It is good to catch up with other enthusiasts from long ago.

* * *

Sunshine poured down just as brightly next morning when Irene and I set off from Brynteg for the coast, but not until after scraping ice from the car windows. In previous years I had showed her some of the best of the Glamorgan Heritage Coast, from Llantwit Major through Nash Point and

Monknash to Southerndown and Ogmore. This year we stayed further east exploring the beaches and headlands around Barry and Porthkerry. Hailing from the fine cliff scenery of South West Wales and indeed living among it, as a long term volunteer worker on Skoholm, she was surprised and delighted at how much scenery could be savoured on this less well known part of the coast.

Artistic and inquisitive by nature, she loved the little quirky bits exhibited by the natural world. At this time of year the highlights were mostly geological, the unconformity between the sloping beds of ancient Carboniferous limestone and the newer horizontal strata of Liassic limestone above leading to plenty of variety.

We padded over the broad expanse of sand extending out into the Severn Estuary from Whitmore Bay beachcombing, in the pleasant absence of summertime crowds. Highlights in the backing cliffs under brooding holm oaks were crowded spherical pits in the Triassic new red sandstone where crystalline geodes had loosened and fallen away. Some of the local pink calcite or alabaster remained firmly in situ as attractive nodules on rock platforms from which winter tides had washed away the covering of sand.

On Friars Point the older rocks held sway. We followed the footpath to the end of the peninsula, this the central of the three headlands of harder rock reaching out into the sea. Scrabbling around on the sloping strata we located a variety of the marine organisms that had lived on that part of the sea bed when Barry lay at the same latitude as today's Great Barrier Reef in Australia, before the tropical forests burgeoned to supply South Wales with its rich heritage of coal. Here were fossil Crinoids or sea lilies, Brachiopods or lamp shells and corals in transverse and longitudinal section.

We moved on into the next bay to the old jetty, which was high and dry to view Barry Old Harbour beyond the tiled plaque commemorating the steamers, "Balmoral" and "Waverley". Circular clumps of Spartina grass were colonising the sand among boats moored in the shallows or tip tilted on the mounds.

After flying visits to the other headlands, Nell's Point to the east and the Knapp to the west, we drove round the swan pool (drained for cleaning with the usual eighty or so mute swans wintering elsewhere) then out along the beach road between the thickly vegetated, near vertical Bull Cliff and the piled, sea rounded pebbles of the storm beach.

Our picnic lunch in the car was taken in Porthkerry Country park, gazing seawards past the willows and pastureland which afforded a 7.30 am trysting place for dogs and dog owners, to the gap in the coast ridge where a few of the nationally rare wild service trees grew. Close by were bright clumps of celandines and the first wild primroses of spring. A few months hence the white butterfly orchids would be burgeoning in the woodland behind.

We strolled afterwards along the edge of the mini golf course where the sea had formerly lapped back towards the stately grey stone viaduct. Following the tinkling stream, with its water cress, brooklime and pendulous sedge over a little bridge, we watched the brisk flow burbling through and finally disappearing among the pebbles, finding its own tortuous way to the sea.

From here we mooched east along the grassy hollow between crumbly, towering cliff and the gently rising storm beach. In parts hardy plants were creeping up the back of the beach, in others storm-tossed pebbles had been rolled over the top onto the fine grass sward to lodge among the pioneering sea beet and orache.

Back along the Sully road we were just in time to get a cup of tea at the Cosmeston Lakes Country Park café before wandering out along the board walk through the reeds to fraternise with the hungry horde of mute swans, Canada geese, mallard and tufted ducks on the eastern lake. The amber sunlight and cloudless sky lasted through till dusk, but night comes early in February and we headed back to the warm retreat that I was beginning to learn to call home.

* * *

In the next day's sunshine we set off on foot across the Taff and upstream to Radyr Weir and the new salmon pass, admiring the big, contorted black poplars which dominated the riverside thicket. Mighty branches had succumbed to the elements, the fractures healing to leave boughs at anomalous angles. Layers of raffia-like fibres were exposed under the bark of elbows helping to support the injured limbs. I had hoped for years to photograph these master art forms of the natural world, but there never seemed to be enough light.

Up then past the sluices where the feeder canal leaves the river above the weir and out to the curved lily pool where frogs would soon be laying their blobs of spawn, we followed the feeder to the canal proper. There is always plenty to see there, with woodland birds flipping down to the grain feeding stations on fence posts and lock gates.

Mallard and moorhens were about in plenty, mostly in pairs preparatory to the nesting season. Three moorhens were perched several feet above the water in the Sheep's Bane Wood alders, diligently preening and looking quite incongruous as they balanced on one leg among branches beside some blackbirds. Brandy bottle water lily leaves were reaching to the water surface in firm green rolls, the few flattened ones that had made it to the surface likely to get frosted.

A group of rangers paused in their hedge laying to tell us that a rare lesser spotted woodpecker was about. We did not see it. An elderly member of the team came out with "Are you Mary?" and continued with his work. It was years since I was here on more than the occasional visit, but it was nice to be remembered, even though I could not reciprocate.

Our day was 'made' by the intimate views we were granted of a couple of voles busily foraging under a tall rose bush which burgeoned with fresh green leaf tufts. So intent were they in making the most of the short hours of daylight that they ignored us completely. They divided their attention between scuffling around at ground level and climbing twelve inches or more up the thorny rose stems to chomp the sprouting foliage.

This climbing made us think they must be bank voles rather than field voles but there was none of the expected rufous hue on their fur. Perhaps this fades during the winter months when they must spend a lot of time sleeping. They took short breaks in their sometimes frenetic activity, remaining within view but in fact disappearing if we looked away, so perfect was their camouflage when movement ceased. We had to identify the spot by some feature of the background before their cryptic outline was once more revealed.

Obviously the wind was in our favour. Their other senses failed to alert them to the alien presence even when a large man on his way to the bird hide beyond came up behind us. We waved him to silence and the three of us watched together as the little whiskery mammals imbibed fresh victuals to see them through the long night.

We spent time in both bird hides, watching a little grebe diving for provender and moorhens exploring among the reeds, but neither pool produced any kingfishers. Bird seed was customarily strewn over the wooded slope beside the as yet unoccupied sand martin colony and this had attracted a crowd of finches and others. Bullfinches, goldfinches and chaffinches shared the goodies with blackbirds, jays, magpies and woodpigeons, but we saw nothing of the white-plumaged chaffinch that had haunted the area in the past two years. Only the cock reed bunting remained aloof beyond the water.

A young man with a digital camera was taking a series of intimate photographs of the birds, particularly the cock bullfinches with their magnificent salmon pink waistcoats. In such situations one expects a few knowledgable ornithologists to be around to ask questions of. He was not one of them. It was he who asked us what birds he was photographing.

This camera man, unable to recognise the three most colourful and common finches on the British list, was getting far superior close-ups than many an experienced bird photographer achieved. For those who wait for hours in vain, this seems grossly unfair. Folk approach the natural world from many angles. We left him pursuing his new learning curve and wended our way back between allotments and pony field and across the footbridge to lunch, after which Irene set off back to West Wales.

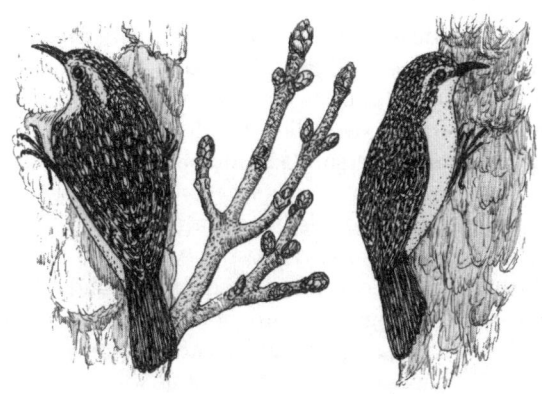

CHAPTER 5

More Walks Abroad

Despite all the new houses being built around my new abode, my choice had been most profoundly influenced by the proximity of rural walks accessible on foot. Not all this part of Cardiff's green belt was being swallowed up by bricks and mortar at such an alarming rate as the localities explored on this side of the river.

Across the Taff beyond the arching footbridge hard by the station was a different world of canal and woodland, where wild communities were not only tolerated but were enhanced by sensitive management techniques.

This was, of course, the Fforest Farm Country Park, overseen by the Cardiff County Council, formerly by its Parks Department, now the Department of Leisure and Amenities as conservation of the natural environment had loomed more urgently on civic agendas.

Within the country park boundaries, part had been designated as an SSSI (Site of Special Scientific Interest) and the canal itself was a designated Nature Reserve. The warden and vice warden were helped as necessary in the management tasks by county rangers and volunteers from the thriving group of lay persons known as the Friends of Fforest Farm.

More or less parallel at a little distance was the backdrop of the fast flowing River Taff, while between this and the surviving stretch of the twenty five mile long canal was the lesser canal of the Melin Griffith Feeder, supplying water power to the mill as well as bringing part of the coal and iron ore from the mines up-valley to the tin plate works in Lower Whitchurch.

Other residents of Brynteg would be encountered on these pleasant walkways - persons not involved in the initiation and/or maintenance of the area like the gallant band of "Friends", but grateful for the amenities it offered.

It was 1962 or thereabouts, soon after my arrival in the area that I had been roped in by concerned elements of the council to do the initial survey of this area, suspected to be rich in species and well worthy of conservation. Too many such historic waterways had fallen into disuse, been actively abused or finally filled in by misguided persons adopting the maxim of "chuck it in the cut" for any unwanted trash.

The "cut" may well have provided swimming holes for the miscreants' forbears and had certainly brought prosperity to projects as diverse as Merthyr Tydfil's ironworks, the Rhondda's coal mines and Cardiff's docks.

Leading lights in the saving of this idyllic relic of past endeavours were Glyn Hopkins, then lord mayor of Cardiff, and Colonel Morrey-Salmon, long-lived bird photographer extraordinaire and much more. They seem now to have been incongruous figures in that unkempt environment, before the "green wellie brigade" became so widely accepted.

I would come upon little groups in urgent discussion by the gently plopping waters, the mayor in his black bowler hat and suede spats, straight from the City Hall, and the colonel, a diminutive but feisty figure in long dark overcoat, with camera and tripod almost as big as himself. Small he might be, but he was a formidable character not to be trifled with and a demon car driver still, well into his nineties. He was held in high esteem by generations of ornithologists and photographers in the years to come.

Robert Hubbard, like Irene before him, came from a more scenic locality than mine, but was suitably impressed by the rural scenes encompassed in these less famed Welsh habitats. We were only about five miles from the heart of the Principality's capital city, but his comment was. "I can see why you chose here."

On his initial visit to Brynteg from his secluded manor in the verdant valley slicing through the Monknash cliffs to the sea, he was fully engaged helping out indoors. The next time he visited we had leisure to explore. We dallied on the Taff bridge after a hot lunch conjured up in my recalcitrant oven, looking for the resident kingfisher. It was not about, but we appreciated the sunlit view of Castell Coch, Lord Bute's attractive 'folly' in the steep beechwood frowning down on the new roundabout in the gorge.

Heading away from the river, we were rewarded by an intimate view of two tree creepers beside the feeder. They foraged on neighbouring branches, working from the bottom up, then flying to the base of the next. Unlike the nuthatches that shared this wood with them, they never worked from top to bottom, but were adept at clinging to the rugose bark to walk along the underside of horizontal boughs in no fear of falling.

We passed the orchid field by the small ponds, no orchids yet of course, and the bare woody flats where water rails can be spotted darting from cover to cover in winter time. Two kingfishers made their appearance as we headed north to where the canal emerged from under the massive M4 motorway embankment, but these were mostly streaks of blue and orange, as so often with these elusive little birds.

There was a time when all the local kingfishers came to fish in the waters of the canal rather than those of the Taff in whose banks they nested. Canal water came rollicking in from clear springs on the slopes of the Border Ridges, bounding downhill over Carboniferous limestone outcrops and spawning crusty tufa along their banks.

Water in the Taff in the 1960s and through much of the 1970s was black with coal dust drained from coal washeries up-river, the fine particles held in suspension. Not only could the kingfishers not spot their prey in the opaque brew, but there was little prey to spot. The sensitive gills of fish and breathing apparatus of invertebrates could get silted up, as did the surviving leaves of many water plants.

Grey and pied wagtails, on the other hand, had found the river much to their liking, paddling through shallows murky with sewage fungi, to tweak out the tiny mud worms and Chironmid midge larvae which thrived in the noxious mass.

Today's canal was being fished by little grebes as well as the equally stubby kingfishers. Mallard were about, as always, mostly in pairs, the eggs evidently not yet laid in mid February. Much their favourite preening places were floating logs, of which there were plenty. Here they could tweak out their belly feathers and clean between their toes without the bother of scrambling ashore' Moorhens were frequent, but we only spotted one heron, although these birds were accustomed to walkers and usually took little notice.

Where we explored the mossy remains of the old canal cottage, I was surprised to find the little colony of big garden marguerites still in place. I thought these had disappeared decades ago, along with the yellow-flowered water figwort. Not only were the plants persisting but they were bearing mini flower heads, anomalously early, and not much bigger than prize conkers, but with perfect, tightly packed little white florets.

From the bird hides we saw reed bunting and an indiscriminate, presumably overwintering, warbler. Also frisking rabbits. I was reminded of a boxing day walk when I had been run into by a rabbit here.. The wee beastie was haring down the main path towards our little group with a not much larger dog in hot pursuit. It canoned into my gumboot, stunning itself, so that the dog's master was able to grab and dispatch it - as a change from the remains of the Christmas turkey, which have a habit of going on for too long.

* * *

The western, Brynteg, side of the Taff was by no means completely built up. The web of suburban roads set well back from the edge of the scarp were often quite steep and the more awkward hummocks and hollows had been left as open land climbing the hillsides towards the Llantrisant Road.

The scarp twixt the settlement and the river was devoid of houses and so steep that sections of the network of paths threading through the enveloping trees had been furnished with staircases reinforced with timber. These were the Radyr Community Woods Nature Reserve, presided over by the local authority but tended by local residents.

Among these were some of my old students of thirty to forty years before, attenders at evening classes held in the Adult Education Centre which took over the Comprehensive School out of hours. I first deployed myself here in this new era of my life on the 18th February. Feeling a little fragile after all the unpacking, I tried to stay on the level, following the sometimes muddy path along the top.

Winter lingered here, the only woody plants showing more than the scantest sign of life being the coppiced hazel. Tight catkins had been produced on these back in December and were, as always, the first to loosen up in spring. By now the yellow pollen had been dispersed by punishing winds some, hopefully, to alight on the cryptic tufts of crimson stigmas to ensure a nut crop for the squirrels. Emptied stamens clung limply to desiccated pendulous axes which were themselves losing their grip and contributing to the soggy mulch below.

Much of the dark wooded slope was bare of plants beneath the trees, the treacherous black mud oozing damp, the prospect gloomy. There were few ways down to the valley bottom and these only negotiable by the most nimble. Where subdued light penetrated little patches of celandines had spread their glossy petals and the first green sprouts were appearing on hawthorn twigs.

The southern section was occupied by the Hermitage Wood Nature Reserve embracing the Hermit's Well, said to be contemporary with the mediaeval motte at Morganstown to the north. It also held a unique species of hawkweed named after the locality *(Hieracium radyrensis)*. Below the bounds of the Comprehensive School the old railway sidings converged under the overgrown Radyr Quarry. It was here that the River Taff swept right in to the base of the wooded cliff from the north-east, bouncing off at a sharp right angle to head away south-west.

The bluff above commanded a panoramic view upstream, past the old engine shed to the functional railway crossing where the waters of the river and the Melin Griffith feeder merged. Further downstream I spied the crossing of the old mineral railway on sturdy iron supports which had formerly opened the way to open fields on the other side of the Taff. In the recent past this bridge had been a much used footway for walkers, but it had been blocked a few years back, for no apparent reason.

A narrow strip of low lying land carrying the still functional commuter line through Danescourt Station to Cardiff intervened between my elevated path and the river from here on. The new suburban sprawl of Danescourt was edging up from the west as I began to emerge into a more open landscape of grass and bracken.

I turned back at a point where a road led off into the new housing complex, meaning to locate this point later in the car and continue my walk from here when more of the vegetation had woken to life.

My exploration through the lower part of Radyr Woods from Junction Terrace a few weeks later was much more productive. A pair of mallard came paddling expectantly towards me as I surveyed the Duck Pond near the goat sheds from the pond dipping platform. In the past these had always slunk away among the mangrove-like alder roots, complete wildlings. The moorhens still did, but someone must have been feeding the ducks. I had no offerings for them and they paddled off into the gloom under overarching brambles.

The first golden kingcups were opening up under bordering willows and a froth of golden saxifrage was displaying shy flowers, huddled together in soft cushions over patches of black sogginess. Across the brisk, sandy floored stream, I circled up along the board walk, past the Iron Age mound under the great beeches, looking in vain for shrews where I had watched them in the past.

Beyond the Kingfisher Pool, half vanished under burgeoning straw-coloured bulrushes, the wild snowdrop flowers had already withered, the green capsules lost among lengthening leaves, but the later spread of wood Anemones had not yet appeared.

I plucked a few sprigs of willow catkins for a vase, avoiding the more mature, which were offering yellow pollen and nectar to the queen bumble bees, now emerging from hibernation. My homeward route was along the junction of wood and field where the planted primroses and daffodils were reaching their prime in partial shade - an idyllic spectacle heralding the awakening year.

The old hedge separating farm fields had been removed. In its place was a spread of short, very muddy grass reaching out from the ever growing housing estate on the railway sidings - inviting incoming residents with suitable footwear to cross to the better maintained paths of the nature reserve.

CHAPTER 6

Lecturing at Cowbridge and Castle Viewing At Fonmon

While my 'in-house' activities had changed fundamentally with the emptying of boxes and crates and stowing of contents, my 'extra mural' activities continued much as before. These were, indeed, closer to hand than when in my former mountain retreat.

Although I now often defaulted in my attendance at meetings of the South and West Wales Wildlife Trust in North Cardiff, I tried to maintain a presence at those of the Cardiff Naturalists' Society, an institution inaugurated in 1867, which were now held in the university buildings in Western Avenue, nearer to Llandaff city than to Cardiff centre.

I had been taken by surprise at the first of these in January, to which I had brought my prized coc-de-mer, as I was to be showing slides of tropical fruits, oil and fibre plants. Some of my good friends and fellow members had laid on a little celebration of my recent MBE award and "not before time" quoth they and others before and after. Following a presentation of a floral tribute - a basket of Azalea, Kalanchoe and trailing ivy - Rob Nottage gave a short slide presentation on "The Life of M E G."

Mostly this showed aspects of the last forty five years of my life based in Cardiff but there were others. Me as a toddler clutching a bunch of flowers (I had started early on the floral path), as a teen-ager standing on my head at a family camp and as a land girl on leave, doing a hand stand on the diving board by the River Thames at Hurley. I seem to remember a stimulating weir just upstream from there. There was another of me posing on the sea front at Aberystwith in gown and mortar board on graduation day.

These 'throw backs' had been acquired for a small commemorative compilation entitled "The First Eighty Years" and presented at my eightieth birthday party in 2002. They had been acquired by subterfuge from my brother in London, unknown to me. Both occasions were very heart warming.

Half way through February I was scheduled to give a talk to the Cowbridge and Vale of Glamorgan group of the National Trust. I offered a travel talk but they prefered to hear about the Welsh Sea-bird Islands nearer home - a subject I had already explored with the Cardiff City group of the National Trust.

By chance their chairman, Professor Malcolm Davies, who had offered me a lift to the venue, lived in Radyr, so he was gratified to find out that he would not be shunting his car around the Gwaelod Mountain in the dark. As a walker, he had often passed Brynteg on his way to the Taff crossing and the Taff Trail, leading along the opposite bank from Cardiff to the Brecon Beacons and beyond, so he knew where to come for me. He, it transpired, had been at a lecture which I had given recently in Cardiff on the wildlife of the Hebrides, and wanted more of the same, but not the same.

The rendezvous was the baronial hall in the Duke of Wellington Public House, High Street, Cowbridge and it was, indeed, a baronial hall. Another two storeys could have been packed in between the chairs ranged in the auditorium and the ceiling. I was glad that I had been promised a lapel or hand held microphone and that I was not expected to fill that great space with sound unaided.

On the front wall was a massive tapestry, which became hidden by the great screen pulled down in front. Soon the lights went out, so it was obscured anyway by my slides - I like to think of even more desirable panoramas on Wales' doorstep. The hall was full: maybe I had left at least some of them rearing to visit these lovely marine outliers so close at hand.

So many people mumble in their 'drawing room voices' nowadays when holding forth in a spacious hall, that it was gratifying to be informed that my offering was authorative and clear as well as skilfully illustrated. Is it me getting deaf in my old age that makes me so critical?

In his letter of thanks and request that I return next year the Prof. wrote; "My wife and I are regular walkers in Radyr and its environs and, although now inspired to go further afield, will maybe meet you on one of our walks.". They did, twice, before many weeks had passed.

Another pleasure for me on that crowded evening was meeting many old friends who I had not seen for years, some of them past students from my evening classes and expeditions.

* * *

I continued to attend the Tuesday lunchtime "Food for Thought" meetings that I had been enjoying for many years. Run initially under the auspices of the Workers' Education Authority, these were now independent. Around fifty or so folk, mostly pensioners, because this was a daytime activity, met for a jacket potato and salad lunch with cheese, ham or pate, followed by an hour's talk by a different lecturer every week. There was no natural history or any other special bias and we all learned a great deal in other fields. Occasionally I contributed, often at short notice when a speaker dropped out.

By the strangest of coincidences, just as I was writing this on a Monday afternoon the group organiser came through on the phone, saying that tomorrow's speaker had defaulted and asking if I could fill in. I could and dived under the bed where the metal slide boxes were stored. A pleasant scrabble through a local coastal set and the phone rang again. "He's just come back to me. Thinks he can manage to do it now after all. Keep yours for your regular patch next term."

Two or three times each term we enjoyed a coach trip to some place of interest. Our visit on March 5th was to Fonmon Castle and grounds a short distance inland from Gilestone and Aberthaw at the eastern end of the Glamorgan Heritage Coast - and not far from Cardiff Airport at Rhoose and the R A F Base at St. Athans. It was a super day of sunshine and blue skies and my only complaint was that we spent so much time indoors there was not enough left to thoroughly explore the spacious grounds and gardens.

The land had been allocated for this baronial hall in the tenth century but most of the building materialised between the eleventh and the thirteenth centuries. The tower set a little apart was an eighteenth century folly. Our coach took the coast road, curving round past the famous Blue Anchor Pub, recently renovated, at Aberthaw. As we turned up the little lane beyond the Cement Works, I peered through the window down into the huge quarry excavated in the soft Liassic limestone which formed the basis of the cement used in many famous buildings countrywide. Yes, the lake was still there, the marginal willows larger than when I had been working in this area but the ducks still paddling around, unworried by the massive quarry machines and civil and the military aircraft zooming overhead.

The tourist map on the Fonmon brochure exhorts visitors not to attempt to access the castle via Fonmon village. That accounts for the warning notice "High Security" where our coach turned off the approach lane. Something to do with St. Athan's airfield, perhaps? I had wandered around there with impunity in years gone by. We entered the grounds past a delightful wildfowl pool dominated by a splendid weeping willow beset with pointy yellow buds, and followed alongside a tree-filled bosky gully to the car park.

It was Lord Hugo Boothby, former land owner and well known local figure, who had carried the banner of the red dragon of Wales at the investiture of the Prince of Wales in Caernarvon. We saw the banner hanging in the great hall, but the present owner is Sir Brooke Boothby.

This is one of Britain's few mediaeval castles which is still lived in as a private home, but it is opened for a wide range of public and private functions, from concerts and wedding to fairs and the Rare Plants Show, which tours the great estates and was to be held at Fonmon in early May in 2008.

The building is not as imposing as some from the outside and a goodly part had been coated with cement to hold the crumbling stones in place. Fatal cracks are feared if this was removed down to the original structure. At least there is an almost inexhaustible source of cement just across the level grazings extending seawards.

Bats roost in the castle, but our guide did not know which species, only that their numbers were monitored at intervals with automated bat counters as they moved out at dusk.

Our indoor tour was comprehensive, up wide staircases and down, receiving brief life histories of the ancestors depicted in the rich wall portraits and descriptions of the many paintings by Sir Joshua Reynolds. Apparently the property had only changed ownership once. Built by the St. John family around 1200, the castle was bought by Colonel Phillip Jones, a direct ancestor of Sir Brooke Boothby, in 1650 during the civil war.

Half way through the afternoon we were mustered for a lavish tea, eight to each round table, enjoying here, as everywhere, the sight and perfume of vases of magnificent tropical orchids in pristine condition.

Afterwards we were led to the historic kitchen, a feature of which was a fine old dresser fashioned from a single length of home grown elm, fifteen metres long and of generous width. The kitchen staff had eaten their meals from this for three hundred years, the front edge embayed to accommodate their legs.

The family had run a brewery here and we handled some old bottles sporting raised images of the castle arms. Lifting the big dark pewter plates ranged along the wall, we found them astonishingly heavy. No kitchen maid would carry many of those very far, laden with victuals,

Eventually we escaped to the extensive grounds, where the sun shone as benignly as before. Individual walled gardens were scattered through the parkland, which nurtured some fine, straight-trunked pines and beeches. Quite magnificent specimens, these would make fine timber trees, but we hoped the timbermen would spare them as living monuments in this historic site.

There were plane trees and holm oaks, also Garrya elliptica from New Zealand, bearing long dangly catkins, and Magnolia buds sprouting among old fruits resembling decrepit corn cobs. Admiring an ancient yew, I was told there was a yew a thousand years old in St. John's churchyard at Danescourt near Brynteg. I must investigate

Some of the walled gardens contained spring flowers, the usual popular hellebores and blue periwinkles, Scillas and lungwort (*Pulmonaria officinalis*). The trumpet flowers of these graded from pink to blue as they matured, like so many of this borage family, and the leaves were decorated with the white spots that have resulted in the alternative name of students' tears.

Neatly trimmed beech hedges holding their leaves through the winter and Gunnera plants mounded up with juicy compost provided focal points. There were said to be twenty five varieties of apples in the orchard, as well as the spreads of Ericas and drifts of daffodils at the height of their springtime exuberance leading away under the avenues of trees.

Big marquees were set out on open grassland beyond the carpark and a few smaller ones near the house. One blocked a path up from the wooded gully but had a handy flap in the back allowing us to creep through rather than retrace our steps.

A pleasant visit this and my first although I had explored these lower reaches of the Thaw and Kenson river valleys in some detail in the long ago. The key feature of interest here on the lowland adjacent to the castle is that tidal flow is manifested more than a mile inland from the sea. The infiltration of sea salt enables salt marsh plants to grow astonishingly far up the Thaw Valley, adding piquancy to the fat lambs thriving on the riverside paddocks. More recently I had attended the annual Cowbridge Show, which is held on more substantial land adjacent to Fonmon Castle.

CHAPTER 7

Garden Centres and Wild Daffodils

Now that I lived so close to the "Food for Thought" rendezvous other members tended to 'pop in' after meetings for a repeat of the tea or coffee and biscuits with which we topped off our lunch before the talk. Folk who were aware of my propensity for collecting things and throwing almost nothing away, were interested to see how I was coping.

Better, thank goodness, than an old friend, Kathleen Chambre, daughter of the family doctor who had brought me into the world. After leaving the rambling family home she had lived cheek by jowl with the stacked, unopened packing cases, sidling round them with difficulty to get from room to room, for the rest of her life! That beautiful rambling old house and garden with its lavish crops of raspberries and other delicacies in South Ealing Road, was demolished like so many others to make way for blocks of flats.

Some visitors came bearing flowers. The oversized yellow primroses, with calyces like small parasols, kept on blooming merrily for three months with new flowers pushing up among the old, before the still prolific survivors wilted and gave up the ghost. Sometimes we sipped our cuppa in the restaurant of Pughs plant nursery a mile or so up the road at Morganstown and from there, too, we were likely to emerge bearing plants.

On one occasion Madeleine Beswick took me off on a trip around other garden centres, all of which tempted would-be shoppers with tea and cakes and an unbelievable array of gadgets and ornaments for the garden. With all those flower-orientated gardening programmes appearing on television, gardening was becoming quite a cult - and one for the well heeled if the range of pricey products for sale was anything to go by.

We started with the Caerphilly Garden Centre on the road east over the hills from the old Nant Garw Pottery. I could hardly drag myself away but had no garden now to replenish with new slug fodder. The range of colour and form in newly developed types of primroses was mind boggling, all the dazzling displays out in the open, buffeted on this occasion by half a gale, although the sun shone, as so often on these blustery spring days. These were not Polyanthus, with the umbel of flowers topping a single main stalk.

We visited other sites, penetrating into Monmouthshire or Gwent, through Machen and Tredegar towards Newport. I had known these roads long ago, when I used to drive to Ealing to visit the family before the first Severn Bridge was built to shorten the distance.

All these years later the cables of that bridge had rusted and been repaired by some new fangled technique, though much of the traffic between Wales and England now crosses by the new bridge further west, nearer to Caldicot.

The decades roll by too fast. No wonder I failed to recognise most of these roads. I had known many as penetrating wooded countryside bordered by high, straggly hedges. Now there was new development everywhere but, laudably, often well back from the verges of the widened highways with green belts between. Those were grassed and daffodil strewn in parts, with a decorative element of ornamental trees. All is not lost. Both Cardiff and Newport councils are to be commended on their efforts at landscaping around inevitable new developments.

We turned back towards Cardiff, stopping for more shopping and afternoon tea at "Blooms" south of the main highway. Modern garden centres such as this are a very different kettle of fish from the old plant nurseries with just the odd diminutive gnome as light entertainment. They are geared as full blown visitor centres, with café and shop, garden furniture and tempting extravaganza to hold their customers for long enough to make their visit a pleasurable as well as a business experience. Tourism rather than basic industries had become the most significant mainstay of the economy in this affluent age.

Even our pleasant "Pick Your Own" and vineyard by the River Taff in Radyr has graduated from the hot coffee and ice cream at outdoor tables by the currant bushes to fully blown bed and breakfast, not to mention the maize maze and the festival of home grown pumpkins in the fall. One day perhaps, when our guest suite is occupied, I might avail myself of the b and b.

On another occasion we took ourselves to Castell Coch at Tongwynlais after the lecture, taking tea in the café there without doing the tour of the premises with their famous Aesop fables room. Instead we followed down the stone steps to the south and up to the west, admiring the many venerable beeches spilling down the precipitous slope to the A470 roundabout below. We were in the gorge here, atop the old quarry face backing the big spread of the Coryton roundabout at the M4 junction a little to the south.

* * *

I reciprocated by taking Madeleine to the Wildlife Trust's springtime showpiece of the wild daffodil wood at Castle-upon-Alun north of St. Brides Major near Bridgend. It was another of those brisk winter days, the 25th February, and the elongated woodland clinging to the steep Carboniferous limestone slope bordering the Alun Valley was at its prime.

There had been years when the panoramic display of wild daffodils had failed to open in time for St. David's day celebrations on March first, but this was not one of them. A few decades ago boy scouts had picked limited amounts to sell for their funds, on St. David's day and Mother's day, but that had been phased out when the area was granted the conservation status that it so richly deserved.

As always when possible, I avoided the main highways, looping northwest along the traditional route through Creigiau, Talbot Green, Llanharan, Pencoed and Ewenny. Parking in the muddy layby by the Trust plaque opposite the pack horse bridge over the locally expanded stream, we strolled back along the narrow lane.

The padlock had been removed from the gate so we didn't have to climb over as in the past. Spread before us was the rare delight of truly wild daffodils, the individuals not much bigger than the cultivated tête-á-tête variety and more decoratively distributed as Mother Nature decreed.

They had opened ahead of the associated wood Anemones this year but little clumps of white were beginning to appear among the yellow in the cosily damp mass of flowering dog's mercury and ferns. Moss was rampant, creeping inexorably over crumbling rock and ancient timber supporting the downhill side of the contoured paths on steeper sections. These humble plants also romped over the "ecological piles" of branches from past coppicing, intended as homes for the smaller furry and six-legged inhabitants of the wood.

Narcissus pseudonarcissus, the wildlings, differed from most cultivated ones in their daintier mien. The central trumpet or corona is a darker yellow than the surrounding perianth of sepals and petals. The corona is the same colour as the rest in the only other wild representative of the genus, the Tenby daffodil, subspecies obvallis, found naturally only in West Wales.

We spotted no violets or moschatel flowering as yet and few primroses, those formerly romping through the bracken meadow across the river having been ploughed up along with the bracken and irrevocably lost some years before.

Brightest exhibits of all were the scarlet elf cup fungi (*Sarcoscypha coccinea*) opening fleshy saucers to the sun on fallen sticks, some nibbled around the edges by small rodents or slugs. Somewhat flabby flanges of pink Jew's ear fungus (*Auricularia auricula-judae*), deflated by the previous night's frost, clung to moribund, barkless elder branches.

Bluebell leaves were pushing through, particularly at the north end of the wood, and the pick-a-back plants (*Tolmeia menziesii*) continued to produce new little plants at the base of the leaves in the shallow pond by the lower wall.

We wandered across the stone slab bridge spanning the crystal clear waters of the Alun with its fine crop of fool's watercress and followed the river until turned back by unwelcoming mud and puddles. Then back to the car and on past roadside drifts of white violets yet to flower to the ford and stepping stones for our picnic.

We left the ford crossing to a passing land rover and walked between the lofty railway embankment and the stony floored watercourse under the tall railway bridge and through the lych gate to the disused quarry well above.

This huge, flat floored gash in the side of Old Castle Down was a traditional site for clay pigeon shooting. The end where we entered was partially strewn with shattered orange fragments of the flying targets fired from the gun. These created sheets of colour as brilliant as parts of New World deserts clothed with Californian poppies, a site once seen never forgotten. Beauty is in the eye of the beholder. Stand well back and half close the eyes and the imagination can run riot.

Deviating nearer the backing cliff than usual, we found ourselves walking over the wintry remains of a mat of wild lady's mantle. There was little else apart from low gorse in full flower and arching brambles. Two buzzards hung low over our heads, wheeling idly in a thermal rising from Carboniferous rocks rich in fossil Brachiopods.

I seldom came this far without visiting my favourite part of the Heritage Coast at Southerndown so we climbed back up the lane and on past the Charolet beef farm and golden plover roosting field to the Farmers' Arms and the road to Ogmore-by-Sea. There was no sign of the usual resident mute swans on Pitcot Pool by Pool Dairy Farm in St. Brides Major, only Canada geese and ducks.

From the top of the panoramic drive down to Dunraven Bay, we cruised along behind a jaunty little pied wagtail on the way ahead, but all was not as tranquil as usual. Doubts had been expressed about the safety of the road, which followed quite close to the cliff edge, and a replacement was being constructed alongside further inland. Mighty bulldozers were at work churning up yellow gravelly soil and pale chunks of Liassic limestone.

These rocks were more collapsible than the older ones underlying the daffodil wood, knitted together as those were by verdant plant life. The cliffs here sometimes had fierce seas pounding at their base, leaving new falls of yellow iron-stained rocks at their foot, these bleaching as the minerals leached out.

Nobody was about at the Heritage Coast Centre tucked into its valley below the drive to the ruins of Dunraven Castle. After inspecting the healthy dollops of frogspawn in the little pond and paying our respects to the ginger cats, the storm beach and wide expanse of sand, we wended our way back up the hill.

It was a little unnerving passing almost beneath the great bucket of sticky soil swinging towards us from one of the mechanical diggers. Instinctively my foot pressed a little harder on the accelerator. At the top we intercepted chief warden Paul Dunn shepherding a party of school children and not a little apprehensive about their safety, but their coach was waiting in the clifftop carpark out of danger's way instead of down by the beach. A police car following us up cut short our chat and we continued, back westwards now, to Ogmore-by-Sea.

Opposite the great embayment of Merthyr Mawr saltmarsh by the River Ogmore I turned sharply up the steep lane running through Norton pinewoods to the Heol-y-Mynydd upland, almost grinding to a halt half way up. (Last time I had been in a more powerful car). My current Toyota Yaris responded and we cruised the tiny lanes atop the plateau to emerge near St. Brides Major.

Time did not permit an exploration of more coast, so we sped eastwards through Wick, turning north at St. Donat's Castle and homeward through Ystrad Owen and Llantrithydd to Cowbridge, Pontyclun and Creigiau.

CHAPTER 8
The London Visit

When awarded my MBE in the 2008 New Years Honours List for services to nature conservation in Wales, I was told that my invitation to the palace to receive it would be within the next five months. In fact it was quite soon, for mid March. So soon, in fact, that the papers confirming the date got lost in the house move. They were clearly labelled and securely packed but were in one of the last boxes to be opened. After sleepless nights and fruitless searches I had to apply to the palace via the Welsh Office for more. Both London and Wales were very understanding of an old woman's bungles, so I had a duplicate set when the originals eventually turned up.

There were other snags relating to this early date. One was the state of my feet, which had been faithfully tended by a podiatrist in Rhondda-Cynon-Taff during the years since the installation of my new knee in 2002. I had now moved into the administrative district of Cardiff and the Taffs Well Health Centre had cast me adrift. Although wasting no time in enrolling at the Radyr counterpart, I was informed that there was a twenty four week waiting list.

Elderly feet get worse rather than better. Did I have to wait for all those in front of me on the list to die? Already my toe nails were uncomfortably long, only the most clod-hopperish of shoes at all wearable and scarcely suitable for the expedition in mind.

"No worry" said the optimists. "The chiropody students in the University in Western Avenue practise on the likes of you." I rang up. "Sorry, students are just breaking up for Easter and they don't treat customers in the summer term because of exams. I'll put you on the waiting list for October when they return." That same twenty four weeks waiting time!.

Exhaustive search in the motley of telephone directories that have replaced the once simple "yellow pages" and help from friends and I found a podiatrist willing to take me on. I was leaving on the Tuesday morning and she came on the Sunday afternoon, just in time, but causing me to miss out on an arranged excursion with Martin Doe to visit the section of railway line that he and a group of amateur enthusiasts were constructing at Cynheidre, north-west of Llanelli. (I had been involved there since volunteering for the initial ecological survey required by the planners and liked to keep in touch).

I scoured numerous shoe shops for walking shoes and elegant town ones, returning with the two most expensive but far from comfortable pairs. Subsequent days were divided between trying to break them in by wearing and subjecting them to shoe stretchers, these exercises only partially successful.

Garments didn't bother me. I had just the right navy and white three piece outfit bought for a party in the 1970s and scarcely worn since. It fitted perfectly, as well as conforming to modern styles with a low neckline to accommodate my triple row of pearls. Even those who had insisted that "If you haven't worn it you don't need it" approved. I should be wearing a navy straw hat so a special hair do was not called for.

I could have done with a lot more time to recover from the trauma of trying to deal with too many things at once. Those first six weeks passed in a whirl of humping boxes around, correspondence with official bodies, notifying change of address to all and sundry, although I had paid the Royal Mail to forward my letters for three months, and apologising where approriate for failing to send the usual Christmas cards.

Utilities paid for by direct debit were usually in credit, so there were sums to claim back, and for property insurance paid in advance by both vendor and purchaser. I was in the throes of a long drawn out verbal war with BT which had made an exorbitant charge for connecting only one of my telephone lines instead of two. Their policy was to request me to phone, so that they could spend the next twenty five minutes telling me how busy they were and that I had been put in a queue! Also I was on a steep learning curve as to how to sell surplus books on the internet, of which I knew nothing.

There were other matters to complete before I took off, the most urgent the correcting of the final page proofs of a book for Halsgrove, my Somerset publisher. This was the third in the Island Trilogy that I had embarked upon after completing my tome on the Welsh Islands, this one concerning the Inner Hebrides.

Other commitments were requests for two articles. One, from my old school, attended in the 1930s, requested a 'pep talk' aimed at senior students on how to qualify for an award - to put it crudely. The other was from a bright schoolboy in Gwaelod whose history project on "What did Britain's women do during the Great War?" required a letter from one such woman who was there. Both were interesting assignments, except for the bottleneck.

The mouse had escaped from my not so new computer during the move and was difficult to replace in the fast moving computer world without endless hassle. The new shelf was up to accommodate it, thanks to the indefatigable Clive, who was my moral and practical mainstay during this whole period, but all the wires seemed too short - more cheese pairing - and required considerable ingenuity in getting it all wired to my new monitor with crucial switches within reach.

* * *

It was a case of 'out of the winter thermals and corduroy slacks' for the three day trip to the metropolis, which coincided with the coldest spell of the winter. My glad rags would have to be worn throughout, to cut down on the luggage.

The rain held off, but the arctic wind did not. I padded down the hill to the station, unsure of the frequency of the local services and so leaving far too much time in hand. A freezing half hour was spent on Cardiff Station, watching three Paddington trains leave before the one on which I was booked and which my god-daughter, Rosemary Hufton, was meeting arrived.

The tryst was kept in the seething mob of commuters surging along the platform. A happy reunion this as we seldom met and we spent the time in the slow moving queue for the taxi catching up.

She and her husband, Dave, had nobly taken on the organisation of my visit, although a great deal shorter of spare time than I was. They had recently spent three weeks touring New Zealand - Rosemary's sixtieth birthday treat - comparing what they witnessed there with my hardback book "A Naturalist in New Zealand", relating to my year spent there in 1957. Fifty years is a long time in a country as 'young' as this!

Almost immediately on return they had gone off for a week's skiing in the Austrian Alps. Sadly the snow was washed away by rain and the trip evolved into a week of walking rather than skimming the slopes. Soon after my visit they were off to their cottage in the Lake District, for mountain walking as well as catching up with some craft work. This is where they experienced the snow!

Crammed into the gap between, they had booked me into the Cavendish Hotel between Jermyn Street and Piccadilly in St. James's, just opposite Fortnum and Masons. I was able to wander in this famous emporium while Rosemary queued to pay for a 'pinta' for a 'cuppa' to be taken in her London flat a short distance away. She had travelled up from her home in Reigate and the flat was stocked only with a minimum of non-perishables.

I tried to avoid supermarkets when possible, on principle, because of the poor way they treated their farming suppliers. Used as I was to Spars and Co-ops in Welsh villages, this emporium with so famous a name was a revelation.

My mouth watered as I viewed the venison and game pies in all shapes and sizes, fancy cheeses, exotic fruit products in sparkling jars and confectionery to suit the most fastidious palates. All was tastefully displayed among a range of exotic orchids and other gems of the plant kingdom. The window layout, I gathered, was frequently changed.

The Hufton flat, which I had expected to be a small sanctuary near Dave's office to cut down on constant commuting, proved to be a fine two bedroomed establishment bigger than my new humble abode in Wales. It was tastefully furnished with unusual pieces, modern, sometimes curvaceous and of mellowed beige timber with none of the metal and glass monstrosities which are deemed fashionable but are certainly neither beautiful nor comfortable to live with.

My hostess was a prominent figure in the world of arts and crafts with her own boutique in a Surrey village, so the wealth of three dimensional wall hangings and other original works by famous artists came as no surprise. The amount of time-consuming details worked into the designs was mind boggling. The more I looked the more intrigued I became, philistine though I am about much modern art. Some of these were a joy.

Dinner was taken in style at Green's fish restaurant across the road, with husband Dave, brother Anthony and son Michael, who, like his two married brothers, had his own London flat to supplement the spacious family home in Surrey.

Back at the Cavendish, I acquainted myself with the electronic room key - not just a card, but a metal contraption which had to be whisked rapidly in and out of a hole in the corridor wall to release the lock and then placed in a container inside before the lights would come on.

I selected two from the assembled pillows and cushions on the double bed and lay back, admiring a huge monochrome photograph of a chap leaping across a spreading roadside puddle and so poised that the viewer was set to worrying whether he made it or not!

Four of us re-assembled for breakfast in the Cavendish. This special day started with a hard to believe range of dishes and accessories - fruit, flesh, fish and fowl eggs in lieu of my normal cornflakes or toast.

* * *

We were close enough to walk to Buckingham Palace across Green Park, which was adorned with drifts of daffodils smiling up at a sunny sky. When I had brought my friend Joan Raum with me to a royal garden party seven years before, we had sat in a traffic block in the Mall for ages, waiting to filter through to our goal. This was not going to happen again, and not because the congestion charge had thinned the traffic.

The wind was slight and my hat only blew off twice. The lawns were not even damp and my renovated feet, temporarily accommodated in suitable shoes, presented no problem. We emerged at the Queen Victoria Memorial opposite the palace at the junction of the Mall and Constitution Hill, both of which are closed to traffic on Sundays, but not Wednesdays. A crowd lined the railings, photographing the patient sentries in their coffin shaped sentry boxes. The necessary security checking was carried out by police and palace officials at entry into the outer courtyard and again at the steps leading inside and through to the inner quadrangle. Photographic proof, as on passports, was required as well as our entry passes.

From cosy cloakrooms with sofas for shoe changing, we were ushered into grand rooms decorated with statues and hung with priceless pictures - 'candidates' one way and 'visitors' another. There were a lot of us and proceedings necessarily rather long drawn out over some three hours.

Marshalls put us through our paces, reminding the men not to curtsey by mistake, and other minutiae regarding etiquette. We sipped orange juice, chatted with fellow recipients and made efforts not to look as if we were posing when one of the press cameras pointed our way. Some of the military men were wearing silver spurs - not presumably needed in battle any more, these possibly part of the ceremonial cavalry.

We had closed circuit television screens, so could watch proceedings until our turn came, but this was denied our companions, who were shepherded into banks of seats resembling those of a grand cinema auditorium, from which there was no escape to relieve necessary bodily functions.

Orchestral music was provided by one of the orchestras of the Royal Artillery Household Division from a balcony at the rear of the hall throughout. The constant procession of unknowns to the dais must have proved tedious to the audience after the first few, who were receiving knighthoods.

These knelt, like King Arthur's knights of old, on a velvet investiture stool to receive their accolades. The sword laid on both shoulders was the one which King George VI used when, as Duke of York, he was colonel of the Scottish Guards.

It was a disappointment that the honours were not being bestowed by the queen. She was in Northern Ireland, to hand out the Maundy Thursday bounty. The Prince of Wales stood in for her, producing sunny smiles and meaningful comments for what must have seemed an endless line of recipients, with infinite patience and obvious goodwill.

I was delighted that he remembered me from a meeting in 1982, twenty four years earlier. He had come to open the new headquarters of the County

Wildlife Trust when I was taking my turn as president, so I had had the honour of showing him round and introducing him to others.

A few weeks after that when I had had a wildlife group on the Scilly Isles, we had encountered him informally. (He came here as often as he could to scuba dive and escape the raz-ma-taz of his position). He had asked one of the students where they were from, commenting that he had been with a wildlife group there only a few weeks before.

On the 2008 occasion, as recognition flashed onto his overworked countenance, he asked me how long I would be keeping on. It was twenty four years ago, but he remembered having written a preface to my "Swansea Bay" book, after enjoying reading its predecessor on "Gower".

During our slow passage to the dais, four Gentlemen Ushers to the Queen saw that we were headed for the right place at the right time. Formalities of the proceedings were as follows:-

The prince entered the ballroom attended by two Gurkha Orderly Officers - a tradition begun in 1876 by Queen Victoria. On the dais were five members of the Queen's Bodyguard of the Yeomen of the Guard, which was created in 1485 by King Henry VII after his victory at the Battle of Bosworth Field. This made them not only the oldest royal bodyguard but also the oldest military corps existing in the UK.

Prince Charles was escorted onto the dais by the Lord Chamberlain who, after the national anthem, announced the name and achievement of each recipient. Then the prince, attended by an Equerry in Waiting and the Master of the Household or his deputy, took a token of the decoration to be awarded from the proffered velvet cushion. The actual medal was collected on the way out, an ornate silver cross on a red silk bow in a neat casket. Had he stopped to pin it on each lapel his fingers would have been very sore and the audience even more bored.

After the ceremony participants and watchers mingled on staircases and in vestibules, stepping back to make way for little posses of soldiers on ceremonial duties or admiring their unwavering stillness as they stood at attention at crucial point while the mob swirled round them.

Outside in the Inner Quadrangle three long queues waited in the icy blast for the attention of the professional photographers. The crucial snippet of the long-running TV record would be too difficult to come by, but we could take photos of our own little group without the body chilling wait.

After so doing, we strolled out round the Queen Victoria Memorial and along the Mall. The impressive range of palaces was bathed in sunshine, which glinted the brightest on the magnificent black and gold wrought iron gates leading from Green Park.

On the boundary walls of historic mansions were effigies of Queen Caroline Queen Mary &c. Lancaster House, Clarence House, St. James's

Palace, Marlborough House, the Horse Guards Parade and Admiralty Arch, they were all here, with the twinkling waters of the wildfowl lake in St. James' Park on the other side of the famous thoroughfare.

Unlike some cities that shall remain nameless, there was no hint of atmospheric pollution here. The businesslike wind cooperated with unobstructed sun rays to dispel any repeats of those old fashioned London smogs of my childhood, when I was sent to walk in front of the family car to show father at the wheel where the kerb was. Londoners have foregone their wood and coal fires for the benefit of all, while we, in our far flung outposts, can still enjoy them - and our garden bonfires.

Our lunch had been booked at the RAC club, from where Rosemary and Dave's oldest son had been married a few years earlier, but we arrived too late. We bundled into a taxi in Pall Mall, which runs parallel to the Mall and emerged at Pesces, another busy fish restaurant for another grand repast. I could manage only the starter of crab meat and avocado pear with tomatoes on the vine and crusty bread, which was quite delicious.

Afterwards Dave returned to his office and Anthony to Winchester, where he had just retired from the post of physics master and much more besides in the arts field on the staff of Winchester College.

Rosemary took her streaming cold, acquired in rainy Austria, to bed for a few hours and I bought a book in Hatchards bookshop at 187, Piccadilly, established in 1797 and claiming to be the oldest and most famous bookshop in Europe and booksellers to the royal household. With this I snuggled into my multitude of cushions for a quiet read after brewing up a pot of tea.

Dinner in the Cavendish was with Rosemary and her youngest son, Tom, who was off the next day to join his siblings on a different ski slope in Austria. Dave joined us later after a business dinner with a client. What busy and exciting lives some people do lead! It made me feel like a real country bumpkin, but tis said that every dog has his day and I'd enjoyed a good share of the big wide world during my eighty six years.

Next morning, Maundy Thursday, Rosemary and I breakfasted in Fortnum and Masons, where I indulged in "the Welsh breakfast". No, not laverbread with my bacon, but Welsh rarebit with tomatoes and mushrooms. We parted at Paddington, she to Reigate and a dental appointment, me back to my frugal life in the Principality.

Due to vagaries of the "First Great Western" ticket system, I had been issued with a first class ticket for my return trip as a second class one was only available at much greater price. My booked seat was opposite a most interesting gent and we conversed all the way back.

An art critic and lecturer, he had a house in London and a holiday cottage in Penarth Marina on Cardiff Bay. More interestingly, he was the ex-owner of Cwrt-yr-Ala House, lakes and estate near Dinas Powis and a knowledgable amateur naturalist. He had recently discovered an inscription of historic significance on a newly exposed wall of the ancient building which few could have known about and knowledge of which he wished to share. I put him in touch with Dr. Joan Andrews, obstetrics surgeon and resident of Dinas Powis, on whose history she sometimes lectured. Friend as well as ex-student, she was one of the few whose address I knew by heart, so hopefully they got in touch.

CHAPTER 9
Easter 2008. Sully, Swanbridge and Merthyr Tydfil

The 2008 Easter Weekend will be remembered for its unseasonality, undermining the general trend of global warming. True it was earlier than usual, Good Friday falling on 21st March, but during the whole of late March and the first three weeks of April bitter gales came pounding in across the North Sea, holding back milder air streams from the Atlantic.

Warm weather earlier in the year had brought flowers into bloom ahead of time and it could be quite warm in the sun out of the wind. Elderly residents were often to be seen lounging on the garden seats outside the front door enjoying a sunny gossip, like their counterparts in the Mediterranean.

If that layer of carbon dioxide that we hear so much about stops the Earth's heat from dissipating into the upper air, how is it that it lets so much of the sun's heat through in the opposite direction? During at least part of any day spent in the open one was bound to be inappropriately dressed.

Good Friday started with snow warnings for South and East England and rain, hail and sleet was promised for the West, spurred on by the gales. We got one icy storm, but this did not linger. An earlier counterpane of hailstones had melted during daylight to cover the lawn as dew. This melted during the evening and then refroze as hoar frost so the ground was still white by morning. The atmosphere seemed empty of particulate matter, early sunrays unobstructed as they illuminated the rosy tints of chaffinches and long-tailed tits engaged in their trapeze acts.

I was amused to see the visiting ginger cat, who shall be called Ginger Pop, streaking back home uphill into the teeth of the worst hail storm, spurred to supreme effort by the elements.

As the Good Friday precipitation ceased a rainbow arched across the sky, its eastern end reaching out of the Taff Gorge to bathe the hillside above in a felt of melded colours, the texture softened as though the myriad water droplets were individually visible.

My breakfast time bird celebrity was a sparrow hawk passing low over the garden. The small head, hunched shoulders, slender body and narrow wings, grey like a cuckoo's, were unmistakable. Crows still came to 'my' lime tree to tweak off bark for their nests, so I was interested to learn that the inner bark of the common lime was traditionally used in the manufacture of ropes and netting.

I availed myself of one of the fine spells on the way back from Taffs Well to stroll in the fields between Pugh's floral displays and Gelynis Farm's soft fruit plots. The sap had scarcely begun to rise in the hedgerow between the field and the track leading to Station House, located dangerously on the other side of the line with commuter trains passing every ten minutes and no road access from the other side.

Things were very different at the edge of the flood plain below Morganstown. A brisk stream came rollicking down here from the tapering end of Pugh' show area, to follow the junction of flood plain and scarp and on under the M4 bridge to Radyr. Kingfishers have been seen here, but not today.

Alongside were thousands of chunky, pollen-packed cones of giant horse-tail thrusting up through the long grass. Young cones of this primitive relic from the ancient Coal Forests shed primrose-yellow pollen onto the breeze at the gentlest touch. Older ones changed through ginger to dark brown before the brittle stem collapsed.

This giant species, unlike the lesser one which sometimes ramps through gardens as a noxious weed, is quite uncommon, although likely to become invasive in propitious habitats. Later in the summer the stream here would be bordered by its two foot high stems bearing whorls of linear branches, brittle with their content of silica, their green chlorophyll standing in for that of the absent leaves in the manufacture of food.

Moister, more open ground nearby supported golden saxifrage sprinkled with starry yellow flowers. Elegant tutsan plants, their young leaves a mellowed crimson, sprouted from among the tangle of alder roots washed free of soil in former floods. Below the ancient, wooded motte the riparian spinney was bordered by young meadowsweet plants and brightened with daffodils.

On Easter Saturday I had hoped to join a party of Cardiff Naturalist members crossing the causeway to Sully Island at low water, but the gale was phenomenal by then and I chickened out.

Next morning I made my initial sortie into the back garden a few days after the first lawn mowing had been undertaken - quite un-necessarily as the grass cover was impoverished, with more exposed soil and moss patches than sprouting blades. As I pushed open the tall wooden gate a ferocious gust slammed it back onto my body. Quite a heave was needed to re-open it and leap out of the way to prevent a repeat.

Among the purple shoot tips of dwarf Hebe shrubs were the clear stars of an open ground cover of greater periwinkles. Much brighter were the apical leaves of red robin (*Photinea fraseri*) - the perfect foil for the daffodils ranged beneath. As the golden trumpets faded the crimson of the red robin leaves was almost the only colour left in the garden which was mostly planted with shrubs, needing minimal attention.

Only when outside here, peering over the bounding fence, was it possible to appreciate that the land fell away almost vertically to the level of the station yard. No development could mushroom up from there to block our view. The 'cliff' had no doubt been accentuated by cutting away the base to increase the acreage below. It was still quite inadequate as a station carpark in the current climate of "Park and Ride". Cars were parked along all roads leading away from here on weekdays, making life difficult for locals and shoppers.

My progress was observed through windows by the house manager's black and white collie, Mitzi and, further on, by the fluffy white Persian cat belonging to one of the basement residents on the storey below mine, which was "lower ground", down one from the front entrance, so steep was the terrain.

This furry flat-faced animal did not venture out much but when it did the excessive upholstery did not prevent it from squeezing under the fence and disappearing over the cliff. Despite the blatantly visible coat colour, it was reported to bring back shrews from hunting expeditions. On one occasion, when it was still a long way from the regular ginger visitor, the latter took flight and bolted with the loose bundle of white in hot pursuit, fur flying. The only other feline seen so far was an elderly black cat wearing a collar.

My Sunday afternoon walk was a short one through the wood and football fields on the near side of the Taff. Stepping through the ground cover of ivy, admiring the expanding leaves of sycamore and Buddleia, I came across more of the attractive scarlet elf cups as seen in the daffodil wood, these on partially bare soil near the old badger sett.

The first bluebell flowers of the season had opened on long stalks, but these were alien Spanish ones and not the dinkum natives. Where field met wood was a broad strip covered with the cotyledonary phase of Himalayan balsam seedlings, like a scattering of paired green tiddlywinks. The resulting flower stems, five to six feet high, would dwarf the perforated St. John's wort and knotted figwort currently overtopping them.

Mallard and moorhen were careering down river on the considerable turbulence. The grey wagtail stayed on terra firma, on a shingle bank, with a chattering flock of long-tailed tits flitting among branches above.

I strolled out on the footbridge and encountered Eric, chemist, OBE and a Brynteg resident returning from watching a kingfisher in one of the bird hides. He pointed down to the bramble-draped stone revetments of the east bank and told me of the time when he had watched an otter there in recent months. It took no notice of him immediately above, finally entering the water and swimming off downstream. So far I had had only a brief sighting of one of these elusive mammals a little further upstream at Tongwynlais.

Having known this stretch of river when it was black with coal dust, supporting no fish to support this king of our river systems, none of which were around to be tempted, it was good to know that they were back again, so near to the human presence that they manage to elude so successfully.

* * *

On Easter Monday Madeline and I went further afield, to some of the lesser known parts of the Glamorgan coast, from Sully, through Swanbridge, to St. Marywell Bay. Snow was still lying in South-east England, but we had merely an icy wind, driving scudding cloudlets across the blue vault.

I had hoped to show her the dinosaur footprints in the lee of Bendrick Rocks at Sully. My usual way down hitherto had been past the land based naval station, but this had been blocked to public access by tall locked gates. The adjacent limestone woodland alongside , where we used to find a rich range of calcicole plants was also now out of bounds.

We turned round and followed a potholey road across debris strewn wasteland to seaward of the Dow Corning industrial complex atop the low brink. On the cliff path leading back through windswept, felted fescue grass, we were soon blocked by branches and brambles. Evidently the navy wanted this place to themselves.

Artificial excavations showed the soil to be a sticky clay with blackthorn bushes condensed by sea winds into impenetrable barriers. A botanical surprise here was the spreading carpet of ground ivy peppered with blue flowers, growing in the open. This is usually a plant of woodland and hedgerow, although also characteristic of soil bared by rabbits, which do not normally eat it. Spearing up from the carpet were a few straw-coloured heads of carline thistles.

The low indented cliff was composed of Triassic New Red Sandstone and we spotted a nice example of fossilised ripple marks on the surface of one of the horizontal strata just below the brink. Fashioned in the sand flooring a shallow tropical lagoon aeons ago, these had been covered over and lithified before losing their shape, to be re-exposed as the covering layers eroded away.

There were places where we could have scrambled down to the stony beach but the bitter wind was not encouraging, so we missed out on the dinosaur footprints.

I had a special feeling for these since showing them to friends from the red Triassic rocks of the same age and in the same latitude in New England. They were scientists and recognised the footprints as replicas of some of their own of similar age on the other side of the "Big Pond".

When the Atlantic Ocean opened up between the Old World and the New, the rift carried land from the old Pangea continent away from what is now the west coast of Britain. Why shouldn't the same dinosaurs turn up on both sides of the break? Even the same animals, we phantasised, "walking" the short way from Britain to America?

Wind or no wind, we stood entranced by the views, particularly when looking up channel with the westering sun behind. The black dome of Steepholm Island rose from water that we knew was brown with suspended silt, but which sparkled blue as it reflected the overarching dome of sky, in front of a backdrop of black snow clouds scudding across the eastern horizon.

To its left lay the lower hump of its sister island of Flatholm with the lighthouse protruding from one corner, and to its right the hump backed outline of Brean Down on the Somerset coast. Up channel what looked like the white line of breaking waves bordering the mainland must have been the sun glinting on the white caravans and bungalows around Swanbridge.

Immediately offshore was the chunky outline of Bendrick Rocks and down channel to the west the little white lighthouse at the end of the long grassed causeway marking the entrance to Barry Docks.

On leaving we explored westwards past a motley of industrial complexes, some derelict, some new, and by mountainous heaps of dark soil and debris. Past clear water, well maintained dock basins towards Barry town and then along the old coal loading bays where fennel used to grow so prolifically opposite the old Fyffes' Bananas warehouse, to the main port complex below the Docks Office.

Old industrial standings here had been grassed over in a land restoration programme, all those wonderful exotic plants that used to grow across the whole complex lost for ever in the clean-up. We emerged at the landmark of the oval roundabout below the bridge under the main line railway.

Taking the winding lane seaward from the Penarth Road we came to the coast again at the landward end of the causeway leading across to Sully Island, where I should have been two days earlier. It was still low tide, the seaweedy slabs beckoning enticingly, but it would have been unwise to cross without finding out which way the racing forty foot tides were flowing. It was too cold to get ourselves marooned!

As we left the car above the tumbled foreshore fronting "The Captains

Wife" Restaurant at Swanbridge we spotted a brown rat scuttling over the broken masonry where the motor road ended to begin again at a different level beyond the rift.

Yellow-green umbels of Alexanders were at prime all along the roadsides hereabouts as we proceeded afoot towards St. Maryswell Bay. There was a marked contrast between the beautifully renovated stone farm buildings into secluded dwellings and the abandoned white block of the former hotel, with overgrown garden.

Quite unusual was the looping straggle of Duke of Argyle's tea-tree (*Lycium chinense*), a woody member of the nightshade family, which would bear unobtrusive pale mauve flowers later in the season. Sea radish was flowering among the sea beet on the rocky shore below the tangle.

Prunus flowers were of two kinds, the common starry ones of blackthorn or sloe on thorny black twigs and the slightly larger ones of bullace or cherry plum on non-spiny green shoots. Among the precocious Spanish bluebells were some delightful swards of white flowered sweet violets.

Herb Robert can produce Geranium flowers in any month of the year and had produced a prolific crop already. Much more seasonal were the yellow orbs of coltsfoot brightening a track curving to the now roofless ruin of the old St. Marywell Bay Hotel among tall trees spilling down to the red rocks of the shore.

We had intermittent glimpses of the packed caravans backing the curve of the bay and the tufty grass and saplings at the west end of the Lavernock Point Nature reserve beyond. Leaves of foetid Iris speared up from the wooded bank inland of the lane, but few of the orange seed heads remained, despite their obvious unpalatability to seed eating birds. Those could help themselves here to the late maturing harvest of ivy berries. There were banks of celandines throughout, these winning hands down as the showiest and most widespread of all spring flowers.

A small white, windowless building, the glass-sided upper storey more capacious than the lower, seemed to be a coastguard lookout like that at Boverton. Although almost surrounded by tall trees there was a clear view out through the treetops, across to the coast of Somerset and the islands between, where so much shipping passed on its way to Bristol and Avonmouth Docks.

The tide was still low when we returned to Swanbridge exposing the great sweep of pebble beach on the landward side of Sully Island, where flocks of waders assembled to roost. We returned due north from here, across the main road and along the lane through Cog and Old Cogan Farm, Morriston and Murch to emerge just south of the HTV Studios below the road junction to Llandough Hospital.

*\ *\ *

I had been a founder member of the Merthyr Naturalists' Society from way back in the 1960s and had kept in touch over the years. Many of the good folk in the South Wales Valleys tend to be part countrymen and part townsmen, with urban jobs but often country pursuits. Some kept ponies, some racing pigeons or poultry, one even emus. Many pursued country pastimes such as rabbit shooting or as beaters at pheasant shoots. I helped with talks and seldom missed the autumn fungus forays.

A long standing invitation from my friend Avril to help her eat a rabbit pie had been deferred. The rabbit had been shot by Gareth, son of the society's founder and long term chairman, Jack Evans, now no longer with us. It had languished in the freezer for months. Easter Tuesday was the day I finally drove north to enjoy the proceeds and the company.

Avril lived in Cefn Coed y Cwmmer, the ridge wood of the two valleys, where Taff Fawr and Taff Fechan joined for the thirty mile or so journey to the sea. Despite the great spread of Merthyr borough, the views from her elevated flat were extensive and fascinating. Many hills, one behind the other, surrounded the Merthyr Basin, with the Brecon Beacons rolling away to the north. The panorama showed how impressive this landscape must have been before the industrial revolution.

Most of my journey was along the A470, which continued over the Beacons to Central Wales. Constructed in the 1970s a little way up the western flank of the valley, it had left the little mining towns away to the east, One of the most attractive parts of the land separating the valley from those of the Cynon and Rhondda tributaries was the Quakers Yard landslip - a natural geological occurrence unrelated to the catastrophic landslip at Aberfan, this manifested now as a tumble of mossy boulders flooring mixed woodland.

The road was lined for mile upon mile with golden gorse, at its floriferous best in late March. Here, too, the blackthorn bloomed. Most of the autumn-flowering western gorse occurred in higher country, with heather and purple moor grass.

Snow lay on the high tops. Good to look at but not enough for the tobogganing and even ski-ing that had been enjoyed in certain winters of the sixties and eighties.

My hostess had forgotten until today that a few society members were meeting in the afternoon, but we did full justice to the rabbit pie before joining them. The function was a litter pick around Gethin Pond, one of the society's nature reserves in the Gethin Forestry Commission area west of Troed-y-Rhiw. Another nature reserve here was Cwm Woods, adjacent to some fine tree grown stone ruins surviving from the days of the smoking iron furnaces.

We travelled half a mile or so of forestry track taking us above the trunk road to the picnic and barbecue site where we met the others. There was no fungal foray this time, but not much litter picking either. We were equipped with long-handled "tweezers", as used by parties of volunteers cleaning Britain's beaches of litter, handy implements, ideal for capturing tins and bottles and tweaking out crumpled polythene. There was little to scavenge, as cleansing trips happened fairly often. "Mostly stuff left by the kids and fishermen"

The path wound down though a mature larchwood, soft underfoot with repeated increments of fallen needles from this, our only deciduous conifer. A pleasant walk this and much improved physically since my last visit. Where before there was mud to be squelched through and broken down stiles and gates to negotiate, all was now ship shape.

Members of the Merthyr Groundwork Trust had been busy surfacing paths and installing new metal kissing gates, also short lengths of board walk covered with non slip wire netting bordering quagmires in the lower, deciduous, wood, with its fine durmast oaks. Marginal trees had grown out beyond the rosebay willow herb fringe into the boggy meadow, which boasted many botanical rarities. It was no good looking for these now. In summer there would be ivy-leaved bellflower, pink pimpernel, lousewort, whorled caraway and cow wheat in swards of devil's bit scabious and sneezewort. Today's only flowers were the ubiquitous celandines and a few primroses and coltsfoot.

The dark waters of the pond lay clear and tranquil, steep sided and fringed by water plants and, in places, trees. Great crested newts were one of the highlights, but they were still hibernating, like the frogs. Two moorhens were paddling around, but no ducks. Four boys had fashioned a fine, ground level tree house back among the conifers, sawing and hacking bits from a sizable tree felled by recent gales.

I had forgotten the formal stone sculptures and was intrigued to examine them again. Some had images of four or five wildlife specimens carved into a single chunk of rock. A heron, the society's logo, came first, with a flying bat, dragonflies and fern fronds. Elsewhere frogs, toads, newts, water boatmen and more had been carved into the protruding faces of half buried blocks of the native pennant sandstone.

The most interesting birds seen were those little green and yellow finches, the siskins, along with long-tailed tits. Both fed on seeds from the abundant larch cones, the siskins more abundant this year and featuring in the RSPB's "Big garden bird watch"s' top ten.

Just a week later, on 1st April, an item on siskins and related finches was included in the "Today" programme on Radio 4, the compilation that keeps me informed before I rise from bed in the mornings. They featured, along with redpolls and bramblings, as coming within the same category as the too numerous immigrants being widely discussed on the media at the time.

An RSPB representative pointed out that flocks of these chirrupy little winter visitors from the North were scoffing the seeds and other victuals needed by our native birds - quoting the diminishing numbers of our sparrows, starlings and blackbirds. "They should have flown back to Scandinavia by now." Obviously, like the larger immigrants, they found life too pleasant to want to leave.

He went on to describe the proposed remedial scheme. Live traps were being issued to twitchers with garden bird feeders. "A bird approaching the bait steps lightly on the trigger and the sides close in around them." One at a time we presume to get sufficient for the long haul back to Denmark through BAA's newly opened, chaotic Fifth Terminal. "No problem" quoth he.

"They don't carry hand luggage. don't need to be frisked and wouldn't add to the mounds of mislaid baggage." "Yes, it is contrary to the usual RSPB policy of encouraging the feathered folk but this is, indeed, a rescue operation, entitled "Finches Flying Free", without tickets "to where they belong." I was taken in at first, but is WAS April fool's day and it wouldn't be the first time the Today programme had tried to hoodwink its public on such a day.

CHAPTER 10
Gwaelod, The Wenallt and Radyr Golf Course

On 25th March on my way back from Merthyr, I called into my old abode in Gwaelod-y-garth. This was a conscious decision. Sometimes, like a homing horse, my car decided to go that way anyway when reaching the Ynys roundabout. I had an open invitation to return as often as I liked and wander round.

The new owners were out but Babs was contacted on her mobile phone by the barman and gave me the all clear after partaking of a cappuccino while she finished her training run for the London marathon - with the two dogs.

She was determined to achieve that demanding goal, although no longer young and the brains behind the hotel enterprise - which had won several awards for excellence - as well as achieving much of the hard work. I met Richard after the event and learned that she had run the whole distance, despite wind and rain. She certainly earned her three day respite in London, as well as contributing substantially to her chosen charity.

The red flowering currants, one self sown in a wall top, were at prime, but the pink, cyclamen-like flowers of the dog's-tooth violet (*Erythronium denscanis*) had not yet followed the red-blotched leaves out of the soil. The green spurges were flowering, the brick red ones as yet only asparagus-like sprouts, alongside the long-lived hellebores.

I collected the final bramleys from the cats' sleeping quarters, these to last me until the third week of April. How flavourless and chewy the golden delicious, royal gala, braeburn and pink ladies seemed after those fully ripened, juicy cookers, but I still had some stewed in the freezer.

Certain trees had been lopped and a birch branch was caught up among the apple boughs, alongside a trampoline on the upper lawn. Firewood had been stacked on the honesty patch, blocking the route taken by the village cats down the 'precipice' at the far corner of the upper garden.

For almost the first time since leaving, I came face to face with one of the feral cats, the littlest. She recognised me, I'm sure, stopping in her tracks and gazing at me as if she couldn't believe her eyes. I wondered if she would tell the others. Having nothing edible to offer, I did her no service. Then a dog barked from inside and she was gone.

Barbara had reached home by then and swilled the perspiration off. "A lovely bath that". She came out, barefoot, to help me pot a few plants to take this with a wallpaper stripper that came to hand. Showing me round indoors, she stressed how much they enjoyed being there, despite the fact that it looked as though a hurricane had passed through.

Wallpaper had been stripped from the downstairs rooms. One was lime-washed a pale yellow, another brick red, the third not at all yet. A new double bed was centred in the main living room where the chimney I had had taken away because it leaked, was to be rebuilt to accommodate another wood fire The new kitchen suite was still in the garage. With the hotel cuisine laid on at the bottom of the garden, there was no hurry for that.

I gathered up the last of my belongings, six boxes of travel slides, a long lead for the projector and a summer bedspread and was glad that I wasn't living here any longer. A lot of work was necessary and I really hadn't wanted the hassle of it. I left with as many pot plants as I thought my balcony would accommodate and commandered the help of Eric Williams to get them indoors. (He was 'on watch' to let people in since the lock had been inoperable on the front door from the outside - with the house manager and most workmen absent on their Easter holidays.)

I came again to Gwaelod a fortnight hence, not to the Cottage but to visit a good friend, Norma Proctor at Wood Cottage in the lower village. She was helping me to establish an E mail address in an endeavour to persuade Amazon to sell some of my books on the internet, a process fraught with problems.

The golden light that had flooded through the beautiful flowering cherry into their sun parlour as I sipped coffee with husband Tom, faded as I left, and rain came tipping down. Driving alongside the Heol Beri Green, a sports field conjured out of the old iron furnace land, I sat it out in the car.

My ensuing walk by the river when the sun returned, was well rewarded, by the sighting of the first two goosanders of my winter. These two rare fishing ducks were headed downstream, being swirled along by the current, the glossy green-headed drake in the lead, his red-headed partner bobbing along behind. So bright was their plumage that my initial thought was shelduck, but these do not come so far up river, although having to tolerate fresh water in Cardiff Bay nowadays.

Consulting the official records, published later, I found that only seven goosanders had been reported from various sites on the Taff during the 2007 - 2008 winter by the county's dedicated band of watchers, so I was lucky indeed to have spotted these.

As I walked back through the high class, attractive housing estate that had replaced the old pig farm after heightening the river defences, I had another surprise. A heron this time, not remarkable in itself but for the way it alighted on the ridge of one of the new South Glade houses to patrol back and forth. High stepping carefully with long, gangling legs, it was peering down into an adjacent garden. Finally it dropped off, out of sight.

Was there a goldfish pond down there? After a while it returned to the suburban rooftop. I discerned no bulge in that sinuous neck. A buzzard cruised in and circled low over the stranger, apparently as curious as I was - although herons are treetop birds as well as waterside ones.

* * *

On 27th March I needed to go to Whitchurch, the most comprehensive shopping and banking centre within easy reach. It was further away by road than the crow flies. Getting across the river by car meant a detour north to the Ynys Bridge at Taffs Well or south to the one at Llandaff North.

As in past years, I encountered the 'pavement walking starlings" which are endemic to Whitchurch. This population consisted no longer of common run-of-the-mill birds. Their ancestors had instilled a complete lack of fear of people into their offspring. These, always cheeky, trotted amiably among the feet of shoppers in the vicinity of a certain greengrocer's shop.

It had all started one midsummer, when the cherries, gooseberries and currants were ripe and on offer alongside the less seasonal grapes. All were displayed on outside stands. How could a healthily hungry starling resist? They were coming still, even when there were no soft fruits apart from out-of-season strawberries. Most remained at ground level, often unnoticed by walkers, who might kick them aside. They just trotted out of the way. I never saw one take flight out of the mob and cause a flurry. This strain of birds could have taken a lesson from the pigeons in Trafalgar square via their London roosting brethren, so skilful had they become in tolerating the master race.

.My northern route back took me through the Border Ridges with their wide choice of woodland walks, so I opted to drop off on the Wenallt, north of Rhiwbina, for some exercise.

I drew into the steep approach lane just behind a caterpillar farm tractor and accomplished the climb in fits and starts as it rumbled on to one of the few passing places. The entire hillside was wooded apart from an extensive grass play area with picnic tables were I parked, some hundred yards or so from the top.

Plunging downhill on one of several paths, I had a strange sensation of space - unexpected when entering a mature woodland, but this was beechwood in winter garb, characterised by the paucity of ground flora. The splaying horizontal branches of beeches arrange their summer foliage to intercept most of the light filtering through the canopy. In addition the ground cover of fallen leaves is said to inhibit other plants.

Shrubs were almost non-existent and the only continuous patches of herbs were intermittent carpets of bluebell leaves and lesser stands of wood Anemones. A few delicate flowers of wood sorrel were spotted and tiny clumps of wild garlic. Others were shade tolerant ferns, mostly broad buckler with a few tufts of hard fern. Occasional straggles of honeysuckle were seeking support and there were patches of hairy woodrush (*Luzula pilosa*). Leaves of wood avens and enchanter's nightshade heralded things to come.

Striking features of the slopes above the covered reservoirs at the foot of the hill were the old field walls. Completely swallowed by the woodland, these contained the most architectural of the beeches, planted in long lines as hedge trees, now gnarled and ancient. Parts just above the old walltop were disfigured by intermittent hedge laying, parts below from erosion of soil from around their woody exposed roots. Relics of a bygone age, grizzled and moss-grown, they were reminders of a long lost life style.

Turning east by a weatherworn pile of barkless logs, I followed the south facing slope overlooking the coastal plain. More sunshine penetrated here, coaxing the petals of celandines and Anemones to full spread and allowing in more scrubby ground cover. The occasional larch was a mantle of light green leaf rosettes but I saw no budding cones as yet.

A puzzle tree harbouring small birds could have been hawthorn or crabapple, with leafy branches of the first and leafless branches of the second decked with partially shrivelled crabapples. The one sprang from a crevice of the other; a natural graft.

It was here that I stood awhile watching a pair of jays. Courtship feeding was in progress, one, presumably the male, offering titbits to the other who was not over anxious to receive them. At intervals they fed together on the path.

Another couple in fine plumage were the bullfinches, the cock's cherry coloured breast seeming to concentrate the fugitive rays of sunshine. A more sombrely dressed dunnock was singing away on a pathside bramble while a couple of wrens crossed and recrossed the path, pausing at intervals to announce their presence in no uncertain terms. Here, as throughout, were the inevitable magpies, carrion crows and wood pigeons, but other birds, including blackbird and robin, seemed wedded to this sunnier face.

The rugged contours of the old quarry had spawned more tumbledown walls, one supporting an aspiring yew tree and a holly. This patch was characterised by bilberries or wimberries as the Welsh refer to them, and I was surprised to see that these were already flowering in March.

Not yet the broom bush, which would be a mass of yellow not long hence, to be followed by ranks of rosebay willow herb where the woodland petered out under aspiring contingents of birch saplings.

I proceeded past the stand of noble scots pines, the light emphasising the brick red colour of their upper boughs, and back across the open field. During several hours I had encountered only two other couples enjoying a walk, one with three small boys, the other with three large dogs.

* * *

I came again to the Wenallt Woods almost a month later, on 23rd April, this time with Robert Hubbard. Hailing from the exposed cliffs of the Heritage Coast, where trees huddle in hollows or grow lopsided leaning away from the wind, these arboreal stands should seem luxurious.

After lunch we trundled some boxes of 'extraneous matter' to the back of Oxfam in Whitchurch, where flourished a remarkably fine border of blue-flowered green alkanet, and then headed for the hills. We went right to the summit this time, to the foot of the great radio mast, which is a landmark for hikers following the Ridgeway Walk or from the coastal plain.

He was driving his favourite 44 year old car, small and white, bought in 1962. Despite a new engine, installed eight years before, strange noises emanated from the entrails and hand signals of intention seemed appropriate, but we made it up the tortuous hill. No caterpillar tractor this time.

At this season we were in the traditional British bluebell wood - of the sort that the literature tells us does not exist in Europe, so that these are our especial trust. Entry was not quite as dramatic as I remembered because some bigger shade trees had disappeared, a low spread of bramble stems romping across in their place. Growth of the bulbs had not been quelled, but these had put up fewer flowers from the dense carpet of leaves, whereas the stands within the wood were seas of deep hyacinth blue.

It seemed the straggly thorns did not provide the necessary midsummer shade as do the dense but seasonal stands of bracken fronds which protect the flowers on the Welsh islands, where bluebells grow lusher and cover more acres in the complete absence of trees than in many a woodland.

As we penetrated under the tall, still leafless, beeches, piercing whistles drew our attention to a nuthatch, hurtling between the upper boughs, with only desultory attempts at bark probing. Apart from this bird life seemed scarce. This was afternoon siesta time.

Ramsons, the hallmark of limestone soils and providing a full ground cover on Rhiwbina Hill to the west, was sparse. Although in alignment with those limestone rocks, a kink in the Border Ridges along the valley on whose flank we walked, had resulted in the 722 ft. (220 m) high Wenallt being composed of the underlying zone of Old Red Sandstone.

This was its uppermost layer, of hard quartz conglomerate. Small boulders protruding through the carpet of fallen leaves were of this "pudding stone", the quartz 'sultanas' paler than the reddish matrix and giving the appearance of a natural concrete.

This rock is particularly hard and forms the weather-resistant capstone of the Brecon Beacons, where the beds curve up again in the North after their passage beneath the Coalfield. Here in the Wenallt, they dip down to the north beneath the limestones that surface around Castell Coch to the west, the two providing the cradle underlying the Coal Measures that brought prosperity to South Wales.

We trekked up over the tumbled hillocks of the old quarry on the south face, crossing first the middle strata of the Old Red Sandstone, the more fertile Brownstone that lies beneath the harder capping.

Here we were in the unexpected bilberry patch, a species more likely to be encountered on acid rocks further north. At this season the fresh yellow-green foliage was particularly conspicuous. Plants bore more of the pendant, globe shaped red flower bells than I had seen a month earlier.

For those with a taste for bilberry jam or, even better, bilberry pie, this would be a good place to come in autumn. It reminded me of the bilberry picking forays that I enjoyed on family trips to the heathy Surrey sandhills during childhood. Those, and these, bore their fruit at a comfortable height for plucking, unlike the more extensive but ground-hugging wimberry swards of the Coalfield hills, where severe sheep grazing limited both this and the surrounding heather to a height of a few inches.

More old walls, of chunky conglomerate survived here, telling of past industry and demarcating an old track. Fat pink flower buds were just bursting from the leafless twigs of a nearby crabapple sapling and yellow ones from underlying archangel. Attractive young foliage was sprouting from the rowan trees, while sycamore and maple were in full summer attire.

The only fungi seen were the hard, long-lived domes of cramp balls or burnt potatoes on a fallen ash, carbonaceous of texture like polished graphite. Concentric semicircles on broken surfaces indicated the number of years of growth, just an eighth of an inch per annum.

Three kinds of insects came to notice, apart from several indecipherable hover flies. Most attractive was the holly blue butterfly, the first of the season for me, but followed by more in various habitats in the next few days. This flitted round us as we took a break on and beside a bench which had been placed on a high point from which to view the coastal plain and the Holms, until the trees grew up on the slope below and obscured them.

The upper side of the wings were a clear blue, as with later emerging blues, the underside much paler, as though dusted with cornflour, and speckled with black, not brown and orange as in male common blues. This was not a butterfly awakening from hibernation like the Vanessids and brimstones which were on the wing earlier. These had passed the winter as pupae attached to the leaves of ivy on which the caterpillars had fed. They would lay their eggs on holly, from which the second brood of butterflies should emerge in August.

Our second insect was a greater bee fly (*Bombylius major*), with the stripy body of a more bulgeous bumble bee but more tapering and with the transparent, brown patterned wings held at full spread when at rest instead of folded. Like bees, it is a nectar feeder, but it sips as it hovers, as with the more closely related hover flies. Although favouring primroses, it has a predilection for blue flowers and there was no shortage of those here. Bluebells, although insect pollinated, have no visible nectaries. Ground ivy, forget-me-not and violets were other potential food plants here.

Our third species, the common dor beetle (*Geotrupes stercorarius*), was not seen bumbling across the path, as so often, but as a mass of iridescent blue body armour, wing cases and spiky legs, the indigestible parts coughed up by a predator on the path. A dozen or more must have been collected to produce that amount of waste, the crop pellet being the size of that produced by the larger owls.

We saw no live beetles, but they are abroad by night as well as by day. The name 'dor' comes from an old word meaning 'drone' and refers to the humming sound of their night flights, when, like moths, they can be attracted to lights.

Moving back to the car alongside the line of pines that I had watched grow up over the years, we went off on the continuation of the lane by which we had come, to take the northern loop road back. The deeply cut valley of Cwm Nofydd, whose well watered, sunlit grassy floor had beckoned during our walk, continued to the left as we undulated up to Thorn Hill, the highway between Cardiff and Caerphilly.

Sharply down and up again to the Caerphilly Mountain summit, we took two left turns to run down the opposite side of the valley and turn off Rhiwbina Hill to the right and return by the wiggly lane going by the name of Heol-y-Fforest. This passed Castell Coch and the old vineyard, now a golf course, and leads into Tongwynlais.

For just a brief while on the mountain top we had been in a different type of country, bleak moorland, still winter-brown, on the less bounteous soils of the Coalfield. The last lap was through the lush greenery of the more southerly Border Ridges, past that popular watering hole, the Black Cock, mustering place for many a walking party over the years.

* * *

Clocks changed to British Summertime on the night preceding Sunday 29th March and the official spring was greeted with sunshine. I strolled into the garden and spotted my first butterfly, a peacock, then set off further afield. I had learned from Anette, a fellow resident, that there was good walking to be had on the Radyr golf course.

She was the owner of a delightful little shaggy Tibetan terrier, who needed exercising two or three times a day and there were few places she had not explored on foot with Lucy, her small consort. Anette came from a nursing background and Lucy had been recruited to bring weekly comfort to the seriously handicapped children accommodated in Sully Hospital on the coast. The children loved her and she tolerated them good naturedly, so she earned her keep. It seems that most Tibetans, however poor, keep these little dogs for hunting, presumably for small game. The Dalai Lama is said to have owned one.

Her mistress told me I would find a path leading from the top of Windsor Road, which ascended steeply from the main Heol Goch. The little wooden gate beckoned as I left the houses behind to follow a little track switchbacking over the lower ends of undulating spurs of land sloping down from golfing grounds to the north.

Those looked too steep to accommodate a little rolling ball with satisfactory results and I saw no players as I followed along under a belt of trees planted to hide the built up land to the south. At one point there was a stream crossing in a bosky hollow, the water oozing from an underground spring bubbling into a quagmire in the furrow between two ridges.

Emerging from the spinney on the opposite slope I had a fine view of the prehistoric tumps on the thousand foot high Great Garth, on whose flank I had been domiciled for so long. From this angle it was not obscured by the five hundred foot high Little Garth.

In the middle foreground was the footbridge over the M4 motorway that I had sometimes followed when trekking home from the Tuesday weekly meetings. Evocative mewing calls came from a buzzard circling overhead, now as then. Here, too, were the familiar Corvids, jackdaw, magpie, carrion crow and raven.

I emerged onto a narrow lane curling through two sections of the golf grounds and crossed to examine two species of Eucalyptus planted side by side. Breaking cover I spotted some golfers, unexpectedly driving balls across the hedged lane, and took evasive action. The two footpaths heading towards the Llantrisant road and shown on my map seemed not to exist on the ground, so I played safe and set off along the lane.

This had an aura of old fashioned rurality, embroidered with celandines and Anemones. The human touch was provided by a lady jogging along astride a mount almost as ponderous as my old Land Army cart horse, with quite as much 'feather' around the fetlocks but too small for either Shire or Clydesdale.

This seemed in keeping with the way the golf course used to be. Completely out of the blue I had a phone call that week from Ray Sturgess, past president of the county ornithologists. He used to play golf here and had found the rich wildlife an integral part of the enjoyment.

"A lizard sunning itself on almost every post, pheasants breeding, fifteen house martins nesting on the clubhouse and sparrow hawks and buzzards always about. The course was ploughed up during the war to grow crops. All that had returned since its reinstatement, but there's nothing there now." Nevertheless, another told me that he saw foxes here in the early morning.

I had known Ray Sturgess only by name, but he had got in touch to say a number of nice things about my third book in the Cardiff trilogy, on the Rhymney-Roath River corridor. He was a Rhymney boy and a friend of Ivor Penberthy, who figures in my early coastal chapters, and had enjoyed reading about his home patch as it used to be, before the saline river ox bow was converted into the freshwater Lamby Lake at the beginning of the new millennium.

A remarkable beech tree by the golf course lane was completely barkless on the near side, which was festooned with orange bracket fungi, although the other boughs were covered with swelling buds. Nearby was a fantastic oak, with greatly exaggerated elbow joints on all limbs, giving the crookedest overall outline ever.

Past a water tank behind a padlocked gate, I came out into Fford Las, which carries on to Pentyrch according to my vintage map and may still do so. I enjoyed a short rest on a seat set among daffodils and mown lawn at the junction with Bryn Derwen back in suburbia. This led to Drysgol Road, which ran between the golf course and a line of large houses and gardens and across Windsor Avenue to the main road.

CHAPTER 11

Flatholm Society, Anomalous Spring and Riverside Walk

Monday 31st March was the day after the clocks changed to British Summertime but it was more appropriately a late winter day than the first of summer. At least the extra hour of daylight enabled us to find our way through the network of major new highways associated with the much disputed creation of "Cardiff Bay" down in Dockland as was.

I had ferreted out a route to the AGM of the Flatholm Society - which had previously been held in Barry - but was offered a lift at the last minute by Carol Sharpe, widow of former secretary, Tony. She lived at the foot of the climb to the Wenallt, so I met her there.

The meeting was held in the ultra modern 'Environment Building' in which steel and glass loomed large This had been built on a limb of land extended now as the eastern end of the Barrage. We crossed the channel connecting Roath Dock and Roath Basin and had to state our mission to the security official 'on guard' to travel down Cargo Road and slip sideways across to Locks Road.

This brought us to the neck of land adjacent to the exit lock from the Queen Alexandra Dock, the only one from which boats sailed out to the open sea direct and not through the great locks on the Barrage. We were locked in behind iron mesh gates, a man who wished to leave early having to phone a sentry to come and let him out. Why this particular spot should merit such high security, we knew not.

The lecture following the business meeting and reports on developments on the island was given on the merits or otherwise of the recently revived scheme for building a Severn Barrage to generate power. In the current climate it seemed logical to try and harness those great tides on our doorstep, second largest in the world.

The project had come up twenty years before and been rejected as impractical. Local environmentalists had been roped in to survey different sections for their wildlife value, wading birds particularly, but also the brackish water plant life. The patch allocated to me was around the mouth of the River Rhymney 3 miles east of the Taff-Ely Roads.

The route currently favoured was not, as we had envisaged, from Lavernock Point in Glamorgan via Flatholm and Steepholm to Brean Down in Somerset, but one which left Flatholm on the freshwater side and Steepholm on the seaward side.

No new study had yet been made of the great host of wading birds which would be displaced by the loss of so many hectares of tidal mud. A number of redshanks had been caught and marked and their welfare followed up when they lost their old feeding grounds within Cardiff Bay in 2002. It was discovered that marked birds displaced to the flats outside were underweight and undernourished when recaught by the cannon netting method and reweighed.

Different bird species with different lengths of bill and legs feed from different depths in the muds and all sites were currently occupied, numbers of the thousands of wintering wildfowl increasing to exploit the available food potential while leaving a sustainable population for another year.

Needs of displaced populations had been at least partially met during enclosure of the Taff-Ely Estuary by creating new lagoons on the Gwent Levels at the mouth of the River Usk. If the Bristol Channel itself was blocked or altered by an incomplete barrier, there would be nowhere else to serve the needs of birds which were only "ours" for the winter, nesting as they did in countries further north.

Our speaker thought the project would be a non-starter on grounds of cost alone, as with most such major projects. Sale of the electricity generated would take many years to pay off the cost of construction, as with profits from the Channel Tunnel and Millennium Dome.

I had taken some of my Cardiff and Island books to sell but demand outran supply, so Quentin Chesham, the society's treasurer, arranged to collect more the following day (when he would be travelling from his home in Penarth to his son in Pontrypridd), and deliver them himself.

Lean and sinewy, he was a mountaineer as well as an islander, also a bookaholic with a special interest in a bookshop in Penarth. One of the peaks 'conquered' was the one which bore his name, Chesham, the highest on the Hebridean Island of Harris. His blue eyes twinkled as he reminisced on other mountains and other islands. He stayed most of the morning, drinking coffee and discussing books - a pleasant and unexpected diversion.

* * *

A couple of days later, after more shelves had been fixed and more pictures hung, thanks to the indefatigable Clive Thomas, the temperature soared to 18 degrees, but only briefly. The first brimstone butterfly was flitting round the garden like an airborne primrose and I saw my first buzzard, which had at last located a thermal powerful enough to take it up to where it wanted to be.

I discarded winter woollies and ventured into Cardiff on the bus, which took me on a tour of Fairwater, Danescourt, Llandaff and Canton en route. Business accomplished, I found myself at the entrance to Cardiff Market and went inside for the first 'real' shopping expedition for months - as opposed to picking up securely wrapped packs covered with tiny writing that the wrappers fondly imagined their customers stopped to read.

This was shopping as it should be, naked and unadorned. The middlemen take a lion's share of the profits just to make life difficult for the recipients, who paid for all the extraneous matter which finished up on tips. Not to mention the bad language engendered as one tool after another failed to release the goods from hermetically sealed wrappings.

Gazing my fill on red snapper and kingfish my mind made the leap back to those fishing expeditions around the atolls of the Indian ocean. The mussels reminded me of boiling up a billyful of the shiny black shells and orange flesh on a rocky New Zealand headland. The kippers - where else but Mallaig, the taking off point for the Inner Isles of the Hebrides?

I took my pick, then chose three inches of farm produced Caerphilly cheese, a wedge of cambozola, four inches from a slab of caraway seed cake, just like mother used to make, some mixed dried fruits and a cut from a succulent chunk of pork. It was approaching five o'clock, packing up time. "Two punnets of raspberries for a pound. What about these lovely strawberries lady?" Who could resist?

As I approached the Rugby Millennium Stadium, where I was to pick up the no. 33 bus, I saw it already there. I was on the wrong side of the road. Could I run, heavily laden as I was? I found I could, spurred on by the knowledge that the next was not for half an hour. The long queue to be dealt with ahead of me detained the vehicle for the necessary time. Thought of what I might have for supper and where it came from sustained me on the way back.

Two more days and Clive finally succeeded in gathering all the parts together and wired up to get my computer working. I should now be able to get going on "The Archive", requested by my god daughter, who also kept a diary. I needed a break from books about islands, something more homely and chatty seemed more appropriate for my second retirement.

*   *   *

Next day I visited Joyce Lloyd in Llandaff and the weather was so balmy that we would have sipped our coffee in the garden, had it not been for the bother of carrying it out. Her plot faced south towards the Cathedral Green, where the resident lesser black-backed gulls were already prospecting for nesting sites on the surrounding roofs. Tulips and Azaleas gave an illusion of summer and buds of Wistaria were already showing colour along the bounding fence.

Back home I was just completing lunch on some of my goodies from the market, herrings and green beans, rhubarb and custard, when my attention was diverted skywards. The air was full of graceful, hurtling bodies, zooming back and forth, circling, yet drifting gradually away to the north-east.

The sand martins had arrived - always the first of the Hirundines to find their way back from tropical West Africa or other delectable climates further south, sometimes even in March, and this was 5th April. They passed through, careening from side to side, like yachts in a gale, sunlight glinting from their white bellies as they changed direction.

Each used a series of rapid wing flaps for motivation, followed by brief periods of free wheeling through the air corridors. What was remarkable was that they had battled in against a headwind from the north, at least on this last leg of their great journey.

Were they headed for riverside nesting sites further north or would some peel off and take up residence in the Fforest Farm 'high rise block? The tunnels in the vertical sand face there had been cleaned out but the usual residents had not moved in during the 2007 season. I looked forward to spells in the hide alongside, watching the aerial cavortings of a population such as the reserve had hosted in former years.

Jackdaws came ricocheting through the midst of the flock, borne on the wind. Only the gulls sailing past seemed wholly under control.

I saw no swallows until 21st April nor house martins until the 24th. No doubt there were others about before that. Migrating flocks passing through can easily be missed, even when they linger, circling as they hawk flies rising from the river below.

Next day, just three hours after chatting with an elderly couple sunning themselves on the seats at the front porch, hailstones up to half an inch across were bouncing off my window sills. A magpie tried to battle through the falling ice pellets but was driven back tail first, before regaining equilibrium.

Deep purple clouds had followed up the blue vista of half an hour before, these swinging together and coalescing as a grey shroud. Most of the hail stones were smaller. Sometimes they came in parallel white streaks from the east, then vertically or from the north, when their angle would not have been discernible.

They soon topped up the plant pots on the verandah to their brims, around the unfortunate, once cosseted, indoor plants, and piled up in the well of the garden chair and two inches deep in the further corner. Those balancing along the rail were soon pushed off by others.

The grey pall, which had obscured everything beyond the garden trees, withdrew as suddenly as it had assembled, revealing blue sky again. Sunshine transformed the pristine carpet over lawn and paving stones to whiter than white, the air too frigid as yet to sponsor melting.

This was the day when I might have accompanied a party of Cardiff Naturalist members to the London Wetlands Nature Reserve at Barnes, but I had opted out, having visited there the previous year.

In two hours the celestial ice had melted and the lawn sparkled with pseudo dewdrops, but patches remained on the retentive bark mulch of the shrubberies well into the next day. I took this as proof that little of my internal warmth was escaping through the double glazing. The low angle of the sun's rays and the steep angle of the flower bed dictated that the solar energy made only brief contact before being deflected back.

The local song thrushes spent an unusually long time foraging between bouncing hops and rapid little runs on twinkling feet. I wondered how the sand martins were faring and if they were hankering after the torrid sunshine which they had so lately left. They were familiar with wet, but not cold.

The house manager's prize blue hyacinths and tall red polyanthus weathered the storm as well as the twiggier Rosemary, but the entrance drive was littered with flat-ended ivy berries blown from plants adhering to the wall above. They bore an uncanny resemblance to the tiny acorns clinging fast to the shoot tips of the evergreen holm oak across the path. Ivy fruits were a favourite of the wood pigeons and blackbirds.

More hail fell after lunch next day, again after the menacing purple clouds had dissolved into a pale, off-white haze. Stair rods slanted from the west this time. At least those powering winds should be warmer. Hailstones bounding up several inches from the lawn emulated some modern garden water features. Or was it the other way round? The aftermath resembled a sprinkling of dry icing sugar rather than yesterday's more substantial layer, as on a Christmas cake. Fortunately such storms were short-lived and were the exception rather than the rule.

* * *

A pleasant place to observe the onset of spring was the environs of the parish church, which were tended as a garden. This lies at the heart of the community, between the parish hall and the health centre. Conspicuous on the corner was a huge *Magnolia soulangeana*, its pink and white flowers like outsize tulips covering the boughs through much of April. From the very start of my residence there were snowdrops, crocuses and daffodils, these soon followed by a fine clump of aquamarine grape hyacinths by the side porch. Somebody had been busy planting sapling shrubs and trees. Volunteer species decorating the lawn were violets, lady's smock, wild strawberry and creeping speedwell.

On 11th April I stood quietly beneath one of the twelve monumental pines bordering the back lawn, watching a mistle thrush. I had heard the three to five challenging notes of this species in the Brynteg garden but had not yet spotted it with the everyday song thrushes.

It is larger than those more familiar garden birds and draws itself up to its full height during bouts of feeding, the better to see any movements in the grass. With the military demeanour goes a more assertive attitude and general boldness. So fearless is this species in defence of its nest that it will attack a hawk.

Busily foraging over the unmown lawn, it was making little runs after each erect pause for viewing, to probe into the turf where movement had been detected. The prey was mostly slender worms one to two inches long, tweaked up and swallowed at once. Intermittent showers from the rain clouds bowling across the sky had moistened the soil, attracting worms to the surface.

When a longer one was hauled out more force was required and the backward lean, thrusting out the conspicuously spotted breast, was accompanied by a fluttering of the wings, but not to their full stretch. People passing back and forth, and me putting on a head scarf against a shower, did not distract it.

Humans were a familiar part of the bird's environment, as I realised when it flew up to its nest in one of the lofty pines. This was not in a crotch of the main trunk, as often, but where two substantial branches crossed and a few lesser ones radiated outwards, making a firm foundation. The bird just stood there for a while, cogitating. Evidently there were no eggs as yet.

In fact the edifice seemed only half built, a somewhat unkempt tangle of dry grass, roots and moss with traces of stabilising earth and wisps of lichen. While March and April are familiar breeding times for mistle thrushes, many are known to start as early as February.

I strolled up three weeks later to see how the birds were faring, but I had picked the wrong day. It was 4th May, bank holiday weekend, with people everywhere - for the Radyr Flower Festival, being held in the church on one side and Saturday afternoon tennis club teas on the other.

Wandering up to the overgrown garden of the Old Rectory I encountered chaffinches and blackbirds but no thrushes. Most intriguing of the natural phenomena there was the intricate patterning left by what may have been a considerable number of large garden snails grazing on the coating of green algae covering the lower section of a derelict garage door.

The sweeping curves of the interlocking zig zag pattern about an inch wide were composed of lesser zig zags about a tenth of an inch wide - very like those left by grazing limpets on intertidal rocks. I was transported back to the Triassic sandstone platforms of St. Maryswell Bay, where I had first noticed similar tracks in equal profusion among the smoother ones of edible periwinkles. This, of course, when the tide had fallen and the limpets were safely cemented onto their home plots.

A grey squirrel was skipping lightly along the top of the paling fence bounding the lower garden, on which were some of its meal leftovers - pine cones, with half the scales stripped off to release the seeds.

Young whitebeams on the church lawn were dressed in softly felted leaves and yellow and white flowers had appeared on the shrubby cinquefoil, white ones on laurestine and guelder rose.

* * *

The showers forecast to disrupt my Saturday morning walk on 12th April did not materialise: instead there was bright sunshine and a brisk wind. I headed down river to Velindre and back along the canal, looking out for signs of the advancing spring.

Two foals were nibbling at the meagre grass cover by Taff Terrace at the top of the steep paddock, an adult, possibly their dam, in the soggy bottom behind the Junction Terrace back gardens. The youngsters were unusually shaggy coated, they must have been out all winter to grow such generous insulation, The feed was meagre, few grass blades more than an inch long, but obviously preferable to the lush border of robustly flowering celandines along the inner base of the surrounding fence. Though freshly green and turgid, these were strictly avoided. The foals were not too young to know about the poisonous alkaloids present in members of the buttercup family.

A collared dove was preening on a tall sycamore across the road. We were but a few hundred yards from Brynteg but I had not yet seen one of these in the garden. Young sycamores were mostly in full leaf by now, older ones so and so, this one not at all. One observed later overhanging the canal had a full complement of foliage on all the lower branches and a few dangling yellow tassels of flowers, but upper branches exposed to the elements bore no more excrescences than the withered stalks of last year's winged fruits.

This prolonged period of bud burst is beneficial in accommodating the varying hatching dates of insects depending on them for food.

Over the footbridge I turned south, taking the lower path further from the river rather than the one atop the embankment. I was glad that I did, because I straight away came upon a much larger spread of moschatel clumps than I remember seeing anywhere. Otherwise known as the town hall clock, these have a greenish yellow flower on each of the four faces of a square inflorescence and another pointing upwards 'for the birds'. Conspicuous only by their abundance, they were much more so than the backing meshwork of ivy-leaved speedwell with its tiny speckles of blue florets.

Wild Arum leaves which push out of the soil in the dead of winter had achieved their victualling function and pale green spathes were already pushing up through the sward of flowering dog's mercury protecting the vital organs within.

Soil was fertile here, as it should be on an alluvial plain. I approached the river on the slope providing access for machines used in dredging, leaving footprints in the deep, soft layer of sandy silt stranded by higher floods than now above the river-scoured pebbles of the current margin by the churning water.

In what I call the Fforest Farm redwing field were scores of outsize molehills of finely sifted black loam, with more on the rough grassy flats across the river among the hundreds of vegetated anthills, which labelled this ground as having suffered no ploughing for decades.

Soil thrown out of the occupied rabbit burrow was of pale clay, but this was on the old mineral railway track which may have been stabilised with soil from elsewhere. Yellow archangel spikes were just showing the colour of the hooded flowers and there were a few bluebells, both genuine and illegitimate Spanish.

A distinctive bird song halted me at the entrance to the sports field and I found myself watching two nuthatches working over the boughs of an ash and flipping and fro so rapidly that there may well have been three. They were being harassed by a flock of blue and great tits with at least one marsh tit, always giving way to the swooping attacks of the smaller birds.

An event was about to commence at the sports centre but a discontinuous string of cars bringing participants immediately below, followed by a bus, had not the slightest effect on this avian pantomime.

I moved over to the riverside by the survivor of the two pollarded black poplars, whose upper branches held a full crop of chunky catkins. The very dead, barkless subsidiary bole was punctured throughout by the half inch incisions made by a feeding woodpecker, digging for wood boring insects.

Peering into the garden of the two old cottages so unkindly surrounded by new red brick homes in recent years, I was pleased to see that one still housed four bee hives. They seemed still closed for winter but a few bees were crawling in and out of lower slits despite the nip in the air. There are said to be fewer and fewer bee keepers in Britain at present.

The plague of Veroa mites which has hit the USA honey bees so disastrously, was becoming an increasing worry in Britain, particularly in the South-East and the Midlands, where 25 to 30 per cent of the hives had been lost. The subject kept cropping up on the media, and not only in the farming programmes. Leading apiarists were particularly worried that no money had been forthcoming for research on eradication of the pest, claiming that many bee keepers were amateurs and insufficiently well trained to deal with it.

"Money can be found to study the structure of the atom and for the exploration of outer space but not for this problem, which is an impending disaster for the whole of mankind if our crops are not pollinated as Nature intended."

Rogue bees came to rob other hives and spread the mites, while many domestic swarms were said to be holed up in trees and likely to be harbouring the pest. The chemical recommended for control is toxic and can be dangerous if it gets into the honey. What is more, it was ineffective, the mites having developed an immunity. Inspectors were employed to find out if the poison was being used illegally. Sadly the Veroa mite was now regarded as endemic in Britain, as well in America.

While bumble bees had been common enough during the past two months - singly and mostly queens newly awakened from hibernation - I had not recognised any honey bees patrolling flowers.

* * *

At the mounted Velindre Millstone I turned back along the canal. The few mallard encountered along the river had fled at sight of me, but the many canalside ones came out to meet me in the hope of provender. Were these a different population or the same birds behaving differently depending on where they were?

Two small boys left some bread on the towpath. The duck and drake for which it was intended made several attempts to scuttle past me to reach it but were unable to pluck up sufficient courage. Then the duck had a bright idea. She slipped through the wire mesh into the water, swam past me and climbed out where she knew the bread must be, but had not quite solved the problem. The lower meshes where she emerged were smaller than the one she had left through and she got wedged, ruffling her once pristine feathers backing out and toppling back into the water. She had done well for a bird brain, so I threw the bread in after her.

A nearby moorhen perched six feet above the water regarded me in alarm, although I remained still. One long-toed foot after another was lifted and the neck bobbed to and fro while it made up its mind whether to go or stay. When it finally took off for the short flight to the water it honked hysterically all the way down, as though scared at its own boldness. This bird brain had not worked out that people on the towpath did not enter the water to molest birds.

All the bird feeders by the lower canal were empty but there was grain on the mid capstan being consumed by blue and great tits and on the lock by wood pigeons and magpies, with squirrels sharing both. The only canalside flowers were milkmaids and early violets, the less common *Viola reichenbachiana*, with purple, not cream coloured spurs and a few blackspikes on the bordering pond sedge

A circuit of the old scout camping field was made delightful by the generous drifts of wood Anemones scattered throughout. A few patches had dark purple leaves instead of the usual lush green. With these were greater stitchwort flowers and the insignificant white dots of barren strawberries.

Most of this old reverted field was covered with Himalayan balsam seedlings and the trash over the ground which simulated dead bracken from a distance was the pale massed hollow stems of last season's six foot high inflorescences. Emergent plants of rosebay willow herb, hemp agrimony and red campion would have to fight their corner in the impending thicket. Beautiful and appearing in every shade of pink, the balsam was an invasive alien and reviled by many, including the warden, as such.

A rabbit scuttled into the thicket at the base of the Long Wood Scarp, which rose as sharply above the flood plain as the Radyr scarp did on the west. A localised drift of broad-leaved garlic flowers was creeping up the base of the scarp near a decrepit elder which supported a fine crop of the upturned cups of Jew's ear fungus.

CHAPTER 12
Insole Court, Llanelly Waterfront and the Welsh National Botanic Gardens

On Monday 14th April I had a date with Madeleine Lewis, widow of David who had run the Cardiff University Gardens for many years, growing material for class work and providing facilities for botanical research projects. She lived between Llandaff and Canton, so I opted to spend the previous couple of hours exploring the Insole Court Gardens.

George Insole, the first member of the family to live in Cardiff, resided there during the middle 1800s, having acquired his wealth from the Rhondda Collieries. Bits were added over the years, including some mouldings from the cathedral when that was being restored in 1862. The main edifice is of yellowish Pennant Sandstone from the Coalfield, with additions of Bath stone.

This turreted building is a treasure, always much admired, but was recently under threat of partial or complete demolition. Happily public pressure to conserve both the buildings and the gardens prevailed. It was disturbing, therefore, to find a mechanical digger shovelling soil against a partially roofed stable yard building bearing the historic clock tower when I arrived. Evidently it was only piled earth being removed. The remaining roofing slates had been protected with wind-tattered plastic sheeting. Hopefully the apparently sound walls were to be reroofed.

The gardens fronting the main house, with its menagerie of stone animals gambolling around the eaves, were in good order. The main side beds had been planted with deep maroon, yellow-eyed Polyanthus on one side and yellow flecked with maroon on the other, while yellow semi circles highlighted the Cordyline 'palm' at the mid point of the central path.

The one remaining veteran cedar was as stately as ever, the broken wall where its sibling had been felled not yet rebuilt. Little bowls of white hyacinths stood atop stone pillars at wall junctions.

One of the evergreen *Magnolia grandis* trees on the front terrace had thrust a two foot length of woody root up through the tarmac causing a crack from house wall to lawn edge. Such is the power of the infinitely slow growth in plants so much more permanent than our mortal selves. The red-brown trunk of the small-leaved evergreen alongside labelled this as a myrtle.

I moved off along the terrace to the eastern garden and came upon a handsome stand of snake's head or crown imperial *(Fritillaria imperialis)* thrusting up from a yellow and blue carpet of encroaching celandines and introduced lungwort.

Overhead snaked spreading branches of *Sophora microphylla,* or Kowhai, New Zealand's national tree. I don't remember seeing this in Britain before and it brought back nostalgic memories of my year in that green and pleasant land, lecturing in Palmerston North University and researching the bird islands around its shores.

To my surprise I found another, with the same blocky yellow pea flowers, by the steps leading down to the east lawn with its central bed of pink tulips.. Even more surprising was to find a third in Madeleine's garden and, to top it all, there was yet another in the National Botanic Gardens of Wales visited the following day. I must have visited before at the wrong season to see the characteristic Caesalpinaceae flowers and failed to recognise the attractive repeatedly pinnate leaves.

A fine Magnolia spread flower-filled branches across the stone staircase leading to the second kowhai, with an attractive spread of summer snowflake below. Twigs of cherry trees had disappeared under a snowstorm of white blossom. The big white bracts had not yet expanded around the tightly packed dark buds of the neighbouring flowering dogwood as they had in the bush across the garden, but the peachy pink flowers of *Cydonia japonica* were at prime.

A collared dove, perched in a yellow-leaved maple, kept reiterating "I told you so", more insistently than the still rudimentary spring calls of the larger wood pigeons. As I moved past the bamboos at the start of the streamside rockery, a little band of greenfinches came lolloping over the yellow and mauve Azaleas to perch in the mighty beech, whose spreading roots gave harbourage to crocuses and Cyclamen in season. A dunnock hoovered up insects from among blossoms fallen from the southern Camellia thickets. Flower of Berberis and mock orange were at prime, Wistaria buds mostly furry ellipses with only a hint of mauve as yet.

Unable to get into the rose garden through the stable yard, I went through the roofed grotto of huge rocks into the cul de sac of a narrow terrace, which was floored with gentian blue alkanet in partnership with equally brilliant celandines. Two strangers among the wall creepers resembled spindle and yellow Jasmin. Outside one major branch of a cherry tree had died and was covered from top to toe with closely ranked flanges of bracket fungi.

Moving out to what had been the rose garden, I found some of the beds grassed over and others filled with a fine composty tilth ready to receive a sprinkling of wild flower seeds. This would produce a summer display similar to others produced by an innovative council at crucial points on the roads around the city and out as far as the Radyr turning. Young trees insinuated into the turf around these beds were another step towards transforming this into an open arboretum.

Circles of flowers had been spared by the lawn mowers under big established trees - celandines, alkanet and one delicious spread of blue and white *Anemone blanda* . I got into conversation with a young ranger about the changes and he told me that these last were planted as recently as the previous autumn. He was working at a thesis on garden history in Pencoed Horticultural College and was particularly interested in types of man-made rockery stone. I was unable to help, not having recognised any such among the ornamental rock fragments and ice-rounded or river-rounded cobbles used here.

Well established bushes persisted under the bounding wall, including a range of members of the pea family with bottlebrush and Jerusalem sage interspersed with plots of white and pink hyacinths. Two gardeners were busy raking a thick layer of red sand over the muddy marginal path. The garden was in good hands, and I learned that a tender had been accepted for doing up the buildings. Insole Court was going to survive to retain some of the borough of Llandaff's past elegance into the crowded future.

* * *

The next day, the 15th April, was that of our Tuesday group's excursion to the coast at Llanelli and the National Botanic Gardens of Wales in Carmarthenshire. Weather was kind at the beginning and the end. The hours of rain in the middle of the day were successfully deployed in the restaurant and the great glass dome sheltering the Mediterranean plants, so offered no hindrance.

The Llanelli Waterfront, recommended as being well worth a visit, was as unknown to our coach driver as to any of his passengers. It was part of a new development, known as yet only to the few.

The several thriving tin plate works and steel works that had brought prosperity to the town were much diminished although not quite yet defunct and hundreds of hectares of coastal flatlands were being cleared of industrial plant and redeveloped for settlement, recreation and tourism, this from different foci, with long empty stretches between.

After several enquiries and a couple of turns our bus driver was put on the right track along one of the several major new roads threaded with roundabouts that promised yet more roads. Our destination must remain nameless. All I know is that it was on the coast where a carparking area and a length of promenade served a long block of what appeared to be multi-storey apartments, a tourist nucleus said to house "A Discovery Experience", a restaurant and toilets, these closed because of lack of water, making tea urns and toilets unusable, also an ice cream parlour, which didn't serve hot drinks.

All but me wanted coffee and conveniences so were thwarted and mooched along the prom instead. I can drink coffee at home and was here for a brief "seaside experience" in a place not visited before. It was not one of the most exciting seaside resorts, but was certainly spacious, with grassed sand onshore and bare sand offshore - several miles of it and all as flat as a pancake.

I headed off over the narrow belt of marram grass and sand sedge, scarcely worthy of the name of dunes, the two dominants the only dune plants seen. Others would have been as much at home on the industrial wastelands - dandelion, cat's-ear, mats of clover and a soldierly stand of common horsetail sporing cones.

The uplifting part of this modified dune landscape was the skylark. Small, brown and speckled, it rose in front of me, up and up, singing the way so many of its fellows used to when there were so many more about. This was certainly my first this spring and I hope not my last.

Hundreds of acres of sea-smoothed sand flats stretched away seawards, to link with the Llanrhidian Sands on the north coast of the Gower Peninsula opposite. The River Loughour curved northwards towards Whiteford Burrows and then south around it to empty into the greater estuary of the Severn off the end of Gower. All the tourism and holiday hot spots had been on that side while industry flourished along this northern, south-facing shore. Now times were changing and the north bank was sprucing up its image.

We moved on, I know not where, none of the names on the sign boards tallying with those on my map. My visits to this stretch of coast in the past had been divided between two contrasting habitats, which were certainly not those seen today.

One was the Welsh National Wildfowl Centre embracing the creeks and salt marshes further upstream to the east - a sophisticated enterprise modelled on the lines of Slimbridge further up the Severn Estuary.

The Other was Pembrey Burrows, just beyond Buryport, down channel to the west. Much of that great expanse of mobile sand had been planted with stabilising conifers - which confine the invasive sea buckthorn bushes to narrows strips along the margins of the rides. It embraced dune hollows, full of wild flowers and guaranteed to produce a wealth of butterflies if the sun was shining.

I kicked through the dry sand of today's upper beach and returned along the most profitable driftline, beachcombing. Almost all the shells deposited among the dry wracks were common cockles, tiny ones, quite unlike the fully grown ones found at Llanrhidian, centre of the ancient, still thriving cockle industry which supplied the Swansea markets.

The gentle waves dumping so many of these little ones were obviously not strong enough to move greater weights this far upshore. There was little else apart from the limbs and carapaces of shore crabs and a few lightweight clusters of whelk egg cases.

Knowing the rest would be feeling unfulfilled, I didn't go far and Madeleine and Jan Fife came to round me up. The coach proceeded across more flat land, partly derelict and partly renovated with tree plantations and ponds. A few ancient upstanding industrial chimneys had been left standing, a nostalgic reminder of times past.

We ended up at "Porth Gieglidion", an extensive area of mown grassy banks around a large freshwater lake behind an establishment called the Sandpipers' Cafe. That was unusual in having a large area set aside as a kindergarten, full of mothers with toddlers crawling all over the floor.

There were plenty of facilities here, but I was not the only one who headed for the lake. Intermittent bordering trees had been planted between the visitor path and the wild fowl beach, where a drake mallard sat atop a pile of debris pretending to be on nest duty. Most were willows and alders, Herbs were filling in the gaps - yellow Iris, pond sedge, water dropwort and greater willow herb'

Quite a few people were feeding the wildfowl - mallard, tufted ducks and a lone muscovy duck, a family of mute swans, the few juveniles with smoky bills, but only one retaining buff feathers, coot and a single Canada goose. All the common gull species were cashing in on the goodies, some of the black-headeds still in winter plumage, some with the full chocolate-brown heads of summer.

One tufted drake escaped their dive bombing attacks by submerging with his quota of bread at each onslaught from the sky. It was useful being a diving duck instead of a dabbler!

There was no sight of the sea from here, despite the name of Porth. The rising ground in the suspected direction was topped by trees. As we drove away we followed a narrow, winding and deeply recessed creek for a while. This, as we moved east, spread out as a clear stream snaking across the sands of the estuary. A major road took us across the main line railway and into the closely built up area of Llanelli town proper.

* * *

From here it was but a short hop to the National Botanic Gardens covering five hundred acres of the Middleton Estate - a regency parkland developed by Sir William Paxton in the late eighteenth century at Llanarthne not far from Carmarthen.

Once through the gatehouse, some of the less able boarded a little buggy for a mechanised guided tour and the rest of us set off on foot. We were four, Joyce, Jan, Madeleine and me, brought up short at the first waterway by a magnificent clump of North American yellow skunk cabbage *(Lysichitum americanum)*. This is an outrageous wild Arum with huge leaves and a bright yellow spathe around each club-shaped spike of florets. Its classic site in Glamorgan is in the grounds of Margam Abbey near Neath, with more in the Valleys country Park on one of the four tributaries of the Neath.

This waterway drained the Garden Lakes, alongside which was the Aqualab Discovery Centre. Professor Terence Turner, who had lectured to us in Radyr the week before on "Green Medicine", had his laboratory here and would have shown us round had he not left for Australia by then.

His approach had centred round the use of plants in primitive medicine with slides of ancient manuscripts, advertising many uses in picture form for the illiterate masses, who suffered their use or, occasionally, recovered. We learned of the doctrine of signatures - like ailing organ, like healing plant part.

The double walled garden was an obvious lure but we left that till later, proceeding past the Mirror Pool at the top of the long stream which wiggled down along the rising central path, past boulders from different geological regions. It was time for lunch, some delicious thick parsnip soup with poppy seed bread in my case. This was a wise choice as the rain came down just as we moved into the stable yard with its display of magnificent pots in the entrance constructed of mosaics of broken fragments of old Welsh china.

We timed things wrongly to catch one of the theatre shows but wandered round the Apothecary's Garden and storeroom of medicinal and culinary plants, complete with whole specimens. Many recalled memories of outlandish places where I had seen them growing

Walking across to the great domed glasshouse, which is the crowning feature, I recalled a display witnessed on the nearby lawn on a former visit. This was the herding of Indian runner ducks by a trained sheep dog. The well known ditty says "And God must have laughed when he made the duck" He probably laughed a little louder when he decreed that the Indian runners should run with body as well as head erect. (An attribute arising from the placement of the webbed feet at the end of the body, penguin fashion, to increase their swimming skills.) The dog drove his little flock along corridors, up over bridges and through loopholes in most exemplary style - not a duck strayed. A faultless performance, with everyone laughing.

Plant contents of the dome were as intriguing as ever. They hailed from six different parts of the world which enjoyed a Mediterranean climate - ie. wet warm winters with westerly winds and hot dry summers with easterly winds. I had visited six of these countries and enjoyed seeing their products.

South west Australia and South Africa were my favourites, with California not far behind. The other known two were the Mediterranean itself and the Canary Islands, destinations of regular botanical sorties with students in April, before the May sunshine shrivelled most of the goodies up. The one I never got to was Chile, a grave ommission.

Here were the African Proteas, milkwort bush aping a pink pea and neatly dichotomising succulent trees reminiscent of the Namibian desert, also Australian Banksias, bottle brushes and Grevilleas. Many of the blackboys or grass trees had died, showing the complex structure of the trunk and the myriad leaf bases from which resin is extracted. The noble kangaroo paws had reached their full height but were not flowering as yet.

Some were incredibly beautiful, some bizarre, all nostalgic of places where I had known them in the wild. Many were an unbelievable mass of colour. After exploring some of the educational annexes we sipped tea in the presence of scavenging sparrows and robins which made free of this haven of warmth and plenty during our inclement winters.

The main feature on our return was the walled garden - which I had seen transformed from a wilderness to a tropical garden and now into an 'evolutionary' exhibit with the tropicals gathered into a fine new glasshouse. There, too, were many old friends, from the most exotic beauties to the wispy strands of 'Spanish moss' living on fresh air alone - as on the telegraph wires of the New World. Japanese Garden, Bee Garden, Ice House and much more had to be left out this time, as our bus awaited us beyond the garden shop.

CHAPTER 13
Danescourt, Fox, Rabbits and The Taff at Radyr

On 21st April I set out by car to link up with my mid February walk through the Radyr Woods to Danescourt and seek out the old Radyr Court Road which had been closed to traffic and engulfed in a sea of new houses.

My map showed a blank area of unspoiled farmland here with the district name of Radyr Court. The term Danescourt was conjured up later. A station was built on the Cardiff commuter railway and a shopping precinct had mushroomed up beside St. John's Church. A new pub had taken over the name of Radyr Court, cheek by jowel with Somerfields and other stores, the old road, now a walkway, petering out as Woolmer Close.

New housing estates seem always to be composed of a maze of cul de sacs and I explored several without making contact with the spot I had reached before. I finally located it on foot, after leaving the car at a promising looking gate into one of two broad strips of tree-bordered but manicured grassland.

A peripheral footpath led downhill from here to a sunken lane leading under the railway to turn abruptly on meeting the bank of the Taff, which it had followed as Quarry Road. I recognised this as the formerly much used through route to Llandaff North. Crossing it I headed along a muddy path bordered on both sides by impenetrable brambles, to the junction I had reached two months before.

Here I took the right turn, leading down through open woodland across a series of ridges and furrows ploughed obliquely across the hillside. Their purpose I failed to fathom; maybe some attempt at drainage. The ridges were obviously old, crossed by fallen branches and covered with moss and algae.

This led me under an old, curve-topped stone bridge carrying the Cardiff

Railway and not wide enough nor high enough for any but the smallest farm cart. Very likely this was for the movement of livestock.

I emerged onto the gravel track alongside the river leading south from the old Radyr Quarry and old Shunting Yards, past what had been a rubbish dump, with some interesting plants such as the poisonous thorn apple, with white angel's trumpet flowers, and so to the old lane, where it passed under the railway by a much loftier stone bride, to turn and continue alongside the river to Llandaff North Bridge.

I had fleeting glimpses of a green woodpecker and a few starlings, which are no longer common, but much the most frequent, as usual, were members of the crow family, jackdaws, crows and magpies, with blackbirds and the common tits. I saw no waterfowl on this rather more turbulent than usual stretch of the Taff.

Most special here was the sighting of my first swallows, just a few, flighting over the treetops, their long tail streamers marking them off from the sand martins, which had arrived some days back. One swallow does not make a summer, but there were more here. Had spring really sprung at last? Another incomer was the blackcap, warbling away among riverside Buddleias, where a song thrush was pouring out its oft repeated phrases.

Where the track diverged a little from the Taff I took a lesser path, approaching the river where the soft peat of the banks had been undermined and eaten into by flood waters, leaving dissected blocks of land several yards across and the same high.

Bare cliffs of friable black river alluvium cut back into the bordering spinney, exposing the woody root systems of ash and sycamore. New sprouts of the dreaded Japanese knotweed were already three to four feet high down at current water level and would probably provide some stability against summer spates.

Riverside willows bore exhausted male catkins and ripening female ones, not yet ready to fluff out their seeds. Tight red buds were beginning to open on the ash trees and white may blossoms had appeared, forestalling the month for which the hawthorn trees are named. The first flowering candles were appearing on horse chestnut trees, while opportunist ground elder or bishopsweed provided ground cover in the shade.

Exit from the riverside track was barred to traffic, but walkers had made an escape route at the end of the barrier. I sidled round and followed the old lane uphill and across a major bus route to the old churchyard.

St. John's Church, which once had stood among fields, now abutted onto the shopping complex, but a plot of grassed play area stretched away south, parallel to the one closer to the river, providing welcome green lungs for occupants of the rows of houses. Some groups of trees and old hedgerows had been preserved and ornamented with little plots of daffodils. So much for the basic geography of the new layout.

* * *

Following information received at Fonmon Castle, I sought out the thousand year old yew tree in the churchyard, the larger of a pair and apparently male, the ground below it peppered with fallen pollen bearing cones.

I estimated its red-tinged trunk to have a diameter of about nine feet from the solid base right up to the tangled mass of branch junctions at a height of at least another nine feet. It was certainly a magnificent specimen, but I am no judge of age. Several sets of spread arms would be needed to span its circumference. The other was also a fine tree, but much less impressive.

Clumps of pine trees grew equally tall but less massive both inside and outside the church wall. The yews were safely inside, with an additional cypress. This had been cattle grazing country and the old farming communities did not risk their livestock by exposing them to the poisonous foliage, which their natural instincts seemed not to warn them against.

There were other trees, including a bushy holly with the few prickles mostly on the lower leaves, the ones in no danger of being eaten above being smooth-edged. An ash tree about twenty four feet high was growing from the centre of the grave of an evacuee from Woolwich who had died aged nine in 1945. "Suffer the little ones..."

Most intriguing as an arboreal miracle was the silver birch rising from a minute crack between two granite slabs of a grave containing the mortal remains of a Mr. Lewis who had lived from 1850 to 1916. During the subsequent hundred years a tiny winged birch seed had insinuated a minimal root through a minimal orifice and absorbed sufficient sustenance to have produced two bifurcated horizontal woody boles passing to left and right before turning up to thrust perfectly normal trunks into the air. A plump woody root followed down the outside to spread gratefully at ground level and thrust absorptive anchors into the soil alongside.

Other neglected graves had been taken over by bramble or ivy, but those in the new burial ground west of the original wall were well tended, one having a superb multiple clump of pink Primulas which had produced a crowd of supplementary plants.

I was amused by the antics of a preening crow here, fluttering on a low perch before flying up to the modest bell tower. There was neither steeple nor major tower here. A small paddock intervened between this and the old lane, separated by a trimmed beech hedge. Silky spires of Timothy grass flowers formed a matrix for the lady's smock and tall field woodrush - which last should appropriately be refered to by its alternative name of Good Friday Grass in a site such as this.

A bumble bee was busy with the dandelions and primroses and a yellow blob topping a grass blade proved to be a harlequin ladybird. This alien is a new arrival in Britain, probably already more abundant than the common seven spot ladybird. Heavily spotted, it had eight or nine dark yellow marks on a paler background on each wing case. Several times it raised these to make short flights, the transparent wings unfurled from beneath.

It seemed the congregation must enter through the church hall. The small wooden gate towards the shops was securely jammed into the stone wall and the paired lych gates under the wooden canopy did not fit the space allocated and were clamped at one end. Alongside was a traditional stone slab stile, which could be stepped over by most of us, but not some of the aged and infirm.

Back in the lane spring was well advanced under the ancient hedgerow trees, their woody roots exposed by the march of time. Feathery cow parsley was showing the first flowers among the unfurling fronds of broad buckler and male ferns. Regiments of wild Arum spathes were at prime and there was a little clump of triquetrous garlic, the white umbels topping stems triangular in section.

Bluebells and a few white bells were of both kinds, with probably some hybrids between the two. The inevitable carpets of celandines co-habited, as so often, with the miniscule flowers of ivy-leaved speedwell. Showier ones of creeping speedwell favoured the short grass in the churchyard. A fringe of mauve-flowered storksbill seemed confined to kerbsides where the original lane had been 'updated'. This drier, sandier situation being in keeping with its normal affinity for dunes.

Cryptic signs pointed to Danescourt Station, which I failed to find on my way in through the labyrinth. On the way out I spotted a sign pointing down a narrow path with an iron railway bridge at the end. I wondered if there was road access the other side for those who wished to "park and ride" like so many up the line at Radyr.

* * *

Yesterday's swallows did, indeed, usher in the spring. I brought a group back after the Tuesday lecture, Jan, Anne and Madeleine, and our tour of the garden had a spice of summertime about it. When they went I sat outside with a book. Glancing up I found myself looking into the eyes of a fox, who seemed to be regarding me with equal interest.

No more than a few paces away in the bottom of the hedge, it seemed in no hurry to leave, before slipping quietly away down the wooded cliff. Lightly built, I assumed her to be a vixen or possibly a youngster from last year. She, no doubt, was a maker or user of the well worn track leading under our fence to the foot of the steep road.

Not five minutes had elapsed before the ginger cat appeared. One of the friendly sort, he came to the further side of the concrete standing and rolled across it, stretching and squirming luxuriously until he arrived at my feet. Very pushy in his greeting - we had not met before - I felt I was being used as a rubbing post.

Repeatedly he jumped onto my lap, pushing my book aside to make sure he got my whole attention. When I tried to read in spite of him, as with Snowball of old, he grabbed my wrist with both fore paws and bit my hand. I pushed him off and he got the message the second time. When my old feral brood got well launched into their play sessions they invariably finished up with mock fights. This I could do without.

Reynard appeared again the next day, strolling across the lawn under 'my' lime tree He wandered along the slope and slipped through the hedge by the red Photinea, followed a few minutes later by Nigel the house manager, who had also spotted her.

Ginger Pop disgraced himself next day by catching a blackbird. Breakfasting a day or so later I watched him stalk a wood pigeon which had alighted on the low bird bath for a drink. The plump bird turned in the nick of time, but the would be predator leapt into the air, paws stretched, as the bird flapped overhead.

The twenty fourth of April dawned mild and murky, Spring had come as the wind swung round to the west, having picked up moisture on the way. Nevertheless, the rain held off, not inconveniencing the mini bus trip to the Museum of Welsh Life at St. Fagans engaged in by a group of Brynteg residents after the weekly Thursday coffee morning.

I didn't go with them but the sunshine drew me forth for a couple of hours in the afternoon. I set off for a riverside walk which turned into an unexpected mammal watch. The grey wagtail had come up from the river and was wagging his long tail, rather incongruously, on one of the topmost spikes of the tall iron fence leading down to the 'hollow way' under the railway. A lively little wren was chattering away in the bushes by the station yard opposite. Both were there again when I returned from my expedition into the world of Brer Rabbit.

I lingered on the river bridge, as always, looking up as well as down. The air was full of cavorting house martins, shooting across at high speed. My third hirundine of the spring!. Soon it would be the turn of the swifts.

Four days later, on the morning of the 29th, there was a breathtaking influx of house martins - several hundreds would be an ungenerous estimate - hawking flies with their characteristic alternation of flaps and glides. This was a repeat of the same mass movements that I had observed each year from my eyrie at Gwaelod-y-Garth. The Taff was an important flyway for both these and swifts, but not for swallows, nor the rarer sand martins.

Turning upstream along the public walkway and cycleway, which was part of the Taff Trail, I focussed my attention on the landward side and was completely captivated by the abundance of rabbits. Beyond the extended hedgerow were rough paddocks such as one seldom sees in today's intensively farmed landscape.

Nowhere apart from Breckland in Norfolk, do I recall seeing so many rabbits in a mainland site. I could imagine myself on the Pembrokeshire Islands except that I was peering out at the wee beasties from the cover of tall trees and hedgerow shrubs which do not survive in those more rigorous habitats.

Bramble patches had been allowed to get away on these fields, the clumps many yards across and quite impenetrable by humankind, but perfect cover for the lapins. Neighbouring grassland had been nibbled to lawn like consistency by hundreds of chomping incisors.

They fed mostly in little groups of three to six and so long as they kept nibbling they were quite difficult to spot, their coats merging with the shadows of the wind scorched turf. The slightest untoward movement and they were off, what had seemed like empty spaces suddenly becoming a sea of bobbing white tails.

They were obeying two opposing ecological laws here, first to be as inconspicuous as possible to avoid detection, second to be as conspicuous as possible to warn the rest of the clan of danger. My mind flipped back to that girl guide song that we used to sing around the camp fire in years gone by.

"Oh remember little bunnies, you must keep an open eye
And must scamper scamper scamper when you see the signal "Fly".
There are terriers who will chase you, there are dangers day and night
But you know the danger signal for your daddy's tail is white."

In the first field I counted groups of up to eleven, then swung around and spotted nearly as many again, all heads down, biting into the short grass like sewing machines. All were within a short sprinting distance of a bramble clump.

Looking more closely I spotted other groups sitting erect on bare ground at the edge of the thickets where the marginal loops of bramble were dead, possibly after cutting back into the tangle. These might have been the timid ones scared to venture further or the replete ones who had. This was mid afternoon with bright sunshine and rabbits are normally crepuscular, dawn and dusk feeders, or nocturnal. It must be quite a spectacle at 'busy' times.

Some groups were obviously of youngsters, so breeding must have begun early. A few of the older ones were lying stretched out in the open, blasé about disturbance. One little one was standing erect by a vegetated anthill, resting forepaws on the top to get at the greener grass that grew there

Such anthills are often used as meeting grounds for members of the colony to gather and exchange pheromones. Those commonly used for this often develop a different vegetation from the surroundings and many were certainly greener as viewed from a distance. Their very presence was an indication that the fields had not been ploughed and reseeded for decades, this borne out, of course, by the presence of the thickets.

Intense pressure such as this is likely to have altered the composition of the sward. All I could see from my stance in the hedge was that isolated patches of daffodils and forget-me-nots had been left alone, presumably as unpalatable.

I beckoned to a young Mum with two small girls who passed me for the second time, hoping to show the little ones these creatures that are so much a part of childhood. Mum was excited to see them, but the girls remained apparently unmoved, possibly not able to focus on them or not recognising what they saw. Maybe they were still at the stage when they needed a close up rabbit in a hutch or a picture in one of their books.

As they waxed older they would learn that wildlife spotting was something of an art except in big game country. Our wildlife, very wisely, likes to keep a low profile when there are people about. This population could not have been unaware of all the noisy cyclists and walkers on the bordering track but, like town foxes, had learned that it is only usually in the countryside that someone might have a gun to harm them.

Chatting with Mike Wiley, long term warden of the Fforest Farm Reserve, awhile later, he agreed about their relaxed attitude. He told of one lying on its back sunning its white underside. "Prime target for buzzards!"

Evidently he and his colleagues sometimes tried to intercept poachers who visited these fields with ferrets and dogs for a free meal. Dogs would probably not get far into those dense bramble retreats. Ferrets could, but unless entry holes were right on the margin, popping them into a hole might prove a problem.

With numbers like that there could have been a veritable honeycomb of burrows under the canopy and no pursued rabbit would be likely to bolt into the open if put up by the little white hunter. Alternatively there might have been few or no burrows. Rabbits living above ground in thick cover were the ones that escaped Myxomatosis in the early days. I didn't enquire if the poachers had shot guns, but they certainly couldn't net all the potential escape holes as in classic ferreting sessions.

For Brynteg's fox this living larder was only a short hop away but it was on the wrong side of the river. I wondered if her hunting circuit allowed her to trot across the footbridge in the silence of the night to come foraging here.

The rabbits' companions by day were three horses, a fair sized flock of probing jackdaws and the usual quota of carrion crows. In one field it was a song thrush pulling out worms, in the other a mistle thrush.

By following the boundary of the northern field where it abutted onto the bridleway by the old mill feeder, I came to the junction of rabbitry and allotments. The vegetable growers were taking no chances. A stout wire mesh fence intervened between field and garden, with more light weight barriers around individual vegetable plots.

Rabbits were free to come through the wooden slat fence to the bridleway and feeder, but there was little incentive in the way of palatable plants apart from a temporary fall of oak twiglets with tender new leaves and dangling male catkins which had been ripped from the trees in a gale.

The spear leaves of yellow Iris and Typha bulrushes were alongside the allotment, but both growing in soft mud in the main channel. Rabbits don't like getting their feet wet.

There were mouse or vole holes at the base of fence posts but their excavators would not be serious competitors for food. I picked up a few hazel nut shells with neat round holes nibbled in the side so, whichever they were, they ate nuts as well as herbage.

* * *

In my passage up river not all my attention was focussed on rabbits. The curvature of the river here was such that interesting features of varying sediment deposition were plainly exhibited. Also, of course, there was further burgeoning of spring flowers as I made my way up to Radyr Weir. Arum and archangel were well into their prime by now, spherical buds of the latter like little yellow peas trying to burst their way out of the pod. Hedge garlic or Jack-by-the-hedge, a cress, co-habited with wood Anemones and the less striking greater stitchwort, violets and herb Robert.

I explored little deviations to the river bank along this stretch, anxious to see what the almost vertical face leading up from the railway line looked like from this side of the water. The cliff must initially have been cut by the river, the present downstream flow being directed straight at it, on the outside of a bend, leaving beaches deposited in slack water on the eastern side.

The further bank subjected to the main force of the current had been artificially stabilised to prevent undermining and the loss of both railway line and the houses on the brink, which were just visible through the trees. A stout concrete wall buttressed the critical stretch with revetments of big boulders taking the strain upstream and down. Were the southernmost buildings those of Windsor Crescent? Further north they must have been alongside the main through road.

The earth bank on my side was stabilised by tall bordering trees which terminated downwards in an eroded clifflet several yards high. At the start of the bend the broad beach deposited below this was of river rounded pebbles. Further down, where the current slackened, it was of smooth sand, darkened by water-borne silt - no longer by coal dust as in the past.

The belt of mature osiers leaning out over the water from both was partially submerged during spates, as shown by the flood-borne debris caught up in the branches. Behind the osiers, again on pebbles or silt, was a burgeoning belt of invasive, alien knotweed. Not unattractive at this season, the young shoots bore reddish maroon leaves on brittle canes one to two metres tall. Later in summer these would form an impenetrable barrier several yards high.

Riverside trees here were mostly sycamore and large sallows. The fabulous black poplars, currently shedding their male catkins (which have no female flowers here on which to lavish their charms) grew a little further upstream. Water shallowed on the stretch below Radyr Weir, the lone fisherman casting his line in midstream being only up to his knees.

The Taff was racing through the salmon pass, but this, of course, was not the season for the salmon run. All the mallard seen today, on both river and feeder canal, were drakes, suggesting that the ducks were away incubating eggs at last. Two were allowing themselves to be bowled downstream, tail first, by the current. As I watched to see them slide over, they gripped the rim of the weir with their feet at the last minute and pushed off back upstream to savour another run, like schoolboys enjoying an ice slide.

There were no goosanders this time. I had been lucky with that chance sighting at Gwaelod a week or so before. Only seven goosanders had been reported to the county recorder from different sites along the Taff this winter.

In the mounded beechwood where the old leat by-passed the weir a score or so of molehills had been freshly raised. The soil thrown up was a delectable sandy loam. And I hadn't even got a plastic bag to take a little home for the orchid that had arrived by post the previous day from a past student!

This remarkable complex of mounds and gullies where the sluices and penstocks controlled the exit of the Melin Griffith feeder above the weir, was a playground for young cyclists. The middle section of the old channel leading water back into the river had been excavated some years back and remained bare of soil and floored by river rounded cobbles.

I wondered how many decades it had taken for that great depth of alluvium to be deposited for use by moles and voles. Certainly enough to support some fine trees. Four were gean or wild cherry, overtopping all else so that the current mass of blossom could not be seen from below and I was puzzled for a while by the carpet of white petals under my feet.

Another remarkable tree in this beech spinney was a sycamore, with seven trunks rising from the top of a four foot high wigwam of woody roots that must have been below ground before so much of the deposited matrix had eroded away. The ancient coppicing at ground level had almost evolved into a pollarding by default. There were likely to have been no large herbivores in this once busy industrial site to munch off the young sprouts and make pollarding a necessity.

CHAPTER 14

Local Ramblings, A Squirrel Family and Cwm Nofydd

On 26th May, two days after my look at the west bank of the Taff from across the river, I strolled along its base as far as space allowed. The land below Brynteg in the south had been levelled to accommodate the station yard and extensive carpark continuing upstream, hence the precipitous nature of our boundary. Part way along, a section of the flat land was cordoned off to accommodate "The Radyr Workshop and Body Shop".

Beyond this a long drawn out narrowing triangle of gently sloping land intervened between railway and cliff, merging upstream into a regular sixty degree slope going all the way up. The lowermost ten foot belt above the track had been shaved of all vegetation; the upper part was swathed in deciduous woodland. This pattern continued out of sight around the bend.

The lofty pines along the summit occurred only at the south end, as a backdrop to our lower garden, their encroaching branches removed. Much of the rest was sycamore, but there was oak, ash, hazel and birch, sweet chestnut, dogwood, cherry laurel and holly, linked together with strands of old man's beard Clematis. Other woody plants were sallow, Buddleia, rose and bramble. Regiments of stripling ash saplings along the base looked as though they might provide some handy garden stakes.

At herb level neat bishop's croziers of hart's tongue ferns lagged behind those of their frondose kin in their uncoiling along the 'forest fringe'. Not so the upstanding cones of common horsetail spores. Few flowers were out as yet. Among those to come were red valerian, looking a bit limp, as though herbicide may have been applied to quell them. Others were herb Robert, enchanter's nightshade, knotted figwort and wood avens.

Under our garden sitting out place the land bulged outwards two thirds of the way down under a tangle of blackberry bushes. The upper section was hidden beneath a dense evergreen shrub which looked like the alien *Lonicera nitida*.

Having got down our precipitous approach road I thought I might as well continue over the bridge. Once again I met Eric Williams there, going the other way. I was watching a midstream fisherman, knee deep in water where he or another had been waist deep a few days before. Salmon and trout are available here in season but Eric thought grayling comprised the main catch.

Two grey wagtails were interacting in chasing flight low over the water - the joys of spring mating, perhaps - while a wren trilled from among the massed yellow-green flowers of field maple at the end of the bridge. There were two holly blue butterflies here, large and small whites on the other side.

I noticed vertical yellow stripes on some of the Japanese knotweed leaves, one each side of the midrib. These would have been the outer layer in the bud stage, when the sides of young leaves were rolled inwards towards the midrib, like a double scroll. Exposed through late winter, these are often discoloured by frost. This year it was likely to have been by the bitter winds.

Taking the subsidiary path to the farm alongside the allotments, past deep blue forget-me-nots, I met up with some arable weeds, Buxbaum's speedwell, tower mustard, thale cress, hairy bitter cress and red dead nettle. Contemporary with the latter in southern England is the white dead nettle. Here in the west that is rare and local, we have yellow archangel in lieu - usually a woodland and hedgerow plant, but cohabiting here with its arable kin.

Newly planted apple tree saplings, little more than unbranched wands, in the "Redwing Field", were bearing fat pink flower buds. They wore protective guards, which was just as well as two rabbits grazed perilously close by the adjacent hedge. The last redwings were recorded here as a hundred plus, with just two fieldfares, on the fifth of January. No wonder I had not seen any here this winter. That imposter of a mild spring had sent them packing early.

The Wild Flower Patch towards the farm had been a disappointment after the first few years, the colourful introductions succumbing to brash aggressives. This last few weeks a generous sprinkling of cowslips had saved the day - these always a favourite flower.

From the riot of green I picked out a generous assemblage of ox-eye daisy leaves, so there would be moon daisies through the summer. Sadly nettles were far and away the most abundant, with thistles, docks and goose-grass or cleavers not far behind. Another patch alongside, newly cleared of scrub, might accommodate more interesting newcomers.

I sat here awhile, listening to the endless, repetitive warbling of a song thrush and alarm pips of blue and great tits disturbed by a marauding magpie. The cavortings of an elegant hover fly and more solid looking drone fly kept me entertained for a while, also a garden carpet moth, white with buff triangles and about the size of a holly blue.

Mostly I was following the erratic movements of a low flying beetle with scarlet thorax and wing cases. The long legs, transparent wings and short, searching flights were bee like, but not those scarlet appendages held at an oblique angle in flight. Much smaller than the cardinal beetles, I judged this to be a lily beetle *(Lilioceris lilii)*, but where were the lilies? I knew of none in the farm garden (where I later came upon the finest cowslip plant I have ever seen.)

These leaf beetles emerge from their winter shelter as early as March when the weather is sufficiently warm. The species got a recent mention on national radio as being unusually abundant in this year of 2008 and on the increase. Although white lilies are a favourite food plant, making them unpopular with gardeners, they feed on other members of this family. Ramsons and bluebells were likely food plants hereabouts. In my Gwaelod garden they had preferred the various lilies. Here they seemed to be settling indiscriminately on bare ground and non food plants.

I spent awhile in the farmhouse garden where many country crafts are demonstrated to groups of youngsters. Live willow weaving was not the least of these - an advance on hurdle making and fences of woven hazel laths. The living willow bower, several years old now, was burgeoning with fresh green growth, the wands tied together high overhead and the entrance still open, but the 'throne' gone from the corner. Maybe the new sprouts were too uncomfortable to sit on.

The most colourful flower bed was a medley of red campion and intensely blue alkanet, with white guelder rose blossoms to add patriotic flavour. Brown-leaved fennel, spiky cladodes of butcher's broom and much more provided a foraging ground among the barbecue sites for the chirruping house sparrows - these a relatively uncommon species now, but always abundant here around the old farm buildings.

Lingering in a more substantial bower of brick and concrete, I was diverted by the somewhat chaotic courtship feeding of robins. Male and female plumage is the same. I could only assume that it was he who was having to chase her back and forth around the timbers with every beakful of titbits. Was she playing 'hard to get' or did she really want him? The backdrop to this avian pantomime was neatly trimmed box and lavender bushes under a central Kerria.

* * *

On 28th April I made a circuit of the Old Shunting Yard developments, admiring the profuse flower spikes of bird cherry alternating with the splaying clusters of gean along the approach road. During my first few decades hereabouts this more elegant member of the cherry group was only to be encountered in the wild as I moved north, to the Brecon Beacons and beyond. Recently it had found favour with urban landscapers here in the South.

It seemed that there were to be three recreation areas running along the centre of the main development beyond the new bridge over the railway. The naked beds of the first, seen earlier in rudimentary outline, had been planted with shrubs, including a dwarf Hebe, a daisy bush *(Olearia haastii)*, a bush rose *(Rosa max graf)*, a yellow-leaved dogwood and a grey-leaved member of the Convolvulus family with white trumpet flowers. Deciduous trees bordered the circular central layout.

The second block was a continuous grass sward with irregular clusters of little trees, pines in opposing corners, beech, hornbeam, hazel and cedar. The third block, beyond the extremity of the current building, had not been divested of its native turf, when all around had been scraped bare for more foreign intrusions.

The view from the junction of plots two and three just showed the smooth summit of the Great Garth, all the rest hidden by three to four storey houses in two different coloured bricks. From plot one the view came from slightly further east and showed the red rock of the Walnut Tree Quarry faces on the left and the somewhat ravaged beechwood of the Little Garth on the right.

The only buildings currently at the downstream end of the site were the four storey blocks bordering Radyr Woods. There was not a single amenity, no shop, school or post office, yet the planning permission notices referred to yet another thirty seven blocks of dwellings.

With no way over the Taff to Whitchurch, our one little grocer's shop in Whitchurch was going to be very busy. Worse. When the twelve apartments still to be sold in Brynteg were filled, there might be twelve more cars wanting space in our already full car park. The puzzle would be to find a patch of flat land to accommodate more. There was a large block of wasteland populated only by the white daisy flowers of mayweed which could usefully be added to the station carpark - from which parked cars spilled out along all the local roads during the office hours of their drivers.

A few days later I heard it rumoured that no more houses were to be erected on the cleared land because of the drop in house prices and falling off of sales. Those already started would be completed and then the whole project would go into abeyance. For how long? It would be interesting to watch the succession of pioneering plants on the abandoned acres.

* * *

It was the next day, 29th April, that the great wheeling flocks of house martins passed through, three and a half weeks after the first sand martins and a week after the first swallows. A cormorant flapped ponderously through their midst, like a naval corvette among keeling yachts. Further upstream a cohort of gulls was spiralling in a low thermal.

Another diversion that breakfast time was the first appearance of four baby grey squirrels, which arrived for a prolonged play session in and under 'my' lime tree. This was not their natal base, there was no drey in the branches, but they had adopted it as their early playground, chasing each other back and forth from chunky base to wispy twigs, among the still tiny, late developing leaves. They were already capable of prodigious leaps, with brief intervals to scratch, but no attempt to feed.

These would be the product of a mid winter mating in late December or early January, when we see pairs of adults chasing madly around, the two obviously at variance in their immediate desires. Gestation takes six weeks and the young are suckled for another seven, after which their milk diet will be supplemented by opening leaf buds and the like. The mother is likely to come into season again in May or early June to produce a second brood, from mid July to late September. Birth occurs in a quite substantial, roofed winter drey, which might have been anywhere on the wooded cliff below the garden. Oak is preferred, for the gnarled configuration of its branches.

Lime trees are famous for the amount of sugary sap which passes out through busy swarms of aphids, to drop on parked cars as honeydew. Maybe this little family had homed in on the sweet rising sap of the late burgeoning lime for a purpose. Most other tree leaves were more mature by this time.

The average number of young per litter is three, so this was a success story. The group of siblings stayed together in the garden for only a few days before moving out of my range of vision. They would be sexually mature between six and eleven months old. Those who research these matters state that the average life span in the wild is about two years, although captive grey squirrels have lived for twenty.

The morrow was a day of low pressure and scudding cloud. Martins were still passing, but in smaller numbers and the squirrels were still playing, but were less closely tied to the lime tree, exploring out over lawn and flower beds. It was as though the first exuberance at escaping into the big wide world had passed, and they were starting a more serious investigation of the terrain where they were to gain their living. How long, I wondered, before they discovered the Brynteg bird table (which was beyond my viewing area in the bottom corner under the pine trees) whose seeds they so enjoyed.

The night's rain had softened the soil for worm manoeuvres and robin, dunnock and song thrush were busy along with two cock and two hen blackbirds. Where the upper lawn sloped down to a wooden edging water lay an inch deep above the poor, mossy sward.

I saw my first house sparrow in the garden and the long-tailed tits were busy, as always, among the lime twigs, joined by the resident wren. There must have been a gale in the night because the turf was thickly strewn with leaves ripped from their hold.

A collared dove passed through, not infringing the territorial rights of the two pairs of fat wood pigeons that frequented a few favourite perches in the lime tree for their daytime snoozes. This was not the immediate territory of either because when I saw them carrying twigs for their insubstantial platform nests, they were always headed elsewhere. I had a good view of a jay this morning and a poor view of a pipit-like bird which must remain nameless.

* * *

A favourite walk a few decades ago to view an association of plant rarities was along Cwm Nofydd, the valley separating Fforest Fach in the west from the Wenallt. The wish to revisit had been awakened by vistas of the bright grass sward shining through the leafless beeches on my Wenallt walk with Robert. None of the rare plants would be flowering yet and it was doubtful if I could have reached their site in the squelchy, alkaline fen peat after the recent rain, even assuming they still survived.

Entry was along a path leading from the east side of Rhiwbina Hill, between Rhiwbina Farm and the start of the more steeply rising land. I parked in a spacious lay-by, well clear of an unsavoury gateway through which passed the daily ration of slurry from the cowsheds.

A powerful pong rose from the slurry pit in the field corner - well above the Nant Nofydd stream which flowed across the eastern grassland and might have carried the over-nutritious mixture on to pollute the Taff. The loud pumping noise of machinery on my return came from a tractor, hub-deep in the marginal mass, chopping the soiled strawey waste into small clods to merge more readily with the general gunge.

A good country smell this and one which brought to mind past ploys of my own. For me it was standing on the back of a horse-drawn cart with a curve-tined dung fork, raking the fortunately rather more solid cleanings of the byres over the tail board into heaps as the cart moved on a few yards at a time. The next job had been to throw the muck out from the heaps - with a straight-tined dung fork. Mechanical tractor-drawn spreading came later. This slurry mulcher was a still newer innovation to me.

To the left of the step-over entry gate (which detered motor bikes) the fine old garden beech tree soldiered on. To the right the little old cow byre still stood, the mangers with their neck chains for the milch cows removed, the double space apparently sometimes used as horse boxes.

Swallows had previously nested here, with free entry above the three quarter length doors, but I saw none there now. No more than a dozen or so were about, some perched on roadside wires, others hawking flies at a fair height. I remembered standing here on a day of low pressure when their prey species were flying close to the ground and the swallows were swooping under the horses' bellies to scoop them up. The horses were still there, in the same field, but there had been no big fly hatch as yet and some of the beasts were still wearing blankets against the lingering winter chill.

The brick pigsty adjacent to the old milking shed was intact, but overgrown, and a long arm of bramble stretched across the water in the full tank alongside, supporting a line of healthy young, well watered sprouts. Wood pigeons were cooing, as of yore and a cock greenfinch zizzing away in the hedgerow at both my going in and my coming out.

A major difference was that there was no longer a way in to the lovely old quarry intervening between path and lane a little further on. The quarry had been cut into the red dolomite of Fforest Fach. It contained a fine old apple tree, its boughs sweeping to the ground and laden with pink blossom at this season. There were wild cherry trees and a sward of sweet woodruff under the trees in spring, knapweed and St. John's wort across the open amphitheatre in summer.

Work ceased in the quarry around 1928-30, but it was used for the storage of explosives and ammunition in 1939-40. We used to enter along a clearly cut pathway crossing the little overgrown paddock by the main track during the latter decades of the twentieth century. This wound up through the scrub to a line of fine old beeches into the cliff bound arena.

It was a calling place for all natural history parties, including a delegation from the BSBI (Botanical Society of the British Isles), here to view the rarities further up the valley. I had watched an adder here, a pregnant female, newly emerged from hibernation and warming up in the sun prior to giving birth to her young, free from the chilly winds outside her cosy sanctuary. Adders are ovoviviparous, laying eggs which hatch immediately on emergence.

Whiskered bats domiciled in the nearby house, sought insect prey here by night. Hopefully both species were still enjoying sanctuary from the human race in their man-made habitat.

A little before reaching the most massive of the bordering beeches, I flushed a busily digging rabbit from the path verge. A number of shallow holes had been dug in the soft black loam, possibly to excavate the fleshy rhizomes of the prevalent wild Arum. Certainly something had been feeding on the Arum flower spikes here. Some had the whole of their purple spadix and the overarching cowl or spathe eaten away. Others had the spathe half eaten and pushed back to give access beyond, to the male and female flowers investing the base of the spike which had also been eaten.

The bizarre spadix is rich in starch, which is converted into sugar when the flowers are ready for pollination, the resulting smell attracting midges to enter and do the job. Such a source of nutrients is a temptation to many larger creatures, birds as well as mammals.

We were on the limestone here, so the entire wood was floored by a white carpet of ramsons or wild garlic - in contrast to the bluebells of the Wenallt rising steeply on the other side of the valley. Bluebells occurred in small patches by the track, with some fine primroses, stitchwort, archangel and all the usual spring flowers.

A series of springs oozed from the limestone shales where they abutted onto the harder rocks. The dissolved calcium carbonate melded into the valley peats to form scraps of calcareous fen more characteristic of Derbyshire and Yorkshire than Wales. These nurtured unusually tall golden saxifrage and marsh violets.

The rare broad-leaved cotton grass and other sedges, helleborines, fragrant orchids and red rattle occurred further up, but had been succumbing to the increasing tree growth in the natural course of plant succession and had doubtfully survived into the twenty first century. Wartime grazing of their commoner competitors may have helped their survival in the years before - a time when less water was being drawn from the underground source.

During the first part of the walk the valley bottom below the path was grassed and grazed by heifers. During the latter part it was completely overgrown by even-aged saplings and quite impenetrable except where patches had been lopped, the cuttings bundled up and left in piles.

Mostly these were alder, willow, birch, field maple and guelder rose, with hazel, dogwood, elder, sloe, ash, old man's beard and several types of wild rose. Hart's tongue ferns were uncoiling among the commoner frondose species and patches of Anemones, strawberries and campion.

Throughout the walk I kept spotting bird boxes, with metal guards around the entrance to deter thieving woodpeckers. These were nailed to trunks and there were plenty of blue and great tits about to take advantage of them. Robin, song thrush, blackbird and a single nuthatch were seen. Many well worn mammal tracks led uphill through the carpet of garlic stretching up to Rhiwbina Hill Road.

The main track that I followed was part of a network of paths. One branch led over a stile, back along the valley bottom. Two crossed Nant Nofydd, one by a double plank bridge, the other by a series of stepping stones. Both led on, over stiles and up into the sloping Wenallt Wood. Slabby liverworts plastered marginal rocks, but there were few water plants other than hemlock water dropwort and Angelica, the drifts of garlic dipping into the water in parts.

The prize plant treasure was a small patch of marsh valerian, its pink-tinged bobble flowers simulating those wood sanicle. This is rare, unlike the much larger cat's valerian and invasive red valerian. I was looking especially for this, as it was long ago feared that it would be squeezed out by the more vigorous meadowsweet and burgeoning shrubs, which included green-twigged spindle bushes.

The menace of the former Japanese knotweed thicket beyond the junctions had been removed by constant lopping, but much of this ungrazed field on the limestone side of the valley, including the lower orchid bog, was now partially overgrown by native shrubs. Characteristic grasses were tussocks of tufted hair grass and elegant wisps of wood mellick.

The animal find of the day was a bloody-nosed beetle *(Timarcha tenebricosa)*, largest of the British leaf beetles and as big as a bumble dor, but less cumbersome and with a series of fawn flaps on the two forelegs. These and the red liquid sometimes exuded from the jaws when taken in the hand (but not from this one) are diagnostic features. This is one of the earliest beetles abroad in spring. Here it was clambering among wood bitter cress and bush vetch..

Kicking aside piles of horse dropping, I exposed no dung beetles. The snails huddled in the damps embrace of golden saxifrage flowers and moss were brown-lipped hedge snails *(Cepaea nemoralis)*, the basic colour brick red with dark stripes, like the majority of those seen on the similar garlic-clad slopes of the Little Garth, where the red dolomite crops out on the other side of the Taff.

Dead wood had not been cleared. One fallen trunk had brought its own epiphytic garden down with it, another its complement of peacock's tail bracket fungi. These had changed their orientation from across the erect bough to along it when the angle of the host changed. Or, more correctly, they had righted themselves when their support upset their equilibrium. Ash saplings wore football socks of soft, greenish-yellow moss to a foot or so above ground.

The valley grass was lusher than most at this season and the heifers that had been busy feeding on my way out were lying down chewing the cud on my way back. So were members of Rhiwbina Farm's dairy herd on the rising ground to the south-west.

CHAPTER 15

Lamby Lake, Cors Crychydd Canal and Floral Tributes

I had met few Cardiffians who were aware of the admirable recreation sites created at the mouth of the River Rhymney in the first few years of the new millennium. Much as I lamented the loss of the salty ox-bow and the original reens that are no more, I must give credit where credit is due for the two freshwater landscape features constructed to replace them,

At least three miles intervene between the mouths of Cardiff's two main rivers, but both are within the bounds of Cardiff city. Cardiff Bay at the mouth of the Taff-Ely Roads seems to be known to everyone. I made it my business on 1st May, 2008 to acquaint at least two others with part of the Rhymney Mouth development.

Jan Fife, who had spent her childhood and teens on the Falkland Islands and had travelled widely since, joined Madeleine and me in visiting the new but nicely grown in lake and canal on what might generously be called the "city's eastern seaboard".

In fact we saw no sea. A decade before, the low sea wall holding the waters of the Bristol Channel at bay would have been clearly visible from both sites - across a level expanse of pony-grazed saltings. Ponies were removed and saltings drained, to make way for a landfill site. There was no hollow here to fill, so the Council made a hill instead. This was contoured, grassed and planted with trees and bushes towards the end of the 1990s, replacing the panorama of the estuarine mudflats with an undulating landscape retaining no trace of the former salty tang.

We approached the lake from the old entrance via Brachdy Lane, which continued as a footbridge over the main London to West Wales railway line.

A day of sunshine and roving storm clouds ensured optimum lighting effects.

There were no longer horses in the Shetland ponies' field, just a few mouldy hay bales and coarse vegetation at a height that their presence had never allowed before. The laneside oak opposite, famous for its knopper galls in the years soon after this phenomenon first arrived in Wales, showed no signs of those at present, just a generous crop of dangly male catkins and pinhead sized acorns.

Across the footbridge, with its heightened metal sides decorated with seabird sculptures, we arrived at the elevated lookout point. Sounds of admiration and pleasure issued from the two newcomers to the scene. The essentially rural nature of the site, with its extensive recreational grasslands and spinneys on the further bank, came as a pleasant surprise after battling through this busy end of the city with its big industrial edifices, now out of sight behind the still extant Rhymney Pottery by the tidal riverside.

I missed the spontaneous display of wild flowers on the embankment that had kept the tidal river from inundating the railway. The pinks and blues of crown vetch, campion, viper's bugloss and tufted vetch had been replaced by a double belt of trees with a broad track between. We moved past both and circumnavigated the lake in an anti-clockwise direction.

There were not many birds about, but we had good views of a cormorant and several great crested grebes diving for fish. Another cormorant was drying its spread wings on one of the fishermen's wooden platforms, and was not anxious to move as we approached. Tufted duck accompanied the ever present mallard, along with a few swans and coot and the inevitable gulls, but not so many of those as on the mudflats of the river just over the bank. Those we saw as we drove round later.

Returning across the curvaceous duckboard bridge delimiting the eastern end of the lake, we spotted the nest of one of the pairs of grebes. It seemed scarcely above water level but must have been. The patiently incubating bird would not have been too troubled by a wet stomach but it would not have helped the eggs to hatch. Although well away from the tall reeds bordering this end of the lake, there seemed to be a raft of low vegetation extending out from the skimpy platform.

A little beyond was the swan's nest, well out of the water among the reeds, some of which had gone into its making. The pen was doing incubation duty, the cob was patrolling the offshore waters, on guard and ignoring the lesser neighbour.

Reeds and bulrushes had grown up among marginal bushes to hide the subsidiary pool where moorhens had nested even before these lesser pools had been linked to the lake. I could not see in but did hear the harsh, distinctive song of a cetti's warbler here, an explosive, metallic, rattling song, unlike any other and surprisingly loud for so small a bird. Uncommon and confined to Southern England and Wales - an extension of its West European range - it was, as usual, invisible among the dense growth.

A sinuous path that was new to me followed round the back of these outlying pools through a burgeoning but restrained thicket of hornbeam and alder. Aquatic vegetation was unimpressive at this season, with none of the handsome Butomus flowering rush evident, just great water dock, old stems of purple loosestrife and fresh leaves of yellow Iris among teasels and prickly ox-tongue. No fresh shoots had yet sprouted from the submerged water milfoil.

A peacock butterfly cavorted by the lake shore and a holly blue over the railway bridge. We drove out past the upstream nature reserve along New Road (which was 'new' a hundred or so years ago) but was looking its best with the double row of red horse chestnuts just coming into bloom.

* * *

We looped back into the reen country along Rover Way and Lamby Way to the official lake carpark opposite the smaller "Fishermens Pond". On past the decently respectable entrance to the Municipal Rubbish Dump, we soon came to the cluster of huge boulders half blocking the layby at the landward end of what was referred to as "The Mitigation Reen".

This was intended as and still is, a pleasant rural walk of a little over a mile to the sea. The layby, which still allowed us to park between the boulders, was blocked to exclude gipsy lorries, as was the nearby carpark for the lake in the early years.

Entry into what should have been an important tourist attraction was through a narrow gap in the tall wire fence, partly overgrown, as unimposing as could be and certainly incapable of attracting the attention of anyone not 'in the know'. The ornamental stone cairn, with its plant fossils from the Coalfield, had been divested by vandals of its plaque announcing the site as a Nature Reserve. This had depicted the image of a heron, created by Rhian Kendall, a talented young artist in the Cardiff Naturalists' Society. One wonders what motivates those mindless individuals who go to such lengths to thwart the efforts of our local councils to create a pleasant environment for their citizens!

Once through the tatty barrier a pleasant waterscape presented itself, the broad canal winding sinuously away into an open landscape, the newly erected buildings by the road decently obscured by trees,

Mostly these were osiers, bearing their long catkins and leaves simultaneously. An impressive oak surviving from more pastoral days bore an impressive crop of attractive pink oak apples. With an appearance and name like that it is not surprising that the uninformed might regard these as the fruit of the oak. Children who know so little about the origin of the food they eat might be excused for not having heard of acorns.

The spongy flesh of the oak apples grows around the developing grub of a gall wasp, *Biorhiza pallida*, whose unisexual generation causes not dissimilar galls on oak roots. This parasite has been always with us, unlike the ridged knopper galls, *Andricus quercus-calicis*, which grow from maturing acorn cups, green and sticky at first and then hardening. These arrived in Britain from chilly mountains in South-east Europe in the late 1970s or early 1980s.

The lofty black poplars a little further on had flowered earlier than those by the Taff at Radyr. Their shrivelled red catkins carpeted the towpath on this, the first of May, while those others were still at prime. Both trees contained bulky nests of sticks, not roofed like a magpie's and probably those of crows.

Plants growing in the chilly waters were mostly late developers, but there were some unusual flowers on the banks. One was trailing St. John's wort *(Hypericum humifusum)*, which usually does trail, but was reaching up here through long grass, showing its distinctive leaf glands and stem ridges to perfection.

Two of the others were yellow cresses related to the oil seed rape which was currently clothing so much of the countryside by the eastern leg of the M4 motorway with sheets of acid yellow blooms.

One was the early flowering yellow rocket *(Barbarea verna)*, often a denizen of river banks, the other was wild turnip *(Brassica rapa)*, also of river banks as well as arable fields. A extensive patch of coltsfoot, formerly as bright, was now in its fluffy fruiting phase.

To our left as we progressed were open, reen bordered horse paddocks, one with two patient, statuesque herons. To our right was the now respectably covered old tip, from which methane is extracted for fuel. Beyond it was the great mob of shouting gulls that marked the site of current dumping.

The ominously purple-black bank of storm clouds hovering over the mudflats ahead, started edging round to the west and closing in on us. We judged discretion the better part of valour and turned back, proceeding east to "Blooms", the garden centre on the Newport Road for afternoon tea.

Home produce was on sale at outside stalls. I wished I'd bought twice as much of the delicious farm butter, and came away also with an iced slab of ginger and lime cake and some rhubarb and ginger jam, just like mother used to make.

* * *

On Sunday 4th May I finally got to the Christ Church Garden Festival - proceeds in aid of repairing the church tower. Various groups had contributed floral arrangements, the main ones illustrating various biblical themes.

Outside the entrance both guides and brownies had contributed a water feature, the first including goldfish, the second tadpoles, with paths in both cases of tiny fragments of slate. Red flowers banked on both sides of the entry vestibule represented the Israelites' passage through the Red Sea, the adjective more appropriate for those than for the actual. Here were Protea, Leucobryum and Anthurium, Carnations, Zinnias and Photinea.

Moses' burning bush was cleverly depicted with more crimson flowers splaying from a flickering red electric light with dark background and with red hot pokers splaying all ways from the top. Sand, stones and cacti represented the desert where quails came to feed the hungry, their eggs cleverly depicted but the seashells a little out of context.

A modern garden feature formed the rock from which water gushed to feed men and beasts - and nourish superb flowers with a pitcher to conserve the overflow. Fishy garden ornaments had been collected for the great catch of fish and the feeding of the five thousand.

The one that appealed to me most was the land flowing with milk and honey. Basic products in bottle and jar were overshadowed by suspended furry yellow bees, their wings fashioned from the transparent septum which divides flat honesty fruits into two halves.

Paul's conversion and the resurrection were more complex scenery-wise, but all these and many more exhibits were monumental flower arrangements. The white bouquets at the end of every pew throughout the church must have taken an age to arrange, with sufficient water to keep them going for four days.

With our floral eruption of home grown daffodils finished long since, all but a few evergreen and bamboo backgrounds must have been imported from abroad, by air. Nevertheless, I heard that sponsorship was such that all costs had been covered.

Walking between the two halves of the village centre, I sometimes took the half way track along the back of the Station Road shops. This passed the old established orchard that I had often peered into to admire the intermittent carpet of primroses after Tuesday meetings in years gone by. Now, in early May, the lofty apple trees were a mass of pink blossoms and the primroses were still soldiering on through their third month of flowering.

The crowns of the misshapen old trees were buzzing with pollinating bees - also bud-tweaking house sparrows and blue tits. Trunks and lower branches were sometimes shaggy with a mesh of defunct ivy stems which seemed not to affect their productivity.

Such ancient orchards are frowned upon now - if not already uprooted to try and persuade us to buy those flavourless woolly yellow balls grown by the French under the pseudonym of 'golden delicious'. Maybe it was something to do with moderns not wanting to go up ladders to pick, or their employers not wanting to pay them, or the 'health and safety' Nanny State not wanting to let them. Baby trees bearing fruit in their lost infancy were all the rage in the orchards now. I was told the apples had not been harvested for years except by birds and squirrels. The soil beneath must be wondrously fertile with all those incorporated windfalls.

There were black bee flies, not the common greater bee flies, but hovering like those as they sipped nectar from the primroses. Their greatest love seemed to be the snapdragon like flowers of the ivy-leaved toadflax which had been blooming prolifically in all the walls through March and April.

Also in these walls, along with the common little wall ferns such as black spleenwort, were some neat rosettes of rusty-back ferns. White-lipped hedge snails *(Cepaea hortensis)* banded in black and yellow, had cemented themselves to walls here, to tide over the daylight hours.

Capacious yards backed the shops, some used as car parks on weekdays but others completely overgrown with brambles. Brynteg's car park had eighteen parking places for eighteen car owners and no more flat land for when the final twelve apartments were filled. Maybe we should be negotiating for some of this unused land.

* * *

At one of the early May coffee mornings, it was decided that Brynteg needed a gardening committee to introduce a little more colour into the gardens now that the daffodils had finished. Blue periwinkles and purple Clematis did not show up well from the windows, and bright touches were currently limited to a few tulips and small Azaleas.

I volunteered, along with Pansy and Louise, under the chairmanship of Rita. Thus it was that on Saturday 10th May I spent the morning digging up specimens from my old Gwaelod garden - with the new owner's permission, of course. Babs helped by rescuing two of the four fine ice plants that had got fenced out by the barrier put through the middle of my choice grow-bag flower bed. The phlox, Japanese Anemones and Doronicums on the wrong side of a higher fence were unreachable and would have to flower unseen and unloved.

Mostly I worked alone in the upper garden, with a fork lacking three of its six tines, before finding my trusty old garden spade stuck in the ground in the lower garden. Lilies of the valley had marched out a couple of feet across the lawn and were flowering merrily from underground parts that I had beheaded regularly when mowing the lawn in previous years, but mowers had not been used in either garden this spring.

I dug up token plants of the most rampageous, purple Iris, scarlet kaffir lillies and the Montbretia, whose corms had had to go in the landfill bin as being unkillable, however long they lay among the squishy compost. The splaying corms of yellow Hemerocallis lilies and fat scaly bulbs of tiger lilies should surely be unkillable, likewise the fleshy rhizomes of variegated yellow Arum.

I extricated lengths of roving rhizomes of three spurges, including my favourite *Euphorbia polychroma*, also Welsh poppies bearing buds to shed their seeds in the hope of more. Pink Astilbe and white Spiraea, rampageous yellow loosestrife and the related floriferous creeping Jenny, with white flowered Geranium, golden rod and a few of the Doronicums that had already thrown up tall flower stems, also most of the Michaelmas daisy bought last year.

Titbits for my balcony were a favourite little tuft of roseroot and a fine clump of primroses, these last to join the burgeoning thrift clump which was throwing up its first flower buds from the only survivor of three cuttings taken several years ago. Lastly there was one of the offspring of the pink bush rose that my mother had always called 'great grandad' - the gentleman from whom it had come in the first place!.

Some were already wilting by the time I got them into the car, so I was grateful for help from sales officer, Suzanne, fetched by Rita, who arrived at the same moment from a shopping spree and declared herself incapable of helping physically. Buckets and bowls were found and the sink filled - where but in the laundry, the only place where containers and water came together? Nigel was not looking too pleased when I encountered him later mopping wet earth from the floor, but he rallied round with the planting and watering.

I helped with the planting for a couple of hours on the Sunday evening - also in his official time off - Pansy and Louise were nowhere to be seen nor any of the men - who had not volunteered anyway. Added to my contribution was a hundred pounds worth of plants bought by Nigel with cash from the residents' 'leisure fund'.

My trowel had a pointed end but it penetrated the solid clods of clay unwillingly and only after much sideways manoeuvring of the cutting edge. The matrix under the mulch of bark chippings was unadulterated clay subsoil, thrown up initially, no doubt, during excavation of the station yard and containing river-rounded pebbles, the largest of which we heaved back over the edge.

Two bags of composty soil contributed a little sustenance at the bottom of each hole excavated. I took on the initial night and morning watering of the patch outside my windows, teetering up the slope with a slopping watering can or following the contours around to apply the elixir of life from above. Fortunately there was a tap in the wall immediately below my balcony. Unfortunately it was a long walk to get to it, whichever way I went. It was good to see Nigel out with a hose pipe on the Monday evening.

When I took Clive and Lynne up to the garden later, after a spell of doctoring my computer, hanging pictures and fixing hooks for mugs, even the main garden gate was bolted. Clive, the perfect gentleman, had to get down on all fours for Lynne to climb on his back and reach over to release the bolt.

Ginger Pop was waiting on the gatepost for whoever might come in to amuse him, and he did his best to entertain us as we occupied the three garden seats above. My friends' two cats were elderly and took life as easily as they could, so they enjoyed sparring with our lively youngster - as Joyce and Lena had when we sat up here the previous day.

During this hot dry weather of the second week of May, the local blackbirds turned their attention to stripping the bright blue berries from the *Mahonia japonica* bushes at both ends of the garden. A lavish crop of these, known as Oregon grapes, had been plumpening up during recent weeks, their supporting stalks radiating horizontally from the top of the main stem like the spokes of a wheel.

There must have been a wonderful show of yellow flowers here back in the winter to produce so generously. It was all over by the time of my arrival in late January, but was something to look forward to next year while waiting for the daffodils. Formerly included with Berberis, the Mahonias are much more robust. This species flowers in December and January, the similar *Mahonia aquifolium* in March and April. Either might have been called 'aquifolium', meaning spiky, shining leaves, as in holly.

With so few pollinating insects around in winter one suspects such complete ranks of fruits must arise from self pollination. If the blackbirds eat them all, the plants can spread with their underground suckers. Conversely the birds may help by defaecating their seeds on new soil after digesting the investing flesh.

Mayflies were habitually settling on my glass doors during May, wafted up from the river in the still boisterous winds. Most were the regular shape with two or three long tail prongs and transparent wings held obliquely at half mast. One seemed to have the hefty thighs of a young grasshopper, but these were probably deformed, crumpled wings - confirmed by the fact that it remained in the same place for several days. Nothing else has similarly long wispy legs and those long tail prongs except ichneumon wasps and it was certainly not one of those.

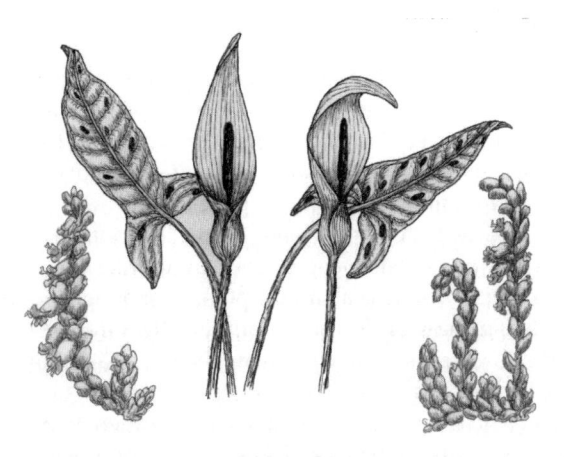

CHAPTER 16

Ledbury and Eastnor Castle, Roy Noble, Blackweir and the Old Cardiff Canal

Weather was somewhat negative over the early May bank holiday, mild, dull and with the odd shower. On Tuesday the 6th, when most people were back at work the sun came out with serious intent and temperatures soared into the early seventies Fahrenheit. This was the day of the Tuesday group's sortie into middle west England - the sort of day when coats could safely be left in the coach

M4 roadside flowers included the last cowslips of spring and the first ox-eye daisies of the summer-long display to come. Turning off at the Coldra roundabout, we travelled up the Usk Valley and then the Wye, past Ross and Monmouth, with the swans sailing the river at Dixton, Much Marcle and so to Ledbury near the junction of Herefordshire and Worcestershire.

Ledbury, which I remembered only vaguely, proved to be one of the most delightful town in this beautiful part of England. It was the sort of place that epitomised the best of Britain, more English than the polyglot English of today and the sort of place that attracts Americans and Australians to view our, and often their own, beginnings. Each has its own character instead of conforming to modern global angularity.

Cherry trees in the hedgerows and apple trees in the orchards were in full flower. Many old apple trees nurtured a heavy burden of mistletoe balls, which preferred these to their wild host trees. A few apparently dead trees still bore large overlapping clumps of the parasite. How long would those survive without a fresh current of sap in the host trunk to sustain them?

Interleaved with the old orchards were new ones, planted with close rows of sapling trees less than a yard high, sparingly branched yet full of rosy pink blossoms. Would they be allowed to bear fruit so young. I noticed no orchards with the white flowers of pear or plum.

Huge fields of rape were at their brilliant prime, their intense colour brightening the valleys and more gentle slopes. This species had been flowering for some weeks, the owners worrying about the possible shortage of bees available to pollinate so huge a mass of flowers to produce the oil-rich seeds desired. Perhaps other insects would stand in for them. There was certainly no shortage of those to judge by the density of flattened corpses on the coach windscreen.

Other crops of these fertile red loams were hidden beneath acres of polythene, shimmering in the sun like lakes - probably tomatoes, strawberries and other soft fruits. Would there be bees to pollinate these, so much more protected from wind and weather?

Approaching Ledbury the country became hillier, wilder - grassland with scattered spinneys and individual trees, all incredibly beautiful. England at its old fashioned best, with a few rabbits and pheasants for good measure.

We had three hours in Ledbury, with its attractive Tudor style black and white timbered buildings, imposing stone ones, such as the almshouses with the glimpse of their colourful gardens, and a plethora of narrow cobbled walkways and walled alleys among quaint huddles of red brick buildings in all shapes and sizes.

So pleased were we with the small tea garden at the back of "Mrs. Muffin's Little Shop" where we sipped coffee, surrounded by pink and white Clematis scrambling up the walls, that we returned there for lunch. Menu items, most locally grown, included wild boar. Of the home reared Gloucester Old Spots pigs it was said that they traditionally grazed in the orchards to scrunch up fallen fruit, bruises caused by larger windfalls accounting for their spots!

We followed on up this particular cobbled way with its museum. heritage centre and craft shops to the church. This was huge with a lofty steeple, deserving of cathedral status, while the spacious churchyard and general environs were much as one expects in cathedral cities. In addition was a multiplicity of statues, lofty stained glass windows and fresh floral decorations.

Lawns were not too severely mown and were draped with a generous counterpane of field daisies, augmented with germander speedwell and ground ivy. I had been looking out for shepherd's purse, formerly one of Britain's commonest weeds, since learning from the media that it had become so rare that it was being cultivated to save it from disappearing. This old childhood favourite with the purse-shaped seed capsules was here, together with the now commoner, long-fruited thale cress.

There were some fine yew trees, none hugely ancient but their red trunks attractively ridged, some in the church precincts and more over the further wall, where ivy-floored woodland reached back to the foot of wooded hills. A big Magnolia was shedding the last of its petals, the pink and white ones of the flowering cherries were at peak. Red horse chestnut candles were just igniting and there was beech, ash, elm and silver birch. The morning radio had warned hay fever sufferers to beware the birch pollen, and the population generally to beware the unaccustomed sunshine, the incidence of skin melanoma having been on the increase in recent years.

Among the fluttery white moths were small white butterflies and I had seen an orange tip from the coach. A spell of bird watching, peering through the railings into the wood, revealed some newly arrived 'willow-chiffs' flying and foraging. They could have been either of these tiny, mouse-coloured migrants but we heard the unmistakable calling of chiff chaffs at Eastnor Castle a mile or so away.

Others in the spinney were tits, chaffinch, blackbirds, song thrush, house sparrows, wood pigeons and pheasants. Most of the ivy berries had been stripped from the wall coverings in this remote part of the churchyard, those where church-goers passed were still adherent to the vines.

Before setting off that morning I had seen my first swifts of the year, unmistakable shapes sailing over the river where the hirundines had been before them. Here there were more, wheeling around the motley of town roofs and the church where they may well have nested. Two of us sat briefly in a pleasant walled garden beside beds of unusually tall green alkanet, pink tulips and stripy grasses usually referred to as gardener's garters. A final wander along the high street after lunch and a few purchases from the stalls in the traditional old market hall and we were away.

* * *

A few miles along rural lanes we came to the great turreted edifice of Eastnor Castle. The yellow rock of which it was built had been quarried in the Forest of Dean and could well have been Pennant Sandstone from the Coalfield. It had come by canal to Ledbury and on mule back from there - this in the ten years from 1812 to 1824 when the present building was going up.

Two of the splendid fireplaces had been constructed from beautifully figured black and white marble found in the grounds. Like Fonmon Castle, visited a few weeks before, it was still lived in by the owning family, but their ownership could not go back as far as the middle ages, as with Fonmon. They had struggled to get the interiors and contents renovated after years of emptiness and neglect.

This must be one of the most remarkable of such edifices that I have visited over the years. The craftsmanship that had gone into both the internal structure and the furnishings, in wood, metal, stone or tapestry, was mind boggling. In addition, our guide was knowledgable and clearly audible and many of the great chambers provided sofas and chairs to sit on while we listened and admired. Why is standing still for long periods always so much more tiring than walking?

The indoor tour finished with a cream tea in what had been the old kitchens - separated from the main building because of the fire risk. After this we could escape into the sunshine. Several sets of steps took us down some of the terraces below the level of the living rooms, to gaze at the curved elegance of the great lake, still a long way below.

This had been constructed at the same time as the castle, encircling the then owner's original house, now on an island. His goal had been to produce something more ostentatious than aspired to by any of the neighbours and he had certainly succeeded.

The lake view was divided by tall trees but was splendid, with wild fowl sailing its waters and lawns sweeping up to arboreta. Fine trees included a treasured collection of cedars and a giant Sequoia. We saw no gardens as such. This was a carefully landscaped parkland with waterside and woodland paths, which we had no time to explore, and a rolling backdrop of some of Middle England's finest countryside.

Under the walls three rabbits nibbled contentedly at the short grass to the accompaniment of the chiff chaff's bisyllabic song, tediously repetitive but a sure sign that spring was here. The first part of the homeward journey was through this same countryside with rabbits and pheasants, broad bean and three inch high cereal crops, country churches, attractive cottages and the fine, non stony red soil being ploughed or cultivated for more crops to come.

We emerged onto the more mundane routes by the famous Beef Eater Inn and returned through Llandaff, where Lena was dropped off, where she had been picked up after misjudging the meeting time by nearly an hour. What would we do without mobile phones? Silly of me to wonder, as I don't use one myself, but it is a good job some people do!

* * *

The weather continued perfect for the official opening of Cwrt Brynteg House on the eighth of May by Roy Noble of broadcasting fame. We turned up in our glad rags to sip champagne and partake in the opening ceremony and first class buffet lunch. Despite summer frocks, all the windows and doors of the communal lounge had to be thrown open to keep the temperature down, as more and more chairs were brought in to accommodate an over full house.

For those who had been in residence for as much as three years, it was an odd time to be 'opening', but it could scarcely have happened when there were only a few participants and there were still a dozen or so apartments not yet sold.

Roy Noble was first class, as always, and kept us in fits of laughter for well over half an hour, as he addressed us in his inimitable Valleys accent. A favourite interviewer on radio, and sometimes TV for many years (and always ready to introduce a new book to the reading public), he was most entertaining when he had the field to himself.

As we were all 'over sixties', it was appropriate that he talked about life in the old South Wales mining valleys, with all its quirks and foibles, 'old hat' for those of us with a South Wales background, but presented with such finesse and humour that we wished he had gone on longer.

It was outside then, for group photographs in the sunshine, brandishing the new brass plaque, before we did justice to the excellent cuisine and got chatting with some of the visitors from McCarthy and Stone and other walks of life.

* * *

On May 9th, following a hot lunch with Madeleine at Danescourt, we drove to Staples, the office supplies store in the Tesco shopping complex off Eastern Avenue, for two bits of equipment. My ulterior motive was to explore along the River Taff and the old Cardiff Canal from this spot on the downstream side of the Cardiff ring road.

We would be following the East bank but for more than half the distance this was actually the North bank, as the meandering river was flowing due east here. It starts turning south again at Tal-y-bont, a short distance upstream from Blackweir, where we branched off to follow the Docks Feeder Canal and return along the track of the main Merthyr to Cardiff Canal. There were sundry places to wander between the two main footways.

Parking near Tesco, we entered the long, leafy avenue under tall trees, with brilliant spring foliage - a veritable cathedral of a different sort. The urban fringe vanished by magic as we entered, to enjoy the patterning of sunshine filtering through the canopy.

A lesser path took us to the river bank by a tall bamboo thicket, over a ground cover of dog's mercury to one of ground elder with broad-leaved garlic and Anemones. Pushing through investing undergrowth we spotted a drake mallard skulking under the bank and then his family of eleven ducklings spinning round their dam on the smooth but fast flow. These were the first of the season and pretty obviously a full clutch as yet unmolested.

The botanical hotspot came soon after while Madeleine was selecting a walking stick from fallen timber. Toothwort *(Lathraea squamaria)*, an uncommon complete parasite, had reached the fruiting phase, the pink flower spike changed to a white fruiting one. Some spikes were beside fallen logs, one ornamented with Jew's ear fungus, most were pushing up through the ground cover of ivy and Anemones. This bizarre member of the broomrape family, with no green leaves, was always a notable find.

Limes were particularly common when we rejoined the main river path, with basal domes of densely proliferating twiglets, masked by leaves, around their trunks, like small bivouacs. There were fine beeches, oaks, horse chestnuts, ash and even a plane tree rising from an open sward of sycamore seedlings.

Past the attractive old timbered dwelling house, where a wren trilled insistently from the fence, we crossed the suspension bridge over the weir. A cormorant was fishing upstream. Downstream water ran smoothly over the salmon pass installed in 1980 and replaced in 2009.

Diversions here were a little dog having fun in the water and a dense shoal of small fish. About two inches long and streamlined, these were probably minnows. The shoal was unusually large, several layers deep and clustered along four or five yards of shoreline. The shimmering mass of protoplasm extended a few yards out into knee deep water, lying quietly over pebbles away from the main stream.

The old stonework of the outlet to the docks feeder canal was embroidered with mounds of pellitory of the wall. A grey wagtail flipped up from the dark water beyond the penstock as we took to the path along the southern bank of the lesser, wooded waterway. This was reminiscent of the Melin Griffith feeder canal taking off from behind the Radyr weir up-river.

A line of lofty sweet chestnuts topped the bank, their leaves still small at this season. On the ground beneath were residual spiky burs from last year's nut harvest. The bank leading down to the grassy expanse of Bute Park was colourful with massed red campion and blue alkanet, with the first tall meadow buttercups opening to the sun. The alkanet, formerly regarded as rare, had been popping up everywhere in recent years and a clump here bore almost white flowers in profusion.

Leafy tufts of onion-scented crow garlic splayed from among the white flowers of the somewhat misnamed hedge garlic and a sprinkling of bluebells and violets. This bank dipped steeply down to the feeder, where the big red Rhododendron bushes were already in full flower, alongside the attractive narrow leaves of a turkey oak.

A spritely orange tip butterfly intruded among the small whites, some of which may well have been females without the orange flashes. Mayflies were abroad, reflecting the sunlight like floating golden spangles. Tiny midges, resembling moth flies, were getting caught up in spider webs spread across foliage and bridge rails alike.

On our return we headed off towards the old Glamorgan canal, obtaining a fine view of two handsome jays as we entered another patch of ancient woodland threaded with paths. The first ended against the canal wall, skilfully constructed of local stone and still in good condition. Another of the same calibre followed along the opposite side of what had been a vitally busy waterway in its heyday.

This old highway had been constructed well above the flood level of the river alongside and had been re-invented in recent years as part of the Taff Trail, popular with cyclists and walkers, particularly students commuting between hostel or digs and lectures.

Arum spikes, abundant throughout, had frequently been chomped off by birds or mammals, some right to the base. Squirrels we saw, rabbits we didn't, but they were probably about. 2008 seemed to be a good year for them. A great bank of the circular leaves of winter heliotrope occupied one stretch of verge, and of the related butterbur another, those much larger but the patch smaller.

We returned to a warm muggy evening, seventy three degrees Fahrenheit in the shade, with banks of soft black nimbus rolling round the sky, the last of the sun's rays squeezing out between them. By 10.30 pm we were treated to a fine thunder storm, the frequent lightning flashes lighting up the whole of the sky.

* * *

On Sunday evening, when commuter trains were few, I took my secateurs down to the station yard in search of garden stakes. Several live saplings had been felled and left at the foot of the wooded cliff, providing me with a good range of stout supports, some forked at the tip for lifting tired, newly planted herbs.

My choice tiger lilies were particularly grateful, but it was hard work trying to force even a half inch diameter support into that intractable clay. I tried tweaking out weeds, which broke off, unable to free themselves from the glutinous grip. Another visit with a trowel was called for.

I found evidence of three dead birds and wondered if my small ginger "helper" had anything to do with these. One was the corpse of a cock black-bird, flattened but intact, one a gawky naked nestling, with skin-covered eyes protruding from an over large head, the beak shape and size suggesting a pigeon squab.

The third was a generous scattering of the tail and wing quills of a wood pigeon beside the low bird bath, where I had witnessed the near miss some days before. Ginger Pop was inclined to creep into the thicket beside this drinking place, to wait. There was no corpse, but a pigeon missing all those feathers would be at a distinct disadvantage.

CHAPTER 17

Afoot In The Country Park and River Walk To Tongwynlais

Ostensibly at the station to buy a train ticket on seventh of May, the sunshine lured me across the footbridge to see if anything was afoot. Activity centred round a pair of nest building carrion crows.

They flew relays under and over the bridge, collecting sticks downstream for their nest upstream near the top of a tall oak on the east bank. One shot through the metal superstructure overhead, manoeuvring a couple of twelve inch long twigs and bunch of smaller ones through the obstacles with ease.

A cock and hen blackbird, crossing and recrossing the river from potential upstream nesting cover, were likewise engaged. Summer was a'cummin' in. The high spot, species wise, was a pair of spotted flycatchers a little downstream, migrants homed in from Africa to benefit by and add benefit to our Maytime landscape.

Perched, rather erect, on low waterside vegetation, one kept flipping out over the shallows to snap up an insect, possibly one of the smoky-winged mayflies with trailing tail appendages. The partner flew across and they changed places. Could there be a nest over there, claiming their attention?

Leaving cormorant and mallard, I peered over the nearest farm gate, as was my wont on these mooches abroad. I was surprised to see at least three quarters of the 'redwing field' knee deep in flowering ribwort plantain. Normally this was closely grazed by horses - which may have disadvantaged almost every other plant except this species, with its flat, spreading leaf rosettes, beyond reach of their incisors. Those had availed themselves of the rare opportunity to send up a bumper crop of flowering heads, on taller stalks and longer in themselves than normal.

I crept through a gap by the ill fitting gate to investigate. Grass was reasonably lush in between, with a few cocksfoot and sweet vernal flower spikes and budding heads of common sorrel. Buttercups here were of the tall meadow variety, only leaves as yet. On the sward kept low by rabbit grazing towards the farmhouse, creeping buttercups predominated.

Subordinates there were small, mouse-ear chickweed and thyme-leaved speedwell, while lush, untrampled swards of nettles occurred elsewhere, particularly in the shade of big trees, where livestock had formerly sheltered and added fertility. My shoes were covered with pale yellow plantain pollen on emergence - this loath to be brushed away.

Grazing had been curtailed to allow the little apple trees to get away - in the 'leggings' that protected them from rabbit gnawing. On past a rusted cattle crush and other farm equipment, I had another surprise - a new pond. This was dug out from yellowish clay, or had that been added as a water-proof lining over the permeable alluvium?

Obviously new, it was by no means lifeless. Pond skaters skipped over the surface film, leaving four pin-prick shadows of their feet on the bed, over which scurried numerous small water boatmen. Others on top were Gyrinus whirligig beetles. More solitary than usual, these were zizzing along less tortuous routes than the norm. Small flies were hatching at the surface by a fine flowering clump of kingcups and I spotted one black tadpole pursuing a lonely course across open mud between clumps of Canadian pondweed.

Two floating straw bales were scummy with green algae, but the water was clear. Bogbean, yellow Iris and greater spearwort had been planted marginally and I noticed some submerged, circular water lily leaves

Groups of logs provided marginal seats for pond dipping groups and a more distant pile of logs yielded a few fronds of split gill fungus *(Schizophyllum commune)*, generally rare but formerly locally common on logs dumped around the nearby timber yard. Scarcer at present, perhaps it was early in the season or perhaps this fungus was associated with a certain stage of decay of the substrate and was on its way out.

The pond was handy to the Fforest Farm garden, but I continued across the hummocky field and climbed the new padlocked metal gate. Today was the second time that fair weather had persuaded me to exchange my winter slacks for a skirt, no hindrance but no help either. Last time I had ruined a new pair of stockings on marginal brambles trying to avoid the puddles! Men, excluding the wearers of kilts, don't know how lucky they are.

* * *

Past fine stands of green alkanet being pollinated by bumble bees and hover flies, I visited the old pond dipping site, now almost dry. The depression was still there and water had flowed into a small experimental pit. Talking later with the rangers I learned that they had decided against digging it out, this entailing the loss of much well established marsh vegetation. Marginal reeds and sedges remained, but this was likely to be a mass of golden greater spearwort flowers by summer, these formerly rare, but very handsome wildlings, now spreading merrily where introduced. A little water mint was surviving.

And then there was the once rich animal life. My mind went back to the old days of pond dipping from the platform provided. Prize specimens then were three-spined sticklebacks and common and palmate newts. Among smaller fry were water scorpions, saucer bugs, freshwater shrimps and water hog lice. On still summer days the air had been whirring with dragonflies and damselflies. No wonder the wardens hesitated to endanger such a rich community. But how were they going to make the bed waterproof without? This was just one of the many problems facing practical conservationists.

I sat awhile on a pondside bench, butterfly watching. The speckled woods were out in force, my first this year, this early brood richer in colour than the later one. Copulation was already going on a few feet in front of me. Both butterflies clasped the same grass stem. tail to tail, their folded wings overlapping. That second brood was already on the way, on what must be very near the emergence of the first. Adolescent development all went on within the chrysalis. No time was wasted.

Large whites were present in good numbers, although no obvious Cruciferous food plants were about. Pairs were spiralling up over the old pond bed in mating chases. It seemed these, too, were wasting no time in producing pollinators to help combat the loss of honey bees.

On emergence I found yet another freshwater habitat -a tiny one this time, cut into the bank by the building serving as an office for the various bodies using the farm as an H.Q. Steep sided and no more than six feet long, this was disastrously eutrophic and green with algae. A nice find alongside was the uncommon shining cranesbill in full flower.

I moved on to join three wardens, who informed me that Mike Wiley - head warden for some forty years - was back after best part of a year away on sick leave. He wasn't in at the beginning, in the 1960s, but he was soon after - the right man in the right place, if ever there was and able to lay a hedge more neatly than any of his colleagues.

I found him in the cubby hole used as his office in a corner of the old barn. It was good to see him back. He owned a smallholding of six acres near Hirwaun on the Brecon border, at the head of the Cynon Valley, so had had plenty of opportunity to recuperate in the great out of doors.

He said the plan for the ribwort field was to fence part of it off to contain the horses without endangering the little apple trees at the further end.

The heatwave of the second week of May came to a sudden halt on the sixteenth, when the temperature dropped a full ten degrees, from seventy four to sixty four degrees F. Low cloying cloud and a gentle rain brought the cavorting swifts down to hedge height, presumably because that was where the flies they sought were suspended. I have still not fathomed how such wisps of protoplasm can remain airborne during rain, when every drop is the equivalent of a whole bucketful to us.

On Saturday the seventeenth, I joined the monthly RSPB bird walk around the Fforest Farm Reserve. The regular leader was indisposed and an individual by the name of Andrew took over. Usually there were only about twelve on this walk, spotting about thirty different species of birds. We were twenty five and we spotted only twenty two species, plus rabbits and squirrels.

We walked from the farmhouse to the Taff by the pollarded poplars and up river to my home bridge at the start. The cormorants were not perched along their favourite pylon wire, but one of the mallard on the river had three tiny ducklings in tow, my second this season on the Taff although, strangely, we saw none on the canal.

The prize sighting was a kingfisher, perched low on the opposite bank. It faced towards the water, so that the image was a warm orange instead of the usual metallic blue, like a plump robin. We were not close enough to put it up so we did not see it in flight. Grey wagtails could be relied upon by the bridge, as could the house martins and swifts flighting low overhead.

The prize sighting here and the first for me on this particular stretch of the river was the dippers. I spotted them a long way off downstream, two dumpy black forms zooming closely side by side up river, just a few feet above the water, wings whirring too rapidly to see. They shot under the bridge and I got to the other side in time to follow their undeviating clockwork flight upstream and out of sight. My only other dippers, strictly mountain birds, seen on this stretch of water had been on the Taff at Tongwynlais and Taffs Well and by the water racing through one of the canal locks.

From the first hide we watched an adolescent moorhen, seemingly the sole survivor of its brood, and five herons flew past at intervals. The bank where the passerines were fed throughout the winter, was now knee deep in woodland herbs, so no birds attracted would be visible. We saw not a single finch all the morning.

I was expecting sand martins, after being told by the warden that six had been seen investigating the artificial burrows, but, sadly, we saw none. It looked as though the high rise martin block so laboriously constructed and lived in for a number of years was going to be empty again in 2008. This second hide yielded only a willow warbler. The kestrel box mounted on top of an old telegraph pole looked very empty.

The feeding station where the path emerged onto the canal bank was busy, the usual blue and great tits accompanied by coal tits and robins, and so used to people that they took little notice of us. Long-tailed tits were not tempted, remaining in the tall trees opposite. It was a grey squirrel which stole the limelight here, returning doggedly to the same fence post only a foot or so away to feed. It sat comfortably back on its haunches, each corn grain brought politely up between delicate forepaws.

The canal yielded no ducklings and only one newly hatched moorhen chick, which seemed to be the only survivor of its family. While its mother swam between the lily pads, the baby swam at them and over them. The leaves were not yet capable of supporting its almost negligible weight, sinking hock deep at a swift passage and belly deep with a more lingering one. It was all the same to the chick, although that loose black fluff did not look particularly waterproof.

An apparently very new moorhen's nest was blatantly obvious only a yard from the bank, the uppermost layer of fresh green composed of neatly severed Iris or bur-reed leaves. I was reminded of the days when water voles were abundant on this stretch of canal and I photographed one which had climbed onto just such a moorhen's nest to nibble at the fresh greenery. Sadly these delightful furry creatures are as extinct here now as almost everywhere else, despite the nurturing of the site as a nature reserve.

The only woodland birds of note were jay and nuthatch. Stars among the flowering shrubs were guelder rose, crab apple and spindle. Rowan was past its prime, may blossom as fecund as everywhere at this season. The rose bush where we had watched bankvoles in February was still a mass of tight green buds. Floral stars by the river were comfrey, red campion and forget-me-not.

The tractor mower had been busy and many river and road banks were shorn down to mud level, with tractor wheel tracks mounting seemingly impossible slopes. A higher cut had been made over the greater part of the wild flower plot, leaving two patches intact, one of budding ox-eye daisies and one of meadow cranesbill. The cowslips had apparently been beheaded before they had a chance to set seed. Rabbits were spied in several places, some very tiny, almost too small to be allowed out on their own and not very wary of the admiring audience.

* * *

I was tempted out by the warm weather of the 21st May and memories of the little path snaking alongside the Taff between the Iron Bridge and the north of Tongwynlais village. Leaning over the home bridge, wagtail watching and checking over the trails of false river crowfoot for early flowers, I became aware of shimmering movement of a darker hue over the feathery green fronds.

This was the first of many pockets of beautiful demoiselle damselflies that I was to come across in my passage up river. The sparkling blue, green and purple body and wings, some of the latter the warm brown of autumn bracken, was visible to the naked eye from my greater elevation, but I needed binoculars to see that these were *Calopteryx virgo* and not the banded demoiselle, *Calopteryx splendens*, where the dark pigmentation of the wings appears as a partial band and only in the male.

I was not to see more until I diverged onto the narrow bridleway between the Taff Trail and Longwood Drive, upstream of Radyr Weir and the divergence of the feeder. Here, hedged about with all the leafiness of spring, I came eyeball to eyeball with them at close range, and what eyes they were, bulging from both sides of the metallic sheened head. How I wished for my camera.

Their hovering flights were short and intermittent, their rests on the leaves of bramble or dogwood longer. The fluttery flight was very like a butterfly's when first glimpsed, but the only butterflies seen were brimstones.

Depending on my viewing angle, the wings of the male glinted first blue, then green or sometimes with a violet-brown tinge. Those of the female were copper coloured, sometimes with the same violet tinge and the black veins showing more clearly on the paler background. Unusually, the female was slightly larger than the male with a wing span of 63mm (2.5 ins) to the male's 58 mm, just under 2 inches.

These, the most handsome of all the damselflies, are on the wing all summer, from mid May to early September, so these, hopefully, were the first of many. It was good to see them here over the now sparkling waters of the once so turbid Taff, their habitat described as "Clear, fast running streams with pebbly bottoms." They are more or less confined to South-West England and Wales, much rarer northwards.

The bridleway threaded this strip of tall woodland, completely out of sight of the main routes to either side - from the weir to the approach to the M4 bridge - and then for a short spell beyond. All the choice limestone shrubs were here, spindle, dogwood, guelder rose, these bulging inwards in places, although hoof marks in muddier spots showed that there was sufficient width for a horse and rider.

One small patch of Japanese knotweed showed a conspicuous white marbling of some of the leaves, which I took to be a virus infection. As I emerged northwards into a broader, more open stretch, stout fronds of bracken dominated, already head high although only the basal pinnae had unfurled from the coiled crozier phase. The path was broader here, with fine comfrey plants, mostly purple flowered, but some white.

I was particularly struck all the way by the spreading blue patches of germander speedwell, in closer canopy than others of its genus and sometimes alongside upstanding wild strawberry flowers. Notable taller plants were two of the St. John's worts, the tall hairy woodland species and tutsan.

From a viewpoint on the narrow walkway by the big iron pipe river crossing on Iron Bridge, I watched a heron come in to land on a pebble bank upstream and was surprised to see it run out into the water with wildly flapping wings, sending a mallard duck and her six ducklings scuttling away in disorder.

I assumed it had duckling in mind for supper - they were no more than a mouthful - but evidently not. When the bigger bird had retreated to the shallows, the duck brought her brood in again, apparently unworried. Maybe they had been trespassing on the heron's chosen fishing spot. They took little notice of each other after the initial skirmish and there seemed to be plenty of fish about, to judge by the number surfacing and big enough to create ripples expanding to circles several yards across.

The air was full of swallows, swooping under the iron superstructure beneath my feet. That was where the clouds of midges were suspended, not glinting in the sun like the spangled mayflies, but shimmering in a grey cloud, with often less than inches between the hovering bodies. A swallow with open beak could scarcely miss. There were fewer over the land, though plenty of hover flies and a lone clouded border moth *(Lomaspilis marginata)*.

I sat awhile on a grassy mound, well north of the bridge among much more delicate speedwells, the thyme-leaved. Its white florets were decorated with blue lines like a mini version of the delicate porcelain we had seen being cleaned the day before at Tyntesfield.

Moving on I got close to the heron and had a fleeting view of a kingfisher on the further bank. Four mallard came flighting downstream to join another seven on the pebble beach opposite. These were mostly drakes. I did not see the duckling family, but would not expect to if their dam had taken them ashore to merge with the pebbles. Two jays and three wood pigeons crossed the river, as well as the usual blackbirds and Corvids.

As I approached the ancient, whitewashed Ivy Dean Farmhouse with its gothic windows, I spotted a magnificent specimen of a giant sulphur polypore or 'chicken of the woods' *(Laetiporus sulphureus)*, the same as I saw at Tyntesfield the day before. A brilliant lemon yellow, this consisted of four attractive wavy-edged flanges a handspan across and a few lesser ones.

I had seen this here in other years, long ago, with as many as a dozen shelves, but had forgotten how striking it was. The big oak tree that supported it seemed healthy enough. It leaned out over the river, but that was more likely to avoid the shading of the larger sycamore and wych elm reaching out towards it from the steep bank behind. In this fresh stage, before fading to white, it looked good enough to eat and is, in fact, regarded as a delicacy in Germany and America. Most bracket fungi of this size are harder and perennate from year to year, but not this one.

On my return I passed a tutor with a big group of children paddling one man canoes upstream in the slack water above the weir, this the first time during many years of spasmodic visits. This was probably the only stretch deep enough for them not to run aground when the river was not in spate, and with little turbulence as the water backed up behind the weir. The other boating site, used by the University Rowing Club, was in the stiller, deeper water above Llandaff Weir downstream. So calm was the water the children occupied that it was actually scummy. Surprisingly the 'fast water' damselflies were as abundant in the little bay where they had launched their boats as elsewhere along the banks.

* * *

On 24th May, when in Taffs Well, I reconnoitered my old riverside haunts below Gwaelod-y-Garth. I approached along the path leading between the recreation ground containing the famous "well" and the Ffynnon Taf Primary School. This leads to the Pont Sion footbridge over the river.

New fences had gone up, a patch of grass had been newly mown and there were major alterations to the east bank immediately downstream. Trees had been felled there and the bank recontoured with a broad shelf half way up, having bare earth slopes above and below, the latter spilling over the river revetment, which was four large boulders high here.

Presumably this would be grassed over and added to the informal footpath following the outer face of the tall flood bank protecting the warm spring of the well on its inner side. It seemed to be fenced off from the property intervening between the two areas of public access and formerly alive with large dogs, though none were seen or heard today.

River water was at its lowest, with broad pebble banks exposed above and below the footbridge as the river curved out around Glan-y-Llyn, cutting into the steep wooded slope under Gwaelod. The resulting pebble beach held the remains of a monster bonfire where the felled river bank trees had been burned.

Another beach was exposed under the west bank a short distance upstream under the oblique railway crossing, where the river approached this bend from the north-east. That was the point where the county boundary between Cardiff to the south and Rhondda-Cynon-Taff to the north took off westwards across the rolling glacial moraines of Lan Farm and up over the Great Garth Mountain.

All was as before at the foot of the steep winding path down from Gwaelod. The clear stream flowed out of the Cwm Dous Mine, as it always had, entry by inquisitive children under the stone arch barred by vertical iron railings. Men, women and children had toiled underground here for the sixty years between the opening of the tunnel in 1847 and its abandonment in 1913. How very different was the sylvan scene today, my only encounters being with a few lone dog walkers.

Spreading over the stony woodland floor, the stream escaped the stygian gloom to burble between celandine leaves already yellowing with the passage of time. It joined a larger rivulet running along the terrace bearing the path, to turn and gush over the tall bank down into the Taff in a tinkling waterfall.

Cwm Dous was the central one of three levels leading into the coal seams penetrating under the Garth Mountain. Down River by the Garth Garage was the bricked entrance to the Llan Mine. Upstream, burrowing under the north of the village at Ffygis and responsible for not a few cases of subsidence, was the Rock Vein Mine. What history this quiet shady stretch of woodland had seen.

Other vertical stone walls mellowed with green algae and punctuated with brick-sized drainage holes were currently holding up the valley side, which was almost as unscalable here as at Radyr, hence that tortuous zig zag path giving at least the more active villagers access to shops and medical facilities in Taffs Well across the bridge.

All were relics of the industrial age. Some, two ranked, were the walls of the old stables, of a few dwellings and of their gardens. Robust lines of hart's tongue ferns sprouted from the rich leaf mould burying their foundations. Frowning down from above were mighty beeches, their complicated root systems exposed to view as the covering of soil slipped progressively away from smooth barked struts, these as sturdy as the branches above.

Following down river, the only changes on the bank were a new stream crossing piped under the path instead of flowing across it, and an ancient oak, toppled from above to dig its broken top into the ground and continue to produce leafy branches and twigs as though nothing had happened.

Its tenuous hold on the soil above was enough, although soil water with its content of necessary minerals was now flowing down along the trunk instead of up. So expertly does our national tree respond to near catastrophe!

CHAPTER 18

Tyntesfield Gardens, Bristol, Whitsun Weather and Picton Castle, Pembroke

The last of our "Food for thought" summer term coach trips took place on the 20th May. It was to the National Trust property of Tyntesfield at Wraxall west of Bristol and south-east of Portishead on the Somerset coast.

This glorious Gothic extravaganza had been created piecemeal by four generations of the Gibbs family. It was modelled around the outside of a previous Georgian structure, the Gothic preferred, as more ornate and churchlike by the deeply religious owners. It seemed that they were part of the Gothic Revival that swept through Britain in the nineteenth century, persuading those with the wherewithal to explore an architecture scarcely practised for two centuries.

With my research background centred around the guano producing islands of the world, in the Southern as well as the northern hemisphere, I was interested to discover that the building had been made possible by revenue derived by the original Gibb owner from the Peruvian Guano Islands off the Pacific coast of South America.

Before the manufacture of so many artificial fertilisers, Europe's agriculturalists were hungry for this source of easily manageable manure, rich in nitrates and phosphates, that was produced by the hosts of sea-birds feeding in the plankton-rich ocean currents flowing along that desert coast. Proceeds from each new shipment went towards the next phase of building. The original Georgian house had apparently been built by proceeds from the West Indian sugar trade, by the then wealthiest commoner in Britain.

It had been very run down when taken over by the National Trust and the extensive premises were now undergoing another phased rebuilding, with heavy machinery and scaffolding much in evidence and the upper floor of the main building closed to visitors. We were able to witness the conservation building project in action as the property, in its beautiful Somerset Valley, was saved for the nation.

Negotiating a few awkward corners after leaving the B3128, our coach came to rest by a sloping field of oil seed rape, its yellow petals falling as seed developed in the long green capsules. This car park was fifteen to twenty minute's walk from the main buildings, but with minibus transport there for the less able.

There was no guided tour as such. We were allocated different time slots for our indoor visits and moved from room to room in small groups to have features pointed out by volunteer guides in each. There was no restaurant as yet, just buffet food to be eaten at outdoor tables or in a white marquee in the yard of the Home Farm as weather dictated. Those needing sandwiches had to order them in advance. Most of us took our own and ate outside, with hot drinks, surrounded by a collection of colourful plants which were for sale.

The land, an undulating series of limestone terraces and slopes, had been purchased in 1843. Work on the mansion and estate commenced in 1864 and was completed around 1888. The property was purchased by the National Trust in 2002 on the death of Richard, the second Baron of Wraxall, who shared his name with that of the adjacent village.

Our little group set off up a path paved with limestone chippings, past a lusciously tall hay crop, coming first to the chaplain's house and the lodge. These, rented out since 1910, were now being reinstated as holiday cottages. Also under reconstruction here was the old sawmill, which had produced the power to run the estate and was destined to become a learning centre for schools and groups of adults.

Along the north drive we were skirting the gardens with tall woodland to our left. Owners had adhered to the current custom of collecting plants from overseas and we spotted some fine trees - monkey puzzles from Chile, coast redwoods from California, yews, both as craggy trees and neatly clipped hedges, cedars, copper beeches and golden maple.

The avenue of enormous hybrid lime trees appealed to me in view of my affinity with the lime tree outside my window at Brynteg. These were fruiting, the long wings bearing stalked, bobble fruits showing as paler streaks against the rich lime green of the leaves.

I had wondered when this was going to happen with the Brynteg tree. When I got back, I found it already had, unnoticed, because only the upper branches bore fruits, again much paler than the leaves, so visible from indoors although not when walking beneath. There were said to be glow worms on this leg of our walk to the steps leading down to the chapel, but not, of course, visible by day

Currently there was a fine showing of bird's-foot trefoil flowers here in a rich turf, and a temporary fence excluding heavy vehicles such as the one that had scarred this lush green bank with the ruts of its wheel tracks.

An ancient, very dead tree stump, was ornamented with a splendid growth of yellow polypore fungus or chicken-of-the-woods - an agglomeration of multiple brackets, the same as I had spotted two days earlier in home territory.

Later that week I picked up at random a 1996 issue of "The Countryman" and found an article referring to this "bracket fungus which has a texture very like the breast of a chicken", hence the alternative name. It had been served up as the piece de resistance at a fungal feast given by an expert, sauted in butter and served on a bed of fresh salad. Perfectly delicious.

Not far into the pudding course, six participants had complained of tightness in the upper chest, dizziness, loss of concentration and feeling excessively hot, followed by the onset of nausea and vomiting. The victims soon recovered but I, for one, never experiment with strange fungi. I am partial to field and horse mushrooms, but not to the more leggy toadstool like objects served up in restaurants as 'wild mushrooms', and this because of their unpleasant taste rather than mistrust of their producer's expertise.

One of the exotic trees by the church was a Judas tree, which usually bears its deep pink flowers before the leaves, but was holding both together here The chapel interior with its fine stained glass was explained before we passed on into the house - the throughway said to be used by family members late for church.

We peeped into certain rooms, but this route was not for us. Retracing our way up the steps, we circled more trees and descended the hill to a lower front entrance. Like Cwrt Brynteg, the church and house were built on such a steep slope that it was not clear what was the official ground floor. After an explanatory talk in the courtyard, we entered a fascinating interior. The main staircase had been moved from the centre to the side of the main entrance hall "to make more room". Fine carpets and carvings, huge vases and library shelves full of books were here, but not the grandeur that we had enjoyed at Eastnor Castle a fortnight before.

A homely touch was the two ladies taking the fine porcelain from a cupboard, piece by piece, and polishing each meticulously with cotton wool pads and cotton buds for the corners. The kitchen, with its huge zinc and wooden sinks and draining boards, wooden tables, scrubbed white, and shelves loaded with modern tinned foods, were in much less elegant style than that of yore.

The bulk of our time was spent wandering in the stately gardens, which had received much recent care. Beds of late flowering outsize pink tulips provided the main colour, the attractive striping of the petals apparently the result of a virus infection. Especially beautiful was a Solanum shrub, its purple blooms as of an oversized woody nightshade.

On the lawn by the old aviary, a white St. George's mushroom *(Tricholoma gambosum)* had pushed up like a genuine field mushroom, but with white to cream gills instead of pink through cocoa to black. This is quite edible and easy to identify, being one of the few peaking in spring, although usually a week or so later than St. George's day, 23rd April, for which it is named.

We climbed the hill again, past the rose garden, which was set out with colourful bedding plants. Apparently roses can no longer be grown there, because of depredations by wild deer. Beside the path were massive boulders with large inclusions of transparent white calcite crystals, similar to those excavated from the Carboniferous Limestone in Cardiff's Taff Gorge. The only interesting birds I managed to spot were two great spotted woodpeckers.

Regrettably there was insufficient time to join the official tour of the garden, so we missed a lot, but enjoyed the distant panoramas stretching from the formal house terrace away to the arboretum known as Paradise, the pond to its south, the stable yard with the arched connection between the two halves, the kitchen garden, the orangery and the Jubilee Garden, named for Queen Victoria's Jubilee. Then back to the farmyard for a few purchases and a quick cup of tea before boarding the coach for home.

* * *

Why does the weather so often let the British people down at holiday times? Easter 2008 was characterised by bitter cold, rumbustious gales. The early May bank holiday weekend I had recorded as 'somewhat negative, mild, dull and showery', with the sun bursting forth again on the Tuesday when most folk were back at work.

The late May bank holiday, the old Whitsun, was a great deal worse. During the week before I was carrying cans of water to my new additions to the Brynteg garden, some seriously wilted by more than a week of unrelenting sunshine. Bank holiday Sunday and Monday were distinguished by their roaring gales from the north and east, accompanied by steady rain, with gale warnings for the South-west and parts receiving in one day more than their usual rainfall for the whole of May.

This applied only from the 'waist' of Britain down. The TV weather maps showed the North of Scotland and the Isles to be bathed in sunshine. It was at this time the previous May in 2007, that I had been enjoying a fortnight of fabulous weather on the islands of Coll and Tiree in the Hebrides. That was not a 'one off'. Tiree's sandy acres are renowned for enjoying more hours of sunshine in April and May than anywhere else in Scotland.

The natural history groups that I led to Scotland's Outer Isles during my working life were almost always in May. We returned with colour slides of azure skies and coral-white sandy beaches that could have been taken in the Tropics - but these did not record the strength of the often chilly winds.

The noise of branches clashing together in the gale kept me awake on Sunday night, accompanied by the gentle tinkle of my normally silent mobile of semi transparent slices of geodes. (The word 'mobile' no longer signifies what it used to). The little birch tree in the upper garden was bending almost at a right angle on the down throw of each gust and the view was non-existent. All was shrouded in grey.

Lawns and flower beds became littered with sycamore leaves, usually fallen pale side up, accentuating their abundance. Smaller lime leaves were less vulnerable, but twigs had been severed and a six foot branch snapped off and lodged in the canopy for a day, finishing up astride the fence. I feared for fragile birds' nests.

Supping my home made vegetable soup in my usual window seat on the bank holiday Monday I noticed that all the saucer-based pot plants on the balcony were awash. A fawn slug came up for air from the roseroot clump. I almost saw it take a deep breath as it surfaced and began to glide gratefully down the outside of the pot. I helped a spider to terra firma before tipping out the excess water and collecting up the redundant saucers.

But there was a good side to this. All the plants I had brought from Gwaelod which had been seriously wilted recovered and were thriving when I returned from a week away. Another crop of small dark brown toadstools with sooty gills had appeared on the lawn. These were one of the mottle-gills *(Panaeolus ater)*, a species with no English name but one of the few to surface in spring and summer, on lawns and short grass in the shade of trees.

Rain, but not the gale, had ceased, when I went out to post a ninetieth birthday card to Syd Johnson of Neath, in memory of our many expeditions together producing the sixteen millimetre wildlife films for the Glamorgan Wildlife Trust. He was the major domo, the camera man and ornithologist. I wrote and spoke the script and advised on plant life.

Sadly the days of his big screen film performances came to an end with the coming of the small TV screens and the disappearance of spare parts for sixteen millimetre film equipment. Syd changed to industrial archeology photography in his ninth decade in lieu of those long, patient waits in bird hides and still soldiered on.

I returned from the post by the back lane and found that the gale had broken the fixing on the gate to the apple orchard, providing my first opportunity to make a sneak viewing. The area was not abandoned, as I had been led to believe, the uneven sward under the trees having been recently mown, leaving the primroses beheaded, but hopefully with enough substance left to beautify another year.

Some of the dead apple blossom had been blown off, but embryonic apples remained on most and were already as big as marbles. The cherry tree had suffered serious loss, the ground beneath strewn with bunches of well developed green cherries. The trunk of this tree was invested with killed ivy stems, but that and most branches of the adjacent apple tree were draped with a veritable tent of living ivy, with few branches protruding and most of these dead. Ivy is not a parasite but it can be a very effective competitor and strangler.

A certain amount of lopping had taken place, the dead branches piled on a potential bonfire site. It seemed someone was interested in the apple crop after all. One corner contained a fine growth of raspberry canes, full of promise in the form of white flowers among the white-backed leaves. There was also the beginning of a good blackberry harvest.

Back in our carpark I spent a while brushing young green-winged field maple fruits from the roof and bonnet of my car. The previous week's dry winds had brought down a fluff of yellow maple flowers, piled up on the windscreen wipers and insinuated into crevices.

* * *

Once again I set off on my travels on the Tuesday following the disastrous bank holiday weather, but for a week this time. Weather was mixed, to put it kindly, with intervals of fine sunshine, very little rain, but a lot of grey skies and several days of swirling sea fog, making the beach barely visible from the cliff above, while sunshine poured down on farms and fells beyond.

My goal was South-west Wales and the famous Pembrokeshire coastal path, my hosts Irene, who had stayed with me soon after I moved into Brynteg, and her husband Martyn. Their warm hospitality made up for all the defects in the weather.

Irene met my train at Haverfordwest on the 27th of May and we drove a few miles south-west to where two rivers, the Eastern and Western Cleddau, joined forces at the head of the ria or great drowned valley that is Milford Haven. We were headed for Picton Castle, near the junction of the two branches, but first we had our picnic beneath stately tall Scots pines, watching the sun break through the grey pall of cloud to bathe the afternoon in golden light, right through till dusk.

So colourful and tastefully planted were the Picton Castle grounds that we found no time to view the castle interior (which I had visited with the Tuesday lecture group just twelve months before.) This was the 27th May, that had been the 8th May, but the flowers seen among the burgeoning Rhododendrons and Azaleas were very different. As the garden covers forty acres, this was not surprising.

We were drawn at once into the bluebell wood with its mighty oaks, and deflected around what was referred to as 'the Peep In Walk', but deserved much more than a peep. Rank upon rank of deep purple candelabra Primulas followed the little water courses, sometimes competing with the great shining leaves of the American skunk cabbage, whose bright yellow Arum spathes were beginning to fade.

One stream had disappeared below a wealth of white Arum lilies, taller and more elegant relatives of the last. Some of the clumps had been felled by the bank holiday wind and rain but were beautiful still. Regarded as a rampant weed in its native South Africa - and a feature of some of the offshore sea-bird islands I had worked on there - its regal beauty belies its unflattering local name of pigweed. This is an outstanding example of familiarity breeding contempt.

Some of the Primulas were interplanted with delicate variations of the always stately royal ferns (Osmunda). Ferns generally were well served here and most were named by someone who knew a great deal about this difficult group. The culmination of so many versions of this frrondose fraternity was the spreading growth of Australian tree ferns. I almost expected to see a lyre bird emerge below the Dicksonia canopy.

The nearby Myrtle Walk was of Luma trees from Chile with cinnamon tinted bark. Most striking of the great array of Rhododendrons were the abundant yellow Azaleas emitting a beautiful and all pervading aroma. These cropped up throughout.

Elegant tufts of cypress-leaved feather moss *(Hypnum andoi)* invested the young twigs of the Azaleas right to the start of this year's spring growth, signifying unusually moist conditions. These elfin fronds, glistening in the sun, cushioned the fragrant blossoms. It was like being in a cloud forest on a misty mountain in the Tropics, the abundance of lichens in this unpolluted atmosphere adding to the illusion.

Rare and endangered conifers were cherished here as part of an international conservation programme, some never before grown in this country. It was a long time before we could drag ourselves away from these magical glades east of the castle - yet not so long ago the whole of this area had been overrun by rampageous evergreen cherry laurel bushes.

We left via the dew pond and filter beds which supplied the castle with fresh water from 1800 on. Fine trees included two soft-barked giant Sequoias from Western USA and magically contorted Western red cedars (Thuja), one rising from the centre of a circle of its own rooted offspring.

There were Tsugas and dawn redwoods (Metsequoia), thought extinct until discovered in a small grove in China in 1941, Californian redwoods, New Zealand cabbage trees and kaka beak legumes (the kaka is a New

Zealand parrot), Australian bottle brushes and South African milkwort bushes. So much to hold our attention, but eventually we made it to the walled garden.

Reclining awhile on a seat, we watched a willow warbler flitting in and out of a pale leaved shrub surrounded by various spurges (Euphorbia). Then on past the central lily pool to displays of giant viper's bugloss plants such as are seldom seen in Britain outside the Tresco Gardens in the Scilly Isles.

Stooping under creepers, sniffing our way across mint beds and dodging Madeiran Geranium clumps and Jerusalem sage bushes, we slipped through a doorway in the high wall that we were following into a magical fernery. This stretched back along the other side of the wall. Here were ferns of every shape, from epiphytic stagshorn fern on tree branches to little shade forms by stream and waterfall.

There was also a remarkable mouse-tail Arum here, like a monster version of the cryptic rarity I had cherished in my Gwaelod garden for many years. But what a difference. The mousetail appendage tapering off from the purple flower tip was just over a yard long!

Outside the castle we watched the colony of house martins swooping in and out of their mud nests under the eaves, with rapid changes of place, before reluctantly making our departure.

CHAPTER 19

Picton Salt Marsh, Lockley Lodge, Monk Haven, Sandy Haven and Little Haven

From Picton Castle on 27th May, Irene and I continued south for a whiff of the briny. Although by no means true sea coast, we found ourselves on genuine saltmarsh, with flowers of scurvy grass fading to give way to greater sea spurrey and thrift bursting into bloom across the salt marsh turf.

We were near the head of Milford Haven, that classic drowned valley where the sea has invaded the land for twenty miles or more, to separate South Pembrokeshire from the main block. The great inlet simulates a ten mile long Y, its stem running north to south and continuing as an ever widening, twelve mile long extension leading off to the west. That begins to broaden as it passes between Pembroke Dock and Neyland and then more significantly between the oil refineries of Milford and Angle Bay. Here its brackish waters mingle with those of full sea strength between Thorn Island Fort and St. Ann's Head, with its naturalists' mecca of the Dale Fort Field Centre.

The two arms of the letter Y are the Western and Eastern Cleddau Rivers, the first flowing through Haverfordwest from north-east of St. Davids, the second from the Prescelis National Park. Picton Beach, reached through a wooded landscape from the castle, is about a mile above the confluence of the two at Picton Point,

A concrete ramp led across a ballast beach to the water near the head of a firm, narrow gravel spit protruding out through soft mud. On the opposite shore at Landshipping was an old, castellated building and a public house, this the obvious place for a ferry in olden times.

Terra firma was protected on our side by substantial stone walls, the woodland continuing alongside the bay downstream. Beyond this was an ancient settlement on the strategic site of Picton Point, from which any invaders from the sea would be fully visible.

Salt marshes are often grazed, to produce that delicious salt marsh roast lamb, but not this one. The succulent plants that go to the making of that repast were untouched and at the height of flowering. Seldom is it possible to compare the tall spike inflorescences of sea arrow-grass and sea plantain so well, the florets of the first loosely aggregated and of the second tightly packed.

Bobble fruits were already forming on the scurvy grass - this an inappropriate name for a cress, but referring to its use as a remedy for scurvy by old time sailors reaching port after a long voyage of hard tack, lacking that all important vitamin C.

One clump of thrift or sea pink had white flowers instead of pink. Sea Aster leaves were abundant. Those flower later, some producing purple ray florets like those we see in the related Michaelmas daisy, and some with just the central boss of yellow disc flowers. There was no means of knowing which they would be at this stage. A notable species here was the grey-leaved sea purslane (Halimione) of the salt bush family, this another which cannot survive grazing.

Had it been later in the year we might have found the lax-flowered sea lavender *(Limonium humile),* so abundant hereabouts that it colours the late summer salt marsh with a soft lavender blue haze but not, of course, a lavender scent, as it is not related to the true lavenders. Found nowhere else in Pembrokeshire and in not many other places, this species is spread generously around the edges of Milford Haven.

And then there was the cord grass, (Spartina), that invasive, salt-loving, spiky-leaved grass that has romped around so much of Britain's muddier seashores. The culprit is a cross between a non-aggressive British species with a relative brought to Southampton Water by ship from America. This cross showed hybrid vigour and has been introduced since to many a muddy sea coast around the world to 'reclaim' land from the sea.

Shiny dark green plants of sea beet overtopped drier parts of the grassy sward of red fescue and salt marsh grass, characterising the change from halophytes or salt-lovers to plants of the land.

A generous driftline of brown seaweeds had washed across the lower saltings onto living patches of green algae, some showing the inflated fronds that so often occur in brackish water. There were not many sea shells this far up river, just a few blue-black mussels and small white cockle shells, also some stranded jellyfish.

We returned to the leafy layby where we had left the car for a leisurely sit on a bench beneath a gnarled and knobbly oak, gazing out over the water.

Evening sunshine glinted from the silvered mudflats, fretted with a meshwork of steep sided creeks wandering inconsequentially across their yielding surface. Beyond was a scattered flotilla of small boats riding at anchor on mirror calm water. There was no murmur from a lapping tide here, nor even the cries of wading birds, just the tinkling calls of lesser beings from the backing spinney.

Just as we were leaving Irene spotted an acquaintance, Stuart Devonauld, an ex member of the Skokholm Island Advisory Committee and retired headmaster, a stranger to me but apparently not I to him. He had been, long ago, on some of my 'nature walks' around the countryside, including some as far from his native Pembrokeshire as Dinas Powis. No doubt the years between had altered us both.

His sunny presence added to the pleasure of this addition to our Picton Castle visit, particularly as Martyn and I had tried to reach the shore of the great inlet the previous year and failed. That was on the occasion of my short stay in Pembrokeshire to join the founders' visit to Skokholm of the first of August.

I had visions of little wooded creeks by the salty river then, in 2007, the sort of secret place one finds by the River Dart in the West Country, but we failed to make it to the coast. The lane we had followed to Little Mitford beyond Freystrop on the Western Cleddau gave us opportunity for a delightful woodland walk in a hilly National Trust property, but no path we followed there led us to the river bank. No matter: the durmast oakwood and bordering Maddox Moor on the hill above were very satisfying.

* * *

Martyn and I tried again next day, after taking Irene to Lockley Lodge at Martinshaven, where she was in charge of the Wildlife Trust shop for the day. We watched a boat load of island visitors leaving at 9.30 am, half an hour before the scheduled time. The boat took fifty people at a time and when fifty hopefuls had arrived and trudged along the narrow cliff path to the improvised landing ramp, there was no point in waiting.

We were still there, browsing among the motley collection of displays and sales goods, when the boat returned. Four students, who had been overnighting on Skomer after taking part in a gull count on neighbouring Skokholm, had come ashore and wandered into Lockley Lodge, the effective 'shore base' for islanders.

Inevitably we chatted about Skokholm gull counts in which I had participated, fifty to sixty year ago in the later 1940s and early 1950s. A deal more than gull numbers had changed in the intervening decades!

One of them lived on the Channel Islands and knew the "Five Humps off Herm" where I had conducted a brief sea-bird survey. My chief memory of that exploit - in a small boat belonging to a tomato grower - was of the shags' nests. Incorporated among the dry seaweed and driftwood were a number of beautiful sea fans or horny corals - ornate growths found more commonly in the Tropics.

Intricately branched in one plane and some twelve inches (30 cm) across, their white limey coating made them appear brittle, but the horny core bearing the coral polyps gave pliability - to withstand both wave movement in life and the trampling of the gawky chicks in death. Had the parent birds plucked these from the seabed in their under water sorties, or picked them up from the drift line?

The years between melted away. I seemed to be one with the youngsters, savouring the delights of discovery - of matters new to ourselves though not to science. The three boys slipped easily into the shoes of my own student contemporaries, now eminent ornithologists at such prestigious institutions as the Edward Grey Institute for Ornithology at Oxford University.

And what observational opportunities the new generation had now that were not available even one decade ago. The huge cam-corder movie screen in one corner of Lockley Lodge provided an ongoing panorama of what was happening, currently, on the island they had so lately left.

Manipulation of the screen revealed all, from the various cameras stationed at critical points - as panoramics or close-ups. Panning in on a chosen spot, the thousand black dots on offshore waters became lively puffins; 'whitewashed' rock ledges revealed rank upon rank of guillemots, razorbills or kittiwakes.

A flowery rockscape of red and white campions could become a little knot of munching rabbits and then the chomping jaws, grazing selectively on scurvy grass. No way would they be suffering the old sea-goers' malady of scurvy.

My work had involved finding out the grazing preferences of the great army of rabbits - one of the major influences on the composition of the plant cover. My deductions came from the state of the plants themselves during different phases of their life cycles. And here I was, comfortably indoors, out of the wind, watching it all happen at close quarters. - the fastidious turning up of the whiskery, questing nose at the less palatable, to seek out something more succulent.

Thanks to the skill of those who had set the movie cameras in position, some of them inside nesting burrows, where shearwaters or puffins could be watched turning their egg or feeding their single chick, the rest of us could witness it happening, instead of recording just their comings and goings and leaving the rest to conjecture.

Life had, indeed, moved on, though not for the animals whose secrets were now revealed. I could not repress a chuckle as the rabbit on the screen lifted his head, looked me straight in the eye and wrinkled his little snout - in distaste? There were no 'customers' present, just Irene and Martyn, and I found myself breaking into song. I was back round one of those girl guide camp fires again!

"There once was a rabbit developed the habit of twitching the end of his nose.

His sisters and brothers and various others said "Notice the way that it goes."

Then one little bunny said "Isn't it funny; I'll practise it down in the dell".

The said "If he can, I'm positive we can" and did it remarkable well.

Now all the world over where bunnies eat clover & burrow & scratch with their toes

There isn't a rabbit that hasn't the habit of twitching the end of his nose."

Clearly, it was time we left, for the world of reality. We found two bewildered caterpillars undulating across the floor, well grown lackey moth larvae (*Malacasoma neustria*), with longitudinal orange, blue and white stripes from head to tail. They had been scooped unwittingly into a student's garments as they brushed through the undergrowth. We put them outside on some brambles among the red, white and blue of campion, stonecrop and sheep's bit. Such accidental transfers show how easily animal and plant life can get transported to and from isolated island communities.

Soon after we left Irene for our day's exploring, a 'woolly bear caterpillar was spotted crossing the lane, at the remarkable speed that these little animals are capable of, even though they have little need to hurry, being unpalatable to almost all bird predators except cuckoos - which are themselves, regrettably rare nowadays.

* * *

On my visit here the previous summer, Martyn and I had walked a short stretch of the Pembrokeshire coast path from here, starting at the Old Deer Park and following the cliffs past the causeway to Gateholm Island, to the environs of Marloes. This time we were headed back to part of the intricate coastline of Milford Haven. The weather was better than at Brynteg, just mild and still with fine rain falling almost throughout the day. There was so much to see that this seemed to bother us very little.

Skirting the well trodden beach at Dale village, stamping ground of countless marine students over the years, we came to the coast at Monk Haven, the next little bay beyond Musselwick. This was not my first visit here, but it looked softer and fresher in one of those prolonged dampeners that 'falleth as a gentle rain from heaven.'

The name commemorates a religious past, but the early monastery buildings have been lost without trace. The cove had been chosen as a convenient landing place for pilgrims headed for St. Davids but afeared of the turbulent sea passage through Jack Sound. The ancient land track that they followed across the peninsula to Little Haven is called the Welsh Road.

Massively tall stone walls encountered along the path funneling through the valley mouth to the sea, are relics of the eighteenth century Trewarren Estate. In common with most of the northern shore of the outer part of Milford Haven the bedrock is Old red Sandstone. At least six small stone quarries had been dug from the hillside for walling stone, the scars now healed by the hummocky surface of the bluebell wood, rich in ferns and with much of the 'gentle rain' waylaid by the dense early summer leaf canopy.

To seaward of St. Ishmael's Church and a lone dwelling, we came to a woodland pool. It was tempting to think of this as a monkish fish pond, but it was, in fact, a more modern irrigation feature made by the local farmer to trap the stream waters in a part of the country more subject to drought than most. Cat's tail bulrush, pendulous sedge and yellow flag Irises encroached from the margins but left plenty of open water.

There were two gaps in the great wall, one for access and one for the stream outlet. The beach beyond was mostly of smallish, dark red pebbles, flattened, suggesting the slaty cleavage of a mudstone, as on much of Skokholm, but not sleek enough for a bout of 'ducks and drakes', though the sea was calm enough.

Other pebbles of different hue and texture may have been transported hither by glaciers. The dark red cliffs dipped at an angle of about forty five degrees, and provided a home, like the great wall, for an attractive assemblage of seaside plants.

Stately spires of small white bells erupted from among the succulent leaf pads of wall pennywort or navelwort. With these was equally succulent rock samphire - a chunky representative of the usually more feathery carrot family. The wispy foliage here belonged to the massed daisies of sea mayweed growing among beet, fescue and thrift.

Yellow patches of lady's finger or kidney vetch were an attractive feature, a foil to the stocky seaside form of ox-eye daisies. Swooping trails of fruiting scurvy grass glissaded down the steep vegetated faces, where the grey-leaved sea purslane of the salt marsh grew high and dry among sea campion, common sorrel and robust clumps of sea plantain.

Much of the cliff towards Musselwick in the west was tree covered, sycamores forming a closed leaf canopy across the land surface three to four feet beneath. The hazel canopy also followed the contour of the land - much closer to it. Such dense low thickets, along with those of wild privet and sloe, are quite impenetrable but not firm enough to walk on.

We explored downshore, where some of the sandstone took the form of conglomerate, with veins or irregular inclusions of white quartz, or pitted with holes where the latter had eroded out.

Animals seen in this upshore zone were mostly the tiny *Littorina neritoides* periwinkles and a few scarlet mites scuttering among the channelled and spiral wracks. Out at sea, well beyond the mouth of the haven, we saw the massive Cork:Swansea ferry ploughing past between St. Ann's Head and the southern limestone.

We returned through the big wall, crossed the stream and followed a path along the gentler wooded slope to the east towards Watch House Point. Here were some fascinatingly contorted trees. One ash bough curled over to grow into the ground and rise again, like a supporting elbow. Below against the valley wall, Martyn was particularly intrigued by ancient graffiti carved into the otherwise smooth grey bark of twin hollies. Each set of initials was half overgrown with a callus produced by the affronted living cambium layer just below the corky bark.

Wild rose blooms illuminating the cliff face thicket where the wood petered out were a deeper pink than common dog roses and the green parts downier. This was probably sweet briar. Looping strands of honeysuckle would soon be adding their floral excellence to the display.

A few of the sloe bushes had fared less well. Some of their usually firm, sour fruits had been replaced by hollow, inch long bags of palest green. These inflated, stoneless sloes had been caused by the bladder bullace fungus (*Taphrina pruni*) - a relative of the better known species which causes peach leaf curl. Other names for these puffed up galls are mock plum, starved plum and bladder plum. (Martyn gathered the wherewithal for his autumn production of sloe gin elsewhere.)

Some cryptic, overgrown holes penetrated the ground to landward of the path, their origin obscure, and we came upon a half ruined lookout tower of stone and brick on the next headland. This seemed to be a folly, castellated but with a small modern fireplace, as though used as a picnic spot by the builder. The artist, Graham Sutherland, is said to have been inspired by this spot, and also by Sandy Bay, which we were to visit next.

We continued a little further up the cliff path, over a stone stile where all but the basal rock step had been replaced by a modern kissing gate. On the return walk we explored St. Ishmael's church. Founded in the sixth century, it was enlarged by St. Caradog around eleven hundred AD, further modified in 1660 and restored in the nineteenth century.

The bell cote was a tall, rectangular wall with two elongated apical slits to contain bells, but one of these was empty apart from trails of ivy and bramble. Apparently this replaced a former four square tower. Some intensely coloured stained glass graced the interior. Walls were hugely thick in parts and we saw a slit window suitable for launching arrows at an aggressor. Someone had fashioned a charming wooden model of the church with its two annexes.

It was still in use and furnished with electric fires, although nearby parking space for the congregation was negligible. The stream sliced through the grassy churchyard, burbling fast and clear over pebbles and supporting shivering tufts of water starwort.

* * *

We lunched in the small parking bay at Monk Haven, gazing at a ferny cliff under dripping trees through a rainy windscreen, then followed narrow lanes with the usual passing places to Sandy Haven beyond St. Ishmaels. Our intended way to the shore bore a notice stating there to be no turning place at the end. We passed on, enquired of a local, were told that this was not true and returned.

There was room, but only on the beach, a pebbly one already occupied by two Water Board vehicles and the moistened green scum auguring ill for good tyre grip. We lingered only briefly below the concrete boat slip beneath the long wooded ridge to the west. Beyond the pebbles was the sandy beach that gave the haven its name.

There was formerly a ferry here, now replaced by stepping stones. A century ago this little creek was a hive of activity associated with the lime kiln on the approach road, this preserved to show the crucible and the two draw holes. Nearby was the lime burner's hut and an old weighbridge used for weighing livestock. We missed these, Martyn extricating us from the beach before we lost our hold on the slippery surface.

From here we headed north along byeways across the peninsula to Little Haven, tucked in the southern corner of St. Brides Bay. The continuing rain suggested an indoor activity and we walked back along the main street to the village hall where an art show was in progress.

Pictures were by local artists, mostly local views but also some exquisitely achieved flower studies. This was my sort of art, a depiction of the natural world as it is, rather the sometimes bizarre ways that the artist interprets it, this not always coinciding with the viewer's impression. Old fashioned, yes, but amply satisfying. Had we wished, we could have taken tea and cakes here, served by local ladies, but we desisted.

South Haven is situated where the Coal Measures backing St. Brides Bay surface close to the older Old Red Sandstone rocks of the main peninsula to the south, and ships formerly sailed from the busy little harbour exporting coal from the local pits. Today it was full of little pleasure craft. The recent excavation of an Iron Age fort at Strawberry Hill above, confirmed habitation from earlier times.

We explored the headland terminating the south end of the beach, up past the Swan Inn, where a fine walkway had recently been refurbished. Tastefully planned, it was of shaped stones and bricks, odd corners floored with flattened pebbles, and led to a rectangular stone, earth-filled construction at the seaward end. Seats set in all sides of this ensured havens out of any wind that blew, with others in cosy alcoves along the way.

Rising from the southern flank was a lush bank, colourful with thrift, lady's finger, sea campion and ox-eye, plus many another. Barer patches supported English stonecrop and sheep's bit, resembling a little blue scabious.

Steps led down to a small seaweedy cove in the south, the various wracks exposed by the tide retaining their form and texture in the caressing rain. Away to the north, upshore rocks gave way to a wide expanse of tidal sand, where a few walkers braved the weather.

It was back then across country to Martins Haven to collect Irene. Beyond the dripping foxgloves, red campion and cow parsley that characterised the lane verges hereabouts were fine stands of main crop potatoes - we had already had the "Pembrokeshire earlies" in Cardiff shops. Some of the grass harvests, pressed into shining bales wrapped in black or pale polythene, was in the form of haylage - a long lasting fodder crop, half way between silage and hay in its harvesting.

While Irene counted the day's takings from the till and Martyn swept dried mud spilled from many boots off the floor, I concentrated on the big screen. Two rabbits were interacting, a bit of sparring and a bit of mutual preening around the head and neck, parts that were difficult to reach. Special attention was being given to the long hind feet that had gathered mud from tracts worn partially bare by close-packed, jostling puffins.

As predicted long since, the grazing selected palatable red fescue grass and rejected the hairy Yorkshire fog with its distasteful acrid sap. Every now and again one of the pair sat back on its haunches and indulged in rapid mock boxing of empty air with furry forepaws. This seemed as pointless as the accompanying nose wrinkling, but I supposed they knew what they were at.

There had been a major kill by the Myxomatosis virus on Skomer the previous year, so these were survivors. Long may they continue to be so. It is not in the interest of any disease organism to kill all its hosts. Hopefully progressively more bunnies will prove immune to maintain the low swards needed by so many of the island's tiny flowers.

CHAPTER 20

Brynberion, Whitesands Bay, St. Davids, Llanerchaeron, Aberaeron and Newport

Brynberion, in the heart of the Preseli Hills National Park, where my good hosts lived, is equidistant from Fishguard in the west and Cardigan in the north-east. The nearest coastal site, just four miles away, is Newport Sands. Their ancient farmhouse, much improved over the years, not least by the skilled hands of the present owners, is set in four acres of land. In the past it has served as a field centre for natural history students and it boasts attractive wildlife in the vicinity.

All but the paddock, the extensive fruit and vegetable garden, the orchard and the lawn, was overshadowed by mighty trees, each an icon of natural craftsmanship worthy of study by human sculptors. Marshy depressions, a half excavated pond and a temporary stream add to the diversity, but the water sometimes cascading off the road, along a self made runnel down the entrance drive is in excess of optimum requirements. Tadpoles in the home pond had been washed away in a recent flood.

Nowhere in my extensive countryside wanderings have I seen such a wondrous mass of primroses, as along both sides of their approach road. Now, after spring flowering, the leaves had enlarged, building up the wherewithal for another bumper display of yellow in 2009. Protruding ferns added dignity and there was a sprinkling of red campion, herb Robert and yellow pimpernel.

In the grape vine trailing along my bedroom window sill was the neat grassy nest of a pair of spotted flycatchers - rare birds in my home territory. They made up for their rather nondescript appearance by their erect stance as they took breathers during their dedicated activity of fly-catching on the wing. The speckled white breast, constant movement and familiarity with humans made them easy to watch.

Just below the nest was a riot of shrubs, where bumble bees came to sip nectar from the Fuchsia flowers as soon as the light of dawn began to illuminate the distant hill slope. The busy pair perched more often, however, on the black wire stretching from the eaves, making the most of this added domestic facility in providing a more open view. No doubt they intercepted many of the midges making a beeline for my open bedroom window.

They took turns to keep vigil on the nest, only the head of the sitting bird visible over the neatly woven rim, so that the nest contents were best seen with the aid of a mirror. Three nestlings had fledged the previous year. When Irene took a quick peep from a ladder this year, she saw four chicks. This was during the heatwave a few days after my departure, when she moved a vine leaf slightly to cast a shade on the panting youngsters. The parents were feisty and house proud and had recently seen off a grey squirrel, despite their diminutive size.

A baby rabbit lived beneath the thicket of Fuchsia, budding rambler rose and snowberry, and used a rabbit-sized track beneath to reach the path verge. Another lived by the newly dug vegetable plot and was seen scampering over the lawn and along the top of the wall alongside in the dawn light. Martyn's first job on my departure was to buy rabbit proof wire netting to protect the seedling crops now developing in the new greenhouse.

Another resident in the Fuchsia clump was a wren. Blackbirds came and went all the time, while nearby was the bird feeder with its visiting tits and robin. This was indeed, a room with a view, including a magnificent collection of multicoloured Violas and some yellow Sedum occupying surprisingly shadowy conditions for a sun-loving succulent.

Sundry outhouses fostered mini communities, from the mossy tiles shaded by overarching trees to a lush bed of mint running riot through the nettles. A speciality in this essentially acid habitat was the neat spread of shining cranesbill flowers, a limestone rarity of walls, making free here of a pile of evidently limey rubble and mortar. Yellow flags and greater willow herb were already established in the pond-to-be while hawthorn blossom and young fruits of cherry laurel encroached on the lawn. Throughout my stay I saw only one red kite. The local buzzard had apparently seen off the one formerly present.

Apart from staging the occasional barbecue party, Martyn made no use of his tree-lined paddock, but allowed neighbours to profit by the grazing and grass harvests as needed - with goodwill gifts in return as appropriate.

Sometimes I roamed the lane alone, while necessary chores were proceeding, sometimes with Irene, spotting the odd red damselfly or speckled wood butterfly in the hedgetops or beetles among the sculptured roots of ash, sycamore and horse chestnut. A car tour showed something of Brynberion village proper, with its church, capable of accommodating a congregation of two hundred and a small school.

Most of the land was owned by three large farmers. Martyn and Irene had kept goats in the past and were likely to do so again. There was plenty of available fodder, but this would mean more fencing, or tethering. Pigs were no longer a paying proposition in these stringent times.

* * *

The sun smiled on us throughout thursday the 29th of May once the mist had evaporated from the Preselis, and the three of us set off for Whitesands Bay and St. Davids. Little charms of goldfinches flipped across the high banked lanes, populated by chaffinches and blackbirds, with house sparrows around some of the dwellings. Swallows were busy dealing with the gnats, outpacing the inevitable crows, jackdaws and magpies.

All this was just as I remembered from childhood visits, as was the familiar humped outline of St. David's Peninsula as viewed in the more recent past from Ramsey Island. This could not be said of Whitesands Bay, where we had enjoyed family camping holidays with daily dips off those delectable sands.

Two large areas had now been allocated for car parking, these almost full, and the beach was crowded with holiday makers. Normally I tend to shie away from crowded beaches but not this one. There was so much new going on. Since those beach larks of seventy years ago many more people were able to enjoy the escape from the everyday routine to such places.

The new plastic buckets made castellated sand castles instead of the cylindrical ones tipped from our old metal ones. The plastic spades dug canal systems quite as intricate as those my brother and I constructed with metal bladed, wooden handled ones, which would probably not conform with modern health and safety standards.

There were fast flying frisbies instead of gentle rubber tenni-quoits, even faster flying missiles looking like hand grenades and fat, bottleshaped balls with tails which seemed to fly of their own volition. The guyed wind shelters, not really necessary today, were lightweight and colourful compared with our green canvas and wooden tent pegs.

Most of all I was intrigued, not by the regular surf boards - which are in common use along our Glamorgan coast - but by the mini boards used for aqua-planing through the shallows. These required considerable skill and were the prerogative of teenage boys.

These sent the boards skimming through an inch or so of water at the edge of the tide, raced after them, extremely fast, and jumped aboard to continue for surprising distances. Some tried turning the board with their feet, as the experts were doing on the quite small waves offshore, usually succeeding, but putting a stop to the momentum.

The gentle waves were just right for those lying along their boards, but the surfers able to stand up could have enjoyed more excitement. It all looked extremely safe and domesticated, with kayaks out in deeper water and the tide advancing gently but inexorably across the sands, pushing the picnic parties towards the upper beach under the low cliff. There was no driftline, so no beachcombing.

Past seas had cut into mature dunes at the top of the beach - brown layers among the yellow showing where a quiescent spell of no new sand deposition had allowed plant growth to add stabilising humus. Broad patches of kidney vetch, chunky ox-eye and sea campion were doing just that on parts of the present face.

Shaggy, marram type dune vegetation persisted along the brink above. Just beyond was the coastal path, with a flight of steps leading down to the beach, well away from the main ingress from the carparks. A row of big boulders a little way up told of past efforts at stabilisation and there were a few half buried rocks elsewhere.

We ambled to the further, southern, end of the beach, where purplish-black rock strata with occasional orange stains, exhibited slaty cleavage and sloped seaward at an angle of about forty five degrees. Consultation of the geology maps later revealed these as Ordovician on Silurian

The northern peninsula and very tip of the southern one were composed of Lingula flags. The whole complex is Cambrian, with pre-Cambrian tuff (Pembidian) appearing inland. Different bands of rock, endways on, formed outcrops at the back of the bay, these mostly green sandstone and red conglomerate. The last is the oldest rock of the Carfai series and was used in the building of the cathedral.

Returning to the car, we collected our picnic and took it to a grassy mound north of the bay to eat on a smooth outcrop of maritime sward. Unfortunately the springtime spreads of blue vernal squill were mostly further on towards St. David's Head.

* * *

We could not linger to explore, as Irene, a member of the cathedral choir, was due at St. David's for a rehearsal in mid afternoon. Before locking the car, after putting her down at the top of the drive, we had to rescue two large red damsel flies *(Pyrrhosoma nymphula)* which had got trapped inside. These are among our commonest damselfly species and one of the earliest to appear in spring.

After releasing them we explored the precincts of the cathedral, alongside the ruins of the bishop's palace. A sparkling stream hurrying over well washed pebbles at the valley bottom, had spawned more damsels. These were the splendidly named *Calopteryx or Agrion splendens,* as found earlier on the Taff at Radyr. Also here was a single, more everyday blue-tailed damselfly, *Ischnura elegans.*

This part of the stream nurtured fine triangular patches of fresh green water crowfoot, covered with white buttercup flowers. Most leaves were finely dissected and bunched together, like those in the Taff, but a few circular lobed sub-aerial leaves had been produced where the clumps surfaced.

Stretches in full sunshine with bordering grass swards put one in mind of a small scale version of the Cambridge 'Backs'. Further along, where the flow was between taller, closer walls topped by trees, there was insufficient light to nurture interesting water plants.

St. David's was a cathedral precinct with a difference, the neatly mown lawns undulating up a steep slope instead of around and below, as the palace and cathedral had been built in the valley bottom, to be out of sight of invaders from the sea. A rural slant on the average cathedral city was the field of young store cattle and somewhat prosaic dung heap alongside.

Martyn took me on a tour around the cloistered homes and gardens tucked behind high walls. A holly blue butterfly lingered, appropriately, in the dean's venerable holly tree, intent upon laying eggs to produce the second generation, although itself brought up on a diet of ivy. Cabbage whites flirted among flowers.

We reclined awhile in a neat public garden squeezed between a darkened section of the stream and the newly renovated cloisters, both before and after meeting up with Irene. Lacy Hydrangea scrambled up the lofty wall, *Clematis montana* and honeysuckle up lesser ones. Holly-leaved New Zealand daisy bushes formed a backdrop for the garden plants.

We adjourned to the cloisters where we sat listening to the strains of the rehearsal wafting out through open windows. With other lay persons, we joined the songsters at choral evensong conducted by the dean in one of the lesser annexes of the cathedral.

Walking through the knave I was surprised to see no coloured stained glass in the side windows, this often so lavish in smaller churches, but here just a little at either end. Another surprise was to see a life-sized recumbent effigy of a lady who died as recently as the 1990s, beautifully carved and girt about with a latin inscription, but the greatest lustre that of the attractively figured marble from which it had been fashioned. This seemed at variance with the expected torsoes of ancients with their swords or pet dogs, and sometimes without an appendage lost during the course of ages - kings and bishops from the realms of history.

Afterwards we met up with the songsters over a cup of tea in the refectory restaurant. Here was another art exhibition, this time all exhibits by one person, being the originals of pictures drawn for her books on ancient myth and legend and for children.

St. David, 462 - 520, is said to have been borne by St. Non where St. Non's Chapel now stands. The original monastery was self supporting, his monks working the surrounding fields. It was burned down in 645. Despite their cryptic position, invading Danes sacked the buildings in 1078 and they were burned down again in 1088. Lead was stripped from the roof during the Civil War. The first Norman bishop was appointed in 1115 and it is claimed that there has been a house of prayer in this valley for over 1400 years.

Rebuilding started in 1180, leaving an edifice substantially like the one we see now. The stone used was Cambrian sandstone taken from the cliffs at Carfai and Caerbwdy, but the tower fell down in 1220, crushing the choir and transept and an earthquake in 1248 did further damage. The Bishop's Palace, with its row of open arches along the top, had a newly installed rose window at the end.

We stopped off on our return at a favourite fish restaurant, the fish laced with oodles of crispy batter and followed by a piquant lemon cheesecake with elder flower cordial. While there, and quite unplanned, two folk from my past caught up with me.

One, who I failed to recognise, though he did me, was Peter Brown, my co-tutor on a Pembrokeshire field course at Orielton in the early 1970s. It was good to hear him say. "Bought all your books and loved them." The second was Jack Donovan, met in association with the West Wales Islands on various occasions, the last time only two years before at the celebration of the acquisition of Skokholm by the South and West Wales Wildlife Trust.

* * *

On Saturday we would be visiting the cathedral again for the culmination of the St. David's week of pageantry, but Friday the 30th May was free for all of us. We set off to the adjoining county of Ceredigion to visit the National Trust property of Llanerchaeron and then on to the coast, first at Cei Bach and then at the port of Aberaeron. Once again we were favoured by good weather as soon as the morning mist had dispersed.

After a picnic lunch at a table in the spacious green carpark, we set off through trees and Rhododendron bushes to see how the gentry of times past had lived it up with an army of servants and a whole village of outhouses to serve their needs, from butchery to laundry.

Yet the owners of this establishment, set in the beautiful Aeron Valley, were regarded merely as Welsh minor gentry They lived around two hundred years ago in what is regarded as the most complete surviving example of a self sufficient eighteenth century country estate - held by the same family for ten generations.

Starting with the Home Farm, still a working enterprise, the only live animals we saw were the large white pigs, including a newly farrowed sow, other livestock being currently out at grass, The yards were floored with cobbles, set edgeways on, often in neat patterns and hard-wearing under the iron shod hoofs of working horses and metal tipped ploughman's boots, but hard on modern footwear, even hiking shoes.

Horse stalls, still retained, were quite short, the working horses thought to have been Welsh cobs, quite small but powerful, with well feathered fetlocks and ideal for ploughing and other heavy work. The harness room was still full of tack, reminding me of getting the great stuffed collar on over my shire horse's head, upside down, and then swinging it around. The cow byres continued in use until the 1970s - machine milking having replaced our hand milking of wartime days by then. The 1970s equipment was still in use, modified to meet modern expectations of hygiene.

Swallows flitted all over the big barn, swooping around between the saucer-shaped mud nests balanced on beams, while pied wagtails and chaffinches pottered outside. The round-topped entrance to the stable and courtyard for horse drawn coaches had to be enlarged and provided with a squared top when the boss changed to motor transport. Square holes below the eaves of the threshing barn gave access to the dovecote, the doves a valuable source of poultry meat and eggs in the eighteenth century.

The feature that interested me most was the rickyard, reached through the capacious threshing barn. Stacked corn stooks or hay were kept above wet ground by a packed layer of walling stones the size of the rick, but having four channels in the shape of a cross to let air through and prevent overheating and possible combustion.

"My" farms in Berkshire were in a land of fewer rocks and our ricks were held off the ground by mushroom shaped staddle stones.

Through a gate from here we were in the walled garden - the most outstanding features of which were the long borders of gnarled and contorted apple trees lining the paths, the boughs of neighbours sometimes fusing together. Ancient though they were, they still apparently bore good apples.

Lush raspberry canes and black and red currants were reaching out through the sides of the fruit cages and gooseberries were already well developed. Rhubarb came in all sizes. Some of the many vegetables for commercial sale like the rhubarb were potatoes, chard, onions, globe and Jerusalem artichokes and big asparagus beds, the succulent sprouts topping the soil apparently quite sparse, as they have to be plucked every day while tender before burgeoning out into something more suited to floral decoration. Three huge compost bays in an annexe accounted for the lushness.

Angelica was twice as tall and buxom as the wild version, fennel likewise. Mint and catmint were part of the wide variety of herbs. There was alkanet and other borages, monkshood, foxgloves, Pelargoniums, beds of poached egg plants romping along under the apple borders, and much more. Chatting with an Irish gardener by the old glassless, concrete conservatory, we learned that there were few rabbits but that slugs were a pest. Where are they not?

Blue damsel flies and orange tip butterflies were on the wing in the two walled gardens, each of which was about an acre in size. One of the biggest surprises was the lushness of the snapdragon plants flowering gaily from the summit and sides of the walls, which were twice the height of a man and built of home made bricks using local clay.

The clay was dug and moulded in Cae Pwll and fired in Cae Bricks. The longest walls face south and were heated by a system of hot air flues fueled by brick fire pits built behind the north faces. Tropical crops were forced by conducted hot air - pineapples, melons and cucumbers, in a glasshouse, this allowing tomatoes and grapes as well as rhubarb to be sold locally.

We made the routine visit of the house, explained by national trust volunteers and not so very different from many others and escaped into the service courtyard with its herringbone patterned pitching using pebbles from the local beach. Overhanging eaves served as rain shelters for servants passing among the many bordering rooms.

These included the dairy, with cream pans of solid slate, a hob grate for washing and scalding, a cheese pressing room and maturing store, a bake house and smoke house and meat salting room with slate tables and lead-lined sinks, a brew house for making small beer and a laundry with long racks for drying clothes.

The spaciousness of all this, to supply one family with their daily needs, was mind boggling, when so many of us now manage in a couple of rooms. In olden days the elite were the only families who benefited. Now all these aids to comfortable living are done outside the home and for the benefit of all instead of the landed few.

* * *

We left with much unseen in this, one of the most diversely interesting National Trust properties I have visited, and headed for the coast. Our first approach ended blindly on the clifftop at Cei bach and we tucked the car into a corner and walked on down the zig zag cut into the wooded cliff, but not all the way to the beach. The track continued for emergency vehicles and a long flight of steps for pedestrians.

A few holiday makers were gathered round a wood fire on the pebble beach with its small patch of sand and long line of groynes. The rocky headland looming close on our left would probably have caught up the longshore drift without the groynes. Although so calm there was a surprisingly loud crunch of moving pebbles, as each three inch high wave toppled in among them onto the Cei beach.

There was a longer view to the right. This section of sea harbours sea mammals, but we saw none before resuming our journey south to Aberaeron and supper. This seaside town, visited occasionally during my student days at Aberystwyth in the late 1940s, lies at the mouth of the River Aeron, bringing a breath of life to a rather dull coast of pebbles, connected with the town heart by a line of unattractive old houses.

Aberaeron owes its existence, from early in the nineteenth century, to the Rev Alban Gwynne. Centred around the spacious harbour, the building materials had to be brought in by sea, but the busy ship building industry that developed here used timber from local forests.

Later, with the coming of better road and rail transport, the trade died and the town developed as a holiday resort, complete with aquarium. Though never attracting as many folk as Aberystwyth further up the coast, it is still popular with the yachting and fishing fraternity.

The harbour was looking its best, with the evening sun blazing in from the western horizon. Many small boats lay at their moorings and others, mostly inflatables, and often with fishing rods, were coming and going. Attractive Regency houses, each of a different pastel shade, sparkled from beyond the harbour head, imparting a Mediterranean feel.

Walking the main street along the north flank of the river, Martyn and Irene met an old acquaintance for a chat on a handy bench. The south side was less busy, a grass slope leading up to a line of dwellings. A curved wooden footbridge crossed the river near the head of the harbour, an offshoot of which lay to the left.

We explored afoot beyond here, around the town square, returning for an excellent scampi supper with sticky toffee pudding and ice cream at the Monachty in Market Street. We sat, hopefully, on the sunlit decking by the water, but needed to move inside for the set meal, lest the onset of night should chill our victuals.

Returning along the harbour front to the car, the sun still shone on the parties eating fish and chips out of paper wrappings on the strategically placed benches. The long drive home was achieved before darkness fell. The end of a perfect day.

* * *

The final concert of the St. Davids pageant in which Irene was taking part was scheduled for Saturday. She went off to St. Davids with a friend for a day of rehearsals, while Martyn and I set off for Newport, in the bay on the further side of Dinas Head from Pwll Gwaelod.

This is within the Preseli National Park and only about mile from Carn Ingli where the eight blue stone columns were quarried for assumed transport some 240 miles to Stonehenge around two thousand BC.

Newport, Pembs., founded by the Normans in 1115, flourished as a busy herring port but, as with so many other coastal settlements, the fisheries waned and it had evolved into a quiet pleasure-boating centre, with only one fisherman allowed to use a seine net.

The town lies on the River Nyfer, with Newport Sands a mile or so away across the estuary to the east. We visited both the old port and the cliffs above the new resort, of which we saw nothing, because of the dense sea fog which settled all around the coast while the sun blazed down on the town at its loftier elevation.

Throughout our inland travel, the piled domes of cumulus clouds, like celestial cauliflowers, shone whiter than white in the powerful rays against flawless blue skies. The drifting candy floss, mounded above and often flat below, was being lifted on currents of air rising from the sun-warmed earth, the thermals that carried the buzzards and red kites effortlessly aloft on summer days.

We watched the wisps and puffs of greyer water vapour moving below them, separating, coalescing, and swallowing up scenes sharply defined just minutes before. Such rapid movement suggested considerable turbulence up aloft, but all was so still below that I almost set off on our walk without a jacket. Once down at sea level I was very glad I hadn't.

Arriving at the shore of the Nyfer Estuary, I imagined this to be the sea coast, being unable to discern land on the other side of this actually quite narrow waterway.

To our left was a mixed landscape of woodland, hayfields and grazing land, with no trace of seaside holiday development. The marshy land to our right showed little influence of the sea. Some was tufty grassland and some reedbed, with yellow flag irises and hemlock water dropwort characterising both.

Only on the undercut earth bank against the water was there any trace of maritime influence - this a narrow band of thrift, scurvy grass and sea plantain. Beyond were mudflats, extending out into what I imagined was open sea but was, in fact, more of the same, and not very far off, on the further bank.

Eventually some old stone quays and warehouses loomed out of the mist ahead. The beach below the sailing club seemed to have become sanded up, but a motley of boats was moored offshore, or lay askew on sandy mud. Most were pleasure boats, including some long boats built for four oarsmen and used for rowing contests. The estuary is said to be well stocked with sea trout and a few crabs, lobsters, mackerel, pollack and mullet were brought in.

We investigated a lime kiln preserved in good condition, one of the three remaining kilns in the Newport area out of a former total of eight. Burning of lime in kilns, probably for building purposes, goes back to Norman time, the tradition of burning it for agricultural fertiliser probably to about 1500 - the product particularly useful on the thin, acid soil of the local hills.

The kilns were filled with alternate layers of lumps of limestone and anthracite from a loading platform reached up a sloping ramp. The fire burning in the hole which we peered into below, might be kept alight for weeks or months, the burnt lime raked out through the kiln eye, which also admitted the draught needed to keep the fire going. As the level of the contents dropped they were replenished on a regular basis from above - where now was a mellowed growth of fresh greenery.

The corrosive quicklime was carted away and left in heaps in the rain to become hydrated into the more manageable slaked lime. This was used for making lime mortar and whitewash as well as on farmland The little village round about showed no taint of tourism, no shop, just a few cottages, a mown lawn, some trimmed hedges and a way out through a new housing development where an alleyway led across a burbling stream by a footbridge and brought us back to our starting point.

Our route east and north to Newport Sands took us across the estuary further inland, just downstream of a somewhat hazardous crossing by stepping stones. Bird life here consisted of two sleepy swans, a watchful heron and a few foraging shelducks.

When we drove into the carpark at our destination the attendant refused to take a parking fee. "You won't see a thing. There's no point!" It was uncanny watching two cars driving off seaward into what looked like outer space, with nothing visible below or beyond. We proceeded to the seaward limit of the first parking bay, looked into the world of vapours and opted to return into that of sunshine.

* * *

Back to Brynberion to tidy up and we were away again to St. Davids for the gala performance of Haydn's "Creation" by the Festival Chorus and Orchestra, with three soloists, a bass, a tenor and a soprano. The cathedral was packed, with carparks inadequate for such great occasions, but we found a handy farm gateway not too far off in the valley bottom.

Swarms of folk, dressed more formally than the usual holiday makers, surged along the steep paths and beside walls decorated with white as well as purple wall toadflax and pellitory of the wall. Our seats were at the very back of the horizontal seating area but the choir was in tiered stands behind the orchestra, so we managed to spot Irene in the back row of the singers, but not much else - and certainly not the soloists down at floor level in front.

I much enjoy listening to pleasant melody and to rhythm within reason, but there was very little of either here except for a few minutes after the interval. The rest was, to the unmusical, a series of very loud noises with lots of banging and crashing, that made me feel that an understandably angry God was seeking to destroy his world rather than create it.

I have no doubt at all about the expertise of the highly trained orchestra and choir assembled from a wide area, but they could only reproduce the notes that Hadyn had drawn together in what must have been a very disturbed period of his life. This was the sort of sound that mother always referred to as "thunder and lightning music", needing constant readjustment of the radio as sound alternated between too little and too much. I was grateful for the opportunity to experience it live for once in a lifetime but it was good to get outside for a breath of fresh air in the interval. Then back to the hard seats and more of the same.

Is it so wrong to think of creation in gentler terms? An acorn pushing out its first pair of tender leaves, a primrose unfurling its first pale petals, a fluffy duckling taking to the water for the first time, a furry rabbit emerging from the dark into a summer pasture, a newly emerged butterfly pumping fluid into its magnificently pigmented wings?.

A cacophony of sound of a different, more natural, kind greeted us in the great out of doors, as a flock of several hundred Corvids filled the sky, preparatory to settling to roost in the tall trees. Most were rooks and crows, but there were high pitched notes from more soprano jackdaws. All bare branches were full of the sooty black forms, strung out like notes of music. Had they been trying to compete? Later they would drop down into the leaf canopy and quiet would reign again, but it was tempting to feel that those within had roused them into this hysterical display of noise making.

We followed the main road back via Fishguard by the light of a watery sun but deviated after Dinas Cross to visit the coast at Pwll Gwaelod in the little bay where Dinas Head, alias Dinas Island, is firmly attached to the mainland. The coastal mist persisted. Driving cautiously onto the concrete boat slipway in the dark we found ourselves among the blurred images of land bound sea craft looming out of the fog. There would be no romantic path of moonshine on the sea to admire tonight.

God's world was in one of its blacker moods.

CHAPTER 21

Ty Canol Wood, Pembs., Forest Farm, Pughs and Other Local Gardens

Sunday morning was earmarked for a long lie-in for the previous day's chorister. I mooched around locally while Martyn, head cook and bottle washer, produced a splendid meal of tender roast lamb. No: not Welsh. This lamb was being imported from Australia prematurely because of the long drought and shortage of feed. Following my sojourns in that great dry continent I could imagine the suffocating dryness only too well.

After lunch Irene and I renewed our acquaintance with the Ty Canol Wood National Nature Reserve a few miles away. This was a fabulous woodland clothing a Preseli valley: full of great mossy boulders, ferny outcrops and ancient trees, like an outsize version of Devon's famous Wistman's Wood.

On our last year's visit with an elderly botanist who had known it well from olden days, we had christened it The Elfin Wood. Endowed with an acute perception and a sense of fun, she had enlivened our exploratory walk. "There. Don't you see, peering round that rock?" A pregnant pause while we strained our eyes. "There's another, perched in that hollow tree. Elves!" We didn't spot the elves, but every irregularity of our hummocky walk would have made a perfect background for the Margaret W.Tarrant paintings that I had collected in the 1920s and 30s and retained through the last traumatic move for their fragile beauty.

Such a remarkable place had been visited by experts in various fields. Almost four hundred species of lichen had been identified - tree dwellers, rock dwellers and ground dwellers. There could well have been as many kinds of mosses and liverworts; from the pale spongy cushions of soil hugging Leucobryum, upstanding mini-forests of dark green, rock dwelling Polytrichum and creeping yellow-green mats of Hypnum investing tree branches and providing a substrate for the some of the shaggier old man's beard lichens.

Nestled into moss clumps were the delicate white flower bells and trefoil leaves of wood sorrel at ground level, on contorted tree bases or clinging to uneven rocks. Polypody ferns sent exploratory rhizomes along sinuous branches, producing epiphytic leaf tufts getting all the moisture they needed high above the ground. All sounds were muffled, no motorways, no aircraft, just right for the little people.

But there was another side to this harmony. As we entered from the grounds of the old farmhouse cum field centre, we came upon a cluster of great spotted woodpecker feathers, some black, sharply spotted with white, others softer contour feathers of crimson. As we left, we spotted the likely malefactor, our attention drawn by the hysterical alarm calls of a blackbird, followed by the sight of the predator, flapping off through marginal trees with a blackbird sized bird dangling from its talons. We had but a momentary sighting of the raptor, but it must have been a sparrow hawk. Mottled brown, it would have been a hen bird, which is three inches longer than the slate grey male and capable of taking larger prey.

Further on, where bracken fronds and honeysuckle vines increased, we spotted the expectorated crop pellet of an insect eater. The discarded, shiny black debris had belonged to at least one bloody-nosed beetle, largest of our leaf beetles.

Midway the path led across a rushy clearing where we came to the dragonfly pool, so named on our last visit. It was living up to its name and it was not long before we spotted a newly emerged four-spotted chaser dragonfly (*Libellula quadrimaculata*) clinging to a rush stem.

On another rush, a little nearer the open water, was the dry khaki skin of a larva, one of the exuvia from which an adult had emerged. The lifeless legs of this still clung to the support, with the shell of the body split down the back where the mature insect had escaped. This hangs head downwards at first until the legs strengthen to heave it upwards, withdraw the abdomen and bend this below the head.

Our specimen was a foot or two away, the wings fully expanded when first seen but the bright brown body still elongating. Irene took photos on her digital camera, so that we could focus in on the dark mottled brown patches at the base of the hind wings and the smoother amber at the base of the forewings. The abdomen had a yellow stripe down each flank, the total length not far short of two inches, the wing span three inches.

Nearby was another, much shorter, discarded exuvium of a different species, but the only other adult member of the Odonata seen was a blue damselfly. The highly predatory dragonfly nymphs had been sustained by other water creatures and these by water plants. Botanical prize went to the massed border of partly submerged marsh St. John's wort along one bank, the fine down covering of the blue-green leaves making these quite unwettable, the water balling up on them as on a duck's back.

As we drove out along the narrow lane Irene halted the car where we had a fine view of the Neolithic standing stones away to our left. The mighty headstone was balanced on only two of the four apparent supporting pillars, the fourth stopping just short. It was an impressive sight, and beautiful, framed as it was in the froth of white blossom in the nearby hedgerow.

The scene was enhanced by the red, black and white cattle fattening in adjoining fields. A popular beef breed hereabouts nowadays was the Belgian Blue, which is not necessarily grey like the old blue-grey suckler cows of my farming days. Those were a cross between a black Galloway and a white shorthorn, the origin of the new crossbreed I failed to discover. It apparently produces a lot of lean meat with little fat in a shorter time than average.

***

I left this beautiful county on the Monday, the train departing from Haverfordwest ten minutes earlier than expected, so that we only just made it, after a "ride of the Valkyries" following the moment our misconception was realised. It was a leisurely journey then, stopping at Clarbeston Road, Clynderwen and Whitland and then alongside acres of mudflats and tidal sands.

On the estuary below Llanstephan Castle opposite, a flight of ten Canada geese tried to keep up with the train, but I saw few waders. Just across the water here my college friends, Margaret and Jago Morris, farm quick-fattening, continental breeds of beef cattle on the salt marsh turf at the confluence of the two rivers, this a delightful spot, the Pilgrim's Rest, where pilgrims of old rested before and after their river crossing.

Not far from here I spotted two men trudging along a river bank with coracles on their back. The art of managing these unwieldy little craft is by no means dead in West Wales. It was Dylan Thomas country by the Taf near Ferryside, upstream of where tidal sands stretch away offshore where the two rivers and the Gwendraeth meet the sea.

More sandy seascapes sped past as we came to Pembrey, Burryport and Llanelli, with more across the Loughour Estuary to Gower. We were backtracking down the other side of the River Towy to reach these, the train backing out from Carmarthen the way it came in, just as it does at Swansea.

***

On Friday the 6th June five nearly fully grown adolescent mallard were padding around on the clump of river crowfoot at the further end of the Radyr footbridge, scarcely denting it, so much had it increased in bulk. They seemed to be finding plenty of edible titbits secreted among the closely packed, wispy fronds.

The west bank was noisy with a gaggle of young magpies, chivvying the two adults for more and yet more. These two, much maligned providers, were behaving impeccably, tweaking small goodies from among pebbles in the shallows. Only the resident grey wagtails had cause to be aggrieved about this.

Past the four old nest holes of great spotted woodpeckers in the dead black poplar, I lingered awhile in the mini arboretum of the Fforest Farm carpark. The chief attraction here at present was the riot of dangling white pea flowers among the softly pinnate leaves of two false Acacia trees *(Robinia pseudacacia)*. These are mis-named, as Acacias bear clusters of tiny pom pom flowers and these ornamental dangles were more like those of Laburnum. One of the two trees was obviously much older than the other, with canker-like bulges all over the branches, which were bare and sharply angled, like a monster bonsai.

Behind them was a row of big horse chestnuts bordering the sports field. Young burs were already forming and I was surprised to see so many of the old conkers still intact on the ground among iron-hard husks, brown now and without their spines, but seemingly indestructible. So far the parent trees seemed to have escaped the newly arrived horse chestnut disease.

The soft red-brown bark of the giant Sequoia or Wellingtonia showed a few of the oval excavations the size of a hen's egg made by roosting tree creepers. Only three seemed to be in use, each having a dribble of tell tale white guano below. With the pale breast pressed into the hollow, the speckled back and head would merge invisibly and the small but closely packed evergreen scale leaves might keep off the rain, but a crevice under a scalier type of bark might have provided a warmer winter nook. Sadly some of the lower bark of this Californian giant had been stripped away from the wood.

Another conifer close by was from the Himalayas, the deodar or Himalayan cedar. This came to a narrower peak than the other more spreading cedars planted in Britain, but had the same perfectly symmetrical three inch long mature cones and smaller green ones, sitting erect among tufts of needle leaves resembling those of a rather dishevelled larch.

I sought in vain for anomalous leafy shoots growing from the tips of larch cones in the central spinney where these had occurred in past years. No walnuts were visible on either tree but the limes and maples were full of fruit and the unripe fruits on the early flowering cherry plum trees were almost full size but not yet yellowing. A great bank of flowering dogwood now divided the area in two, this bordered with Himalayan balsam, some of which had been lopped as a beautiful but undesirable alien.

The part now closed to cars had become a rabbitry. Seven rabbits were feeding on the short mossy turf laced with rosaceous yellow flowers as I approached. Everywhere around the open area were beds of round-leaved mint *(Mentha rotundifolia or suaveolens)*, more than I have seen anywhere else. The unusually wrinkled leaves smelled as strongly of mint as any other and were obviously not being eaten by the rabbits. These dislike the powerful scent of members of the dead nettle family, although those are the lures that attract pollinating insects and culinary connoisseurs. This mint is native but uncommon in the wild except on south-west coasts of England and Wales.

Hedge bindweed wound its way through nettle beds left in the hope of attracting Vanessid butterflies to lay their eggs. Speckled wood and cabbage white butterflies and small magpie moths were on the wing, but I saw neither eggs nor caterpillars.

Massed black aphids crowded together near the stem tips of docks, and fewer on those of creeping thistles, siphoning off the rising sap. In both instances they had attracted brown ants. Nymphs of froghopper bugs *(Philaenus spumarius)* lurked in frothy blobs of white 'cuckoo spit' on other stems. The foam which they secrete prevents them from drying out and protects them from some, but not all, predators.

Leaning over the gate of the field where the little Dexter cattle had formerly grazed, I was able to watch the foraging of another group of rabbits domiciled in the hedge bottom, also a possie of five fat wood pigeons, three crows and a mistle thrush. A section had been cordoned off for growing bird seed, but I avoided disturbing the foragers so do not know what species had been sown.

* * *

Later in the day I visited Pugh's garden centre to obtain slug killer to save our new lupin plants that were under attack. Exploring the furthermost corner I found that the stream under the Morganstown scarp had been fenced out, beyond a formidable array of sizable young trees awaiting sale. A pity. On one occasion I had seen a kingfisher perched close to the little footbridge there.

I took the opportunity of visiting the fish and aquatic centre next door, now taken over by the thriving firm that I had seen start as Mr. and Mrs. Pugh and two stalwart sons. Since those far off days some of the now large, uniformed staff had volunteered their services scrub-cutting and burning on the County Wildlife Trust's nature reserve at Lavernock Point on the cliffs west of Penarth, to help spare the grassland orchids and spreads of Dyer's greenweed *(Genista tinctoria)*.

The multi-coloured and often iridescent fish in the freshwater tanks were always a delight, their variety of bizarre shapes as well as their colours almost unbelievable. Now there were living displays of coral reef organisms as well, fish and other natural forms, all pulsating with life and bringing back memories of snorkelling off Hawaii, Aldabra and the Seychelles.

The troughs of aquatic plants conjured up other memories of warmer lands but some, like the scourge of the Nile *(Eichornia crassipes)* and water lettuce *(Pistia stratiotes)* I have now come across growing out of doors in Britain. I was surprised to see on sale some of the rampageous water weeds from abroad that conservationists have been warning against introducing for some years now - as unstoppable invaders of our waterways, crowding out the natives.

These were the parrot's feather water milfoil *(Myriophyllum aquaticum)* and the American floating pennywort *(Hydrocotyle ranunculoides)*. At least I saw none of the rapidly spreading New Zealand pigmyweed *(Crassula helmsii)* that has taken over much of the Llanelli Wildfowl Centre's fresh water and has been painstakingly removed from pools in some of the Cardiff parks, where it turned up mysteriously.

Later on the early evening sunshine tempted me out around Windsor Crescent, where I saw that the street trees with their astonishing woody 'elephant's foot' bases were, in fact, cherry trees, as I had suspected from their horizontally banded bark. Upper branches were often cankered and some were dead, the trees showing a general aspect of decline, but a few full blown cherries lay on the pavement below. Some younger ones in good condition had been planted at the further end.

The house on this corner had provided sanctuary for nesting house sparrows, tucked in under the eaves. An attractive little mini garden of maidenhair spleenwort ferns clung to the brick chimney just above. Sparrows as well as jackdaws were noisy on other roofs. The presence of tall trees where I discerned the further ends of back gardens seemed to confirm my suspicions that these backed onto the Taff clifftop.

* * *

Next morning Ginger Pop was out hunting before breakfast. I spotted him racing home (to the next door garden) carrying a dead bird with long dangly legs and the size of a thrush. He did not pause when the local jay flew past, quite close to his head.

Sunday the eighth of June, living up to its forecast of brilliant sunshine, had been chosen by Hugh John, the photographer who had attended the official Roy Noble opening, for a spell of photographing me. This was to accompany a 'commercial' advertising Brynteg as 'a good buy' to potential customers.

I had been misguided enough to state on the occasion of the opening - which coincided with the publication of my latest book, on the Hebrides - that I had chosen to move here because of its proximity to the country park, the river and other potential walks, also its extensive view up the valley. The publicity officer's mind switched immediately to the headline "Botanist chooses Brynteg for its ideal location" or some such. A photo was needed of my venerable self communing with nature in the garden.

Unfortunately almost the only flowers available now that the daffodils and Clematis had finished was a burgeoning wild elder in the top corner by the water tank. I stepped gingerly between the ground cover shrubs and duly admired them from various angles, dreaming of elder flower champagne, as six thousand pound's worth of digital camera equipment recorded my movements for posterity. The same in other sites, including my annexe, now full of books. A good job film is now re-usable.

We spent a pleasant interval on the garden benches, marvelling at the digital world into which I had inadvertently strayed. "Those photos I've just taken could have been reproduced in Australia within minutes of exposing the film." "How?" He didn't know. "Nor do many others."

In his mid forties, he was old enough to marvel at these new mysteries. "My daughter takes it all for granted. They are doing this sort of thing on their computers all day in the class room." We all, like sheep, are in the hands of the few 'clever Dicks' who know how these planetry wonders work.

He had been recording the international cricket match in Sophia Gardens all morning, and showed me the results, along with the later shots, on the crystal clear screen of his long-nosed apparatus. His stated preference was "Why don't we feed the world's starving and cure their aids instead of indulging in all this wizardry." A good point, especially from a participant.

Despite the benevolent sunshine we had the garden to ourselves, but there was the usual bunch sunning outside the front door. A perfunctory chat and I wandered off through the elite suburbs to the recreation ground behind the church, making the circuit up the steps to the roads beyond.

Trees, now thickened up with foliage, obscured the winter view of the tennis courts, which advertised themselves by the constant thud of balls on raquets. The hollow containing the venerable oak was now a veritable thicket, the periwinkles of winter swallowed up by shoulder high herbs and saplings. Among the strategically placed flowering roses were some unusual ones producing attractive flowers almost at ground level.

I noticed that the residential road above was called 'Drover's Way'. This was the approximate location of the old hedged and sunken track identified in my initial survey, which I thought might have been an old parish road. I could now envisage rough-voiced Welsh drovers urging their cattle along it - or something smaller: geese, perhaps, their webbed feet tarred and invested with sand to take the wear on the long walk to market. Yes indeed, the world WAS changing - too fast for the likes of me.

A couple of days later I wandered out while waiting for the washing machine to do its stuff - the third day of our heatwave with temperatures in the early eighties. The tall field maples separating us from the road had stopped shedding redundant leaves and immature fruits over our parked cars below. Wings of the remaining fruits had turned a deep crimson and looked fit to remain attached.

Two juvenile carrion crows were calling repeatedly overhead. A more treble, less throaty call commensurate with their smaller size, came from a couple of jackdaws. Both were fully feathered and were enticed away eventually by an adult. The greenfinch that hopped confidingly from twig to twig at head level was not advertising its presence with constant cheeping, as sometimes.

I was waylaid on my return to the laundry by two members of the new garden committee, Pansy, trowel in hand, with some new additions. Thing were looking up on that front. Rita was extolling the virtues of red valerian, which I had always regarded as a weed. She had sought permission to help herself from a waste plot in a back lane behind the Spar shop, but all plants there were mature, their woody roots insinuated firmly beneath the concrete floor and quite immovable.

I sallied forth with a trowel and managed to find some clusters of seedlings whose roots ramified between the concrete and a surface layer of moss. Bearing them back in triumph, I called the news through Pansy's open balcony doors and we settled the new acquisitions in a bucket of water for a drink, which both they and I needed at that stage.

* * *

Later on, walking back along the Melin Griffith feeder towards the weir, I had an interesting encounter with a buzzard. I was watching a couple of jays when this flapped across the canal, from one low branch to another, turning round to keep an eye on me. I stood for another five minutes, watching the chunky, thick-necked mound of feathers, whose gaze shuttled between me, safely beyond the water, and the ivy-clad bank on his side.

Then the great wings spread, as he plummeted obliquely down onto the bank. With lethal beak and talons attending to presumed prey, all I could see was the uncoordinated flapping of wings, which were presumably keeping the weight off feet that were otherwise engaged. The kerfuffle continued for long enough for him to have gulped down anything the size of a mouse or vole. There was nothing in the talons when he rose to flap away through the branches, so he may or may not have been successful.

Walking back down-river after lingering by the weir, heron-watching, I was alerted by a mixed mewing and crowing. Looking skyward I saw the buzzard, still flying low, but over the rabbit field now, being closely pursued by a protesting carrion crow. Each lunge by the darker bird came perilously close to the more ponderously flapping raptor, but the aggressor peeled off as his quarry disappeared into the trees where I had first spotted him.

CHAPTER 22

Radyr Woods In Summer, Coryton Roundabout and Wenvoe Limestone

Bright and early on a brilliant Monday morning, 9th June, I boarded the car for a shopping spree. Battery as flat as a pancake after two weeks of no mileage to recharge it. I walked round the corner of "Orchard Alley" and enlisted the help of the wizened, curly haired proprietor of Victoria Garage, bent lovingly over a low built shiny sports car. He'd come and get me started at 1 o'clock if I wasn't in a hurry.

I wasn't - and continued afoot along Radyr Terrace in the direction of Radyr Woods. Leaning over the fence to say "howdo" to the mare and two young ponies, I was delighted to see a tiny skewbald foal, mostly white with golden brown patches. and surely no more than a few days old. It picked ineffectually at a few blades of grass poking through the fence while the bay mare, sleek and shiny, replenished her needs on the still meagre sward. The resident cockerel crowed - in triumph? - as I passed from what I found on my return at a lower level to be a brand new hen house at the end of the paddock.

Birth of the new and death of the old. My next wildlife encounter was a dead adult toad at the top of the way leading down into the reserve. A few paces in, past the stile, was an extra large molehill with a fist sized hole in the top where the digger had left, and at least as much displaced earth spilled over onto the hard path.

This was not the usual crumbly loam thrown up by moles but a sticky reddish-yellow clay, incompletely broken down and with knobs as big as walnuts. I refused to believe it was the work of a mole until I found similar mounds under the low bramble canopy above, some with green algae filming the clay. There were no tracks or droppings of other mammals. Moles seldom tunnel under hard paths, usually turning to throw up a line of hillocks along its edge. This one had tried extra hard on the final excavation in unsuitable soil before leaving overland in disgust. The only other mammal signs were halved hazel nut shells left by squirrels, of which there were plenty around.

Similarly sticky reddish yellow clay lined the vertical sided stream spanned by a plank bridge near the bottom of the flight of steps leading down into the valley. Among fat seed capsules of the spring bluebell crop, was the paler blue of wood speedwell with red campion and a single tuft of ragged robin as I turned into the valley marsh.

A prolonged and noisy flapping of wings drew my attention to a pair of mating wood pigeons high in the canopy. Finally the kerfuffle ceased, one left and the other remained, making a single, self satisfied comment:"I TOLD you so", instead of the usual "You two FOOLS, you two".

I back-tracked along the sinuous wooden causeway through the swamp - floored by black peaty silt now. This had been installed in memory of Bill Clarke, MBE, chief warden between 1986 and 2000, the relevant plaque mounted on an upstanding rock of the same reddish-yellow tinge as the derived soil on the eroding slope above.

The main swamp where kingcups had been blooming on my earlier visit, was now covered with their leaves, on much elongated stalks, but not the large size often attained after flowering. Hemlock water dropwort had thrust flowering umbels up through the mass, with arching sprays of lady and broad buckler ferns, these giving way to the lower growing umbellifer, fool's water-cress, in glades with more open water. Here were fine-leaved tufts of remote flowered sedge and shoulder high sprays of pendulous sedge shading spreads of wood bittercress.

A narrow belt of non-flowering mint was pierced by a few yellow Iris clumps beneath veteran alders thrusting skywards to vie with oak, ash and beech. Rugose, patchy bark above and contorted bases provided numerous moss-grown cavities penetrating deep into the wood. These and even more dissected fallen logs created a choice of hidey holes for small animals.

Shafts of sunlight shone between their misshapen boughs, illuminating shimmering pools along the course of the placid stream and playing on the transparent wings of the flies which gyrated through the lower atmosphere.

Peering from the board walk I spotted the curved bodies of freshwater shrimps sidling sideways through clear water too still to stir the silt over which a few small bugs and beetles scuttled. Water crickets tripped lightly across the surface film. This was a magical place at this season with no sound but that of unidentified birds singing high above.

I emerged into a spot with picnic tables and benches within an old mossy wall and was surprised to see the otherwise bare ground beside the benches covered with a close mat of *Lunularia cruciata* liverwort. Its little lunar gemmae cups were crammed with tiny vegetative disseminules, to be splashed out by raindrops and produce more of the symmetrically aerated fronds.

And then the stillness was broken: human voices drifted through the trees and I perceived a jigsaw of colour as I spied on them, unseen. A walking club perhaps, about twenty of them, all mature enough to be residents of a retirement home and just the sort of group I used to trundle round such places myself, but none of these known to me. Their leader was pointing out features of the way ahead. They had by-passed the elfin water world that I occupied. I found their presence as intrusive as the wildlife must have found that of my parties in years gone by. They moved on in the opposite direction to mine. The quagmire was not quite in the valley bottom. As I proceeded south the gradient steepened and the silt-floored wetland stillness gathered momentum into a stony-floored, gushing stream bounding down to the Kingfisher Pool at the woodland edge. I continued towards Hermitage Wood along a broad open swathe cleared through the flowering guelder rose and elder bushes.

A jay flew across in front of me, then thought better of it and flew back. Then a glimpse of a great spotted woodpecker. Magpies were everywhere and a great band of jackdaws was indulging in a communal noise-making session, presumably for some good purpose which I could not guess. How I wished I could interpret bird song. There was little chance of seeing woodland songsters other than blackbirds among all the newly sprung leaves now.

Margins of the broad walkway were composed mainly of robust stinging nettles with some greater willow herb and, as I moved on, Himalayan balsam, some recently cleared. The February snowdrops and April wood Anemones were now swallowed up by mightier growths.

I returned stealthily, as always, to the Kingfisher Pool. It was as well I did because the baby moorhen foraging along the grassy walkway between the landward thicket and the water was not alarmed. Loud honks came from an adult which remained hidden among the weeds

Across the pool, skulking at the edge of the bulrushes, was a young heron. The neck alongside the frontal spotting was grey rather than white, as were the forehead and crown. This bird was well aware of me, watching me from various angles and with much neck weaving, its concentration unwavering, but it held its ground as I moved on, taking off awhile later and flapping overhead with characteristic strongly bowed wings.

The *Typha* bulrushes had increased to take over most of the pond. The original growth in the north included many of last year's cat's-tail heads, the tightly packed, dark brown florets fluffing out to spread more of the tiny seeds. The entire growth in the southern section, however, was of bright green leaves of the same stature but the flowering heads not yet developed.

There were fish here, and in the lower, faster flowing reaches of the stream - two inches long there, a little more in the pond. They looked like tiddlers anywhere, possibly sticklebacks, probably minnows.

It was long-legged pond skaters on the water here, not water crickets, but I saw no whirligig beetles. Typha and water dropwort thickets were full of bright blue damselflies. Whether the common blue or the azure I know not. The difference depends on a few black markings on the thorax. None were flying in tandem as yet and I saw no other species. (Although a larger brown-bodied darter shot under my nose as I plodded up the steep rise home, from its perch on an Osteospermum, that brilliant daisy we called star of the veldt in South Africa.)

My most intimate moments here were standing three feet below a baby greenfinch that I would never have spotted had it stayed quiet. The call was incessant, bi-syllabic, a rather truncated 'peewit' sound. The streaky breast was the same off-white colour as the stubby, broad-based bill, but the bright yellow streak along the base of its wing was seen also in the adult.

Two other youngsters were flipping around the other side of the bush and with them one of the parent birds. None of these were giving voice, like the innocent, who was looking straight at me, seemingly pleading me to help. I did, by moving on and leaving him to his family, the adult only moving in after I was well away.

All about were narrow-leaved osiers, broad-leaved sallows and alders, whose leaves were infested by a rash of nodules over the surface. These were caused by Eriophyid mites, *Eriophyes laevis-inangulis*.

Mounting the steps and moving on, I came to a new development alongside the pond, a fencing in of a corner of the former field to enclose an enlarged waterside plot, with two newly planted, staked osiers. The influx of unrestricted sunlight had made this a different world.

It was a community of shaggy grass with yellow tormentil and buttercups, the butterflies were common blues and yellow brimstones instead of the speckled woods and large whites of the woodland, and those only in the clearings. Free access, apparently little used, was gained via a wooden gate and I went down to the water's edge but saw nothing new except severe algal contamination of the open water.

From here on the reserve was not fenced off from the grassed recreation ground alongside the new houses on the old shunting yards. Two parties were exercising dogs along the edge of the wood followed by the stream so I made a beeline for the old Duck Pond. No ducks today, just an adolescent moorhen and a community of small water creatures swimming below the viewing platform.

I moved in haste from here. I had an appointment with the garage man and had no idea where my spare car keys were. Such are the hazards of moving house, when all small items are pushed in among the large to save space. After following several false trails, I found them eventually among the spare electric light bulbs, just in time. It was not just a flat battery but one which objected to being re-charged. Fortunately the spanners required for change were not far off. At last I could get those ice blocks from the deep freeze and drop them into a glass of water.

* * *

On the evening of the eleventh of June a large proportion of the Brynteg residents assembled in the lounge for a beetle drive. I would have joined them, but it clashed with a field meeting of the Cardiff Naturalists' Society where my first loyalties lay, so I opted for that. This was a joint walk with the Cardiff Council, laid on for members of the public although led by Bruce MacDonald, our field outings secretary.

The venue was the Coryton Roundabout on junction 32 of the M4 at its crossing of the A470 to Merthyr. Always before I had entered over the footbridge from Tongwynlais on the eastern flank. Tonight we were meeting at Whitchurch, on Forest Farm Drive to the west.

This plot of land, an unlikely site for a nature reserve, was the largest roundabout in Wales at the time of its construction in the 1970s, occupying thirty five acres and furnished with a web of footpaths and cycleways. Subways as well as footbridges gave access from different points.

I first knew the area as green fields in the 1960s, then as an amalgam of big machines and dumped soil in the 1970s, this last bringing the disseminules of plants and animals from other areas, presaging an interesting sequence to come.

I kept tabs on the changes during the next quarter of a century until 2002, when my tome on the Natural History of the Taff Valley was published and the site became recognised as one of the finest for wild orchids in the county outside the phenomenal spreads on our western sand dunes.

The initial landscaping involved intensive tree planting - too many too close as it turned out - but when trying to establish a mature community as quickly as possible, this is easily done. Some trees were thinned, most grew on. I had visited very little during the past few years, Now, in 2008, the paths and stairways remained almost the only clearways we could distinguish among rampant foliage and there was no distant view of landmarks. It was a case of not being able to see the trees for the wood.

With such a large party on narrow paths we were bound to split into groups with sub leaders. My little lot drifted to the back, dwindling to five, then to three and we took a different turning from the rest, getting temporarily lost - and very wet when the promised late evening rain came down in torrents.

Having probably once known this plot of land better than anyone else here - taken scores of photos, drawn maps and given talks and tours, I had a hard job living this down. By the time I and my two stalwart gentlemen companions got back to the starting point all the other cars had gone. Nevertheless, it provided a laugh at the next meeting and it was good to see how the man-made landscape had matured.

A new entrance path had been cut through the wood at the top end of the canal nature reserve where we assembled This circled round the back of the garage and bridged the ring road to the western flank of the roundabout, which was always more wooded than the east, some of which is still open grassland - which we missed on the night,

The orchids were particularly disappointing, as none were woodland species and had been largely superceded as the tree canopy increased. Bee orchids, especially, are early colonists on partially open land and we only saw a couple of spikes throughout. Pyramidal orchids, only a few seen, are most characteristic of open dunes and cliffs.

Common spotted orchids, once present in thousands and showing a remarkable colour range, from white to deep red, and a different degree of spotting, are essentially grassland plants. We saw plenty of the usual lightly spotted pink ones tonight, drawn up tall among straggly grass and herbs, but not in the extensive plots of orchids and ox-eye daisies that had dominated wide tracts in the past. Southern marsh orchid and fragrant orchid we saw not at all and only the odd, sad looking twayblade, which is more at home under trees.

But there was much else, not least the upstanding plots of shoulder high goat's rue *(Galega officinalis)*, just opening its pink and purple pea flowers. The former flamboyant everlasting peas and crown vetch were not encountered, but there were smaller purple and white vetches, yellow vetchling and hop trefoil, tall melilot and some lush red clover that we decided must be an agricultural strain, with hollow stems.

Lanky ox-eye daisies, drawn up in partial shade, brought home how very different those chunky seaside natives of the Pembrokeshire cliffs are. Musk mallow, three species of St. John's wort, four of the carrot family and several Geraniums, including the Pyrenean, mingled with the commoners.

Marshy areas were characterised by yellow Iris, water figwort. the larger willow herbs, lesser spearwort and a plethora of sedges and rushes. Blushing pink dog rose blooms were appearing among flowering dogwood, elder and wayfaring tree. Brambles came in great mounds, taller than a man and yards across, with huge white flowers, surely Himalayan giant and certainly a place to come blackberrying in a few weeks time.

Plodding through the rain in the lowering dusk, we three laggards gave up searching for subways and over-passes and took our lives in our hands by crossing one of the ring roads (via a traffic island), where we could at least recognise some landmarks, to trek back round a commuters' path shielded from the traffic by trees.

* * *

A similar sized party, all members of the Naturalists this time, met up the following Saturday morning in the village of Wenvoe, which is by-passed by the main road to Barry south of St. Fagans, and very little known. A delightful village, of smart houses with large gardens and plenty of public green spaces. This was Bruce's home patch and he led us out along residential roads to the hill country in the north west.

Three arboreal highlights seen en route (and also present in the city's Roath Gardens) were Clerodendron, the tree of heaven and the loquat, with big rough leaves and edible yellow fruits half way between a small apple and a plum. The sloping garden of the dwelling now occupying a redundant chapel was entirely filled with upstanding, mellowed gravestones, with a scrap of, presumably unhallowed, ground at the top. Where the road veered away, we continued along a woodland track - our immediate goal two orchid meadows - to make up for the dearth of those prize flowers three days before.

The steeper one, known to the locals as the Sledging Field, had become overgrown with ash trees, which had been cleared but were beginning to regenerate. The sward here had a purple haze when viewed sideways, the colour from common sorrel and the pigmented heads of Yorkshire fog grass. It was full of flowers, including orchids, but all these were the common spotted until we caught up with some twayblades at the woodland edge.

The second, further down the hill, was permanent pasture, unploughed and unfertilised, ideal conditions for wild flowers not overwhelmed by nitrogen-boosted pasture grasses. But there was a snag. The dominant plant here was yellow rattle, a sure sign of ancient pasture, but a semi parasite, sucking nourishment from the roots of others and keeping the sward much lower and sparser than in the other.

Both were on Cardiff Council land, the lower one leased for hay, but it would be a meagre crop. The uphill site was visited first and we followed a narrow path that had been cut around the tree girt perimeter for viewing, this being primarily a conservation site. All was very lush, but the corner where we emerged was more open and liberally sprinkled with cowslips, past their prime but always a delight when flowering.

There was yellow rattle here too among yellow pea, bird's foot trefoil, silverweed, cinqefoil and bush vetch. Specialities were the elegant beautiful St. John's wort, yellow wort with the leaf pairs fused across the stem and the related pink flowered centaury among the leaves of faded primroses.

Bracken, formerly six foot high, was lower now and judicious trimming was carried out in the more exuberant plots. Still to flower there were black knapweed, hemp agrimony, rosebay willow herb and meadowsweet.

From the heights we gained splendid coastal views across the plain to the stark outline of Steepholm Island in the Bristol Channel and Somerset's Brean Down beyond, consulting the O S map to identify the various land features in what appeared to be a predominantly rural landscape with wooded hills dissecting the paler farmland.

A buzzard rode a thermal rising from the sun-warmed quarry floor, pestered, as so often, by smaller fry, and a green woodpecker flew across. Among the usual butterflies were other insects, including both male and female scorpion flies *(Panorpa communis)*, the male with an upturned, bulbous tail tip resembling a scorpion's sting, but quite harmless. Both sexes had the long beak and attractive brown-patterned wings, and feed mainly on carrion, as they did in the larval stage.

Linda Nottage, an adept at catching insects in small glass phials for others to view, also procured male and female thick-legged flower beetles *(Oedemeria nobilis)*. Both were a magnificent, iridescent bottle green, but only the male sported the jewel-like bulging of the upper hind legs. Non-carnivorous, as both larvae and adults, these can often be seen sitting in flowers.

Another green insect, larger, with gangling legs, was a sawfly *(Rhodogaster viridus)*, with green underside and the back transversely striped in black and green. This catches insects visiting flowers and adults are quite short-lived, so we were lucky to see it. There were shield bugs and seven different species of ladybirds, including the cream spot, also a click beetle, which obligingly performed its self-righting leap when turned over on its back.

We did not penetrate far into the lower meadow, but far enough to spot some fine bee orchids, deep purple patches of self heal, wild strawberries and scarlet pimpernel. Some local councillors had designs on the lower part of this field as a potential cemetery and had been taking soil cores in the lower part to see if there was sufficient depth of soil over the bedrock for decent six foot burials. Conservationists were urgently hoping that there wasn't.

* * *

The prime habitat visited during this delectably sunny morn was the Walston Limestone Quarry. Although vaguely familiar with the Wenvoe Quarry on the opposite side of the Barry Road, a supposed haunt of dormice, I had not heard of this one. It proved a botanical paradise, as old quarries so often do, with so much cleared ground open to treasures unable to compete in mature plant communities.

From 'Cowslip Corner' at the bottom of the upper meadow, we plunged into the adjacent wood, climbing a path with useful handholds on uneven sections, to the brink of a yawning gap in the limestone hillside. Quarrying had ceased about a decade before, part of the space below now used for storage, mainly of great mounds of soil.

We worked our way along a broad ledge on the north side with dense woodland to our right and tentative colonisation by Buddleia, sallow and flowering field rose along the brink. A aggressive colonist was ground hugging *Cotoneaster horizontalis* but there was plenty of room for others.

Plucking the sweet wild strawberries as we progressed, we admired the quivering patches of quaking grass or shivery-shakes - a favourite from childhood days when we gathered bunches on the North and South Downs for dried winter decoration. Since then I have grown its larger relative, *Briza maxima,* from seeds brought back from the Scilly Isles, which have survived for five years on the mantelpiece with no visible deterioration.

Others reminiscent of the chalkhills of Surrey and Sussex were tall flowering salad burnet, with its fresh smell of cucumber, scarlet poppies and tall, single headed rough hawbit *(Leontodon hispidus)*. Some really fine bee orchids and pyramidal orchids kept the photographers busy. Upstanding red valerian, blue borage, yellow toadflax and white feverfew defied the rabbits, which kept the sward open enough for tinies like mauve field madder, white fairy flax and yellow hop trefoil.

Most colourful were garden escapes, particularly the multicoloured Antirrhinum or snapdragons, some pink and yellow but most strikingly crimson and scarlet. How good it would be to see colour such as that among Brynteg's sombre evergreens, but plants, like animals, do best in habitats of their own choosing. With them were purple dame's violet, like honesty but with elongated instead of oval fruits, also fennel and feverfew.

Aromatic patches of lemon balm, square-stemmed St. John's wort and a fine spread of white-flowered mignonette, mingled with ox-eye, dog daises or moon daisies among attractive, ivy-draped limestone boulders and modest carnation sedge with blue-green leaves.

Far below, between dumped soil and limestone chippings, was a broad muddy puddle where house martins were collecting wet clay for their nests. They came in little groups, carrying back gobbets of building material to we knew not where. Were they nesting under house eaves in the village or back in their ancestral habitat of limestone cliffs. There was a fine lofty example of such on the opposite side of the great hole.

On the tree-lined path back to the village we came upon a clump of the hoof shaped leaves of coltsfoot, giving Bruce the opportunity to produce a bag of pale brown 'coltsfoot rock' bought in an old time sweetshop somewhere on his travels. Produced as rock-hard sticks about a half by four inches in size, it resembled Edinburgh rock and dissolved in the mouth with a pleasing flavour of liquorice. Said to be a remedy for coughs, it was also a pleasant sweet and new to us.

Some of the party were embarking on a three mile walk to the Wrinstone Salmon Leaps and the promise of emperor dragonflies after a picnic lunch on the village green, but I opted out at this point, well pleased with my morning.

I had intended taking the rural way back through Peterstone-super-Ely and the Llantrisant Road but was thwarted on arrival at St. Fagan's level crossing, to find the road blocked, with no obvious warning at the top of the long road down. So it was back to the maelstrom of traffic and an overdose of traffic lights along this busy stretch of the A48.

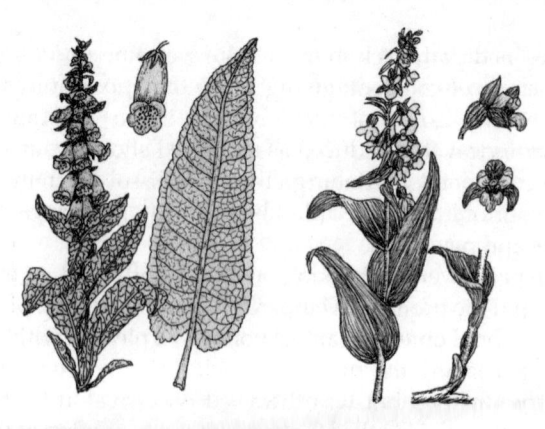

CHAPTER 23

Brecon Mountain Railway, Midsummer Day, Dyffryn Gardens, Bonvilston and Hailey Park

Every now and again one of our number organised an outing for fellow residents to a local site of interest. There had been one to the Welsh Folk Museum at St. Fagans in the early spring which I did not join and another on16th June which I did. Our purpose was to ride on the Brecon Mountain Railway and we had at our disposal a fifteen seater minibus with volunteer driver.

The requisite coffee stop en route had been scheduled for the "Little Chef" on the main A470 near Treharris, but our driver mistakenly turned off towards Abercynon, this entailing a circular tour back down the other side of the Taff Valley, viewing the old mining towns and their leafy backdrops at close quarters, before rejoining the highway at Pontypridd.

A benign sun smiled on the surrounding hills, the old black tips now clothed in heather, grass or trees and the wooded hills behind the Graig-yr-Hesg Quarry looking particularly fine, so no-one was complaining. On reaching the scheduled break, we found that the "Little Chef" had sold out to a garage and an Indian Takeaway, as part of a general contraction of their enterprises, so we carried on to our ultimate goal, where most made a beeline for the coffee shop.

We were now at Pant, a few miles north-east of Merthyr Tydfil on the edge of the Brecon Beacons National Park. The tourist line was sited on the old Merthyr to Brecon Railway, opened in 1859 and closed in 1964 - one of a veritable network of lines in use for long and short journeys when Merthyr was recognised as the largest iron making town in the world, not to mention hosting the trial run in 1804 of the first steam railway locomotive, built by Trevithick.

We had now longer than expected to wait for our train, so I went walkabout while the others sat companionably over their coffee cups. There were fine views from the carpark, particularly to the dark grey cliffs of the disused Morlais Quarry just across the lane and fronted by rolling mounds of spoil, grassed over and kept neat by grazing sheep. The quarry had supplied lime for the great iron smelters, as well as building and walling stone.

Looking back through pylons to the west, the nearer hill was decked with tall gravestones, and still room for more, despite the cholera epidemic that had ravaged the town during industrial times. Beyond this were moorland hills, sweeping round southwards over woodland and grass moor to the Giant's Bite, that conspicuous nick in the Coalfield skyline made by quarrying on the hills above Mountain Ash.

Knowing the carpark had been built on the former branch line to Dowlais, I assumed the three neatly symmetrical stone-built ventilation towers (pepper pots) topped by domed iron gratings to be reaching up from an underground mine, but no. Eighty feet below us was the tunnel of the old London and North-western Railway, which closed in 1958, the towers preserved as part of the industrial heritage.

Strolling along the farm track leading uphill away from the quarry I soon came to an old station with stone built walls rising from grass-grown rail track to grass-grown platforms - so the modern tourist narrow gauge railway had not been built exactly on the old track but alongside it. For the first six hundred yards it followed a totally new alignment, some of which had been blasted from solid rock.

North of the path the railway ballast had been colonised by crested dog's-tail grass with mouse-ear hawkweed and white and yellow clovers and on the sides of the track by more robust tall oat grass. This occupied all the visible part to the south, joined on the old platforms by golden patches of bird's-foot trefoil. The only potential passenger on the old ghost line was a diligently probing pied wagtail. A hundred yards or so on to the north the line curved away to the right and was lost among the trees.

An adjacent field had been laid up for hay, the crop, like the margins of the farm track, dominated by the silky plumes of tall oat grass with ribwort plantain, plus a little ryegrass, cocksfoot and red clover. The rest was typical upland sheep pasture, almost the only vegetation topping the closely nibbled sward being creeping thistle and the wiry stems of dogstail, these almost all that remained after the more palatable foliage had been munched away.

This grazing land, and more especially the sheep fank where the flocks were mustered as required, were littered with tufts of sheeps' wool. It is not so long since this would have been collected up by the women and children for cleaning, spinning and weaving in the close-ranked cottages.

Gnarled hawthorn and elder hedge trees, tortuous from past layering, lined the track beyond the old station, with a massive ash shading a cluster of pens and yards, fenced around with whatever had come to hand, from old gates to corrugated iron and rotten fence posts.

Another mammoth ash on the corner of the cottage wall and more along a rocky bluff, pointed to these as the natural tree dominants of this upland limestone country as opposed to the oak and beech of more lowland sites. Woody bases were nibbled by rabbits as well as sheep. A woodpecker was drumming in the ash spinney while jackdaws, crows and magpies were foraging among the mountain sheep, a few of which were black. Swallows swooped in and out of the low barn beside the small whitewashed cottage.

Walls of local limestone, tumbled in some parts, mossy in others, nourished a thriving colony of shining cranesbill. Thyme-leaved and buxbaum's speedwell, wood avens and field forget-me-not found shelter along their bases and yellowing leaves told of a past spread of springtime celandines. A bald patch had been claimed by aromatic thyme, pale yellow flowered mouse-ear hawkweed and white mouse-ear chickweed.

This could have been a small hill farm anywhere in this part of South Wales, the entrance lane grass-grown along the centre now that this no longer needed to cope with the pressure of horses' hooves in this motorised age. And so back to the carpark, with its newly planted border of rowan, alder, sallow and sycamore. Then up through the engine shed, with its parked rolling stock and heavy equipment and so to the platform where the others had just started to board.

* * *

The original abandoned railway stretched for five and a half miles along steep gradients and through the Torpantau Tunnel which, at 1,313 feet above sea level, was said to be the highest railway tunnel in Great Britain. The present line, inaugurated around 1982, was only negotiable as yet for about half this distance.

The views away to the left along the first lap to Pontsticill were superb, the land falling steeply away to the rocky course of the Taf Fechan River, cutting into wooded slopes, with patches of farmland patterning the fields beyond. The original line joined from the right as we proceeded north and a branch line following below to the left veered away as we gained elevation, the part that had followed just below being replaced by a footway. Also below was a great spoil heap of material excavated from the Morlais Tunnel of the London and Great Western Railway.

Across the gorge was the Vaynor Quarry, still in the limestone belt and from which most of the ballast laid for the new tourist line had been sourced. (The old ballast had been taken for road making, the track and bridge girders removed and most of the railway buildings in ruins, so the enterprise had had to start all over again.) (Vaynor Quarry was famous botanically for the great spreads of purple flowered fairy foxgloves (Erinus) climbing all over the rocky spoil tips)

To our right the mountain rose steeply, partly as a newly quarried cliff, so the distant views were all to the west - away to Ystrad Ffellte and the scenic headwaters of the River Neath. The streams we crossed tumbling down to the smaller branch of the Upper Taff were less spectacular than those.

We rumbled through the first station and on past the Merthyr Tydfil sailing Club Headquarters. About half way to Dol-y-Gaer, by the junction of the larger Pontsticill Reservoir and the smaller Pentwyn Reservoir, we halted on a double section of line where our steam locomotive was uncoupled from the front and hitched to the back for the return. It seemed that either the track or the available rolling stock were not adequate to take us any further.

There was a quarter of an hour break at the Pontsticill Station for strolling, visiting the little café or utilising the viewing seats or children's play area. Then the main party rattled back on the return journey to a hot lunch, ordered in advance at the Pant Cafe. I had opted to take sandwiches and do some local exploration, catching the next train back.

It was good sitting at a sunny table on the platform with my ham and cambozola provender, taking in the view. The long reservoir was as blue as the sky, backed by dark, largely coniferous, forest and forming a tranquil foreground for the Beacons beyond. Constructed in 1927, this can hold 3,400 million gallons of water.

I saw not a single water bird. Even in winter water fowl were scarce here, as a result of the poverty of nutrients in the clear lake waters. These spring from acid, peaty uplands beyond the limestone belt, making little input to nourish a basis for the food chain. The surface was broken only by red and white floats for mooring the sailing dinghies - all of which were beached at present.

It was nice to see the three high tops again. They could scarcely be called peaks, because the upper strata of the Old red Sandstone of which they are composed is extra hard and resists erosion, having been dubbed the ORS capstone. Almost horizontal strata form the level tops. The middle summit, Pen-y-Fan, at 2,096 feet, is the highest point in South Wales. To its right is the Cribyn, to its left Corn Ddu.

Duly fed and watered, I set off down the stony track to the lane running between reservoir and railway with its rusty bogeys, sleepers and the like alongside. Gated beyond the station exit, this was effectively a walkway only except for boat owners, the main road over the pass being away to the west.

Like the Pembrokeshire lanes so lately left, this was decked with foxglove and red campion, other shades of pink introduced by wild roses and the more flamboyant flowers of *Rosa rugosa*, which seems to have acquired the name of Japanese rose. Herb Robert, common vetch and lesser knapweed kept to the rosy colour scheme, interrupted by a lush growth of ferns under field maple and wild cherry trees.

I walked across the dam, following the finger post pointing to The Red Cow Inn, a famous landmark, on the other side. The road was walled along its upper flank and I had to stand on tiptoe to see the water below. The long view was downstream over the roofs of the new water treatment works on the original valley floor far below. There was no rush of water down the front of the restraining embankment, as often. This was grassed, with ornamental trees and Rhododendrons at the west end, the denuded rivulet flowing modestly from its base.

A pied wagtail criss-crossed the road ahead, perching on the rail which was decorated by a series of spider webs, stretched between the uprights and thickly speckled with more tiny midges than any normal spider could be expected to consume unaided. House martins flipped past, scooping up others from the air and I thought I heard a cuckoo. Or did I? These are sadly very rare nowadays except in more remote places than this.

Why, I wondered, were these big dams not used as a source of generating power. So many folk relied on water power in the past, waylaying a river in a holding pond upstream of the point of requirement and releasing the pent up power through a leat as required.

The view to the east was of a sloping, grassy hillside dotted with small hawthorns and grazed mainly by horses, but also some store cattle and sheep, the hilltop terminating in a low horizontal rocky cliff. The road veered away downstream at the dam end, past a mound clothed in lush plant life - a riot of foxgloves at present, with rosebay willow herb to come. Here, too, was yellow lady's bedstraw and white pignut and, on a balder patch, yellow crosswort, wild thyme and ripe strawberries. Maidenhair spleenwort ferns clung to the masonry.

I moved a short distance up the reservoir bank, peering down into the great circular vortex into which excess flood water must disappear when the level rises, to pour over the gently rounded brink. As anticipated, there was practically no aquatic vegetation and nothing very exciting on the sloping beach, which alternates between wet and dry according to the state of supply and demand for the precious liquid.

But time was limited. I had a train to catch and quickened my pace when I noticed that this was already standing at the platform. I made it, with just time for an ice cream, and joined the others at Pant for the homeward drive.

Midsummer day, Saturday the 21st June, dawned grey and murky, so the hopefuls waiting for sunrise at Stonehenge would have been disappointed. There was a healthy influx of birds probing the rain-soaked lawn. The flock of great tits was new, suggesting the recent fledging of a large family. Starlings, even house sparrows from the house next door, joined blackbirds, thrushes, dunnock and robin on the lawn, then an undersized squirrel. Was this from a second litter? It was a darkish brown, or may have seemed so because of wet fur.

Then came a feline newcomer, not seen before, black and white with bushy black tail, causing the avian foragers to scatter. Not only did the interloper chase off the resident Ginger Pop, but he raised a quivering tail to stamp a bogus sign of ownership on the plant trough that was Ginger's lying-in-wait spot by the bird bath. The previous day an unknown black cat had stalked through, followed by the resident white Persian. This territory was becoming crowded, Ginger would have to fight his corner instead of fleeing.

Later on, stretching my legs around Windsor Crescent, I came upon two handsome and unusual weeds. One was a robust flowering plant of greater celandine - a member of the poppy family with orange sap - anchored half way up a stone wall which showed no visible cracks for attachment. The other was a clump of handsome, waist high spikes of purple toadflax, firmly rooted in the ground, unlike its commoner relative, the ivy-leaved toadflax, which seldom leaves a wall uncolonised.

Clive came after lunch to sort out a computer problem and transported me back for a pleasant evening meal. First I was to renew my acquaintance with the two cats, six rabbits and little flock of budgerigars. While he took on the role of chef, Lynne and I strolled around the lovely garden, full of colour although undergoing major renovations -a new flight of steps up the wooded bank, conversion of lawn to flower beds and renovation of the water feature, currently glowing with yellow Mimulus or monkey flower. I left with a haul of young plants of nasturtium (Tropaeolum) and lady's mantle (Alchemilla) and a mini rockery of tall yellow stonecrop for my balcony.

I was out bright and early on Sunday morning planting these on the slope outside my windows, so near and yet so far when it came to carrying soil and water. This was in the teeth of a ferocious wind, coupled with gale warnings on the media. By the end of that wild but sunny day the lawn was strewn with severed lime fruits ripped from their hold, along with a few leafy branches.

* * *

Monday the 23rd June was the perfect summer day, like so many Mondays following wet, windy or grey weekends, so when Madeleine Beswick phoned and suggested a visit to Dyffryn Gardens at Bonvilston, six or seven miles west of Cardiff, I readily acquiesced.

This estate dates back to the seventh century, but it was the shipping magnate, John Corey and family, owners from the late nineteenth century, who were significant in shaping the lovely old house and planning the beautiful estate and gardens. They financed plant hunting expeditions to far places, as did so many estate owners who made their fortunes from industrial enterprises. The gardens, a grade I Heritage Site, were currently being restored with support from the Lottery Heritage Fund.

My Extra Mural Natural History Groups had enjoyed many residential weekend courses here - from early Friday evening to late Sunday afternoon, two evening lectures and two days in the field. At first we had been billeted in the fine old house, in bedrooms larger than any short of dormitories that I had slept in elsewhere. Then a new block was built, with normal, hostel sized bedroom accommodation and a refectory. Now that entire block had been demolished. How time moves on!

The car park had been greatly enlarged and the Soay sheep flock had gone from the entrance field. I also missed the great glasshouse near the mansion, where coconuts had germinated and bananas and lemons bore fruit. Gone, too, was the cactus and orchid house from the walled garden, along with almost all the roses that formerly thrived within the walls. We peered through the iron gate here at the invading undergrowth and learned that this was due for renovation as soon as funds were available. New, tourist type buildings now clustered about the entrance.

We missed the circular pond and the little garden tea house, but the heather bank was still there, newly stocked with small plants of different colours. The great sloping rockery, with its two flights of steps, derelict when last seen, had been magnificently renovated and was a mass of colour, from the deep hues of bloody cranesbill through brilliant yellow to the snowy white of dwarf Parahebe.

Water cascaded down the cliff into a curved, sparkling pool occupied by drifts of dark green water milfoil and pale green stonewort or Chara. This last is a green alga with a difference, the linear branches simulating the feathered pinnate leaves of the other.

There must have been hundreds of great pond snails crawling over rocks, hoovering up the algal coating, or occasionally hanging upside down from the surface film, to which they clung with their big flat foot, maintaining suction because of the absence of intervening air pockets. There were well grown tadpoles and tiny fish, pond skaters dimpling the surface film and leaving quartets of shadows on the bed, also whirligig beetles scudding haphazardly hither and yon.

A healthy population of blue damselflies was on the wing, many of them coupled, the blue male holding his much drabber mate by the scruff of her neck. Sometimes they progressed in line ahead, sometimes with one of the bodies arched to make a heart shape. First the male curved round to transfer his sperm from the genital opening at the back to the copulatory opening near the front. Then she bent her genitals at the hind end forwards and helped herself to his contribution to their potential offspring. Some were depositing eggs among the water weed.

We continued across the Archery Lawn, watching players on the Croquet lawn in front of the house, and so into the Arboretum. Some of the finest trees here were limes, with leafy skirts dipping to ground level, there being no livestock to keep them trimmed back to an elevated horizontal base. Most magnificent of all was a monster double trunked lime seen later between the Australian and Mediterranean Gardens.

At the far end, against the southern boundary lane - a former location for the rare, white-flowered butterbur - we turned back to the old walled stream winding its way across a hummocky lawn. This had been a haunt of freshwater shrimps but was now dry. A nearby walnut tree was loaded with clusters of unripe nuts. Along the Vine Walk, we deployed ourselves in the Folly Garden. Here were four crescentic pools alternating with flower beds. Feathery water milfoil dominated again but there was also attractive wavy-edged curled pondweed *(Potamogeton crispus)*.

The broad four-sided pool at the end of the great lawn was in poor shape with little more than a murky puddle of water on the crumpled lining, but it produced our two best wildlife sightings. One was a cute ginger-brown bank vole, nibbling grass on the margin, then disappearing into a burrow penetrating outside the liner. This was one of many such holes, suggesting a thriving population.

The other was a very active gathering of broad-bodied chaser dragonflies *(Libellula depressa)*. Both sexes are yellow on emerging from the pupa, but the males turn powder blue as they mature. All seen here were mature blue males, with no yellow females around to pursue. The short flattened body of this species makes it unmistakable.

More of these were zooming over the long central pool, where the white water lily flowers were of normal size but the round floating leaves were smaller than in our common native species. Not for the first time, we admired the intricate carving of the sinuous, bristly dragon on the main fountain, the central bowl supported on what resembled an outsize oriental pekinese.

Four buzzards sailed languidly over the great lawn, buoyed up by the rising warm air that caused us to seek out benches in the shade rather than the sun - and Madeleine only just back from Ibiza! Now, at the height of the breeding season, this number wheeling together must represent two newly fledged young with their parents. Surprisingly there were also swifts shooting across at low elevations although it is usually cloud and mist that brings these down to low levels. Both song and mistle thrushes foraged on the lawns, with blackbirds, robins, starlings and jackdaws.

We threaded a series of garden rooms, the Cloisters, the Pomeian and the Theatre room, where chairs were already set out in a marquee for a Shakespearian performance scheduled for the weekend, all tickets already sold. As so often, it was the trees that deserved the greatest accolade, the various Ginkgo or maidenhair trees, tulip tree, dawn redwood, red-trunked myrtles and the green and yellow double conifers, that have featured on the approach lawns for as long as I can remember.

The broad walk between the long herbaceous borders was spanned by a series of wrought iron arches draped with climbing roses. All were pink, most double, but the deep crimson of the single flowers of the American pillar roses outshone them all.

Many of the robust herbs were not yet in flower but there was already a fine show of colour. Giant bellflower and other Campanulas, tall mullein, greater meadow rue, marguerites, tansy and shorter Zinnia and catmint were showing their paces. Purple Clematis and a showy purple Solanum, with the little peak of yellow stamens so characteristic of the genus, scrambled up the high north wall. A workman, precariously perched and well away from his ladder, was sitting his way along the top of this wall, sweeping off debris and weeds.

We emerged by devious ways through sunken gardens to the main amphitheatre, past the Chinese Philosopher, still riding his ox as in decades past, following in part the notices and suspended tree lights which would guide the theatre goers to the leafy arbour housing the performance. We cooled off with an ice cream in the Exhibition Room, where exhibits included a fine watercolour of one of the rose arches linking the specimen flower borders. Prize specimens in the formal beds on the terrace were ice plants, their succulent leaves and stems an astonishing deep reddish purple, set off by vibrant red, white and green associates.

Apparently the ultimate fate of the mansion was still in the balance, awaiting the necessary finance. There was talk of it becoming a headquarters for the Princes' Trust and certainly Prince Charles had been here recently, looking it over.

* * *

Hailey Park, on the east bank of the River Taff, upstream of Llandaff North road bridge and right along to the main line railway bridge where the Melin Griffith feeder canal rejoins the river, was the scene of our natural history walk on 23rd June. The voluntary group, "Friends of Hailey park" and one of the county council's wardens, who jointly manage the area, were hosting a deputation from the Cardiff Naturalists' Society.

My memories of this area were of a splendid show of early spring daffodils on the mown grass of the south and a great expanse of dumped rubble being levelled out in the north-westward swoop of the river between the two railway bridges. The daffodils were safely recuperating below ground and the northern area had developed into an extensive lush meadowland with open shrubbery and mosaic of marshy hollows.

At first we followed upstream alongside the riparian strip of woodland, checking on tree species and admiring a bumper crop of green walnuts and an unusual number of green marble galls on oaks, which were producing the first lamas shoots of summer. These young, red leaves contain a toxin which deters insect pests and compensates for loss of foliage to earlier generations of hungry munchers.

New to me was the way of telling the leaves of Norway maple from those of sycamore. Those of the first exude a drop of milky juice when pulled away from the twig, those of sycamore do not. Sallows were occasionally affected by patches of orang rust fungus, alders were not the native British species, while limes and field maples contributed to the variety of winged fruits. Various poplars, aspen and a range of willows were scrutinised.

I enquired why the half way iron bridge carrying the old mineral railway line and footway across the river to northern Danescourt had been closed to foot traffic. "It was the railway company. They didn't want the liability." Whether the liability of someone falling off or the bridge falling down wasn't known.

Already we had passed the play areas and football pitches and were alongside the meadowland. Overshadowing much else was reed canary grass, tall oat and hard rush with a range of other grasses, false fox and hairy sedge and a liberal spattering of small bushes, mostly sallow.

Big patches of yellow were contributed by greater bird's-foot trefoil and there was melilot, yellow pea, perforated St. John's wort and silverweed. We found common spotted orchids with ox-eye daisies. The southern marsh orchids were over. Later we crept into a woody thicket to admire the broad helleborine orchids, some with green flowers and some with red. Gorse and broom provided winter colour and there was much more.

It was not so long since I had scrunched my way across the rubble on this expanse - which was an old landfill site, with who knows what just under the surface. The "awkward phase" of thistles, yellow composites and other weeds had passed and it was veritably a "brown field site" turned green. Some had been mown, to keep the woody plants at bay and war was being waged on alien invaders.

One of our shaggy dog members played up beautifully when I lightly dropped a sprig of cleavers or goose grass over his neck to demonstrate its clinging properties. Both forepaws were used in turn to dislodge the weightless morsel, which could not possibly have been felt through all that fur but obviously tickled.

Plunging into woodland again, we followed a narrow path and dropped down to beach level on the downstream side of the bridge carrying the northern commuter railway line to Cardiff. This spot yielded all the best sightings of the evening.

A pair of dippers was spotted against the line of revetments on the opposite shore and we learned of several sightings of otters on this stretch. The air was full of swooping swifts and sand martins. The latter were popping in an out of small drainage holes under the railway track, like others in urban Merthyr Tydfil, which build their nests in lower drainage pipes in the river wall. Three kingfisher nests, remarkably close to each other, were known to the locals. River banks were evidently not without nesting holes. Could there be other sand martins there, as in years gone by?

The bridge itself was worthy of note - almost a viaduct with five broad arches. The nearside one was occupied by an enormous amount of gravel and rounded river pebbles at the outlet of the Melin Griffith feeder canal, below the famous pump. We climbed the mound of detritus and slithered down the other side to a very humble stream running out at right angles to river flow to empty under the second arch, previous flows having effectively blocked its direct passage.

We could have leapt across now but the locals reported the flow to be frighteningly fierce in times of spate. It must be, to have moved that amount of material and deposited much more in the river downstream, as ever changing pebble beaches where picnic parties came to paddle and bathe now that the water was crystal clear again and where a line fishermen was currently trying his luck.

The solid stone bridge stanchions did not show that the super structure had been built on three separate occasions, as new commuter lines were added. Young trees had rooted in invisible cracks between the martins' nests. Looking up we were aware of mini forests of dangling limestone straws hanging from the ceiling, water seeping down their hollow centres to help growth by depositing more lime, grain by grain, before dripping off.

Seepages on the walls had deposited layer upon layer of tufa, bulging ever outwards in attractive lobed formations more often seen on the walls of caves. Other, brisker, seepages were nourishing little patches of dark green *Conocephalum conicum*, a slabby liverwort common on the sides of woodland streams.

A railed footpath followed the edge of the line across this bridge, but that was on the other side of the track, accessible from the path alongside the feeder canal. We stayed on the south side, admiring the marsh vegetation with figwort, red valerian and marsh woundwort, where reed buntings had nested.

Some of the pebbly rubble had been left as heaps and these, apparently, were favoured by reptiles. Common lizards had been seen here and a three foot long grass snake, forager in the pools round about. The reptiles which we saw were four slow worms, exposed when the slab of tarred felt put down for their convenience was lifted. This was at the end of a narrow track penetrating a brambly thicket, so was little disturbed. Three of these little legless lizards remained for prolonged viewing.

Our hosts had been busy with their digital cameras, photographing a whole range of insects seen on the site. Portrayed were dragonflies, grasshoppers, beetles, bees and bugs, butterflies and moths, even a pygmy shrew - the fruits of countless hours of waiting and watching.

We parted company under fruiting wild cherry trees where the path emerged onto the road leading out of Llandaff North to the Canal Nature Reserve at Velindre. This dipped beneath the oblique crossing of the railway. Some converged on refreshments here. Bruce MacDonald and I did a shortened version of the walk to regain our cars.

An old acquaintance, not seen for a long time, was present - Harold Boudier from Penarth. He brought the sad news that my ex colleague, John Perkins, had died a fortnight before on 11th June. A geologist and my co-tutor on many a field excursion at home and abroad, John had conducted us around the geological marvels of all the national parks in Western North America and many volcanoes, from Mount St. Helens to others in the Canary Islands and, of course, Hawaii, finest of them all, not to mention our local Heritage Coast and mountains.

Regrettably, though much younger than me, he had to retire early with Parkinson's disease - with which he lived on his own for many years. He did not let it bother him too much - continuing to take long walks with the "Ramblers", who came to call themselves "Shamblers" as the years advanced. I had lost touch, but many of his students, who he had imbued with a love of geology and landscape, had not. A sad loss this, but he had lived a full life and enhanced the lives of many others in the doing.

CHAPTER 24

A 'Townee' Guest, Lewis Merthyr Colliery, Penrhys, Rhondda and Cynheidre Railway Project

The week spanning the transition from June to July was the one scheduled for the visit to Wales of my ninety-one year old brother John. Unfortunately it proved to be almost the wettest week of the summer. Sunny spells intruded on a few days, but the sky was mostly overcast and chilly winds were almost unrelenting.

Throughout his stay he saw my major asset, the distant mountain view as seen through the Taff Gorge, only dimly, shrouded in clammy mist or not at all. This was a pity. He was greatly perturbed at my 'dumbing down' from an eight-roomed house with commodious gardens and lock up garage to a two-roomed flat with a mere share in a public garden which could only be reached by lift or stairs, and an open carpark. I had hoped to persuade him that it was really not as debilitating as it seemed, but circumstances were against me. He left slightly mollified but not convinced.

Telephoning from London at 4.0 pm on 26th June, he said he was just leaving and expected to arrive some three hours hence. In fact it was nearer five hours. His weather deteriorated from the balmy sunshine of which England's South-east corner gets more than its fair share, to a steady downpour pushed sideways by boisterous westerlies.

I spent the two penultimate hours waiting in the public lounge to guide him in, with the occasional descent to my quarters to see if he had phoned to say the line was blocked by a fallen tree or some such disaster.

At last I spotted him, toiling up the steep slope from the railway station, so near horizontally but so far vertically. He came in through the lounge doors with rain dripping from his bald pate where the headwind had blown the hood of his mackintosh cape back. He appeared undaunted. "Oh, I'm used to rain."

Climbing the open steps from the central platform, he had turned north instead of south, heading, very understandably, towards the station's only building, which happened to be on the platform beside the river and the no-man's land beyond. He found the double flight down to the hollow where the steep lane petered out after dipping under the three railway lines, and headed off across the Taff via the footbridge!

Sheltering under trees on the Taff Trail cycleway heading north, he encountered two walkers, who didn't know Brynteg but thought it must be on the other side of the river. So, seasoned rail traveller that he had always been, he made it eventually, but it could scarcely have been under less propitious circumstances.

The traditional 'cuppa', steaming lamb casserole and hot rhubarb crumble made amends, as did his subsequent sleeping accommodation in the next door flat. The one and only guest room supposed to accommodate the needs of 52 flat dwellers when the building becomes full, was already allocated when I tried to book it several weeks earlier. Instead we were allowed one of the fully furnished "show apartments", which happened to be next door on the other side of the stairway and proved much more convenient. He used only the bedroom and bathroom, not even the tea making facility, knowing there would be early morning tea next door after listening to the news on my spare radio.

* * *

All next day, Friday, 27th June, the rain continued unrelentingly. For the first time since moving in, I unpacked my mackintosh, not because it hadn't rained before but because I chose not to go out when it did.

The high spot of the week was planned to be his first visit to Flatholm Island, this involving transit through the great sea lock from Cardiff Bay to the open channel. Highlights promised on the island to appeal to a non-naturalist were the old sunken gun emplacements and underground munition stores, the lighthouse tower and foghorn building and the old Victorian Barracks, Isolation Hospital and farmhouse, with several thousand nesting gulls thrown in for good measure.

It had been a matter of juggling dates to book two passages on the boat. Our booking on the Saturday had to be cancelled because of bad weather and we were offered seats for the following Tuesday, but that trip too, had to be cancelled at the last minute. My back-up programme of less exciting visits had to be expanded.

We spent much of that first wet day cruising round town in the car. As a knowledgeable railway historian who had explored the complex South Wales Railway system intimately long before I moved into South Wales permanently as a post war student in 1945, my guest was saddened at the final demise of the Railway Shunting Yards and the loss of the great part that they had played in getting coal down from the mining valleys to the docks.

Last time he was here we had traversed them on foot, through a riot of wild flowers and burgeoning shrubbery, to the old signal box under the abandoned Radyr Quarry. This time the area was choc-a-bloc with three and four storey houses and flats alongside a maze of cul-de-sacs and slip roads with parking lots but few garages.

This accommodation for hundreds of new residents had been fabricated without a single amenity: no shop, no post office, no village hall, no petrol station, no church, no pub, no bus service. The new bridge spanned one of the two railway lines but there was no bridge over the river to provide an escape to Whitchurch. All those car owners had to thread their way out through Radyr from the exit road converging on the station. Fortunately Brynteg's steep approach road was a one way system which they had no need to use.

Our motorised browse took us by the lower entrance to Radyr Woods. I popped out briefly to see if the new foal was sheltering in the stable. He was, along with the mare and two colts. They came out to see if I had brought them any comfort - permitting my closest view yet of the new arrival.

Our wet exploration of the old green belt's new suburbia extended around the labyrinth of Danescourt downstream. We finished up parked alongside Roath lake, watching swans and geese asleep on the wet grass, the weather submitting them to no more than the fleeting passage of 'water on a duck's back', this rolling off in silver balls.

* * *

Instead of the next morning's early start to catch the Saturday boat to Flatholm, the vacated day provided an opportunity to look at some of the old mining valleys. It was many years since I had been a regular visitor there, exploring the bleak mountain tops, steep woodlands and gully torrents with local naturalists. The wealth of public transport had made their built-up parts a favourite stamping ground for brother John in the years before that. If he came with the parents to visit me at Gwaelod during the sixties and seventies, he was likely to take off on public transport to Cardiff or the Valley towns while we went somewhere more scenic.

Now, in 2008, I had decided to go part of the way up Rhondda Fawr, across the mountain divide and back down Rhondda Fach, the smaller of the two Rhondda tributaries of the Taff. We followed the old valley road through Hawthorn, Tonteg and Trefforest and not until negotiating the Valleys' hub of Pontypridd did I recall the much advertised tourist attraction of the Lewis Merthyr Colliery at Trehafod. Of course! Just the place to interest a non-naturalist.

As we neared the site the railway line ran along the right hand flank of the road close against an artificial cliff cut into the base of the mountain, but there was plenty of flat land by the loop road to the left. Extensive, tree-girt plots had been allocated for the parking of cars and coaches.

Alongside a striking mural depicting the hazards and horrors endured by miners of the industrial age, we explored various rooms typifying those of the close-set cottages to which the workers returned - to the tin bath in front of the kitchen fire - until someone dreamed up the luxury of pithead baths.

Across the 'street' were old time butcher's and hardware shops, depicting the lasts that cobblers used to nail heftier soles onto hefty boots and a host of other DIY tools, flat irons, scrubbing boards and the paraphernalia of that hardworking age, not forgetting the best china teapot and other treasures kept as show pieces in the front room used only for special occasions such as funerals - by the few who could afford the space.

There was lofty winding gear controlling the lifts descending into the bowels of the earth, both inside and outside the massive winding house, coal trucks and vehicles, but also an unexpected feature of natural history interest. The event of the day was a rose festival. Gardens and allotments, a necessary adjunct to lives spent in day-long darkness and with scanty food budgets, had spawned a tradition of gardening in the Valleys, with no shortage of exhibitors among the miners' offspring.

The show did not open until one pm, but I peeped through the crack of the marquee entrance when the panel of judges was at work inside. Bush roses, thick with unopened flower trusses, had been carried out into the open. The big tent was currently decked with a galaxy of rose blooms, of every shape and colour, single and double.

While John examined coal trucks and a Rhondda bus I explored the leafy perimeter of the site and came across two alien alder trees. The poplar-leaved or Italian alder (*Alnus cordata*), with shining heart-shaped leaves, scarcely serrated, was the rarer of the two. It resembles a poplar with baffling similarity until one spots the large but characteristic bunches of green or brown fruiting cones. The other, the grey alder (*Alnus incana*) lacked the smooth-edged, flat-topped leaves of our native *Alnus glutinosa* and was commonly planted on municipal sites and to reclaim refuse tips, because the root nodules enrich the soil by their ability to 'fix' atmospheric nitrogen, as members of the pea family do.

Most intriguing of the botanical highlights was the complex maze of woven living willow wands. Willow weaving was practised at our own Forest Farm, but this circular edifice of osiers struck a different note and was constantly tended, as shown by the weaving in of new sprouts to form roofs over the circular walls that topped muddy trackways worn by the feet of many children as they ran through the maze. This was a more permanent innovation than the annually produced maize maze at Radyr's Gelynis Farm.

* * *

We continued up the valley to Ystrad where I was hoping to recognise the sharply backward-turning road leading up over the mountain to the northern river. I did, but it did me no good. A kind driver waited at the top for me to achieve the first steep, narrow lap, only to find myself thwarted by "Road Closed" signs round the corner. And I had seen the name "Old Penrhys Road" at the bottom, so I knew I was on course.

An awkward turn on a steep gradient and back to the valley floor. Further along a new Penrhys Road branched off at a similar angle. It was not much less steep than the other and cars were passing my little Yaris as they got up speed to tackle the main hairpin bend above.

Things were very different at the summit from those which I remembered. In place of the grassy pull-off at the site of the ancient statue marking the medicinal well, was a new, neatly manicured roundabout and a capacious carpark with embayments decoratively floored with squared rocks and red bricks.

We nosed into the low hedged wall for our thermos coffee. The ridge stretched away southwards to the cairn at Mynydd Troed-y-Rhiw. The golf course on a lower knob to its west, lay at 327 metres - a true mountain, topping a thousand feet. We watched a broad based mowing machine cutting swathes of greener green across the distant fairways and saw a red-coated horseman riding along the horizon, but no sign of the once active hunt.

Penrhys village perched on the summit behind us, was a quite featureless collection of embarrassingly plain council houses - visible from both valleys and almost everywhere else within miles. Occupying the most conspicuous site in the local uplands, it had been dubbed an eyesore right from the start. Even the Prince of Wales, who is not permitted to be too outspoken, condemned it. The houses still stood, after several decades, but the Council had done its best to brighten up the local summit landmark for sightseers.

We emerged into the more than brisk wind to investigate the tall grey monument of "Our Lady of Penrhys". She had been moved onto an expanse of neatly mown lawn surrounded by walls. Below the brink of her grassy platform where I tried unsuccessfully to trace the old well of healing waters was a semi circular auditorium with eight tiers of timber-edged seats separated by grey ballast.

Views in all directions over adjacent summits and the valley towns huddled below were superb. I could imagine classes of children and, indeed, adults seated there having the diverse landmarks pointed out.

A kestrel hovered motionless in the blue void above, watching for a minute movement of potential prey in that vast landscape. Swifts swooped back and forth, quite at home on the windy heights and able to sleep on the wing at much greater elevations than these.

The well, which I recall as always muddy and unimposing, was nowhere to be found. The statue had been set on a new stepped plinth. On one side was a faint inscription including the date 1538; on the other 1953, presumably that of a renovation, and long enough for the circular growths of white lichens to have obscured some of the inscriptions. Walls surrounding the statue were embellished with native ferns, not only the common maidenhair spleenwort and much nobler polypody, but shining triangular fronds of black spleenwort. Sheep had been banished and the whole hillside bore a creditable hay crop dominated by tall oat grass with cocksfoot, ryegrass and Yorkshire fog, lightened with tall meadow buttercup and meadow vetchling with yellow pea flowers.

I would like to have walked along the ridge, but was expecting visitors, invited when I had no idea where we might be heading. We drove down from the ridge as steeply as we had driven up, heading up the lesser valley to emerge in the upper suburbs of Stanleytown between Tylorstown and Pont-y-Gwaith above Wattstown. The 'town' of these names is a mere formality. Housing in the Rhondda Valleys is continuous and there is no knowing where one borough ends and another begins. We hadn't been all that high but we seemed to be driving downhill all the way to Porth at the junction of the two valleys and on down to their confluence with the Taff at Pontypridd.

Next came a pleasant domestic spell at home with Clive and Lynne, who had met John only briefly at Christmas in Gwaelod-y-Garth eighteen months before. Gil Barter of the Countryside Council for Wales visited later in the day to renew her acquaintance. John had known her father in London for many years, both of them being involved in the world of public transport.

* * *

Usually when John visited Wales I put him in touch with Martin Doe, who is deeply involved in renovating an old, full-sized railway at Cynheidre four miles north of Llanelli, as a king pin of the Llanelli and Mynydd Mawr railway Company. Martin was one of only two schoolboys who attended my adult education classes as sixth formers. Both were amateur naturalists domiciled in the Rhondda, the other being Phillip Masters, who worked on hedgerows in the Vale of Glamorgan for his initial research.

As a sixth former at Howardian School in East Cardiff, Martin was one of the founder members of the Howardian Nature Reserve, which started as a school project backed by the County Council, and he took over the running of it when the school closed. He was still deeply involved there, as well as with the railway, having served for many years as chairman of "The Friends of Howardian" and put in countless hours of tree planting, scrub bashing, grass cutting, hay raking, pond digging, step building and the like alongside the County Council's wardens.

Now, as a fully blown solicitor, he was bringing his administrative skills to bear in keeping the Cynheidre Railway project in business, conjuring up generous grants of many thousands of pounds from various charitable institutions, lottery funds and conservation bodies. His enthusiasm for the practical side was no less bountiful than that for the paperwork - well seen when he reminisced about great bonfires of defunct wooden sleepers, huge machines running berserk, spillages, mud and muddle.

Conservationists as well as railway buffs, he and his group had planted many thousands of trees, levelled land, bulldozed vehicle tracks, dug out and renovated old ponds and ditches and excavated new ones.

I got involved initially with the basic plant survey needed to comply with the planner's requirements. The finished railway line will run alongside the countrywide cycle track - the whole tract of abandoned mining land with its colliery ponds and spontaneous woodlands becoming something in the nature of a country park.

The group of amateurs had raised many hundreds of pounds selling salvaged railway lines unsuitable for re-use to the lucrative old iron market. Also the iron 'chairs' in which they had rested on the wooden sleepers, those often rotten and sometimes burned away on great bonfires if they failed to disengage. Much of the proceeds had been used to buy rolling stock, examined by John on his winter visit eighteen months before, when it was in store at Llangennach, four miles north-east of Llanelli. Now they had erected a spanking new shed to house some of it, although their best engine was being overhauled elsewhere.

A new entrance road had been pushed through a hillside, the tall banks sown with grasses and trees. Plots had been protected with new wooden fencing and iron gates with bench and table picnic sites installed.

Some of the money for all this came from weekly car boot sales which the group organised in a Llanelli carpark. There was one on the day of our visit, when about eighty car owners came to sell and a hundred came to buy, their entry fees going to help the railway project. Martin was in charge of this today and had to be on duty from 7.30 am. So, instead of getting a lift both ways by car, John and I went by train and he met us at Llanelli Station at one o'clock. We left Radyr in mellowed sunshine and arrived at Llanelli just as it started to rain!

He drove us around the site, as far as the great dump of old lines, those lying across the heap bowed down at both ends with their own weight. Then he swathed me in a brand new yellow workman's hip length waterproof from his car boot and left me to explore the plant life while he showed his fellow enthusiast round the engine shed, wheeled trophies and new developments generally.

* * *

I set off looking like a police woman, grateful at first for the protection from gusty cold wind and rain but far too hot when the sun finally appeared. As on most 'brown field sites', the land unaffected by herbicides or fertilisers had produced a wide range of plants.

Arid chippings supported pink centaury, white eyebright, red dead nettle and purple tufted vetch. Untrodden soil along fence lines produced taller growths with evening primrose, knapweed, perforated St. John's wort, self heal, a wealth of yellow Composites and scattering of common spotted orchids.

I walked on up the line to the start of the broad bordering ditch, parts of which had been cleared of choking vegetation at different times, my purpose being to see the general sequence of recolonisation by different plants.

En route I passed a new, irregular shaped pond, dug into the hillside and consisting still of largely open water. Tree saplings had been planted on the smooth. shaly slope behind, leaving the shallows towards the rail track open.

There were few truly aquatic plants as yet, apart from a small clump of common water starwort. A submerged stand of water mint seemed quite happy in this medium, which it shared with flote grass. The further end of the pond merged into a bank of mature sallow bushes and taller vegetation, principally hemlock water dropwort.

Much the most remarkable was a small patch dominated by the annual celery-leaved buttercup (*Ranunculus sceleratus*), a not very common species which is more often found in brackish waters bordering saltmarshes. Always variable, depending on the presence or absence and height of neighbours, I had not seen it as variable as here.

The largest specimens had fleshy green stems as thick as my finger but remained no more than knee high. The smallest, though copiously branched, did not exceed two inches tall or broad. Both kinds and throughout the range, were full of flowers. The water form in the adjacent shallows was as different from these as could be, consisting of long stalked leaves with circular lobed blades floating on the surface and no flower stems. The two forms differed from each other as completely as the land and water forms of the much rarer hairy buttercup (*Ranunculus sardous*), which grows in the Howardian Nature reserve and adjacent sections of the lower Rhymney River valley. Was this just coincidence?

Whirligig beetles scudded over the water surface and a two-spot ladybird with black spots on red, skulked on the bank. Tall emergent plants colonising the most recently cleared open water included soldierly stands of completely unbranched water horsetail and less imposing unbranched sprigs of Eleocharis spike rush. Branched bur-reed, with generous clusters of spiky bobble fruits, invaded quite early, often with erect rather than floating flote grass.

Wafting across part of the pond bed was the only slender pondweed (*Potamogeton berchtoldii*) seen, the linear leaves no broader than the attenuated stems. Much more obvious were the tangled cushions of stonewort or brittlewort (*Chara*), three to six inches deep, the main axes beset throughout with whorls of branches. These are the most complex of all green algae, quick to colonise but competing poorly with other plants as the cover thickens.

The names arise from their affinity with the lime in calcium-rich waters, a crisp layer of lime scales settling over the surface. This turns the original fresh green colour to a murky grey and makes the plants brittle. At Cynheidre the Chara competes most successfully in the big lower pond bordered by a wide, solid concrete roadway which is regularly flooded to become part of the pond bed in winter. This must surely have been the source of lime there. Had plants from this established community been transferred to this new pond to get the succession off to a good start I wonder?

Although limestone quarries border the Coalfield to north and south, lime is very sparse on the naturally acid soils of the Coal Measures. There is no knowing what odd minerals could crop up on such intensively used industrial sites, and lime is an integral part of iron smelting at Llanelli, so some may have strayed hither or, more likely, be derived from the limestone ballast of the old railway track.

First to cover the open water with broad, oval floating leaves, often bronzed, was the slender pondweed's larger relative, broad-leaved pondweed (*Potamogeton natans*). Rarer and greener but similar was the water form of amphibious bistort with spikes of pink flowers, and marsh bedstraw, both under and above water. Blue-flowered brooklime, one of the speedwells, was another able to grow in or out of the water. The natural plant succession led on to Typha bulrush, hemlock water dropwort and great willow herb, with jointed rush common through all stages. Subordinates included lesser spearwort, purple loosestrife and meadowsweet. Sections of the ditch not cleared for some years were a solid mass of vegetation. No doubt there was still water beneath, but it was a poor lookout for the initial colonists, now starved of almost all light. Banks might be colonised by yellow fleabane, common horsetail, yellow pea, melilot and clover with saplings of sallow and birch establishing and eventually the inevitable brambles.

Only in the big old pond nearest to the engine shed did open water persist over the years. The level there is thought to be maintained by springs. Underwater leaves of great water plantain were present throughout. Only here did I see dense growths of the two tall emergents, common clubrush, formerly known as the true bulrush, and sea clubrush (*Schoenoplectus lacustris* and *Bolboschoenus maritimus*). Here, too, was more purple loosestrife, marginal gipsywort and forget-me-not, with land lubbers such as yellow rattle, strayed in from the grass understorey of the pine and larchwood which had engulfed the pasture across the road.

I disturbed a moorhen here but the snipe which visit in winter were far away now. While the wind was at its strongest, a buzzard headed into it and hung, motionless as a kestrel, buoyed up by its strength instead of gliding gently on the usual thermal. A collared dove passed by and there was a snatch of song from a blackcap, but birds generally seemed to be lying low at this sleepy time of the day.

Swallows were on the wing, wind or no wind. Formerly nesting in the green farm barn, some were prospecting around the eaves of the engine shed, this as large as an aircraft hangar. A pied wagtail patrolled the new roof.

When the sun emerged in mid afternoon a few butterflies appeared. Some had the orange patterned wings of meadow browns, others were ringlets, much less common and one of the few species likely to be seen on dull days. These were very dark, almost black, the line of hollow yellow rings standing out clearly on the underwings when they settled. Hawker dragonflies and others recorded here were not on show today, nor were the three recorded amphibians and three reptiles.

Part of the site had flooded with the cessation of anthracite mining here in 1989, less than twenty years before. Sustained by a gathering of small but sweet wild strawberries, I settled at one of the picnic tables to ponder the return of the wildscape. The transformed landscape was very different from the infertile hill grazings taken over by industry. Hopefully the diversity would remain when the new railway was up and running.

CHAPTER 25

Rhymney Mouth, Cardiff Bay and Cosmeston

Joining us on Monday June 30th, was Robert Hubbard, who had helped with my home move. He had worked with public transport in both London and continental Europe and had met John before. Between morning coffee and lunch the two of them were busy discussing the technicalities of railways, tramways and even shipping. Robert, like Martin before him, marvelled at the ninety one year old's ability to remember facts and figures regarding transport matters great and small in such meticulous detail.

The mist lifted as we ate and sunshine blessed our afternoon jaunt to parts of the Cardiff foreshore that even Robert, a land owner further along the coast, had not known about. He squeezed himself into the back of my two-door car, leaving the front passenger seat for the chap who always followed our route on the map, however long or short the journey.

Through the north-eastern suburbs, alongside Roath Lake and up Rumney Hill, we came down to sea level at the Brachdy Lane entrance to Lamby Lake. The 'sea' formerly visible from here, was now hidden behind partially wooded hillocks dappled with a mixture of grass and trees, concealing unimaginable quantities of domestic rubbish.

We failed to find any of this year's crop of knopper galls on the Brachdy pedunculate oaks, which were already covered with long-stalked acorns. The ground beneath, however, was littered with the bloated brownish leftovers which I had at first mistaken for the droppings of the formerly resident Shetland ponies. Those, sadly, were no more, their once threadbare paddock now overgrown with what might constitute a useful hay crop, although over-rich in coarse weed species.

Crossing the footbridge over the main London to West Wales Railway was quite a protracted procedure, because sundry goods trains as well as passenger services rumbled through in quick succession beneath. Freight trains carried great slabs of iron or steel, presumably from the Port Talbot Steel Works in West Glamorgan to Llanwern Steelworks near Newport for rolling into those great reels of metal sheeting that I used to see outside the West Glamorgan works when I was deployed along that stretch of coast. The return was necessary to link up with the deep water shipping berths down Channel for export.

John lingered at the viewpoint above the lake while Robert and I walked a short section of the shore looking at plants. His high spot was a first sighting of the handsome pink flowering rush *(Butomus umbellatus)* alongside fruiting capsules of yellow Iris and backed by exuberantly flowering sea club-rush - as seen the day before at another freshwater site. Other subjects worthy of photography were the mauve vervain, a Verbena, stately great lettuce *(Lactuca virosa)*, a plant of Southern England only just venturing into Wales, and the bristly fruit heads of little colonies of sea clover, this last a relic from the former saltmarsh of the old ox-bow.

Back to the main highway and along Rover Way to the other side of the lake, we crossed the still salty section of the River Rhymney at high tide, so no mud banks were exposed for wading birds. Dark red roses flowered in the hedgerow bounding Tredellech park with the lake, and the Fisherman Pond opposite the official lake carpark was showing the water lilies at their best.

We failed to locate the boulders half blocking the layby serving as carpark for the Nature Reserve of the Mitigation Canal which we had walked along on our recent visit here. Instead we continued and branched from the new main highway down Mardy Lane. This was unchanged from the single track byway typical of so much of this reen country.

The tall bounding hedges were relics of a past that some of the new tree plantings around the lake had already almost caught up with - less some of the knotty wooden tangles. Parking by the stables at the end of the road, we walked through to the canal, meeting it by the spinney where owls used to nest.

Upstream was a bridge over one of the penstocks where the flow could be controlled by insertion or removal of planks. The canal was narrow here, with reeds encroaching from both sides and the surface covered with duckweed. Several coots and a moorhen were spotted, these leaving trails of dark water across the mobile green counterpane, marking their erratic passage through the water.

A little further on John rested on a not very comfortable seat under the hedge while we went on to the bridges around the final broad pool of open water behind the sea wall. Clambering up the bank we found, not the great expanse of mud that I had promised my companion, but the high tide lapping right to the base of our bit of the sea defences.

I had assumed that our impromptu entry would connect with the old right of way along the summit, but that was no more, so unused that it had become effectually blocked by a tangle of wire and brushwood to our left. Nor was there any longer the former duplicate walkway along its seaward foot.

Rubbish tipping was still proceeding behind a tall wire mesh fence to our right. It seemed the coastal right of way had been blocked until this section was soil covered and grassed over, and that former users of the mile and a quarter long towpath beside the canal would have failed to find the cryptic entrance through the broken fence at the top and so not be looking for the former much used walkways.

A narrow beach of pebbles with salt-tolerant plants lay below and on it a darkly handsome young man on his knees, scrabbling among the pebbles. "He must be one of us. Only field biologists behave like that." He was. We called out to make his acquaintance and he proved to be a 'Spider man'.

Any new specimen located was captured and popped into a phial of alcohol for later identification, either by him or at the National Museum of Wales with which he liaised, although not on their staff. He recognised me as a fellow crank, so knew he had sympathetic hearers. We compared names of arachnologists and entomologists we had known, but had few in common. My acquaintances in that field were two generations ahead of his in time, most of them retired long ago. It made me feel very old.

Bird life was reasonably lively on our return, but did not include the usual mute swan family of other years. A heron flapped past mounds of stony rubble alongside others of solidified mud behind the sea wall. Hopefully this did not presage another industrial development on this pocket of reenland surviving between past developments and current tipping.

A kestrel crossed the canal from the tip, where it may have been seeking out small rodents, and there were plenty of finches about, the most vocal the greenfinches. I had a possible sighting of a reed bunting among the house sparrows by the old car yard as we left and the air over the stables was full of swallows. Most obvious, of course, were the gulls squabbling over the landfill site, and most obvious of the butterflies were large whites.

* * *

With the planned trip to Flatholm Island looming, I had set out one morning in June to discover a route through the city to the embarkation point on the shore of Cardiff bay. In the past I had always sailed from Barry Docks, in whatever sort of vessel, except for once when we left from Queen Alexandra Dock. That was the only Cardiff Dock still opening to the Bristol Channel outside the Barrage, and we had edged our way out through the original high sided lock which is still used by ocean-going vessels.

I located Jim Driscoll Way Quay, the new embarkation point, on the Taff side of the neck of land between the two rivers - just above their confluence to form the old Taff-Ely Roads. Opposite on the east was Hamadryad's new parkland by the old Seamen's Hospital of that name and formerly the site of the Old Glamorgan Canal sea lock.

The long man-made channel from Merthyr Tydfil in the hill country had crossed from there to the grassy Hamadryad Saltings and mud flats beyond. Once straight, then sinuous, but now no more: once salt, then fresh but now submerged for all time. The channel had been totally obliterated by the oblique viaduct which followed menacingly above the last lap of the old barge canal on which so much of Cardiff's prosperity had relied. Only photos of the sturdy stone walls of the sea lock and the bollards remain to tell of past endeavours.

The west bank area by Jim Driscoll Way had been open land before construction of the barrage. It was the "Marl Recreation Ground" lying to the south of Grangetown, so it was ripe for incorporation in the new scheme with no demolition needed.

Playing fields remained and there was some open land towards the shore, but new apartments had edged ever closer along the section leading upstream to the old Clarence Road Bridge. That had been the lowest crossing of the Taff before the great overpass was constructed. More shoreline apartments stretched south from the quay towards Channel View at the west end of this new "Butetown Link".

Behind the new Jim Driscoll landing wharf were two big warehouse-like buildings, containing a recreation and leisure centre and the headquarters of the Cardiff Aqua centre. Throughout the morning boats were leaving and arriving, tiny single-man kayaks, medium sized inflatables and more solid craft that were backed down the concrete slipway on their trolleys behind the owner's car. The floating gangway leading to the quay responded to fluctuations in water level, though these were minimal, being no longer tidal as at the Rhymney River boatyard.

I followed the path upstream to Clarence Bridge. Gutweed (*Enteromorpha*), drifting among rather tatty water milfoil, seemed to be the last remnant of former salinity, although the most unusual of the marginal plants also had a strong affinity with this formerly salty channel coast. This was dittander (*Lepidium latifolium*), a tall, anomalous cress which dominated the first section of the waterside fringe. Its contemporaries here were freshwater plants, gipsywort, meadowsweet, hemlock water dropwort, great willow herb and tall pendulous sedge. Invading land plants were evening primrose and ragwort.

As the east-facing coast bent round to face south, municipal gardeners had intervened, planting a border of sturdy foreigners to keep the water from encroaching onto the mown strip of clover-rich turf bordering the walkway within. Beyond was a narrow fringe of evergreen shrubs against the walls of the new apartments. Introduced plants were great clumps of New Zealand flax, tamarisk and tufted ornamental grasses more than man-high.

Further from the quay were woody plants, alder, sallow, Buddleia and bramble thickets. The littoral fringe broadened amidships to embrace tall meadow plants and what could be classified as noxious weeds but were all part of the conservation fringe.

A flock of house sparrows, those garrulous birds that enjoy living cheek by beak with starlings in noisy confusion, erupted from the small house gardens beyond. They busied themselves foraging on this patch, clinging to the fruiting heads of docks, sometimes two or three together, tweaking the seeds from the small, three-sided florets. As the docks swayed in the sea of purple-headed Yorkshire fog grass, so too did the finches, clinging grimly on. Co-habiting plants were prickly ox-tongue, lucerne, mallow, feathery fennel and purplish giant lettuce.

It was here that I saw the season's first striking red and black cinnabar moths *(Tyria jacobaea)* warning off would-be predators by flaunting their poisonous brilliance. Cinnabars are more often encountered as the black and yellow, tiger-striped caterpillars that feed on ragwort. There were juicy garden snails about to tempt the thrushes.

A broader, impenetrable waterside strip was fenced off from the recreational lawn with benches to landward, by a barrier entwined with hedge bindweed covered with white trumpet flowers. Quite large trees, singly and in groups, added to this somewhat apologetic but people-orientated waterfront.

Gaps in the shrubs opened up views across the water, where I counted at least twenty six mute swans, one pair with five cygnets, and sizable flocks of mallard. Lines of booms, directing boats to safer, deeper water, were occupied by lines of cormorants, drying spread wings or just cogitating. Shoreline gulls were sparse, but swallows skimmed everywhere, dealing with any midge problem.

A cohort of ten ducks on the water close by, seem to have been indulging in free sex. Most were pure mallard, one, the malefactor, was pure white. A drake with the shining green head and neck of a well dressed gentleman mallard, had a white breast and dark instead of silver-grey back.

On the opposite shore where the river narrowed the little old houses had survived along the landward side of Clarence Road and a new, rather complex landing stage had been constructed at its upstream end. A motorised blue and white vessel labelled "Aquabus, No. 2" drew away from the steps and came chugging downstream with a few passengers.

Great brick and concrete condominiums eight or nine storeys high loomed skywards upstream of the renovated Clarence Bridge where the Taff had been diverted three to four decades ago to by-pass the big flat island that had provided a nesting site for a flock of lesser black-backed gulls. That island and the broad loop of river to its east had been absorbed into the townscape. Redundant loops of meandering rivers could no longer be allocated that amount of space in all this new development - as we had seen more recently on the River Rhymney. The west bank where I walked was gentler, with grass and trees between highway and houses.

* * *

Disappointed at the cancellation of our Flatholm trip because of the gale the previous Saturday, we had been allocated seats on the 1.45 pm boat on Tuesday 1st July, but bad weather forecast for the evening stopped that one too. There were doubts about getting us back.

So much for John's viewing of the recessed Napoleonic gun emplacements, the second world war bunkers, fog horn mechanism, lighthouse tower, Victorian barracks, incoming sailors' isolation hospital and other items of non natural history interest - with several thousand gulls defending their nests thrown in for good measure.

I opted for the mundane alternative of a boat trip inside the barrage. This was viewing Cardiff Bay by default, but a seemingly apt substitute for a 'townee'. We found our way in along new boulevards strung between look-alike roundabouts and drove into the multi-storey carpark in Stuart Street, emerging into the sunshine at ground level in the further corner. School precincts just across the road were peopled with pupils gathered round teachers in little groups.

Walking baywards beside the highly regarded Techniquest Science Museum, John was able to examine the line of visiting coaches parked outside, while I looked nostalgically across at the burgeoning vegetation of the new Nature reserve away to the right.

We were on the wrong tack for boat trips, so circled back from the waterfront at St. David's Hotel around the three graving docks, all water-filled now, and some with lines of moored boats. Reaching Mermaid's Quay Wharf 'on the hour' we were just in time to board the yellow Cardiff Water Bus - a sizable craft, roofed and with seats both sides of the gangway, like a bus.

The voyage on the five hundred acre freshwater lake was brief, just three quarters of an hour, not including the hoped for detour up the River Ely and spending a fair while moored to the barrage on the Penarth side for the exchange of passengers.

Features of interest occurring on the open water, apart from the large number of moored craft and even more red mooring buoys, were twofold, both related to the maintenance of water quality. The upward gushing of water under pressure in parts was triggered by the water aeration system. Stagnation could have proved disastrous in relation to algal growth. The floating glass domes, bigger than the mooring buoys, were where chemists took the samples necessary for monitoring water quality - and possibly air samples from under the domes to see what gases were being given off by biological activity below.

Many buildings had risen around the shores since I was last here, the most impressive being the as yet incomplete components of the new super Sports Centre near Jim Driscoll Quay. It was here that ornithologists had formerly gathered outside the Red House Inn on Ferry Road, for wader watching on the mud flats.

Now the land accommodated the headquarters of the Cardiff Devils Ice Hockey team, a public skating rink, snow and snowballing enclosure and an olympic standard swimming pool to replace the one demolished when the Millennium rugby stadium was erected further up the Taff in the city centre.

All around were row upon row of condominiums and flats as residences or for weekenders with boats, One white edifice consisted of a series of round-ended rooms receding successively upwards to afford balcony space at each level. This had been designed to simulate the Manhattan skyline.

St. Augustine's church atop Penarth Head was pointed out as the highest spot on the whole of the Vale of Glamorgan coast. A red traffic light at the entrance to Penarth Harbour warned that the lock gates were closed - although those were more eye-catching than the light.

Our craft drew into the landing stage under the great sea barrage, some passengers disembarking to return on a later water bus, the service running at half hourly intervals. A pied wagtail foraged among the spider webs strung across the metal super structure that dwarfed the boat.

Swallows quartering low over the water were few. It seemed there were no longer sufficient midges to attract big flocks and certainly not the pestiferous plagues that had been feared by entomologists when the great body of water was being converted from salt to fresh during barrage building operations nearly a decade before.

We chugged on along the inner face of the barrage, which was immaculate now with sloping lawns, little clumps of shrubs and folk at leisure, moochin, lounging or partaking of alfresco lunches. There was a children's pirate pit playground and picnic place and an "Age of Coal" exhibition, as well as the triangular white sails visible from afar.

Cormorants rested on booms and piles and any other emergent object, while other water fowl concentrated around Mermaid's Quay, where human bystanders were a source of provender. Most were mallard, the satisfied individuals sleeping off their victuals on the timbers of the ancient mooring towers offshore. The mute swan cygnets proved as popularly cute as always, despite that fairy tale about The 'Ugly Duckling".

I am no admirer of the plain, blocky New Millennium Arts Building with its jumble of Welsh and English characters writ large across the top, but the sun shining on the great curve of what appeared to be burnished copper at the lakeward end was most impressive as seen from the boat. This was particularly so when the beautiful old Docks Office, now an annexe of the Welsh Assembly Buildings, in the foreground, formed the centrepiece of the tableaux.

Once ashore, we examined the tastefully executed carvings in the red stone of that icon of old Dockland, the ornately sculptured tiles within the entrance and the mosaic floor. Impressive in a very different way was the great plain forecourt of the meeting house of the new Welsh Assembly, made entirely of slate, presumably from North Wales quarries, with banks of solid slate walls, flooring and seating accommodation for many hundreds of loyal citizens. The mind boggled at the thought of that quantity of rock being ferried in down the motorways.

Not far to the left was the headquarters of the Torchwood and Dr. Who television series which were produced in Cardiff, so that one often found oneself watching the inter galactic happenings for the wrong reason of trying to spot Cardiff landmarks as viewed by cameras on those high rise-buildings.

The film makers sometimes strayed further afield. We had come across some perched on scaffolding erected beside the cathedral at the bottom of the Dean's Steps on one occasion. When Cardiff City Council's horticulturalists earned themselves an invitation to produce a show garden at the Chelsea Flower Show in 2008, they produced an extravaganza entitled "Dr. Who. A Garden in Time".

After trying to decipher the rather faint inscriptions of geographic features on the horizontal circle of shining metal at the old Roath Dock entrance, we passed between the great stone bastions into the converted space within, now the white oval of the Roald Dahl Arena or amphitheatre, the site of many flamboyant public functions, with or without fireworks.

* * *

Circling back to the car, we drove across the water on the great new overpass and continued high above the River Ely along its now much straightened east bank. Turning upstream over Leckwith Bridge, the highest point to which small boats can reach, we went on to Cosmeston Park Country Park for a late but leisurely picnic viewing the East Lake through the fringe of trees, some of which were hung with ripe wild cherries.

While checking which of my books had sold and which needed replacing, I was accosted by Steve Latham, the past warden, who I always associate with the horse that he rode around the newly opened reserve several decades ago. Now in charge of all the wardens in the Vale Coast area, he was office-bound and tied to computers, but offered me a land rover tour of the reserve to observe changes, as he had on my last visit, sadly not followed up.

The chief attraction at present was a large colony of white lesser butterfly orchids, these of rare occurrence and known to me only in Porthkerry Park. The Cosmeston ones were on the old quarry waste beyond the two lakes, where fine drifts of outsize bee orchids had burgeoned on the tumbled liassic limestone rubble when the plant succession was younger. I declined, but resolved not to leave it so long this time. An ice cream on the board walk terrace was followed by the ever popular session with the massed wildfowl.

A pair of swans among the many scores were in charge of six half-grown cygnets, surely a full clutch, although a fox had been seen here recently. Coot were present in abundance, their lobed toes shining pale blue through the shallows. Some of the many mallard had green heads but mottled brown plumage. I thought at first that the drakes might be going into eclipse, but it was early in the summer for this. These must be young drakes just growing out of the adolescent plumage that resembles that of their dams.

Many folk were feeding the swans, which were quite unafraid of humans, pecking hopefully at fingers held behind the back as well as in front, but hissing warnings at too inquisitive pooches.

At first it was much too hot to sit for long on any of the benches, but then the promised black clouds rolled up, providing welcome shade. There was still no wind and we witnessed no sign of the promised thunder storm, but the timing of the weather change had been forecast correctly.

We made a double circuit of Penarth front, now part of a one-way system to allow for parking along the slope leading out to the west. Steepholm and Flatholm lay alluringly out in the Channel, clearly demarcated against the still sunlit sea - so near and yet so far. There was still a couple of hours to go for the promised storm. I got in the wrong lane on the way back and found myself crossing the water again, so we had to return by the way we had come.

CHAPTER 26

Cathedral Precincts, Llandaff Weir, Stream By Morganstown Motte and Gelynis Fruit Farm

The 2nd July was brother John's last day in Wales, with nothing particular on the agenda until Joyce Lloyd phoned and suggested a get-together for morning coffee. She, too, had a ninety one year old brother, four to five years older than herself. We were favoured by morning sunshine, the thunder storms holding off until later.

Refreshments and garden viewing were followed by admiration of fine cross-stitched tapestry work and water colours achieved by our hostess, after which we sallied forth to enjoy the serene surroundings of the heart of this cathedral 'city' or cathedral 'village' at the end of her garden.

Buildings surrounding the lawn and flower beds and memorial to the dead of two world wars were comfortably mellowed by time. Most of the walls were of stones of many colours and shapes, put together by master craftsmen. Here were rough hewn rocks and river rounded pebbles of yellow, brown and the red of Radyr stone, dark grey, slaty tinged and the paler hue of Carboniferous limestone. One high wall was topped with a V shaped roof of flat stone tiles of sandy texture, not slaty as seen on roofs in the Brecon Beacons.

A botanical anomaly was the vast amount of Mexican fleabane *(Erigeron karvinskianus)*. This had arisen from small beginnings on the crumbling but massive masonry of the twelfth century Red Dragon Inn, in pride of place at the top of the slope leading up from the cathedral, which, like St. David's in another of Wales' small 'cities', was built in a deep hollow, not far above water level.

This chunky ruin has had many uses during the eight or nine centuries since its construction, including as a site of ecclesiastical meetings and a bell tower or campanile near the lych gate.

The fleabane, massed with delicate purple, pink and white daisy flowers, hails from Mexican deserts and thrives with no very obvious source of water. It clings to smoothly distempered walls, bursts from cracks in pavements and pushes up through tarmac, its wiry stems more slender than a hairpin, its leaves equally delicate.

Bunches were sprouting from the top and sides of the stone walls leading from the lych gate to the cathedral and from many a crevice elsewhere. Sadly the other, larger fleabane, which flourished here a decade before, seemed to have disappeared. That was the tall, blue-flowered Philadelphia fleabane or Robin plantain *(Erigeron philadelphicus)* from North America. It was discovered first on Tintern Abbey in 1917 and here at Llandaff in 1944 and 1975.

We admired the lofty spire, sometimes the home of kestrel, jackdaw or pigeon, from various viewpoints around the ancient inn and watched a group of art students trailing up the slope to settle on the grass above with large sketch pads to portray the scene below in their own diverse fashions.

On past the preaching cross with the mellowed curves of the eleventh century base which supported a thirteenth century shaft, we came to the Old Bishop's palace. Formerly regarded as the Castle of Llandaff, only the northern gatehouse of this, with its slit windows for arrows and the curtain walls leading away in both directions, remain.

As ruinous as the campanile and probably almost as old, it was more or less abandoned after Owain Glyndwr's attacks in 1402 and 1405, but provided sanctuary for frightened citizens during times of stress in the sixteenth century.

Scars of a sloping roof can be seen near the gate with its two ancient wooden doors, these marking the sloping roof of the eighteenth century Bush Inn, which was one of at least nine ale houses at the time. St. Teilo's Spring, just across the road still, is one of many sources of potable water that could have been useful in the brewing of ale.

The courtyard enclosed by the ruins had been dedicated as a public garden, having a central lawn with some black mulberry trees, surrounded by a path and a broad border of shrubs with a variety of creepers shinning up the lofty curtain walls. Lesser crumbling ruins remain in two further corners and the stretch of wall from the remains of the South-east Tower to the gate into the modern Cathedral School has been found to descend well below soil level. Buried at its base is the cobbled floor of an old stable yard.

From here back to the gatehouse, the high wall was decked from top to toe with the lacy flowers of creeping Hydrangea *(H. petiolaris)*, the species which we had seen climbing up the walls of St. David's Cathedral a few weeks before. Here at Llandaff, it partly concealed a colony of wall germander *(Teucrium chamaedrys)*, a rare pink flowered dead nettle said to be native only on the Sussex chalk but present also in a limestone quarry in Mid Glamorgan.

Mulberry trees, both here and outside the residences of the clerics, were bearing unripe mulberries alongside young bobble fruits dangling from giant planes. Other beauties were the maidenhair tree *(Ginkgo biloba)* with its triangular leaves near the campanile and the holm oak with mini acorn cups near the lych gate.

We returned to a late lunch at Brynteg, to the accompaniment of distant thunder storms and a belated tour of the premises before my guest's departure. The local train arrived just after we had got the luggage up and over the tracks and then the rains really came. I was dressed appropriately and wandered on over the river bridge, sheltering under trees during the heaviest bouts, equivalent to those accompanying John's arrival. At least he had boarded the train dry. My town mac failed to keep out the rain, but I had dry things to put on when I got back.

* * *

I was back in the cathedral precincts a few days later, wandering round the consecrated ground, checking on the established and spontaneous plant life. Following the railings to the kissing gate entry from the path alongside the Cathedral School playing fields, I spotted an unfamiliar species. This, the dwarf mallow *(Malva neglecta)*, creeping among flowering sun spurge, bore attractive white flowers streaked with purple.

By-passing the main, well tended part of the burial ground, I turned back north, disturbing two wood pigeons and a blackbird probing earth from a new grave. Mostly the burials along this overgrown woodland belt dividing the cemetery into two had been engulfed by the multi-storey growth of cypress, sycamore and elder or the great domes of blackberry vines reaching out for the light.

Where dates were still decipherable, these interments had occurred around the 1890s. Some of the enveloping growths had been treated with herbicides, most of the tangle of killed stems still awaiting clearance. A few of the head high monuments had been exposed once more to daylight by clearing operations.

I moved through the partially wooded section where ground between the graves was mostly clothed with a dense sward of tall grass and hogweed, knitted together with bush vetch, yellow pea and Clematis.

Cleavers was scrambling up the sides of neatly shaped Irish yew trees, some of which had exploratory ash saplings emerging amidships. More lofty monuments towards the riverward boundary were submerged under mounds of bramble and old man's beard.

The Taff was a whole field's width away now, but had formerly flowed close by the cathedral, making it easier to bring the building stone in by water. It is appropriate that the lower courses of such mature waterways should be referred to as meanders. Two embankments, the taller of which I remember being constructed a few decades ago, now kept the waters in their place.

Unsurprisingly the soil underfoot, was a deep black river alluvium, beloved by moles as an easy digging medium. Three times, however, I came upon molehills thrown up on the earth path, lower than normal and with a firm-edged hole in the summit where the builder seemed to have given up and left, as on that harder clay path in Radyr Woods.

Another feature of these paths, with their scattered river-rounded cobbles and small chunks of masonry, was the abundance of song thrush anvils. Suitable anvils were too numerous for there to be any big build up of smashed snail shells, but the brittle remains of both Helix garden snails and Cepaea hedge snails were scattered throughout.

I sheltered from a shower under one of the great English yew trees perched on the standard two foot high circular stone mound, with a two to three foot high woody root tangle some six to seven feet in diameter between this and the early forking trunk of similar diameter. Low branches dipped to within 4 feet of the ground.

This was the standard pattern for the row of ancient yews down the centre of both this unkempt and the tended part of the ground to the south. Like those, the surface of the walled eminence and of the ground round about was literally covered in accumulations of the tough little shells of old yew seeds. Some had little round holes nibbled in the side, others were split neatly in two. None were whole now.

These have always been a feature here over the four to five decades that I have known the site - and I have seen mice nibbling the nutlets and squirrels splitting them open - yet still there are people who ought to know better who maintain that no animals eat yew seeds, but only the fleshy pink arils, because the seeds are poisonous.

Certainly the thrushes and blackbirds spit them out, as crop pellets, but they are eaters of soft fruits, not hard seeds. And certainly farm animals can be poisoned by the foliage - hence the prevalence of yews in walled churchyards rather than on grazing land - but not those rounded nutlets. Only under pollen producing male trees were these remains of mammalian banquets absent.

Fine circular box trees with branches dipping to the ground mingled with the English and Irish yews. Monterey's and Lawson's cypresses were linked by pink and purple swards of rosebay willow herb and creeping thistles. Lower ground cover was of umbelliferous ground elder which, in such holy consecrated ground, should surely be refered to by its other popular name of bishop's weed.

* * *

There were two ways out from this northern wilderness of forgotten graves to the fields beyond. One was through a decrepit iron kissing gate near the main path past the cathedral, the other, less official, at the end of a dwindling path leading through a gap at the end of the hedge.

From the north end of the graveyard, the river flats changed in character. Leading upstream towards Llandaff Weir was a thick hay crop, dominated by cocksfoot and tall fog grass, with robust hogweed spilling out from the churchyard tangle, and a lower sward of white clover and buttercups used as a tractor way alongside the dense shrubs bordering the river. To the south was the neatly mown rugby field of the colleges strung along Eastern Avenue.

Between the two was the double avenue of oak trees that I had seen being planted many years before. Badly infested by marble galls as small saplings, they were now fine trees, twenty to thirty feet high, with mown grass beneath.

Winding up through the dense thicket of Japweed and balsam to the uppermost river defence carrying the main walkway, I came upon wind damage wreaked by our unseasonal summer gales. Two black poplar branches had been blown down, one with the leaves still unwilted. The Taff was running high and two hopeful anglers cast their lines from beneath a big umbrella, black instead of the usual green, on the further bank.

A lesser path wound among thickets of herbs and saplings towards the river's brink and along one stretch the tree cover lowered on the Llandaff side, affording a view to the cathedral at river level and the steeply rising land to Llandaff 'village' and the clerics' houses high above. Those who had sited these long ago, evidently knew the wisdom of not building on river flood plains that some modern developers have yet to learn. The lane I had driven down to this level formerly led to a ford where men and livestock had crossed the Taff in the distant past.

I continued upstream to Llandaff Weir, this an extra long one because the river broadened at this point and the weir crossed it obliquely. Threading down through alder, ash, maple, osier, and rowan, I got close to the roaring flood below the weir. The broad gravelly islands here that I had seen swept right away in the past, had built up again and were now well stabilised by a willow thicket, which fended off the water successfully. The bordering reed canary grass had been combed flat, the seeding heads undulating in the turbulence, along with the rushes.

Water level had been higher, with drifted branches lifted several feet above the present level and a severed tree trunk had been washed from upstream to become stranded across the top of the silvered fall. Swifts soared back and forth, sometimes through the spray, but the gulls being drifted downstream took off just before reaching the brink. The one speckled wood butterfly seen stayed among the trees.

I carried on a little upstream and, edging through long grass to the acute corner of the barrage at the river's widest point, found myself looking into a quiet little backwater protected by green and yellow booms, along which teetered a young magpie, its ludicrously short tail not helping its balance. The still water was covered with the floating leaves of broad-leaved pondweed, the long edges inrolled and the stalk meeting the blade in a little notch.

I returned along the foot of the towering beechwood leading up to the cathedral green and Joyce's house above. This wood occupied the steep scarp cut by the abrasive force of the river before it worked its way northwards towards Gabalfa beyond the further bank. Now first a willow spinney and then the big hay meadow occupied the new flat land between the old course and the new.

From here I was following the old dry canal that had formerly acted as the leat supplying water to a corn mill sited where heavy traffic now roars along the main highway.

* * *

On Saturday 5th July, I revisited the stream which flows past Pugh's Garden centre from the Ty Nant Inn (which translates as the house by the brook). The scene had changed remarkably since my last viewing on Good Friday in mid March nearly four months before. Admiring the pollen laden cones of giant horsetail on that occasion, I had predicted later growths to two feet high.

That proved a gross under estimate. Most of the silica charged vegetative horsetail stems were now shoulder high, with those deeply shaded reaching to eight feet. The columnar stems were stout, but the generous whorls of branches splaying at regular intervals all round were slender but rigid, making an elegant whole, soft to brush through, resilient to return.

This fairy forest must have been a miniature replica of those created by their now extinct kin in the ancient coal forests, trees which left their fossilised remains in the coal taken from the South Wales mines. Stems rising now in the bright light among the grass bordering the mown playing field, reached only to one or two feet. Where severed by the mower further out, new shoots, a few inches high were trying their luck again - only to be felled by the next mowing.

Modern shrubs, alders, sallows and Buddleia, now covered with leaves, hid the stream altogether along most of the field margin. Meadow vetchling scrambled four to five feet into their branches, to bring its yellow pea flowers to the notice of pollinating insects.

These and tall associated herbs, hemlock water dropwort, Himalayan balsam and great willow herb, easily overtopped the horsetail where sunlight penetrated, that coming into its own again in the deeper shade behind. Was it fanciful to think of this as a reincarnation of the dominance of modern flowering plants over the spore-bearers of Wales' prehistoric forests?

Recent excavation of a short section of the stream had opened up a view to the scarp rising steeply to road level above, revealing precocious horsetail sprouts pioneering well above the water table. Apparently shade was more vital than water in stimulating growth in height.

Further along the marginal thicket was augmented by nettles, docks, hogweed and hemp agrimony, fine cover for wildlife. Tunnels penetrated the lower growths, the maker of at least one having left its calling card in the shape of a black elongated twist of fox dung. Zooming over the riot of foliage were more of those beautiful demoiselle damselflies with iridescent bodies and unbanded wings.

This was an official path along the field margin, marked by a post where it left the track to Gelynis Fruit farm. The inscription was "Ramblers Association, Cardiff Group, More capital walks" with a distance in miles and kilometres. It curved round the woodland edge where flowering meadowsweet seemed to be ousting the fine water mint stand of former years.

This bulge in the woodland concealed the historic mound known variously as the Tumulus, the Castle Mound and the Motte. That was said to have been used by parliamentarians to bombard royalist troops occupying Fforest Fawr on the opposite face of the Taff Gorge during the Cromwellian war. The gorge, leading through here to the strongholds of the wild Welsh, must have been much narrower and more defendable then, before the sides were quarried back to left and right.

A hundred and twenty feet (thirty seven metres) high and eighteen feet (five and a half metres) diameter, the scramble up the motte is helped by emergent tree roots but hindered by dense Rhododendron and the tall trees that finally closed in, obscuring the Roundheads' target of the modern castle's predecessor by the end of the twentieth century, when a few narrow paths were opened up.

It was against the further, eastern, boundary that Radyr's new Skateboard Park for young skateboard users was to be erected during 2008.

* * *

Returning past the footpath signpost to the motte and beyond, I reached the foot crossing of the main line railway to Gelynis Fruit farm and Vineyard, where I used to be a regular PYO customer. I sampled fruit today from a straggling hedge plant by the railway. Yellow raspberries, these seemed to be more pips than flesh and it was not one of the varieties cultivated in the rows beyond.

Traditionally run as a small holding on market garden lines, this forty eight acre property had been split in two at the coming of the motorway across its southern fields in the 1970s. There followed a period of dereliction, the owner continuing to live in the lovely old farmhouse, a grade II listed building, into his nineties, when his daughter, her husband and son, took over the property and brought it to what it is today.

The oldest acquisition is the magnificent sweet chestnut tree at the end of the private garden - said to be some four hundred and forty years old, as old as the house. The newest is the bed and breakfast accommodation at the top of the garden, in the end of the converted building, the masonry now a smart primrose yellow. Across the yard are the renovated old stone barns, where barn owls formerly nested and swallows and house sparrows still do.

I reached these on the occasion of this stroll along the course of the old railway line leading obliquely across country from the direction of the motte. At that (north) end, it joined up with the Taff Vale Railway main line at Station House, to transfer freight to Cardiff and Merthyr.

At the other (east) end, it crossed the River Taff on the forerunner of the present Iron Bridge as "The Pentyrch and Forest Halt Light Railway", which took coal from riverside mines at Gwaelod-y-Garth and iron from the Gwaelod riverside forge to the Tin Plate Works down river at Melin Griffith. The first Iron Bridge washed away in the great flood of August 1887. Its successor carries just a footway and a stout iron mains water pipe.

The part of the track I followed (not a public footway) was floored with fine quality mown grass, the bordering turf covered with circular leaves having scalloped margins. Assuming these to be those of ground ivy, I wondered why there were no blue flowers, until I spotted a few with subsequent leaflets and realised that these were seedlings of hogweed or cow parsnip, the two not related, but uncannily similar at that stage. Along the base of the bordering hedges were cinquefoil, avens, bird's-foot trefoil and white clover. Approaching the farm I passed a bordering wall, with ferns and ivy.

On a river crossing I spotted seven tiny ducklings in the same place as before. That was seven to eight weeks ago. This must be a second brood. Swallows from the barns were dipping to drink under the pipe bridge.

The maize maze upstream was in its infancy as yet, the aligned maize plants not much more than twelve inches high, the elevated wooded stand forming the ultimate goals seeming incongruous in the open centre. Rows of plants to be removed from the walkways would be used as silage for cattle feed.

This went, too, for a second maize field visited south of the M4, the field formerly holding the crop of colourful orange pumpkins used in the autumnal Halloween festival. I reached this field by following the river bank under the great concrete edifice carrying the motorway across.

From the first maize field I viewed the crystal clear outline of distant hills beneath billowing purple clouds. From the second maize field I had to hasten back to the motorway bridge to shelter from the contents of one of those purple clouds.

I returned past another incredible sweet chestnut tree, almost as ancient as the garden one. The shower passed and I picked a punnet of fine big raspberries, trying not to be tempted by the loganberries and tayberries alongside. Only the red currants had been netted against the birds and blackbirds were helping themselves freely to the others.

On then past the vineyard bearing young grapes at shoulder height, to pick strawberries, these, too, elevated at a comfortable height, out of the way of slugs. The fruits dangled from well watered black polythene strips, chest high and protected partially from birds by high domes of stronger white polythene. The rain passed and other customers were enjoying coffee or ice cream under awnings by the kiosk where home produced honey, chutney, jam and white wine were for sale - also hanging baskets of flowers earlier in the season.

CHAPTER 27

Neath Valley, Blaengwrach Garden and Melincourt Waterfall, Bats, Coco De Mer, Lily Pools and Bird Hides

I needed no second bidding when Gil rang on the morning of Sunday, 13th July suggesting a garden and a nature reserve visit in the lower Neath Valley. We took the northern loop, up the Taff and down the Neath from the intervening uplands of the Millstone Grit country around Hirwaun. Our destinations were Bryn Heulog at Blaengwrach and the Melincourt Falls further down the valley near Resolven.

Rainclouds still scudded across the sky but it was the sunniest day of the week and we spent much of it in a delightful hillside garden which was holding an open day as part of the National Gardens Scheme - one of the premises opening to the public to raise money for charity and featured in the famous 'yellow book'.

We left the road down the Neath Valley at Aberpergwm, (where I had first found the rare *Tremiscus helvelloides* orange cup fungus - an incomer to this country with Baltic timber for use as pit props in the Valley mines). A tiny lane led to Cwmgwrach and an even tinier, steeper one to Blaengwrach, fortunately well signed with yellow handbills on posts.

Mynydd Resolven, at 1,257 feet, reared steeply to the south, this a part of the spreading Rheola Forest, while other, open land rose high to the east to lines of cliffs - probably an old quarry - steep woodland and a bald summit.

The garden was exquisite, partly due to its undulating nature with steps leading between different levels, but also to the skilful planting of beds of intractable hill soil, interspersed with almost level lawns, mounded rockeries and little ponds.

The present owners had moved here only three years before, in September 2005, bringing many of the plants from their former garden in Surrey. Previously the property was a small holding, peopled by horses, sheep and chickens, yet the transformation was so rapid that the garden had been featured on the BBC's Open Gardens Programme in 2007, when their open day attracted a hundred visitors and raised seven hundred pounds for charity.

It would be foolish to try and enumerate even some of the plants emerging from the overall mulching of bark fragments, from exquisite lilies to deep purple passion flowers, exuberant hollyhocks to ground-cover creeping Jenny, the leaves as well as the flowers yellow. I spotted specimens of the Dyffryn Gardens puzzle ice plant, these bearing a tag: "Sedum chocolate". Another problem solved, if not very scientifically.

It was good to see a thriving colony of water hyacinth *(Eichornia crassipes)* - rosettes of bulbous-based leaves with dangling roots floating on the surface of a greenhouse pool. One of the plants had produced a lovely pale blue hyacinth-like flower spike but, like our attractive Himalayan balsam, it was unloved in most of its tropical sites, where the better known name of "Scourge of the Nile" indicated its reputation as an invader and obliterator of waterways. Outdoor ponds showed more open water, with room for whirligig beetle and pond skaters to pursue their busy lives.

This was, indeed, a botanical feast, with upstanding Campanulas and spiky relatives of the sea holly, multi-coloured Iberis or candytuft flowers and the bronze foliage of bugle and Heuchera, a vegetable patch, rockeries and small scale water features. Just over the fence, with its newly planted perimeter hedge of native species, was part of the tangle of bracken, bramble and shrubs that had been cleared recently to establish the wildlife garden, where corn cockle ran riot and paper-thin poppy petals reflected the sunlight. This brilliance, we are told, appears as ultra violet to pollinating insects.

Our afternoon tea and slab of one of a variety of home made cakes was enjoyed in the welcome shade of an open canopy. We were unused to such powerful sunshine and had not expected it here in the hills. A short walk was suggested, on up the hill, to obtain great views of the Brecon Beacons, but we had our own walk in mind, further down the valley, so had to forego this.

* * *

We were loath to leave that lovely garden, but had, perforce, to carry on down the attractively wooded valley, one of West Glamorgan's highlights, to the Melincourt Falls just beyond Resolven.

This steep tributary cutting into the south-east side of the valley, had been a recognised tourist attraction for many years. In 1986 it was deemed worthy of designation as a nature reserve and was bought by the Glamorgan Wildlife

Trust, with money from various conservation bodies. Several of us had homed in on this local beauty spot at that time to record its credentials, plant and animal. The scenic splendour could not be recorded in exact terms.

Disturbed then, as now, only by the sound of rushing water, things had once been very different - as in so many of the Coalfield valleys. This was once the site of a busy Iron Works, powered by the falling water. A large overshot water wheel had driven bellows powered by diverted water, so providing the air blast for the main furnace. After a hundred years of service the works were closed in 1808. The water wheel had disappeared during the intervening two hundred years but remains of the furnace and an air exit still existed.

Gil drew the car into an attractive carpark across the minor road B4434, which follows this flank of the valley, leaving the main A465 on the other side. Girt about with broad-leaved trees, this was furnished with bench and table picnic sites in mown grass embayments around the central tarmac. Only one other car shared the space on this midsummer Sunday afternoon.

We set off up the footpath carved into the valley side well above stream level. Erosion of the almost vertical face above had exposed the massive, contorted roots of two trees right at the start. A labyrinth of bark-covered living timber stretched way above our heads to the old ground level where the trunks began.

From there on it became another elfin wood of mossy rock faces like the Ty Canol Wood Nature Reserve visited in Pembrokeshire some six weeks before. Water seeping down vertical rock faces nurtured coverings of slabby Pellia liverworts or feathery mosses, with clumps of upstanding Polytrichum. Other faces, both vertical and horizontal, were covered with sheets of golden Saxifrage, that elegant species that adorns itself with starry golden flowers in February and March before anything else apart from celandines have dared to open.

In places the trefoil leaves of wood sorrel speckled the moss mats, the Irishman's 'shamrock'. Robust bluebell capsules along the brink of the path told of other spring flowers. This brink was now bordered with the tall silky plumes of tufted hair-grass and the widely spaced seed clusters of remote sedge.

Ferns were everywhere, graceful lady ferns, more substantial and slightly darker male ferns and the more triangular fronds of broad buckler ferns. Hard ferns were sometimes plastered flat on vertical rock slabs, but we missed the rarer lemon-scented ferns, because we didn't remember they were here, waiting to be recognised. Nor did we see the royal fern, reputedly here but scarcely missable had it been on our route.

The uncommon and highly esteemed small-leaved lime, for which the Neath Waterfall Country further north in the Brecon beacons is famed, was one of the dominant trees of this lush woodland. With it were wych elm, oak, ash and sycamore, with less alder and rowan.

After several weeks with so much rain, the eight feet high waterfall crashing down its vertical precipice, was as impressive as either of us had seen it in the past. The Coal Measure rocks that it was cutting into were of two kinds, the tough, blocky Pennant Sandstone and the softer more friable shales, which crumbled into slaty fragments. A massive bed of the tougher rock, as always, formed the lip of the fall, chunks falling away only as the underlying beds of shale were washed out from beneath, leaving them unsupported. Brilliant shafts of sunlight penetrated the open amphitheatre where the tall, vertical and largely unwooded cliff curved round to the right, bringing out the rich orange tinted yellow of dry rocky slabs contrasting with the wet black shales.

Further down the valley we recognised narrow beds of this harder rock running through the other, where ancient floods had brought sand instead of silt into its making. This gorge, cut through the hillside over millennia of time, must descend much further than we could see, because the broad valley of the Neath into which it emptied, after flowing alongside for about a mile according to the map, had collected a deep layer of ice-borne deposits during glacial times, burying the sculptured parent rock.

There was something mesmerizing about that silver torrent of mixed air and water, a sense of power battering the chunks of sandstone fallen from above into the plunge pool. In complete contrast was the equally high but more gentle flow swilling down the mossy cliff to our right as we viewed it from the end of the path.

A lone dragonfly, with yellow thorax and yellow body patterned both sides with black and with a black tail tip, was hawking over the pool, keeping well clear of the spray, then zig-zagging up the little tributary that flowed from the base of the weeping cliff on the right, never once settling while we watched. Not big enough for the familiar golden-ringed dragonfly of this hill country, the colour fitted that of a young male or mature female black-tailed skimmer *(Orthetrum cancellatum)*. The abdomen changes in later life to blue as the male matures.

We were on the lookout for dippers, so characteristic of such torrents, but saw none, nor even a grey wagtail, or the pied flycatchers known to nest here. The only birds recorded throughout our visit were a jay in the carpark and a buzzard just after leaving. We did, however, see a rufous bank vole sidling across the stony path and into the undergrowth along its brink.

The flower species I have always associated with this site is cow-wheat *(Melampyrum pratense)*, a member of the foxglove family, but we had neither the time nor the energy to climb the flight of steps to the upper path leading round the top of the falls where it grew. I had to be satisfied with the more mundane, tall attenuated herb Robert, broad-leaved willow-herb and enchanter's nightshade.

It seemed a different river as viewed from the road bridge. This was the same water, propelled from above but flowing gently now along an almost horizontal bed of rock fragments. Where had all that power been dissipated?

Rather than carry on down to Neath and return along the motorway, we headed back up the valley by the way we had come. Passing clouds, from pale grey to deep purple, had darkened our view on the way in. The present peerless cloud-free blue sky allowed the July sunshine to highlight every innuendo of that delightfully wooded valley that I visited much too seldom nowadays. Rolling foothills stretched away both sides, the rounded tops of deciduous trees incorporated among the spires of conifers.

And then a sudden change, as we came abreast of the great belt of Carboniferous Limestone harbouring the cave systems and waterfall country of the Upper Swansea and Upper Neath. The bald sweeps of calcareous grassland undulated away east to the headwaters of the Taff Fawr and Taff Fechan, not forgetting those of the Cynon. Turning south past the great stone viaduct as we skirted Merthyr Tydfil, we returned down our own valley. A day well spent.

* * *

Coming in through the front entrance, I disturbed a fluttery yellow moth, which pranced erratically away into the open, arousing the attention of three house sparrows. These came at it from different angles from the summit of the tall, ivy-clad wall. There ensued a complicated chase, until the three finally drove it into the shrubbery. A hen bird emerged from the melée with the moth held firmly in her bill, still flapping.

Similar chases after aerial prey came within my ken at the other end of that day. Gil and I were gossiping in my lounge when she noticed a group of bats cavorting outside the window. These were weaving in and out and around the multi-trunked lime tree at the incredible speed always adopted by bats, making them difficult to identify at the best of times.

It was ten o'clock, with the sky over the Taff Gorge still light enough to show their silhouettes clearly. They were large by our bat standards and we surmised that they were likely to be noctules, the largest of all, or brown long-eared bats. Both have been recorded by the river below in the Country park.

I kept my eyes open after that and found that little groups were likely to occur between 9.30 and 10.30, flipping back and forth for a while and then moving off as a group. Some were smaller, the size of our commonest species, the pipistrelle, now divided into two sub-species distinguishable only by their calls, which human ears are unable to detect unaided.

One night I sallied forth over the footbridge for the hour between ten and eleven, hoping to repeat the past experience of a "bat walk" which I had joined with the experts carrying bat detectors. These slowed down the calls to make them audible to the human ear and recognisable to those in the know.

On that occasion we had watched noctules overhead as we gathered on the footbridge and Daubenton's bats skimming the water beneath, dipping occasionally as they spotted likely prey. No luck. One meagre little bat, probably a pipistrelle, hovered round to pay its respects before passing on for the night's work, and then no more. I walked on down the towpath on the further brink until the trees closed in, so that I would no longer be able to discern their silhouettes.

Mostly overcast, there was a brief interval when half a moon was visible across the river in the southern sky. Rounded on the right and straight on the left, like a wedge of Caerphilly cheese, it occupied a gap in the nimbus where streaks of white wisped across a residual patch of blue. Then the grey pall closed in again, less orange in this direction than to the north, where the incandescent lights of the M4 and the A470 were reflected back, to lighten our darkness and obscure the stars.

No-one was there to see but me, just one lone jogger, passing twice, his eyes on the ground watching for puddles. Three days later a daily habitués of Forest Farm informed me that a big cat had been sighted by both canal and river on two occasions. "Big! As long as my bike, spotted and with tufted ears". A lynx is not as big as a bike, but this is something to bear in mind. I returned to the accompaniment of distant rolls of thunder, part of the "warm front" that was engulfing us in its pall of grey.

I was 'turned on' to bats, having just watched a TV documentary of them, or rather the large flying foxes of the Comoros Islands north of Malagasy (Madagascar) - the islands famous for the discovery of live Coelacanths, the legged fish thought previously to be extinct.

* * *

That site connected too with a short talk I had given on neighbouring islands in the Western Indian Ocean, Aldabra and the Seychelles, a few nights before. The occasion, entitled "Pot Luck", involved twenty or so of the residents gathered in the communal lounge listening to three volunteers discoursing on tangible objects or remembered experiences.

My choice as a botanist, had to be the largest seed in the world, the coco-de-mer, my most treasured possession since returning from those islands. It met with appropriate approval as it was passed from hand to hand, while I unfolded its life history and inability to float and be a sea coconut as its first discoverers had dubbed it when it appeared on a beach on the Maldives - Not its one native island, which is Praslin in the Seychelles.

No-one had heard of it before except George - a loner who I had not seen at any of the weekly or other gatherings in the lounge, but who was persuaded to come at the last minute. He brightened visibly as the object came his way. A working life spent in the Far east had made possible several visits to the Seychelles when going on leave. In conversation with him over the strawberries and cream which followed, I found that it had evoked happy memories. Perhaps he will join us more often in the future.

For the ladies, who had no such memories, I discoursed briefly on other goodies from those tropical islands which I stored within the great hollow palm fruit. These included cinnamon bark, pods of the vanilla orchid and brown nutmegs wrapped around with red mace. The other entertainers were a gentleman on an overland desert trek during the war and a lady on the versatile subject of cats.

One of my rare visits to town found Cardiff in a state of disarray, with many of the central buildings knocked down and high rise blocks going up, swathed in scaffolding and polythene. I met Christine Mullins of the Cardiff Naturalists' Society in the High Street. Her comment was: "When I hear of anyone hoping to visit Cardiff, I tell them to wait till next year - or the year after."

But, there is always an upside as well as a downside. It was 11th July, graduation day and university students were wandering about in gowns and mortar boards, fresh from the ceremony. This was the generation that might help to put this chaotically overpopulated world to rights.

My bus had been diverted from its expected route, taking me on to the crowded bus station where some of the pulling-in places had disappeared under the great heap of rubble that had been the Wood Street booking office and other emporia. Back there after a self indulgent session in the Cardiff covered market, I waited three quarters of an hour for a half hour service. The expected vehicle had suffered a puncture in Danescourt. The man who brought the relief bus changed places with a lady driver and we were away at last. Other passengers had tales of other chaos. I never did like 'going to town' but 'needs must' occasionally.

* * *

I was out afoot for four hours on Wednesday 16th July, the morning so brilliant that I couldn't wait to get away, but clouds had rolled up by mid morning. Some of the anglers had beaten me to it, but the only fish I saw when peering into those translucent waters were a shoal of minnow-shaped tiddlers at the head of the Melin Griffith feeder and deep-bodied sticklebacks in the canal.

There were no waterfowl on the stretch of the Taff up to Radyr Weir, just a particularly pale buzzard low over the water, indulging in slow, regular flapping to keep itself aloft - too early in the day for a thermal to have developed to bear its weight.

I spent a deal of time exploring round the lily pools on the extensive lawns of the Automotive Electronics Ltd., hoping I had timed it right for the migration of the tiny frogs. Speaking later on with Mike Wiley, I learned that I was too late: it had all happened a month before.

How well I remember the occasion when thousands of tiny, bluebottle sized froglets not much bigger than tadpoles, despite the absorption of that long tail, had been scrambling out of the water and hopping across the lawn. All were headed towards the thick vegetation by the river, like baby turtles heading for the open sea, en masse, as they dig themselves out of the sand. Why would they not want to stay by their nursery pool? A few opportunistic magpies, a carrion crow and a moorhen were cashing in on the sudden glut of food.

To attain their goal the little amphibians had to cross a road built to carry heavy lorries. There was no problem tumbling off the kerb and hopping across, but they were incapable of leaping up the four inch kerb on the other side. Discovering their dilemma, conservationists had helped with brush and dustpan and the wardens followed to construct a couple of ramps. These did the trick, because the little adventurers worked their way along the barrier until they found an escape route.

On one occasion Mike had arrived just ten minutes too late to save the population from a mechanical road sweeper, driving his vehicle with a revolving brush sweeping everything from the gutter. That was some time ago but, later that morning, he reported that froglet numbers had dropped this year. During his routine clearing of the drains, he had found few froglets, just the odd adult frog and toad, palmate and great crested newts.

All I saw in the way of animal life were the usual whirligig beetles and pond skaters, a fair sprinkling of common blue-tailed damselflies *(Ischnura elegans)*, and a single blue damselfly. Circles of expanding ripples marked where a water boatman had surfaced for a gulp of air. The only recognisable water plant, rampant throughout, was a tired looking population of curly leaved Canadian pondweed, scummy with algae.

Surrounding plants were more reassuring and there were fine rafts of pink and white flowered water lilies. Gipsywort, greater bird's-foot trefoil and common spotted orchids infiltrated among the Typha bulrushes, most of those with fine young cat's-tail heads of dark brown female florets topped by four inches or so of naked stem vacated by the fluffy yellow male florets. Those would soon break off. Both greater and lesser bulrushes were here, the male and female spikes contiguous in the first but separated by a short length of stem in the second.

Sharp-flowered jointed rush and common soft rush formed a matrix for meadowsweet and hemp agrimony, flowers of the former a magnet for nectar seeking hover flies. The meadow browns preferred the purple self heal.

An exuberant belt of the huge circular leaves of Peltiphyllum *(Darmeria peltatum)* with a radius of sixteen inches, simulated a smoother version of the Gunnera often planted in such sites. Topping these were spent sprays of two-valved brown capsules, gaping after release of their seeds. The species hails from Western North America, where it is known as the umbrella plant for the big circular leaves mounted on metre long stalks. I had first seen this quite recently in the Cefn Onn Park on the Border Ridges inland of Cardiff's coastal plain.

Principle waterside shrub was the Siberian dogwood. The white flowers were normal but the young ripening fruits were a rather bilious purple, like unripe bilberries, some turning white. Later on white flowers and white berries would occur side by side: later still the berries would darken to purple. Bushes had self seeded here and were thriving, a whole bank of them now trimmed to form a flat-topped waterside hedge. Unusual trees alongside were Italian alder and whitebeam.

* * *

From the lily pools I followed the main path alongside the feeder canal, not the bridleway as last time, to the country park. Beside the way two grey squirrels were busy on a felled beech log which had been liberally strewn with what looked like the crushed oats that I used to feed to my cart horses. By this time a sore toe required adjustment of the padding and I made for the first bird hide to put things right. No seats! I learned later that vandals had used them as battering rams to charge the wooden walls. The warden replaced them. Next day they had been dragged out again and dumped in the pond. He gave up. Where, oh where, is the pleasure gained from such anti social behaviour?

This pond was more than half covered by fringed water lily *(Nymphoides peltatus)*, the fringed yellow flowers most attractive but the plants unacceptably aggressive - as we had first learned when they took over Broad Pool on the Gower. Four moorhens were pushing their way through it, two of them youngsters.

Tall rosebay afforded colour beside the hide, perforated St. John's wort in front of it, codlins-and-cream and meadowsweet on the other side. After several years with no sand martins in residence in the 'high rise block' built to accommodate them, three pairs had moved in this year. Earlier on, I had assumed 2008 would be another empty year.

I moved on to the second hide, along a path thickly strewn with the fallen scarlet berries of rowan or mountain ash. There was a heron there, a mallard duck and several moorhens. An astonishing self sown crop of meadow cranesbill was flowering in front of the hide. Isolated emergents in the water were purple loosestrife with bur reed and Iris, both fruiting well. Reeds were occupying far too much of the pond area, attractive with their silky purple flower plumes, but 'eating up' the open water where kingfishers liked to fish.

The constant zizzing of a greenfinch emanated from the bordering sallows and the scratchy notes of reed warblers came across thinly from the far side of the pool. Every now again one of the fawn-coated warblers topped the reed plumes, one returning always to the same spot as though feeding young. Mike Wiley joined me on his rounds and said there were probably three nests here this year. He had handled one last year after the builder had left for warmer climes and he waxed lyrical about the perfection of its weaving.

He told of the time when he had seen a sparrow hawk grab one of the little songsters in this spot, only to drop it among the reeds, from where it was irretrievable. Feathers had been ripped out and the victim did not reappear.

We remained there a long time, watching a large blue dragonfly coursing back and forth, usually a few feet above the water, occasionally soaring higher, never settling. We saw no other airborne insect life but it was obviously catching something. It looked like an emperor, but may have been a hawker. It was impossible to tell through binoculars.

He spotted a crop pellet on the window sill of the hide, thought to be that of the resident tawny owl. Little owls had formerly nested here and short-eared owls had been seen, but not recently. Mike was the only warden on duty today, the others, in a different trade union, were on a day-long strike against their employers, the local authority.

Major physical jobs were not on his day's agenda and he waxed eloquent about his own three fields at the head of the Aberdare Valley on the margin of the Beacons, where rare marsh fritillary butterflies bred on devil's bit scabious. Like that other long serving chief warden, Paul Dunn of the Glamorgan Heritage Coast, he was a keen line fisherman. It would be natural to think that folk working outdoors in all weathers would enjoy their leisure indoors for a change, but not a bit of it. Their addiction to the great out-of-doors was too strong.

We moved on eventually to lean awhile on the gate of the wild flower meadow, discussing the take-over by thistles, good for seed-eating finches but not for the orchids, whose increasing numbers he had been recording over the years. The horses responsible for grazing there had been moved on and replaced by six friesian heifers, obviously replete on what looked like a fair hay crop away from the thistles, as they lay contentedly chewing the cud.

A baby robin was constantly with us, on the gate post, gazing directly at us with both eyes at once beside the narrow beak (binocular vision). The innocent still had his attractively speckled head and back but orange feathers were appearing on the breast.

When we went our different ways I passed several bright pink patches of French cranesbill *(Geranium endressii)* which someone must have introduced. Walking back along the canal, where the yellow brandy bottle water lily flowers were at prime, I encountered abundant mallard, many also changing into adult plumage, like the robin. Patches of tall yellow loosestrife had replaced the yellow Iris brightening Sheep's-bane Wood and purple marsh woundwort mingled with the tall canalside flowers.

Returning between the horse paddock and the allotments, the yellow tansies were just coming into bloom and a single stranger, the purple bugloss *(Echium plantagineum)*, had appeared in the paddock, this a relative of the commoner viper's bugloss of our dunes. One of the summer brood of red admirals had joined the midsummer glut of meadow browns.

CHAPTER 28

Pembroke Waterfront, Stackpole and Bosherston Lakes

I joined a blue coach from Ogmore Vale at 8 am on Saturday, 19th July for another Pembrokeshire visit, this one organised by Duncan Hockridge for "The Friends of Forest Farm". The promised rain stayed up in the scudding clouds and we enjoyed sunshine throughout. After the usual stop at Pont Abraham, we crossed the River Tywi at Carmarthen and left the main Haverfordwest road at St. Clears, past tempting signboards to Saundersfoot and Tenby, to Pembroke town.

En route we had a good view of the noble stone ruin of Carew Castle, on a sideshoot of the same waterway as Picton Castle visited earlier in the year. Picton lies at the confluence of the Eastern and Western Cleddau, Carew at the broadening of the middle one of three waterways which come together as the Carew River east of Neyland, to flow on as Milford Haven.

Pembroke lies at the head of yet another tributary of this drowned valley, the Pembroke River, which broadens into vast flats before squeezing out into the Haven below Pembroke Dock - an industrial complex a little over two miles away from the charming old walled town of Pembroke.

With rather less than three hours at our disposal, I left the rest to shop and dine, while I set off to explore and consume sandwiches in my usual uncivilised manner. I resisted the temptation to go on the official castle tour, preferring natural to human history, and moved first into the grassed HQ of the Pembrokeshire Territorial Force tucked in against the castle walls. An expertly carved wooden crown took pride of place on a central plinth, commemorating Queen Elizabeth II's Jubilee in 2002.

Leaning over the stone balustrade, I traced the likely succession of wild plants gaining a hold on the walls. First must have been the unquenchable ivy-leaved toadflax, then red valerian (with a few white), Buddleia and vigorous sloe bushes with fat green fruits showing the first tinge of purple. Notable absentees were the usual small ferns and pellitory.

Leaving along a wall draped with flowering Russian vine, I almost stepped in a tell tale splodge of guano which pulled my gaze upwards. Yes. Four house martins' nests plastered under the eaves in the angle of the arched entrance porch.

Down to the bridge leading across the river to Pembroke Dock, I stayed on the near side of the water to make a circuit of the castle. On a previous visit, in early May, 2007, I had gone along the other side, coming across the rare meadow sage *(Salvia pratensis)* with blue flowers, early purple orchids and a fumitory with pink-lipped white flowers *(Fumaria capreolata)*. The more widespread Alexanders was in full flower then, now the leaves were withering and the nutlets blackening.

Land rose steeply to the castle battlements, thickly wooded and with plentiful, lush hart's tongue fern in the ground layer. Ash, sycamore, sloe and hawthorn intervened between the path and the water at first, petering out through a tangle of traveller's joy.

Two interesting clumps of plants occurred offshore here, both with seaside affinities but growing here in fresh water, as at Cynheidre. One was the grey clubrush *(Schoenoplectus tabernaemontani)*, a dark, blue-green, the other the yellow-green sea club rush *(Bolboschoenus maritimus)*. More of the latter occurred on the opposite shore as a narrow fringe below sea beet.

The bitter north-westerly wind assailed me round the end of the arced 'lake' until I reached the shelter of the rising land opposite the castle. The thickly wooded slope to windward was topped by a paddock from which peered a pied (lucky) horse. It was two coats warmer here in the sun and butterflies were out in force.

Ringlets were the most abundant, these a dark sooty brown, relieved only by the pale rings. With them were brighter gatekeepers or hedge browns, orange with brown border and an oblique bar across each forewing. A few meadow browns joined in - these the commonest of butterflies, right through to northern Scotland. Hedge browns scarcely extend north of the southern Lake District, while ringlets come between the two, distribution wise. Meadow browns, true to type preferred ragwort on the short grass by the water. The other two species concentrated on the bramble flowers of the bank, with visits to the occasional marjoram and wood sage, along with foraging bumble bees.

This sunny, windless haven also produced the only dragonfly seen, basking on the tarmac with spread wings, affording a good close view. This was another black-tailed skimmer, a fully matured male this time, the black tailed body a clear powder blue. The species, common in South and Southeast England, is fairly sparse in Wales according to the maps but, as I learned a few days later, is proving one of the commonest dragonflies here this year.

The causeway across to the other side was open now for walkers - the water travelling one way only, from fresh to salt. I would love to have followed down the Pembroke River into really salty zones, but padlocked iron gates prevented access after a short distance.

Tidal mudflats below the penstock were dissected by short, steep-sided creeks, bordered above by small angular stones coated with brown spiral wrack, itself coated with a thin layer of drifted mud. Above this on the opposite shore was a substantial belt of medium grey sea purslane *(Halimione portulacoides)* , which can thrive only in the absence of grazing, and above that again a sparser belt of the much rarer, almost white plants of sea wormwood, formerly an Artemisia but now *Seriphidium maritimum).* This unusual silvery-white species formed a belt between purslane and a red fescue sward backed by trees.

On my side of the salty creek it occurred as a few odd plants rooted on the rock wall with great sea spurrey (Spergularia) and big, ungrazed plants of sea plantain. Sea beet was the only one of the creekside salt lovers to occur also by the great arc of fresh water above.

Feeding on the mudbanks were small numbers of black-headed and lesser black-backed gulls. Birds of the fresh water, beside which I lunched, were numerous low-skimming swallows, with the usual few jackdaws and magpies and a single mallard, but house sparrows were the only small passerines seen. Four swans came out of the water to graze the fresh spring grass on the bank, but most of the swans were above the road bridge on the stretch of river bordering the north flank of the old town.

The woodland backing the saltmarsh gave way at the sluice first to attractive new dwellings with alternating red, yellow and white limewash, and then older ones towards the bridge, equally attractive in weathered grey stone. Magnificent skyscapes followed each other above the castle elevated on the opposite shore, propelled by those unseasonally strong winds, the sharp-edged piles of white against the blue the most attractive.

From here I followed the stream running through the valley below the fragmented town wall bordering the southern side of the elevated and elongated shopping centre. Grey clubrush continued here, with purple loosestrife, bordering the scummy, eutrophic water. Alongside were tall prickly oxtongue and mallow with shorter ox-eye daisy and bird's foot trefoil. Up a steep flight of steps then, from the valley carparks to the town on its ridge, with a few cryptic alleyways or arcades, well hidden from the half way point where I entered, but leading through to the main shopping street and the coach.

* * *

The Stackpole Estate, about five miles south of Pembroke, is jointly run by the National Trust and the Countryside Council for Wales and is described as "Surely one of Wales' most fascinating and varied National Nature reserves. Its dunes, grassland and sea cliffs, beaches and woodland, all easily explored by a network of footpaths."

All true, but not for us. The word "Stackpole" for me conjured up that curving stone quay, Barafundle Bay and the beautiful Broad Haven where the three Bosherston Lakes come together and lose themselves in the sand. We were not to see any of that beautiful limestone coast, so near and yet so far. All we did was a lot of brisk walking through tall woodland, with glimpses of a short, heavily fouled stretch at the head of the eastern Lake between two bridges. There is said to be a panoramic view of the best landscape features in the buildings round the quadrangle, but we were not invited inside.

Our two guides seemed to be most concerned with outdoor activities for school children engaged in rock climbing, abseiling, canoeing and recycling of waste, weighed and assessed every day. We were shown the windows of the dormitories where parties were accommodated for a week at a time by the courtyard where we assembled, and then set off smartly down to the "Hidden Bridge".

This lies near the uppermost end of the eastern arm of the lakes, which is some three times as long as either of the other two and not typical because of the recent desilting programme here that I had been reading about, quite by chance, in a recent number of the Welsh Natural History Journal, "Natur Cymru".

We caught up at the bridge, where hosts of house martins were skimming over a lone heron. I enquired about the large blue dragonflies zooming back and forth under the bridge, but our guides were not conversant with those. They did, however, give us some interesting facts about the fish biology and reason for the murkiness of the water.

It seemed that a lot of roach were present, these feeding largely on the animal plankton, water fleas and the like, whose place in the ordered scheme of things was to feed on the plant plankton. This their depleted numbers could not achieve adequately, hence the algal coating on the one species of water plant that I managed to see in the clogged depths. That was the reflexed leaved version of the Canadian pondweed, Lagarosiphon. We saw no infestation with blanket weed.

Two largish brown shapes lying doggo and only just visible in the murk were said to be pike. These and the larger of the tench, which revel in mud, were also prized as being predators of roach and hence partial saviours of the animal plankton. They were helped in this by cormorants, which came winging up from Broad Haven - also otters, which may be seen by the few who manage to get out at dawn and dusk but not by day trippers.

Small shoals of sticklebacks hovered in the shade of the bridge and we were told of a population of eels. The elvers arriving from the Sargasso Sea in spring had difficulty in entering the lake system when the outlet across Broad Haven Beach became sanded up, so this had to be dug out to accommodate them. The sluice could also be blocked with a board to keep the water level higher, and a gravity fed supply of fresh water might be trickled through a pipe to keep the substrate damp. Elvers (or glass eels) are able to travel overland for short distances on damp surfaces.

Another reason for the murkiness was soil run-off from farms upstream - as well as the recent unavoidable stirring by dredging. As we approached the bridge I was astonished by the big mob of cattle on the skyline of the hill opposite. The animals jostled each other as though yarded, but that was open pasture. It seemed that a method of cattle grazing used in New Zealand was being tried here.

This was to turn the cattle out each day onto a piece of pasture only just big enough to hold them, so that they grazed it bare and were then moved on to another small plot. Munching mouths took up a lot less room than all those cloven hoofs and I guessed there must be a lot of waste by treading and jostling. It would also entail a lot of work fencing in the plots substantially enough for the herded beasts not to break ranks.

From "Natur Cymru" I had gathered that the farmers upstream had been gratefully accepting the loads of sludge and limey marl dredged from the lakes to put on their fields, to add the fertility of the organic matter in various stages of decay. Perhaps they were short of clean grassland for the livestock. The locally abundant stoneworts absorb lime from the water, this being redeposited and incorporated as marl when the water level falls and the plants die.

While most of the lakes lie on the Carboniferous Limestone of which this scenic coast is composed, farms at the head of this longest of the arms are on the bordering belt of Old Red Sandstone to the north, so would benefit from the lime input. Limestone, however has overall porosity and the parent rocks beneath the lakes contain cracks through which the water table rises and falls, according to rainfall - as it does so famously in the Irish turloughs. Thus the underground springs that feed the lakes also drain the water away during dry periods when it is most needed.

Average water depth is said to vary between one and two and a half metres, the lakes becoming separated into compartments in a dry spell, divided by the dams installed to hold the water back. Water abstraction through boreholes on the surrounding land will also accentuate drought effects.

The old estate managers created the lakes by damming the three streams which come together at Broadhaven, and modern estate managers were kept busy maintaining levels. Mechanical cutting by a broad-beamed boat with a mower across the bows was used to cut the weed and throw it back into the boat to be disposed of on land, so that the dead remains did not build up to displace -and over enrich - the lake waters. Reeds and bur-reed were only severed above the base by mowing and we were shown a reedbed which had grown up again to its full height when we halted by the bridge further upstream.

Our walk there was along the west lake shore through tall woodland, where handsome stands of hart's-tongue fern formed a complete ground cover in parts and colonies of polypody ferns spread along displaced boughs leaning out over the water.

Along one section most of the bordering herb Robert had white instead of pink flowers - a very rare form of a very widespread species. Waterside vegetation along this section, where visible between the trees, seemed to be mostly branching bur reed and there were two nice colonies of white water lilies. Not for nothing are these referred to as the Bosherston Lily Ponds.

It was further back, away from the lake, that I came upon a thriving colony of black bulgar *(Bulgaria inquinans)*. This is one of the jelly fungi, infesting a fallen log which I was about to pass, assuming it to be the common cramp ball or 'burnt potato' *(Daldinia concentrica)*. Fortunately I tapped it with my toe and discovered that it was rubbery and not clinkerlike. Flat discs, smooth surfaced and slightly dished, a little more than an inch across, tapered inwards below into a short, thick holdfast, the discs massed closely together.

The lass who was tailing back with me took Anna Malarki, one of our leaders back to look at it. Result: A phone call a few days later. "Bob Haycock, the CCW chief says this species had not been recorded here before. Was I sure?" As sure as can be after consulting five fungus books showing only one other that it could possibly be confused with, but which had little in common with the crowded Stackpole colony. An interesting find this, almost missed.

We diverged twice along this shoreline walk, once into an old stone shed which had been converted to a bird hide. There were thirty three of us, so I was in the back row, wondering why the ground was so sloshy underfoot, until I saw the massed swallow dung on the handrail separating the two ranks of bird watchers. The rafters were full of the old mud nests but the families had fledged and no second brood attempted as yet. People at the window in front were seeing mute swans, one with two small cygnets, coot, mallard and a heron.

Our next diversion was into the old ice house where game was hung to mature. Stout hooks attached to the beams had held deer carcases, smaller ones pheasants. Shoots accounted mostly for those but also partridges and a few snipe or woodcock. Big triangular orifices at floor level in one of the thick stone walls were for ventilation. Ice was imported between layers of straw - to prevent it from freezing into impossibly heavy, inseparable lumps.

We were marshalled onto the broad flight of stone steps leading up beside a many-arched bridge for a group photo. The steps were beautifully patterned with large colonies of white lichen showing radial growth, some with old fronds dying in the centre of the circle. It was evident that I was not with my usual sort of natural history party when a discussion started about how best to scrape these interlopers off!

Leaving the wood we came to a substantial, ornate stone building which proved to be 'just a summerhouse', where the ladies of old could sit and preserve their white skin. There was open grassland nearby, full of low-skimming swallows, no doubt the families from the bird hide practising feeding techniques. It seemed we were walking among small flies that only they could see.

Flies which flew by night were no safer and this open space was bordered by a long building pierced by the entrance to the old stable yard. The fine ornamental clock tower housed a colony of rare and highly prized Greater Horseshoe Bats. Stackpole is home to one of the largest colonies of this species in Britain - also to one of the largest populations of the almost equally rare Lesser Horseshoe Bats in West Wales.

With all that water about, the Daubenton's fishing bats had to be here too, also the Brown Long-eared, the ears almost as long as the body, the Noctule and the two Pipistrelle species. (The one of these recently separated from the other on grounds of voice alone is the Soprano Pipistrelle.) Other bats known to be domiciled here but less easy to find were Natterers, Brandts and Serotines.

While winter roosts are often in the buildings, summer roosts are more often in holes in trees or walls or among roof rafters. The little mammals travel along favourite corridors between trees, so work being done to clear the invasive cherry laurel bushes (the limestone country's counterpart of the acid country's invasive Rhododendron) is done piecemeal, not to upset their flight paths too drastically.

From the stable yard we moved on to the walled garden, manned largely by members of Mendcap, but also by fit volunteers. Here, too, bats were present, but not for us to see by day. One of several flights of steps leading down to the old underground housing of the heating ducts, had a notice on it: "Do not enter. Bat Roost". This underground heating labyrinth is ideal as a winter refuge, maintaining a regular temperature, not too warm to wake them from their necessary hibernation when there are no flies around to sustain them.

There were plenty of these for feeding bats in summer, including moths.

Day-flying insects seen by us included the new summer broods of small tortoiseshell and red admiral, meadow browns and whites. Mostly we were captivated by the splendid variety of flowers in well set out beds and rows of glasshouses.

Everything was here, from regale lilies and exquisite two-coloured Pentstemons to huge onions, rows of raspberries and runner beans, glasshouse tomatoes and courgettes or cucumbers. Some were for sale, including bunches of cut flowers. Many of us left with rhubarb - usually unobtainable in shops, and I experimented with a kohl rabi, though not sure how to deal with it. None of the ladies asked knew either, but another resident on my Brynteg corridor looked it up on the internet and presented me with a sheaf of literature which would take an hour or so to read!

CHAPTER 29

Cosmeston Tour With A Warden and Pentyrch Treasures With CCW Personnel

On the morning of tuesday 22nd July I arrived for my appointment at Cosmeston in good time to effect some book transactions with the keeper of the bookstall and with Quentin Clesham of the Flatholm Society who had been helping with sales in Penarth.

We chatted in company with four swans which had wandered through from the lake to snooze on the carpark lawn before too many disruptive humans arrived. Geoff Curtis of the Cardiff Naturalists' Society, a knowledgable local botanist and much more , turned up. He was coming too. Our guide was warden Aaron, Steve Latham having been called away to try (unsuccessfully) to save an endangered tree on an SSSI.

There ensued a fascinating two to three hours hopping in and out of the land rover and executing short walks in our tour of the country park, which covers over 275 acres (110 hectares). On most visits we get little further than the two main lakes, which occupy 12 hectares of the whole, but there was much more - grassland, scrubland, woodland, pools and streams and a newly excavated bit of the medieval village, much of which had been reconstructed.

We went first along the eastern boundary against the golf course - the route of a rewarding late evening walk finding glow worms and bats a year or so before. Our goal this time was the sculpture trail, marked by a series of wood carvings set alongside a circular grassy track carved from a spinney. Painstakingly executed works of art represented figures from the ancient Welsh Mabinogion, including a series of lesser symbols on a forked tree trunk. - a swan's head, a webbed foot, an owl's eye and a heron, with more around the rest of the park including a giant boar's head, an even more giant human head and a Welsh dragon, conjured up from a fallen tree in situ. (Also a witch's cauldron fashioned in metal.)

This leafy arena was the site of the rare white butterfly orchids (Listera) that Steve had spoken of - only a few, but spontaneous arrivals in a new site and confirmation enough that the current management was wildlife-friendly. It was too late for the flowers, but not for another treasure - some little adder's tongue ferns, primitive plants consisting of a single broad leaf bearing a single spike of spores - uncommon and mostly to be expected on sand dunes.

The walkways had been cut through stands of aromatic meadowsweet and corn mint, just wreathing its stems with whorls of mauve flowers. In this woodland clearing a wild harvest in season, known to but a few, was of horse mushrooms, but we saw only 'burnt potatoes'.

On to the north towards Cogan we were in open country of smooth ridge and valley, clothed in a diverse community of low herbs with almost no grass. Grass needs an input of fertility. The dominant ground cover here, where the ground was covered at all, was of the rosettes of glaucous sedge *(Carex flacca)*. The plant succession must have advanced little from that which first colonised the scantily clad landfill dumped on the old quarry floor.

That was during those two unforgettable hot summers of 1976 and 1977 when the country park concept may not even have been thought of. My friend and I spent happy hours swimming in the East lake in those days, trying to balance on the floating, rolling logs. We had cruised along outside the reed fringe, with the wings of low flying dragonflies clattering close overhead, the noisy gulls moving discretely away. The "Nanny State" was in its infancy then, if, indeed, even conceived, but the edict finally came. "No bathing. Too dangerous".

Work had only recently ceased then in this northern part of the quarry complex. The flat slabby stones into which the symmetrical layered beds of Lias fractured were being extracted from 1890 to 1970. The stone was taken across the Sully Road to the Portland Cement, later Blue Circle, Works on the coastal side. That tract, with its wealth of limestone flowers and butterflies during the early 1970s was subsequently covered by a housing estate.

The two southern quarries house the East and West lakes, much of the rest having been used for landfill. The resulting terrain, too infertile for grass or crops, was fine for wild flowers and, as so often elsewhere, was happily designated as a wildlife and amenity site for public enjoyment after the clearing up stage.

This northern community was where, back in the early days of the plant succession, a magnificent colony of bee orchids had appeared - a veritable honey pot for the county's flower photographers. Other orchids followed, but only pyramidal and lesser spotted were still in flower now in late July.

The threadbare swards were composed of eyebright, yellow wort, yellow bedstraw, red bartsia, fairy flax and much more. The blue haze of pale flax *(Linum bienne)*, was still apparent, although but a remnant of the continuous sheet of blue remained, this now represented by massed, circular seed capsules topping the slender stems.

We visited similar communities even more open, these the haunt of small skipper butterflies, as well as ringlets and meadow browns. Here I was shown a species new to me. This was a tiny pink-flowered member of the gentian family, the lesser centaury *(Centaurium pulchellum)*, growing among the common species, which reached four times as high. A rabbit heaven, the lagomorphs were not responsible for the dwarfness of the sward, this shown by the lack of any significant thickening up of growth in a rabbit exclosure.

Spikes of yellow flowered agrimony overtopped most others in these threadbare herbfields, while fluffy fruit heads of mouse-ear hawkweed (Pilosella) huddled at ground level. Marginally taller plants in the lee of Cogan Wood included three members of the carrot family, wild carrot, tall hedge parsley and yellow parsnip, with St. John's wort.

Geoff and I walked across this semi desert valley while Aaron circled round with the vehicle to meet us on the other side. It was as well he did. He was just in time to rescue a lady who had collapsed from unknown cause, and deliver her into the care of the local ambulance team, who were based in the carpark awaiting a call out to wherever they might be needed. A warden's tasks are multi-faceted - not just hard labour in the field and boring spells with computer records.

The biggest trees in Cogan Wood, which we visited next, marked an old parish boundary. A noisy rook roost by night, this shady, ivy-floored woodland, embellished by ramsons or wild garlic in spring, was quiet by day. Lesser trees seemed to be mostly lanky, crowded hawthorns, unusually tall, as in the nearby nature reserve of Lavernock Point on the cliffs.

* * *

A foot detour into open marshland beyond, brought us to the site of three newly bulldozed ponds, a no go area to encourage wildlife. The shoulder high meadowsweet and hemlock water dropwort topped by enormous teasels springing from squishy marshland offered little temptation to intrude.

A kestrel flew into a tall tree on the far side, then another, neither emerging. It seemed they were nesting there. A buzzard sailed past and we saw a great spotted woodpecker, heard the merry 'yaffle' of a green woodpecker and vaguely perceived a little brown bird among gipsywort. It was here that

Aaron had recently watched two herons engaged in aerial combat, tipping their bodies back to claw at each other with flailing legs. Usually these behave with exemplary decorum when fishing in each others company.

This was one of several sites pointed out which were the haunt of water rails. In winter much of the central grassland was tenanted by snipe - a large area having been fenced off here to keep the public from disturbing them.

We trod lightly through the usually forbidden territory around the dragonfly pool, but saw few dragons or damsels, because these normally fly only in sunshine. The forecast was for bright sun all day, but there was no break in the clouds until well after we had left.

The plant interest here made up for this, both wayfaring tree and the related guelder rose bearing bumper crops of ripening scarlet fruits, though the dangling ones had fallen long since from the buckling cherry trees. A tiny spindle sapling bore a disproportionately large crop of young, four-lobed fruits.

Large numbers of undamaged but empty shells of great pond snails lay on the sward, apparently washed up when the water level was higher. The clean removal of their contents with no breakage was thought to have been achieved by glow worm larvae, this reinforced by the presence of intact but empty shells of brown-lipped hedge snails and others.

Other animal life was manifested as galls. Most familiar were robin's pincushions, moss galls or rose bedeguars induced by the gall wasps *(Diplolepis rosae)*. These lay up to sixty eggs in a leaf bud, causing the host plant to produce the attractive bunch of sticky red filaments. Less well known were the tufts of reddish leafy sprouts in the flower heads of jointed rushes. These, known as rush tassel galls are caused by a psyllid or jumping plant louse *(Livia juncorum)*.

The main emergent plants here were the larger of the two Typha bulrushes and club rush with shorter Eleocharis spike rush. A colony of broad-leaved pondweed encroached over the water, bordered by marsh bedstraw. As we left a fine flock of linnets looped across the pool, to harvest seeds on the 'prairie' beyond. Goldfinches were other takers of those, appearing sometimes in large numbers.

Driving along the north side of the western conservation lake, we looked down on the always to be relied on sheet of pink water bistort flowers surfacing from the depths. The peninsula and island further off where we used to encounter water voles was looking very lush, but sadly the voles had gone, as from most of their former habitats. Mink were present and were blamed for their demise.

Black-headed gulls had just arrived from their nesting haunts on lakes and ponds in the Welsh hills and were mingling with the larger coastal gulls on the water. Cormorants occupied emergent posts; the coot and mallard were being tempted by walkers with provender and stayed within easy distance of the shore.

In the field adjacent to the one where the neatly thatched buildings of the fourteenth centre village had been reconstructed - on the site of the excavated ruins - we stopped to view some new excavations. The substantial stone walls exposed in the main trench were believed to be those of the old manor house - removed at a respectful distance from the hoi polloi in the farming settlement. The search was on now for metal or bones suitable for carbon dating to establish their age.

We circled over the Dovecote Fields towards Sully Brook later, peering into a substantial but partially overgrown brook where we spotted fish with red fins, either rudd or roach. The shoals of tiddlers could have been the young of almost anything in this waterway which joined the Cadoxton Brook to flow into the sea at Cadoxton. Gatekeeper butterflies were present here and a speckled wood.

Where reeds encroached over its surface rare cettis warblers had moved in, these recognisable by their loud song. Reed warblers and sedge warblers were also here. Reed buntings, not seen today, often scavenge crumbs on the lakeside picnic tables by the One Mile Drive after the picnickers have left. We trod the curved board walk to another pond at the end of an offshoot wooden walkway.

A moorhen's nest, in a conspicuous site, as so often, had a neatly woven lining of reed leaves and contained two buff eggs. Not far off were two tiny moorhen chicks, stepping lightly over the leaves of a fine display of yellow fringed water lilies, which scarcely gave beneath their weight, but were pushed aside by the adult, busy snapping flies off their surface. We were told that the chicks had appeared five days before and no adult had been seen on the eggs since, so those were unlikely to hatch.

Lagarosiphon in the main body of the water had to be raked out annually. The less obstreperous spike rush sprouting from a shallower ridge and a little marginal greater spearwort were less invasive. One of the other Cosmeston ponds contained a rare stonewort, recently discovered and earning special protection status.

Another rarity which I was privileged to see in the course of my extensive tour was a little colony of round-leaved wintergreen *(Pyrola rotundifolia)* , the only known location in the Vale of Glamorgan and formerly the perogative of Kenfig Burrows NNR further west. At present in full flower, this was a rare find indeed.

The wet shaded wooded hollow as we returned, held no water, but the mud was clothed with a wall to wall coating of duckweed - not the common lesser duckweed *(Lemna minor)* but the smaller more aggressive American invader, the least duckweed *(L. minuta)* which reached Britain around 1977.

***

I had a date on Wednesday, 23rd July with Julian Woodman and John Clark of the Countryside Council for Wales, to explore a tract of species-rich land on the outskirts of Pentyrch. Julian picked me up after lunch, phoning first with the comment "Don't forget your sunhat". This, at last, was the first scorcher of the summer.

He took me first to his home, also in Pentyrch, and proudly showed me round his front garden, much the untidiest in the whole road, but full of wild species, some rare and treasured, but not for their showiness. Weediest of all, and collapsed to boot, was a leggy specimen of the rare Radyr Hieracium "just another of those dandelion jobs" to the average viewer.

There were others in the back garden, though that was allocated more specifically as a play place for his two small daughters. Julian was THE plant taxonomist in his prestigious government establishment, so might be excused the quirkiness that is permissable for the specialist.

On a more down to earth level, I was introduced to the two guinea pigs, shy animals, only tempted out by the offer of some common dandelion leaves, which certainly looked more appetising than the flopped hawkweed, that had been lovingly transferred from my current parish to this, my past one.

When John arrived, we drove the short distance to the abode of Mr. Christopher, a land owner at the head of the Heol Goch Valley, which separated the Great Garh Mountain and the Little Garth Hill. This was way above my old elevation in Gwaelod-y-Garth, which translates as "the foot of the Garth", but well below the summit tump.

Viewing that later in company with the locals, I learned of the tribulations of the postman, who had to effect deliveries to the three isolated dwelling near the tump on three different tracks, not all negotiable by the postal van. There is still an element of remoteness, even so close to Cardiff!

Christopher's house was a new one, on the site of the old farmhouse where his father had farmed from the 1960s, but the old stone barns remained; "A project in mind for those, in due course." Some land had been sold and the rest, a quite delightful stretch of countryside of the sort I used to wander in as a child, was scarcely farmed at all at present.

It was said that a few ponies found a living there, but we saw none and little evidence of their presence. This 'farmland' fitted more neatly into the category of Nature Reserve, as was accorded to the lower section of the valley, The Coed-y-Bedw Nature Reserve and SSSI, owned and run by the County Wildlife Trust.

That had figured largely in my book on "The Garth Countryside", which Christopher was kind enough to say he much enjoyed reading, but I had not ventured on up the valley into the terrain where we roamed today. Its beauty and the ever changing views which it commanded to the rolling wooded hills beyond the Taff Gorge, were real eye openers to me, who had been rash enough to think that I knew the Pentyrch-Gwaelod-Greigiau parish reasonably well after forty five years of residence.

Basically our tour afoot took us across rough hummocky grassland, with an increasing number of scattered trees and shrubs as we proceeded downhill and through a hole in the fence to circle broad-leaved woodland, returning further south through some fine open bogland. Each habitat had its botanical treasure, many of them seldom seen in this age of homogeneous productive pastureland.

At first the slope was dominated by purple moor grass (Molinia), tumpy rather than tussocky and not interspersed with the little pools so common in the over-grazed and over-burned 'Molinia deserts" of the South Wales Uplands. This sward was much more diverse, with a dozen or so other species of grass, among them the unexpected quaking grass (Briza) and the heath grass (recently transferred from the genus Sieglingia to Danthonia, an important component of many Australian sheepwalks).

The nature of the underlying rock was uncertain. Great Garth is on acid Coal Measures, Little Garth is on alkaline Carboniferous Limestone. This was the Millstone Grit valley between the two. Where was the boundary? We decided it didn't really matter, the rolling nature of the terrain suggesting glacial till, deposited subsequently during the Ice Ages, as in the Coed-y-Bedw Reserve further down.

We came upon a lone colony of purple-red betony, large but scattered, also red hemp nettle and single-headed rough hawbit, all with affinities for lime. But we also walked over small clumps of heather or ling and, more conspicuously, pink lousewort, both regarded as acid indicators.

It was certainly water retentive, as shown by the delightful frequency of pink ragged robin, with yellow lesser spearwort, white marsh bedstraw and purple and white marsh thistles. Common and jointed rushes mingled with the more elegant toad rush and a wealth of sedges, including yellow, star and glaucous.

Perhaps the most widespread and abundant herb was devil's bit scabious, food plant of the caterpillars of the rare marsh fritillary butterflies, but these seemed not yet to have discovered what they were missing. Something else, possibly insect, possibly fungus, had made a concerted attack on the scabious leaves, most of which were speckled with dark brown. Invertebrates seen included grasshoppers, green leaf hoppers, red soldier beetles, white grass moths and a carpet moth, also ringlet, meadow brown, hedge brown, small heath and white butterflies, along with spiders and daddy-longlegs (Opiliones).

My best moment here was coming on a dinner plate sized patch of pink bog pimpernel *(Anagallis tenella)*, one of the most delicate denizens of wet hillsides, the creeping, leafy stems massed with flowers. Even more special and more delicate was Julian's special find of ivy-leaved bellflower *(Wahlenbergia hederacea)*, another creeper with blue flowers not much larger and more solitary, so less likely to be spotted. Both are characteristic in bogs of the real hill country from Merthyr north, but I had very occasionally come across the bellflower during ramblings on the Great Garth.

Neat round sallow bushes increased as we moved downhill, many of these being eared sallow, *(Salix auriculata)* with rumpled, round leaves and persistent stipules, the ears.

We were spreadeagled on a dry knoll recovering from our exertions when Gil Barter joined us in the later afternoon. She had been at a conference with CCW colleagues from other regions in Abergavenny and had hoped to catch up with us before we left. We waited for Jack, the zoologist, to finish threading specimens of sedges and woodrush through pages of his notebook, complete with names. Every expedition is a learning process.

Out through the fence, we passed a neighbour's smooth-textured hay crop, the silky plumes of the dominant species being those of tufted hair grass, its bristly-surfaced leaves less tufted than in its normal habitat of wet woodland. This field lacked diversity. "Few if any herbs" quoth the expert dismissively.

* * *

As we entered what showed every aspect of being ancient woodland, my eyes alighted on banks of cow wheat *(Melampyrum pratense)*, that special plant that I had sought in vain by the Melincourt Falls. Others were more ordinary, bluebells, Anemones and violets, all past flowering, wood speedwell, wood avens and enchanters nightshade just coming into their own, among spreads of wood sorrel leaves and Pellia liverworts.

Fine old trees, some double trunked, stood out as an old hedgeline, suggesting that the woodland might have grown up on previous grazing land - as those sallow bushes were currently doing above- eventually to exclude the floral treasures by shading, if not gently curbed.

A more orderly woodland edge to the hayfield was composed entirely of birch apart from a single rowan tree, full of berries. Trees had thickened where we walked or squelched through brief quagmires, excluding light and with it the interesting bog flora. I presumed the two deeply cut streams were those uniting as the headwaters of that forming the nucleus of the Coed-y-Bedw, which received tributaries from both acid and limey sources on its passage down to the Taff.

Back into the sunlight, we were among more interesting plant specialities. Here was a big circle of bog asphodel *(Narthecium ossifragum)* with yellow flowers, orange fruit heads and the little sideways curved 'Iris leaves', by whish we recognise it among the grass before the flower stems arise, grown out into foot long, linear leaves of a gentle pale green.

Another patch bore the fluffed white fruits of bog cotton *(Eriophorum angustifolium)*, officially known as cotton grass, but actually a sedge, with unassuming brown florets before producing enough silky white down to have been collected to stuff pillows by past mountain dwellers.

Gil's special find here was marsh valerian *(Valeriana dioica)*, which I had been so pleased to see persisting on my Cwm Nofydd walk in the spring. This ground was much boggier, with patches of Sphagnum moss and spreading colonies of the circular leaves of marsh pennywort *(Hydrocotyle vulgaris)*. One such patch produced the pale pink flowers of the uncommon water speedwell *(Veronica catenata)*. Other water lovers were square-stemmed St. John's wort *(Hypericum tetrapterum)* and marsh willow herb *(Epilobium palustre)*.

With these specialities were two familiar aromatics, water mint and meadowsweet. Anthills bore a special vegetation of their own, able to thrive in the dry powdery soil lifting them above the water table. A notable change was from lush marsh bedstraw to dwarf heath bedstraw.

As we moved uphill surface water disappeared and we came across the spent heads of heath spotted orchids. Most special here were neat little plants of saw wort *(Serratula tinctoria)* with reddish-purple heads and neatly serrate leaves. Relatives, equally uncommon, were meadow plume thistles *(Cirsium dissectum)*, peat lovers of South-west Britain and Ireland, with cottony, non-prickly leaves.

Particularly interesting in this community were patches of English or trailing tormentil *(Potentilla anglica)* growing side by side with the common tormentil which characterises acid grasslands everywhere. The flowers were twice as big as the normal ones and might have four or five petals. It is a sterile hybrid, producing no seed, so must perennate by creeping, rooting runners. Also in the rose family was lady's mantle, one of the confusing kinds of Alchemilla.

Throughout our walk we lifted our gaze from the ground at frequent intervals to take in the ever changing view. So many wooded hills seemed to pop up in different sequences, giving me some entirely new angles on a landscape with which I thought I was quite familiar.

Most panoramas spread east of the Gorge with its landmark of Castell Coch, to the higher landmark of the great radio and TV mast on the Wenallt. To have so much real countryside with such a polyglot flora, as diverse as nature intended, before humankind moved in and meddled, was a real bonus so close to cardiff. A stile at the top of the hill led us into a housing estate, new to both Gil and me, both long term residents in this community council area.

We were soon back at our starting point. Mr. Christopher came out to learn the NCC's opinion of his patch, while jackdaws probed the lawn and the barn's complement of nesting swallows skimmed over our heads. A great spotted woodpecker came looping in from the marshland and settled in a nearby tree, parallel to the trunk, a fitting farewell to an unknown pocket of real countryside. We can only hope that it is replicated elsewhere in other corners of this so overpopulated land.

CHAPTER 30
The South Flank Of The Little Garth and Home Territory

It was Saturday, 26th July, nearing the end of the first week of real summer and too hot to walk comfortably in the sun, but not in the shade. I took the car a few miles up the road to the Ty Nant Inn opposite Pugh's Garden centre and set off for a stroll in the woods clothing the 590 feet high Little Garth. This forms the western flank of the Taff gorge which cuts through the east to west ridge of Dolomitic Carboniferous Limestone.

Caves lived in by primitive tribes penetrate the magnesian limestone, as do deep mines from which iron was extracted during the industrial heyday from 1620 to 1884. Currently there is a quarrying industry taking roadstone and associated products.

Unquarried faces are clothed by beechwood, the only part concerning me on this hot July day, beechwoods in which little or nothing grows except beech where the trees are tallest and closest. Spectacular when the soft green leaves appear in spring and when these change and fall as copper coins in autumn, they can seem very empty in the seasons between.

These are not just any beechwoods. Charcoal examined from ancient hearths here have shown that beech was present in the indigenous forest, in one of its most westerly sites as a native in Britain. Individual trees have not survived since then, no doubt many being exploited for fuel during the second Iron Age, but there were now mighty trees here once more.

Closely juxtaposed, they were tall rather than bulky or spreading. The phrase "cathedral aisle" has often been used for such lofty, even-aged stands, and seemed more applicable than ever today with narrow streaks of light sneaking through between the trunks as though through stained glass windows.

Moving in from the brilliant sunshine, I saw little at first, even less when a disorientated fly entered my eye and took lot of easing out in the absence of a mirror. Finally, accustomed to the gloom, I set off eastwards to move up to the brink of the old, abandoned Ty Nant Quarry facing onto the gorge, where I used to go for a bird's eye view of plant colonisation of the old quarry walls and floor. No luck!

The brink had been fenced off - the Nanny State again? and the path which started optimistically upwards curved round and down to the road towards the renovated entrances to the old lime kilns. I turned back and followed the track along the lower slopes, skirted at first by the extensive allotments opposite Cwm farm.

Sparse clumps of wispy, shoulder-high beech saplings were almost the only components of the ground flora under those mighty "timberman's trees" with their conspicuous lack of lower branches. A few ferns and the yellowing leaves of a sparse showing of wild garlic and that was it: not even a ground cover of ivy as often in dim deciduous woods.

It was no surprise to remember that the two special understorey flowers that I had found here many years before were both complete parasites, with no chlorophyll and hence no need for light. These were the bird's nest orchid (Neottia) and the yellow bird's nest (Monotropa).

Where the path forked I took the upper one over the sturdy stone bridge which crossed the old Barry Railway line just before it plunged into the long tunnel which took it right through the south-east corner of the hill to emerge in the Taff Gorge. That it had crossed on a tall viaduct, built in 1898 and demolished in 1970.

I perceived no bird or other creature, just a pile of feathers where a raptor had dined, and the scrawtch of a jay. The brown-lipped hedge snails found had almost unstriped shells the same red colour as the rock, as in the beechwood on the north flank of the hill. Was this because the red tinge had gone into their making or because it afforded them better camouflage from hungry thrushes? I spotted a way out through the dense border of ash, birch and sycamore reaching towards their source of energy and escaped into the sunshine.

After several hours, I returned into the gloom along the line of the old railway, overgrown in one part but with a compensatory loop path leading back in. I followed under the bridge which I had crossed earlier and where bulldozers had been at work on my last visit.

A vertical cliff towered on the left, green with algae and with a thin coat of mosses, but with small hart's tongue ferns sprouting from cracks. Rocky soil had been dumped against the lower face on the right, where slabby liverworts clothed moist boulders and a few others found a living. A broad concrete sluice brought water down to a hole by the track from the woodland opposite.

The mouth of the tunnel was boarded up, but it continued right through the hill, directly under the trough of a syncline (a geological downfold in the strata). A vertical shaft of light shone between the two halves of the tall wooden doors so I moved in to investigate.

I got a clear view through the gap to the round-topped blaze of light at the other end, the tunnel itself being unobstructed. Modern excavations only just completed had blasted a way out from the quarry to the road between Pughs and the Ynys Roundabout to the north. I had thought that some of the old railway line might have been incorporated into this, but that would have brought the roadway out at the level of the old viaduct, with a steep descent needed from there to valley road level.

The purpose of the new road, curving out at a smaller roundabout between high walls of newly cut orange-red rock, was to allow the trucks out to the A470 across the River Taff by the shortest possible route. Previously they had emerged onto Heol Goch - the steep and not over wide road connecting Gwaelod-y-Garth and Pentyrch - a traffic hazard to residents, particularly of the latter.

* * *

But, back to my exit from beechwood gloom into the blazing sunshine. Mauve spires of Buddleia erupted towards the light from the woodland edge, where greater willow herb, bracken and ragwort graded out to a feast of meadow plants. The entire swathe of country up to the four farm ponds and the new developments to the west was covered in a tangle of tall grasses, sedges and rushes, mostly dark brown hard rush, but also ginger brown soft rush.

Large round plots of red clover were so uniform in size that I sensed they must have been sown. They were a leafy agricultural form with flattish heads more sparsely invested with florets than the normal kind. Similarly large plots of yellow and orange bird's-foot trefoil added a harlequin touch to the colour, under widely spaced stems of agrimony. This, like everything else here, was more robust than anything on the Cosmeston 'prairies' but there, as here, the semiparasitic eyebright was unusually common.

Tramping through this long herbage was very different from stepping lightly between the dwarf plants at Cosmeston. Here I was on the outer face of a hill which had been disembowelled from above by quarrying but leaving the adjacent face intact. There I had been on the actual site of rock removal and its subsequent covering with waste. Both were on limestone, that of the Garth vastly more ancient than the Lias of the other. The main difference was water retention, as shown by the prevalence of rushes here.

Today this was no problem and I stretched out on a shaded but open patch among self heal and white clover to watch the butterflies. There were crowds of them, just as when I had lain in hayfields of the Home Counties eighty years before.

Mostly meadow browns, as always, there were all the other seasonal usuals, including ringlets, small skippers and the first commas of my season. Also moths, one a shaded broad bar, whose caterpillars feed on vetch, others variously patterned in brown and white which I would be rash to try and name without specimens in one hand and a 'key' in the other.

I had no trouble identifying the six-spot burnets, resplendent in their red and black livery. Some were involved in mating, an exploit usually indulged in soon after their emergence from the chrysalis. Their papery, vacated cocoons were everywhere, secured near the tips of the tallest rush and grass stems, most with the shiny black skins of the pupa from which they had broken free adhering to the torn apex. The delicate yellow cocoons were papery and pointed at both ends - almost perfect replicas of the sheaths enclosing the rush buds, and so affording them perfect camouflage during the period when they were incapable of escaping. The caterpillars had no doubt waxed fat on the abundant bird's-foot trefoil.

Cinnabar caterpillars were munching on the young ragwort spikes where I rested in the shade. It was over a month since I had seen flying adults of these, also red and black like the burnets. Those were of the generation that lays batches of thirty to forty eggs in June and July. There is only one generation a year.

These caterpillars would feed up through the summer months, imbibing the poisons from the ragwort that makes them so unpalatable to birds, while doing themselves no harm, and then pupate in September, overwintering as chrysalids at ground level until the ensuing June.

The black and yellow stripes of the larval phase - transverse stripes as in wasps, tigers and some bulldozers, signifying danger, as blatantly as does the red and black of their fearlessly day-flying elders.

Others wearing a similar, less striking garb today were the Nephrotoma craneflies, their long legs bright yellow, as was the body, topped and tailed by black. Weak fliers, these were mostly floundering in bracken and undergrowth.

My own floundering through the thick vegetation, laced together with creeping cinquefoil, was to discover the identity of a brilliant patch of blue amidships. It turned out to be an unusually fine patch of tufted vetch with exceptionally dark flowers.

En route I halted to watch a small scale battle, the aggressor a furry brown funnel web spider (Agalena), the victim a bright green grasshopper

(Omocestis). The spider, on the firm webbing where the tapering funnel in which she lived broadened out, was making repeated short runs at the victim, which was a deal larger of body than herself but without the spread of legs.

She had got enough silk around it to prevent those neatly folded hind legs from springing into action and effecting an escape. The elongated bundle - her potential packed lunch - finally got knocked off the web into the grass. Would the aggressor retrieve it? The beautifully constructed tapering silken tunnels were locally abundant, opening about a foot from the ground in loose cover, sometimes only a foot or so apart.

Beyond the spider colony the ground was wetter, the hard rush taller and mixed with robust Angelica. Then came an area dominated by field horsetail. Young tree saplings were springing up throughout, so evenly that they, once again, gave the impression of having been introduced.

A vast number of red brick, red roofed houses had sprung up recently to the south, on both sides of the M4 (here deep in its cutting), the houses infiltrating into Morganstown. It is conceivable that this shaggy meadowland, criss-crossed in places by narrow paths, may have been preserved as a recreation area for the big influx of new inhabitants, but there was no-one but me using it today.

Other features had been the two permanent ponds among trees and the two winter ponds, which appeared seasonally to half drown the field boundaries. Or maybe those were casualties of the housing development.

I picked up the trail of the old Barry Railway and followed round past ripening hazel nuts and tinted dogwood foliage with purple tufted vetch and more delicate white hairy vetch climbing six feet up their exposed flanks, to bring themselves to the notice of pollinators. Buddleia, sallow and sycamore closed in as I moved back into the beechwood gloom to examine the tunnel.

* * *

On wednesday 23rd July, when breakfasting in my usual armchair by the window, I thought I was hallucinating. Could that be a small tabby cat doing his morning ablutions in the corner of my balcony? Had one of my deserted 'ferals' tracked me down? How could he have climbed onto my balcony, a full storey up from the ground? I moved out quietly and there was a mutual summing up session.

Puss didn't like what he saw and bolted round the corner onto next door's balcony which, because of the steepness of the garden below, was at ground level on the other side. He wore a little blue collar, the same pattern as two which had been discarded, broken, in my Gwaelod garden - possibly in combat with my three residents. I had not seen him before, nor after for at least ten days.

Oddly enough another cat turned up next evening, when Rita and I were out with hose pipe and water can. This one was twice the size, a big fluffy tortoiseshell, which crouched in the bushes just out of range of the hose, watching us and moving discretely into fresh cover as the spray decreed. At one stage he showed himself, just as Ginger Pop appeared about twenty yards away. They took one look at each other and fled in opposite directions. Ginger was much smaller, but he was the resident. So whose territory was it?

We were likely to be watering for a while yet. Nigel, the house manager was off on holiday for a fortnight. His comment at the weekly meeting was. "If you want your flowers to survive, you'll have to water them." There didn't seem to be many volunteers. For me, gardening was no chore!

Lynne's nasturtium plants, which I had inserted into the knobbly clay with little hope a fortnight before, had not grown any bigger, but had produced half a dozen brilliant orange flowers. I had hopes of them rambling all over the drab evergreens in due course, among the current crop of dark purple Geraniums.

The salmon coloured Polyanthus-rose which I had brought from my old garden was doing splendidly at the far end of the premises, along with the yellow loosestrife, orange Montbretia and pink Astilbe. Ice plants in my own new patch would soon be in flower, but there was little response from the scarlet kaffir lilies as yet, or the Michaelmas daisies.

Rita had sown some unlabelled seeds on a patch of compost and asked me to identify them - in the cotyledonary stage. These first two seed-leaves were each dissected into two slender triangles. No plant had leaves like that. Then a premonition stirred. A dwarf blue and white Convolvulus or Ipomoea with heart shaped leaves from number three on?

With her permission, I potted up six of them for my verandah and in two days the first heart-shaped leaves had appeared. Would I have to stake them or would they wind themselves round the balcony rails, thereby blocking my view? This was the first week I had found the weather warm enough to want to sit outside on this north face. It was certainly much too hot to do so on the garden seats facing south.

Blue butterflies were about again, but not settling to show their underwings. I suspected this was the second brood of holly blues. There was plenty of holly about, but not bird's foot trefoil for caterpillars of the common blues.

A small white-tailed bumble bee came repeatedly to my Cyclamen flowers, a second crop after the first in January. The bee visited every upside down flower in turn having difficulty pushing her head in with little to hang on to. The last of the thrift flowers held no attraction and the massed Geraniums were not even sniffed at, but she was back in an hour to see if the Cyclamen had produced any more nectar.

Sometimes I spotted something new in the garden. Wondering why the supposed pignut flowering just beyond the fence was doing so, this late in the season, I took a closer look. Delicately dissected leaves and spreading 'beard' behind the flower head, this was no pignut but fool's parsley *(Aethusa cynapium)*, an arable weed I had not seen in years in these days of herbicides.

I pulled noxious weeds from the beds as I wandered round, but not those producing even a wisp of colour. Even the tiny pale mauve flowers of the four seeded hairy vetch *(Vicia tetrasperma)* passed muster, as did the small yellow flowers of lesser clover. The 'gardeners', who only dealt with lawns and hedges, eliminated this at intervals from the lawn, leaving bare patches which the thin grass was incapable of covering over.

A fine young green hellebore had appeared outside the fence, but there had been no flowers on the black bryony further along. I had hoped to push a few ripe berries of that under the fence to germinate and hide the unsightly white name plate that marred my view.

While engaged in producing my Sunday lunch I was able to watch a cock blackbird's sun-bathing manoeuvres. After a spell on the railings, making sure no people or cats were around, he dropped onto the sun-warmed lawn, flattening his body on landing and spreading the left wing over his back.

A few minutes later the wing was brought forward for a thorough preening, turning occasionally at a right angle, so that the beak could comb through the feathers from both above and below. Then back to the sunning position and another bout of preening - several times. After ten minutes my pork cutlet took precedence. Preferring hot food to cold, I failed to learn if the right wing received similar treatment.

Unsettled was the word for this week's hot weather, mild, muggy, bright sunshine and sharp showers, punctuated by brief, rolling thunder storms. Gulls were behaving strangely, their horizontal flights interrupted with rapid flaps which took them vertically upwards for five or six feet - presumably to grab a morsel of flying food.

A magpie was systematically quartering the station platforms, with shuffling gait, like a Cardiff railway pigeon. A lone great tit was around morning and afternoon - these seldom having visited since the spring, and another not too familiar at this season was a greenfinch.

Frogs, toads and newts were escaping the heatwave huddled in the mud at the bottom of shallow ponds. How did I know this? Clive and Lynne were cleaning out their garden pool and had to launch a rescue operation, popping them into buckets of shallow water to tide them over the crisis.

* * *

A teatime thunder storm eliminated the necessity for an evening watering patrol, so I went for a walk instead, down river on the east bank, out on the lower path and back on the embankment. My binoculars were trained on a foraging juvenile blackbird when a young rabbit hopped into my field of vision. Then, surprise surprise, the long lean form of a weasel streaked across the path and no more was seen of the small rabbit. Had the predator been a stoat it would have had less chance of survival, but weasels usually hunt small rodents.

In the vicinity of the monumental black poplars, I came upon two unfamiliar plants, already well established. Purple and white goat's rue was shoulder high and laden with tassels of pea flowers. Prior to finding it on Coryton Roundabout a few weeks before, I had only met this species on the spacious wasteland of Cardiff's now defunct dockland.

The other stranger here was a fine specimen of lady's mantle, a garden escape this, *Alchemilla mollis*, which is a favourite 'background plant' with flower arrangers. Buddleia was at its most splendid, full of flowers, but scarcely a butterfly had noticed, despite the plant's popular name of butterfly bush. The bumble bees were not so neglectful of such bounteous forage.

A crab spider (Misnumena), with bright yellow abdomen and pale green thorax and legs, lay doggo on a yellow composite head, waiting to embrace an unsuspecting insect visiting for nectar. These can change colour to white, or even pink, if necessary to maintain their camouflage.

I had another leisurely view of a rabbit nibbling long grass among riverside forget-me-nots - but missed the stately comfrey plants which had been removed by some felon when at the height of flowering.

Having an appointment on Tuesday, 29th July to see a podiatrist at St. David's Hospital on Cowbridge Road East in the city was good news. It seemed I shouldn't be waiting twenty four weeks as told prior to my London visit in February. Not a bit of it. My need was approved and I was informed that I would be contacted eight or ten weeks hence. That brought us up to October again.

Needing to fill up with petrol en route, I left earlier than necessary and had time to kill on arrival. Bright sun, fierce wind and purple thunder clouds hurrying across the sky, I wandered off, umbrella at the ready. The hospital buildings were entirely new. Whether the old stone edifice with its clock tower beyond blocks of new flats was part of it I failed to discover, nor whether there was ward accommodation or just out patient services, but the spacious environs of the new emporium were wholly pleasing.

I spent most of my time in the various car parks with their surrounding and intervening plant life. This ranged from sizable maples to the massed blooms of climbing roses and tall ornamental Fuchsias The basic design was delimited by neatly trimmed, flat-topped hedges of box and many another.

Various Hebes were in flower and fruit, broom bushes which must have been brilliant in spring, were decked with exploded brown pods. The mass of small white flowers lining one side of the main entrance proved to be a composite: I guessed an Olearia or New Zealand daisy bush. Less spectacular white umbels opposite passed the 'leaf dangling test' for dogwood - the halves of leaves split across remaining connected by sticky strands when dangling.

Gulls squabbled noisily overhead. I saw no roof nests, but the intensity of mutual abuse was such that there must have been territories to defend. Car parks were not full, patients and/or visitors were few, personnel businesslike and pleasant and my wait to be seen was minimal.

The dark haired young man who came out to get me was Dr. Mathew King - no intermediate ushers - and the ensuing half hour passed pleasantly as well as usefully. Why did he remind me so of the other dark-haired young doctor who had enrolled me as a patient of the Radyr Health Centre? I must be at the age when doctors as well as policemen look very young. How different was this calm, spacious atmosphere from the frenzied hustle, bustle and long waits for disgruntled patients experienced at the main Heath Hospital.

All the way back along Cathedral Road, the pavements were covered with yellowing lime fruits. Others had piled up on windscreens of parked cars. Lesser floral parts drifting through the air settled on all and sundry, but I saw no signs of aphid stickiness, although cars were parked, of necessity, along both sides. Nor was there a surfeit of honey dew below, on pavements or car roofs, here or elsewhere. Where had all the aphids gone this year?

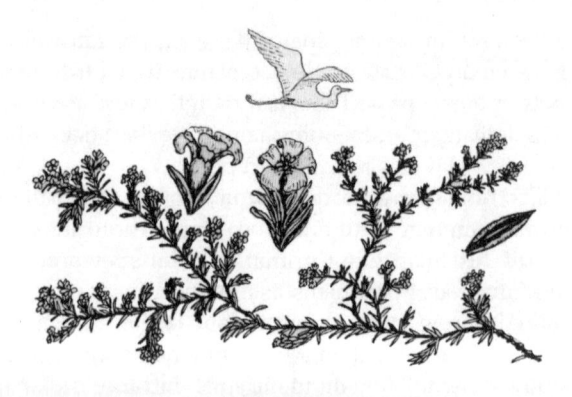

CHAPTER 31
Aberthaw, Gileston and Llantwit

On the last day of July I had a date with Madeleine Beswick for a visit to the coast at Aberthaw, a honeypot for environmentalists but known to few others. The forecast was for rain. Shall we shan't we? The concensus was 'yes'. It rained all day, with a few cool, windy letups, but we enjoyed it immensely. There was so much to see and, for me, major changes to come to grips with since my last visit some years back.

We took the lanes through Peterston-super-Ely, Llancarfon with its water splash and Llancadle, turning down the east side of the Thaw and Kenson Rivers to the old familiar layby close to the bridge across the railway at East Aberthaw.

Tree growth on the land sloping down to sea level was phenomenal, as was that of the travellers' joy knitting all the rest together in a billowing mass of impenetrable greenery flecked with white. The several off-putting notices "Beware of snakes" were unnecessary. No-one could have penetrated the present day thicket. The chance to spot one would be a fine thing.

It was hard to believe that I had conducted a survey on those slopes in years gone by, to measure the increase and subsequent decrease of the massed bee orchids in a series of permanent transects, on what was then open limestone grassland, dotted with shrubs.

The former entrance lane was gated below the lone cottage. We had to search for the tiny obscure track leading round a corner to the lagoon. There was another narrow stile alongside a gate leading to the alternative route along behind the towering lime kiln. That, at least, with its three storey annexe alongside the twin furnaces remained, roofless but unchanged. I chose the lower path to sea level.

The view of the lagoon from the railway bridge, under which still trundled long goods trains, taking coal to the remaining power station, was superb. Neatly fringed with tall, reedy vegetation, it had three or four neatly circular reed islands amidships. The old fly ash tip beyond was higher than I remembered and neatly grassed over, the tide way out beyond the sea wall revealing broad intertidal flats of sand and pebbles.

A little path led through the thicket of sand couch grass, great willow herb, meadowsweet and Angelica to the lagoon shore. The resident mute swan was moulting and his main wing primaries were strewn across the close sward - a suitable source of quill pens! He followed us just offshore, hissing his displeasure. When we left he came to land, once more monarch of his own domain. A few coot and mallard swam tentatively towards us. Were they used to being fed? Obviously the cryptic entrance did not encourage visitors, although we saw two faded boards commenting on biodiversity - well into the site and too faded to read.

Then the bird of the day flapped past - a little egret, neck tucked tightly back to the snowy body and legs trailing. Later, from the shorter vegetation on the opposite shore, we saw another speciality, a cock stonechat, resplendant in his breeding plumage of black, white and orange. What appeared to be reed warblers were flying in and out of the reeds, but there was no singing, so no way of recognising a Cetti's warbler. I spotted no sedge warblers.

A dipped finger showed the water to be still salty. Did sea water seep in through the outlet sluice? Most seemed clear of visible vegetation. That which approached the shore was a very local denizen of brackish water, the tassel pondweed or beaked tasselweed *(Ruppia maritima)*, a sure sign of the presence of salt. Scummy green algae indicated eutrophication or fertility above optimum.

Presumably there were still fish here. People used to bait the big grey mullet with bread, catch them and put them back, but there were several "No Fishing" notices now. During three hours here we saw other people only thrice, two were rod fishermen, in transit, one a man walking his dog and the others a family from the Fontygary caravan site, out of view on top of the verdant east cliff.

The close velvety sward occupying the swan territory between thicket and water, was almost entirely of black saltwort or sea milkwort *(Glaux maritima)*, much trampled but undamaged. Shoots some two inches high were clothed with neat succulent leaves, some still topped with pink flowers. This was very much a seaside species, although leaving its habitual salt marshes at times to ascend spray splattered cliffs. Where it abutted onto the riot of freshwater marsh plants shoots reached to nine or ten inches. Plants liberally covered with swan dung seemed none the worse.

The only associate, and this in the less trampled parts of the sward, was brookweed *(Samolus valerandi)*, another member of the primrose family having an affinity with the sea. The emergent vegetation in the shallows beside the low earth brink was almost entirely sea club-rush *(Bolboschoenus maritimus)*, the main grass a typical denizen of foredunes, the sand couch.

We returned through the exuberant freshwater marsh which was pierced in places by fine clumps of purple loosestrife, wild carrot, tall composites and fleabane. Water mint bordered the path, which was narrow but drier and little used, and dotted with pink centaury and the related yellow-wort of the gentian family, its leaves joined in pairs around the stem. Here, too, was aromatic wild celery.

These persisted beyond the upper marsh, where the sward was kept low by rabbits. Here were eyebright, scarlet pimpernel and self heal with two uncommon thistles - musk or nodding thistles, with more than their share of prickles, and carline thistles, some generously branched, their flower heads surrounded by shining yellow bracts. Taller plants among the scattered liassic limestone boulders included yellow toadflax, hedge bedstraw, pink rest harrow, another typical dune plant, and knapweed, some encircled with elongated florets, true cornflower style.

Here we were walking beneath the sturdy stone wall which was the quay where boats had pulled in. Some were barges, brought in onto adjacent pebble flats at high tide, loaded with boulders for the great kiln and towed out when they refloated. Others would take the finished product away, either as quicklime or more manageable slaked lime.

It was hard to picture the part where we had been walking as a broad sandy estuary, but I had a fine set of panoramic photos illustrating just that, acquired from power station personnel when we, as the Glamorgan Wildlife Trust, were negotiating the nature reserve status of the area in the 1960s and 70s.

Sea water had not only lapped this old quay at high tide, but had infiltrated through the cul de sac under the two kilns, between the hefty masonry of the chutes and the great pile of waste lime beyond, this now comfortably covered with robust vegetation.

We went inside, up the central corridor and peered into the two dark interiors, encircled by narrow passages. The warehouse space beyond had been kept clear of all but ground herbs but, when we returned later past the back, we found it unapproachable now from the landward side.

Circling on around the lagoon, we walked along the inside of the concrete sea wall, which had spelled doom for the old estuary where rabbits had burrowed in sand spits infiltrating the wide river mouth. Just such a transformation from salty estuary to fresher lagoon was to take place in subsequent years in the creation of Cardiff Bay. The main body of water from the two short Vale of Glamorgan rivers, the Thaw and the Kenson, now entered the Severn Estuary along a straight concrete runnel through the power station site beyond the great pulverised fuel ash tip.

Apart from a few grasses and buck's horn plantain, there was little indication of salinity here. Two characteristic plants in the daisy family were bristly ox-tongue and hawkweed ox-tongue *(Picris echioides and Picris hieracioides)*. The first is most often found near the sea, the second on limestone. Another abundant composite with white daisy flowers, was sea mayweed *(Tripleurospermum maritimum)*.

On the outer side of the sea wall substantial concrete groynes reduced longshore drift and provided a roothold for plants. Most ebullient of these was a fine clump of rock samphire *(Crithmum maritimum)*, an atypical umbellifer with stubby succulent leaves to store water not tainted by salt. More usually on cliffs, this is quite at home on pebble beaches. The mosaic of sand and pebble flats reaching out into the channel stretched as far as the eye could see to east and west.

We carried on only as far as the fly ash tip, though the track continued round to Gilestone. Offshore were one tall and two short stone turrets where hot water from the works was exchanged for cold, making the immediate environs suitable for marine organisms from warmer climes. Turning back to recross the underground outlet from the lagoon, we could just discern the grey hump of Steepholm Island beyond the angular, hazy headlands of Rhoose and Lavernock.

Despite the constant drizzle and wind sufficient to turn our inadequate umbrellas inside out when not held by both hands, it was quite mild and there were plenty of insects on the wing. Gatekeeper butterflies were with us throughout, speckled woods in the thickets, whites and skippers over the shaggy meadows.

Brambles, an integral part of all these communities, bore flowers and fruits, their blooms, both pink and white, popular among nectaring insects. Here, as below the Little Garth, there were six spot burnet moths and their vacated cocoons on tall grass stems, also shaded broadbars and other moths. Despite a fair amount of ragwort, we saw none of the usual cinnabar moths.

It was along here that we came upon a dead hedgehog, just the discarded skin, with most of the spines still intact, each held in place by a little white disc at the inner end, inside the leathery hide. It was tucked into one of the many burrows, not all of which belonged to rabbits, which had littered much of the ground with their mini marbles of dung. A fox perhaps?

* * *

We pressed on to where the sea wall abutted onto the cliff, to the concrete steps leading up and over, these unaltered by the passage of time. This was real coast now - Glamorgan's best amalgam of saltmarsh, pebble storm beach, muddy creeks, sand dunes and limestone cliffs.

The sight that met my eyes on emergence from the entry thicket was the most astonishing botanical revelation of the year. Dominating the strand vegetation between cliff and salty creeks was a great spread of ground-hugging sea heath *(Frankenia laevis)*, a species unknown in Wales until R.N.Roberts spotted it in Anglesey in 1965 and then the late A.G.Wade found a single plant by a harbour boom at Penarth, that doomed by the coming of the Cardiff Barrage.

Blamey, Fitter and Fitter's Flora of 2003 states the species to have been introduced to the Dorset cliffs and mapped its distribution as east from there along England's south coast, appearing again in Essex and around the Wash, with none in the West.

The second population in Wales, and, indeed, in the whole of Western Britain, apart from an introduction at Braunton, North Devon, was found by Stephen Waldren at the mouth of the River Ogmore on the sandy strand of the Merthyr Mawr dune system in Mid Glamorgan in 1981. It romped right up the estuarine section of the river in a matter of years, ousting much of the sea sandwort *(Honkenya peploides)* from its niche along high water mark.

It must have been here at Aberthaw for many years to have formed this unbroken sward along the upper driftline, mostly only a few feet wide, where the amount of inundation by the tide was optimum, but stretching for hundreds of yards until the land curved outwards to connect with the seaward storm beach - and possibly there too, where we did not go. A few years before I had seen a colony on a cliff in North Devon, not so far from Braunton, so its need for inundation by salt water must be minimal.

Although reaching but two inches above ground, it was twiggy, the stems and tiny heath-like leaves a dark red as though suffering from water stress.(Few tides come this far in to green it up). Spangled now with starry pink flowers, it made a fitting partner for the smaller but taller patches of rock sea lavender *(Limonium binervosum)* with which it grew, both here and at Merthyr Mawr. Such a vista of rare and unexpected colour certainly made my day, rarity or no rarity, rain or no rain.

Previously this zone had been occupied by a belt of sea radish, all along the cliff base, and there was plenty still. Related to the arable wild radish, this, with its large, purple-veined pale yellow petals and splendid bumbly bobbly seed capsules, was easily distinguished from the many other yellow-flowered Crucifers.

The rock sea lavender was magnificent, occurring across the creeks on the saltmarsh proper, where it would be logical to expect the larger-leaved salt marsh sea lavender of the old Cardiff river estuaries before the sea was excluded. At Aberthaw it mingled with the dominant sea purslane *(Halimione portulacoides*) and coarse sea grasses but, happily, we saw very little of the invasive Spartina cord grass that was romping along the shores of the Severn Estuary.

Below the sea heath belt were all the normal components of salt marsh mud, succulent-stemmed glasswort (Salicornia), succulent leaved sea blite (Suaeda), glaucous leaved orache (Atriplex) and fleshy leaved sea spurrey (Spergularia) starred with pink flowers slightly larger than those of the newcomer.

The succulent, linear leaves of sea arrow grass (Triglochin) presented a problem. Able to grow unusually tall in the absence of farm livestock, big clumps of this had nevertheless been nipped off cleanly at an even height of four to five inches above the ground. Rabbits were unlikely to be responsible, preferring to nibble at ground level and there was no horse dung around to suggest visiting ponies.

I could only think this must have been the work of swans or geese - some of those roving flocks of Canada geese perhaps. One remarkable colony formed a neat circle of about a yard diameter and a hand span across, with smaller plants of other species in the centre - a case of radial growth from a central point with older plants dying away.

Discarded carapaces of shore crabs were scattered with other marine debris over the saltings turf. These did not signify dead crabs, just shells discarded during the normal process of ecdesis or growth. The shell, once hardened, cannot expand and must be shed, as with caterpillars, allowing a new one to grow beneath.

Our growing crab is very vulnerable during those few days when the new shell is absorbing water, expanding and hardening. These little greeny-brown denizens of the shore extend right up the Bristol Channel to the Cardiff salt marshes - such as is left of them - but are apparently unable to breed in water much less saline than that found here around Aberthaw and Gileston.

The backing cliff here is referred to as a fossil cliff, one that is no longer buffeted basally by waves, causing minor falls. Almost as far as Rhoose Point there was little bare rock exposed as a result. The term 'cliff', as appropriately applied in quarries, was no longer relevant here. This was a steep wooded slope, lying under a mantle of ivy and Clematis strung from tree to tree. It was coming to lie progressively further from the sea as deposits of mud, sand and pebbles built up to seaward, fending off the waves. The sea heath was exposed only to gently seeping water from the bordering creeks.

A dune pasture community had existed from at least the mid twentieth century in the angle where the main storm beach left the land to head off down channel and this was still there. A rabbit haven this, because of the easy digging in the dry sand, and it harboured some major warrens.

Sand flora included storksbill (Erodium), salad burnet (Poterium), with its fresh cucumber smell, and thyme, with its aroma of sunny summer banks. Yellow lady's bedstraw and bird's-foot trefoil added colour.

This was a relict dune system, if indeed it had ever been a dune. The Aberthaw and Gileston Power Stations were always cited as having been built on the most easterly sand dunes of the South Wales coast, which boasts so many fine dune systems distributed well up the Bristol Channel from those of Gower - principally at Crymlin, Kenfig and Merthyr Mawr.

But, another major change here since my last visit, was a live and growing sand dune, bristling with marram grass as dunes should, and sited out on the highest point of one of the storm beach ridges of pebbles. We could not cross the creek-dissected saltings to visit it and had not the time to follow along the dry land connection, but it was good to know that Mother nature had seen fit to create a dune system, once again, on the coast of the Vale of Glamorgan - even though it had taken half a century to get established.

My extensive collection of colour slides taken from the early 1960s on, from the old clifftop, showed the ever changing positions of the sand bars and pebble spits, opening, closing and deflecting the channels by which sea water entered the marsh, since the original estuary mouth had been cut off upstream. I had defaulted since the early 1900s. While my back was turned what might be thought of as the greatest change of all had been effected. We recognise major changes that have happened over geological time, but they are going on under our very noses if we can stand far enough back to see the whole picture!

I would love to have carried on towards the living cliff at Rhoose, where water trickling down the Lias rock face dissolved out the lime and redeposited it as tufa, in fantastic formations, but this was not to be. Madeleine wanted her sandwiches. On another day, perhaps, when we would spend less time around the lagoon.

There were too many different ecosystems here to appreciate on one short visit. Each was pursuing a different line of development, recovering from the major impact of the coming of the power stations, one now demolished, but virtually untroubled by the tourist aspect affecting other more homogeneous sites. When Madeleine had told her friends where I was taking her, they had thrown up their hands in horror. "What? All that industry!" How little they knew of their county's hidden treasures!

There was more to come as we trekked back on the inner route. Orchids were past their prime, shedding their tiny seeds on the wind, but the wayfaring trees, actually bushes, were enjoying theirs. The numerous bunches of fruit were bright crimson. As they ripened they would turn black and hard - unlike their fellow Viburnum, the guelder rose, where they remain juicily red - those not confined to limey soils as the wayfarers are. A special limestone beauty flowering on the edge of the thicket was wild basil *(Clinopodium vulgare)*, also the related red hemp nettle.

* * *

Regaining the car and shedding wet garments, we moved on to Gilestone Beach, this quite a wide detour towards St. Athans to get around the river mouth's streams, which had created a flat bottomed valley allowing tidal waters to seep inland for more than a mile - nurturing some of that special salt-marsh lamb for the local farmers. This fascinating community, dominated by salt-marsh rush, followed up the Thaw Valley under the pylons taking electricity from its source on the coast. Salicornia and Spartina, the two marker plants, grew alongside the coastal road crossing a mile from the sea, spring tides submerging a further half mile.

We ate our sandwiches in the car, unable to see over the crest of the storm beach, although parked immediately behind it. Only that kept the sea at bay. A flock of a dozen or so linnets foraged over a 'glade' of smaller pebbles. Binoculars were needed to make out the red on forehead and breast through the drizzle. These also picked out one brighter than the rest, another cock stonechat. It was odd to see this little heathland bird on the ground instead of perched on a sprig of gorse or bramble as in the bird books.

Beyond the birds the view stretched west to where the liassic cliffs rose again as Summerhouse Point. The sturdy concrete blocks that had been put in place to prevent enemy landings during the 1939-45 war had been re-aligned. Still there, they were no longer spaced out to cast long shadows over the rough grassland behind, but moved together by big machines to form an impenetrable wall, except where a gap had been left for a narrow stile.

The wall abutted onto a low lying field leading back to another, which had sometimes been flooded when planted to potatoes, cereals being non-starters here. The hollow between had held some permanent ponds, paddling places for the local cattle when the flies were biting. Now these had been drained.

Attempts to do this before had failed. The surrounding paddock had held mainly meadow plants, but muddy hollows and furrows had always harboured sea purslane, sea milkwort, sea spurrey and common orache. It seemed that sea water might be backing up through the drains buried under the storm beach, the accumulated fresh water insufficient to dilute it.

Floods were nothing new here. There were years in the 1980s when these had frozen and folk had converged to skate. In 1990 diluted sea water had flooded the garden pool of the lone dwelling near the beach and the goldfish had gone exploring up the lane towards the village.

But all that is another story, as is the famous stranding of the hump backed whale in October 1982 - a great crowd puller until it was finally taken away to the National Museum of Wales - appropriately a Welsh Whale.

What pleased me today was the finding of the red or narrow-leaved hemp nettle *(Galeopsis angustifolia)*, still pushing up from dark cavities below the pebbles where the seed had lodged. This is a decreasing arable plant of such coastal sites, sparsely distributed, with most in South-east England and an outlier by the Humber. There are three sites in Wales, one here and two in the north.

Gileston had won an award recently in the county's "Best kept village contest". Well back from the fluctuating shoreline, with its forty foot high tides, it was certainly beautiful, with traditional stonework, neatly thatched cottages and attractive gardens.

I had hoped to visit the saltings at West Aberthaw and we drove around the circular approach road but failed to spot the old parking place where we used to enter afoot to the lush grass saltings harbouring several rare plant species. The ecological puzzle there was- How do the occupants of the many inhabited anthills survive when their grassland is flooded, on high spring tides as I had seen it on past visits?

Being so close, we paid a flying visit to Llantwit Major for a cuppa in the café by the wind surfers headquarters. The tide was out and the surfers were way beyond low water mark where the only decent sized waves coincided with the only stretch of sand at that level, making falls from the surf boards less abrasive.

Most of this vast intertidal spread is of chunks of limestone - the 'delta' formed by the ancient Col Huw River, now a placid stream cutting into the flat infill of ice transported material from the hill country. This, too, suffers floods but of a different sort, involving movements of the boulder deposits offshore.

The low sea wall behind which the cars now parked had, not so many years before, separated the carpark from the grassed valley behind. Now it separated the carpark from the beach in front, part of it smashed up and added to the beach deposit which had covered the old carpark during that night of storm.

At Aberthaw the sea was adding to the land as the storm beaches grew, the marsh behind silted up and new sand settled on top. At Llantwit it was taking away from the established grassland by rejecting boulders of the old river delta and throwing them back.

POSTSCRIPT;-

My impression that 2008 was my first sighting of the newly arrived sea heath at Aberthaw was incorrect. Browsing, quite by chance, a week or so later in my 1998 nature diary, I discovered that I had actually seen the beginnings of its sojourn here ten years earlier. I was with a group of specialists from the BSBI (Botanical Society of the British Isles) assembled from all over the country to scour our best sites for possible rarities.

Just a few plants of sea heath were spotted and these with few flowers, as it was 9th May and the peak of flowering is in August. My aging grey matter had forgotten those few straggles of the humble plant, which I drew at the time to illustrate my account of the excursion.

My elation at seeing so much of it - right along the strandline, only ten years later, however, WAS justified. That plants so insignificant, rising less than two inches from the ground could cover such an area in a single decade was a miracle in itself. In my 1998 account I had written of the new find: "These were overpowered by the rather similar pink flowered sea milkwort and lesser sea spurrey." Both were still present, a decade later, but in tiny amounts. Its arrival here was seventeen years after its arrival at Merthyr Mawr. Are fragments water-borne on the mighty Bristol Channel tides?

The other two newcomers recorded here in 1998, and not seen since so far as I am aware, were fenugreek *(Trigonella ornithopodioides)*, a white clover, and a small-flowered buttercup *(Ranunculus parviflorus)*, which occurs sparsely but regularly further west along Glamorgan's Heritage Coast.

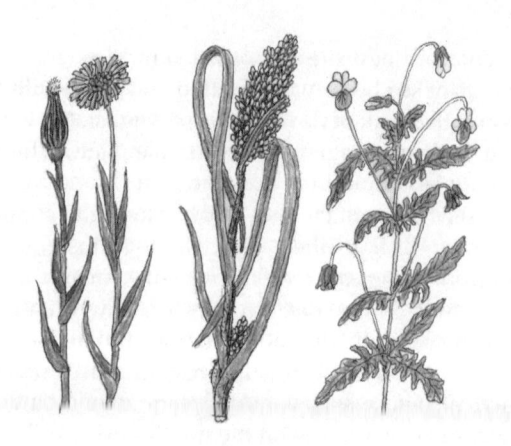

CHAPTER 32

Radyr Farmland, Taffs Well Recreation Ground and Caerphilly Garden Centre

On wednesday 29th July I set off along Taff Terrace - an excuse to see how the little skewbald foal was progressing. Like Maurice Chevalier's "little girls" in the famous song, "she gets bigger every day". Where the road petered out in an amalgam of ruts and rubble at Woodfield Road I was opposite the waymark of a white horse on blue that signified a bridleway.

This is marked as Radyr Farm Road on the map. A road no longer at this end, it connected with a way out onto the Llantrisant Road at the other. After the first restricted lap it led through a landscape that reminded me of years long past. Here was a fine hedgerow flora, bright with flowers now seldom seen en masse and some cereal fields with a healthy range of arable weeds, at least marginally.

The rough track became a narrow path, with a link into new Suburbia on the right. Over a stile by a narrow gate and I was once more on a narrow lane, with fat round hips of Japanese rose in a hedgerow threaded with nipplewort. I passed Radyr Farm on the left, but this was not the old farmhouse of thirty to forty years before. It had been tastefully renovated, like the two properties opposite, "Lower Barn" and "Upper Barn", with their spacious plantings and attractive zig zag panels on an ornamental brick wall topped by a splendid flowering Fuchsia. These were hallmarks of fortunate occupants, enjoying a sequestered corner of old Wales within a stone's throw but out of sight of urban amenities. A green woodpecker was foraging on the drive of one and the properties oozed well being - like so many in Radyr said to be the homes of surgeons, judges and executives.

The real country hedgerow started as I moved on westwards, its most delightful feature the lavender-mauve stands of large field scabious *(Knautia arvensis)*. Here, too, was dark red hedge woundwort, a patch of rosebay and a few foxgloves, basally bordered by creeping cinquefoil flowers. The matrix of dog's mercury was as fresh in July as in February and March, when it was bearing its unisexual flowers, the first of the season.

This riot of flowers partially obscured the laneside ditch and was backed by a high hedge. The opposite road bank was much lower, bordering a cereal crop. The main colour there was from hundreds of attractive pink trumpet flowers of field bindweed or Convolvulus. Long trailing stems might bear as many as twenty flower buds beyond the ones currently offering sustenance to their pollinators, so it looked as though these would be flowering on into autumn.

Their spiralling stems were wound tightly, anti-clockwise, around naked grass stems, each twist less than an inch from those above and below, making a rigid axis rather than just a rope, to bring the flowers above the thicket. The species is obviously invasive, but is much less often encountered than the more blatant hedge and great bindweeds which romp over all and sundry, sometimes sprinkling whole walls and hedges with their flower trumpets, usually white but occasionally pink.

If they were blue and their name was Ipomoea instead of Calystegia, we would hail them as the star characters, as we have their counterparts in warmer lands that have earned the name of morning glory. Their very aggressiveness is what has earned ours such a bad press. The white underground rhizomes can be as exploratory as the green climbing stems, as many a gardener knows to his cost, but I had seen walls and hedges during the past few weeks made beautiful beyond words by their massed flowers. Beauty is, after all, in the eye of the beholder.

Others here were perforated St. John's wort, yellow pea, bush vetch and knapweed, with the uncommon goatsbeard or Jack-go-to-bed-at-noon. It was past noon so the flower heads tapered off to a fine spire, protecting the yellow florets, these not yet sufficiently advanced to have fluffed out into the spherical heads of plumed achenes. All this was against a backdrop of bracken, hogweed, tall oat grass and male fern rather than hedgerow trees.

The gem this side was crow garlic *(Allium vineale)*, bearing hard round heads spiked like mini giant's clubs. These spheres of dark red bulbils were the size of marbles and borne on stiff, slender stems up to a yard high, to top the others on the field bank. One or two, or very occasionally three balls were crowded at the tips. A few had produced three or four pink florets with long floral tubes tipped with tiny petals. Other heads bore wispy green leaves, an inch long among the clustered bulbils, most trailing downwards after the rain.

It is rare indeed to find more than four flowers in a head but, botanically speaking, this is an inflorescence which, as in some of the other wild onions, has switched during the course of evolution from sexual to asexual or vegetative reproduction. Lilies, in the same family, can also reproduce by bulbils, these usually borne in the axils of the leaves. With all this diversity to choose from, it was the blackberry flowers, white or pink, that attracted most of the nectaring insects - hedge browns and speckled woods, bees and hover flies.

Where the narrow lane leading from the three residences debouched onto the Llantrisant Road, a plaque on the telegraph pole read "Povey Farm", this almost engulfed by the tall but smoothly trimmed hedge of field maple and hazel. The bridleway ended there.

Low trimmed hedges lined the highway to the north, but these were set back behind mown grass swards to the south. One by the next but one junction contained a circular wild flower bed, planted with short, inconspicuous white and yellow herbs impossible to recognise from a passing car. This was the municipal pattern this year and disappointing after the previous year's splendid displays of red, yellow and blue, the princesses of arable weeds, field poppies, corn marigolds and cornflowers.

* * *

Fields of golden corn, ripe unto harvest, stretched away on the other side of the road, the haulms at a density never even dreamed of during my farming years in the early 1940s. These were obviously autumn sown.

Only this week I had received a handsome medal depicting a wheatsheaf on its embossed centre. This had arrived through the post in a little black box, with a certificate signed by the Rt. Hon. Gordon Brown, Prime Minister. It was an acknowledgement of nearly five years working in the wartime Women's Land Army.

Somewhat tardily, one would think, after sixty six years! There couldn't be many of us left now, so they made a major saving there. This would seem to be congratulations for surviving thus long after all that hard work, rather than a thank you for services rendered in feeding the nation during its time of trial. Appreciated, nevertheless.

I was hopelessly out of touch with farming matters these days and didn't even know where Povey Farmhouse might be or whether Radyr Farm was still functioning agriculturally. The cereals to either side of my bridleway were spring sown and only a few inches high.

Not the blue-green of oats, the haulms might have been either wheat or barley. To my shame, after gaining a first class degree in agriculture - postwar and too late to benefit my war effort - here was I surrounded by what I mistakenly imagined to be Great Britain's staple food crop and unable to identify it! All my agricultural lecture notes and text books had had to be discarded along with so much else at my move to smaller premises, so I had no means of running my sample seedling down. Wild flower books seem not to get involved with crop plants.

I had to wait for it to mature and look again. Ten weeks later I discovered that it was neither wheat nor barley. Harvested by then, enough had been missed by the combine to show that it was millet, a crop that I had never seen in Britain, although reasonably familiar with the larger millets of Africa. But more of that anon.

Back in July, topping the rise to where the fields both sides were freely accessible, I paused to admire the view. I was south of the two main Border Ridges here, the most southerly, of Old Red Sandstone on which I stood, being less impressive at this point. The entire coastal plain was spread before me.

It was salutary to realise how much of the western suburbs were swallowed up by trees, my view stretching to St. Augustine's Church on Penarth Head, with the forested ridge of Leckwith Hill reaching away to the right, towards the elevated dome at Wenvoe.

Looking eastwards I could see much more than the radio mast landmark on the Wennallt. From this angle I was looking along the grassy, tree dotted southern slopes of Craig Llanishen and Craig Lisvane. These scarp faces of the Border Ridges were scarred in places where the valuable Carboniferous limestone rocks had been quarried, leaving some impressive rock faces. It was gratifying to be able to see all this from my own parish, where I now lived almost down at river level.

Closer at hand I was intrigued, as well as surprised, to see such variety among the few arable weeds along the field headlands. Most attractive were the yellow-green spreads of sun spurge, much showier plants than the petty spurge which squeezed out between walls and paving stones in suburban Radyr.

The blue of field speedwell contrasted with the pink of red dead nettle in a matrix of knot grass, speckled with rosy buds. Here were the glaucous leaves of white goosefoot among annual meadow grass and tall straggles of corn spurrey *(Spergula arvensis)*, with whorls of linear leaves at the swollen nodes. After the white petals of these fell, the five pointed starry calyces opened out, each brimming with hard black seeds covered with little humps and looking horrendously viable.

Wild radish was here, the large white or yellow petals purple-veined, the fruiting capsules constricted between the seeds as in our now more familiar sea radish. This arable species is commonest in South East England: sea radish is a species of western coasts. The most blatant and decorative flowers were those of scentless mayweed *(Tripleurospermum inodorum)*, its feathery leaves not succulent as in the sea mayweed. Shepherd's purse was present, despite the worries about its supposed rarity.

I left the bridleway along a path leading into Radyr's most recent addition to suburbia. A short residential road with lawns and trees led straight to the top of the recreation ground behind the tennis courts. Down the steps past the oak tree dell, I noticed that a narrow path newly penetrated the undergrowth, leading perhaps to the cosy den of some youthful pioneers. The next spinney harboured two ten or eleven year olds swinging on the end of a rope attached to a tree branch - this much more fun than the formal swings with seats.

Some of their contemporaries were in the 'formal' enclosure, but were using the iron frame from which the swings dangled as a climbing frame, sitting their way along the summit ridge. Thank goodness innovative youngsters can still think of interesting things to do apart from gazing into computer screens at virtual reality or vulgar, violent cartoons. The municipal authorities had done their bit sprucing up the environment for toddlers to learn in and lawns and flower beds for oldies like me to enjoy in my leisure hours. Nature too, has much to contribute to the learning environment for all of us.

* * *

Nature was winning the battle, temporarily perhaps, in the recreation ground that I visited a few days later over the border in Rhondda Cynon Taff. Lawns had been mown here and a few of the flower beds were almost immaculate, but the 'wild' was fast taking over in others. It looked as though the gardening staff was one man short. There was certainly enough crying out to be done to keep another man busy for a good many weeks.

The park in question lay alongside the river Taff at Taffs Well. From the elevated roadway, where I paused to admire two unusual white flowered plants of great willow herb, a circle of cobwebby grey inserted into the lawn below caught my attention. Small patches among the grey were a startling china white. I was intrigued.

As I closed in I realised that the bed had been planted with white busy lizzies (Impatiens), but few of these remained visible beneath superficial layers of ivy-leaved speedwell with spidery stems, multiple grey leaves and indeterminate seed capsules rising twice as high.

Tall shrubberies had great stems of bramble arching from their summits, their tentative apical buds rearing to go, arching down the sides, anxious to get their rooting tips to work, like ropes holding down a bivouac. Some of these were reinforced by trumpet blowing great bindweed, while the man-high Astilbe had been knitted into the mantle of overtopping wild traveller's joy.

Wild meadow grasses had insinuated a passage through waist-high Rosemary bushes, great bird's-foot trefoil and tutsan through lower but denser Hebes. Tall, so-called creeping, cinquefoil spread parasol leaves over variegated Euonymus. From tangles of bush roses, Cotoneaster and others speared erect young ash trees, to spread triumphant branches on emerging into the daylight. I had always reckoned ash to be the most prolific seedling weed in my Gwaelod garden. I couldn't resist unthreading some of the Convolvulus winding its way up the flanks of the cypress trees.

As in previous years, I gazed into the tepid, supposedly medicinal well from which Taffs Well gets its name of Ffynnon Taf. Walled around like a small swimming pool, railed steps led down into the dark waters, a quarter of which were covered with rubbish, drifted to one end. Shields on doors and window had been replaced by iron railings.

This is a remarkable natural feature emerging from the embankment of the Taff, but the water bubbling up from deep underground, quite independently of the river. H.G.Morton suggested that Taffs Well was the place to come if one wanted to see a spa in the primitive or healing well stage. He wrote "Every day the visionaries of Taffs Well go down to the riverside and gaze at 'The Smallest Spa in the World', and the cheapest, dreaming of hotels and crutches, bath chairs and gouty colonels." Not any longer.

It had fallen into disuse as a spa at the time of the first world war, but was then renovated in the 1930s, when two hundred people had bathed there. A swimming pool had been built alongside, by previously unemployed men, to use its waters, but that fell into disuse after a disastrous flood in the 1950s. I remember strolling round on the algal coated tiles of the empty structure. Cleaned out in the 1970s, it was subsequently swallowed up by the gardens, leaving no trace.

Citizens had talked over the years about renovating the well to its former glory, but it was obvious that there was not a lot of spare cash around at the moment for such niceties. Even the local pub had changed its name from "The Taffs Well Inn" as though ashamed.

I could no longer climb up the unofficial little path beside the well onto the river bank as in the past and there was no gate at the south end of the gardens to connect with the track leading from road to river, so that part of the Taff remained unvisited today.

A short way beyond the village school upstream, I looked across the mounded field with its sentinel oak and rugby pitch, to survey my old abode on the eastern face of the Garth. The mountain road looked terribly steep from here, but I was younger in those days. Not quite my grass roots, this, but that forty five years was more than half way back to meet them.

* * *

I have been unduly hard here on the tenders of the Taffs Well Recreation Ground, where boys were enjoying the tennis courts and the informal football pitch on this muggy monday afternoon at the start of the school holidays. The bowling green and its hedges were immaculate, as always and the lawns had been mown, though not before time judging by the generously mounded mowings.

One of the circular flower beds amidships had been planted with specimens big enough to look after themselves in the relentless silent war with the spritely army of natives. This was a bed of tropical plants which, even now, in this rainy Welsh summer, were more than a match for the indigenous speedwell and petty spurge.

In the centre was mature maize (Africa's staple of mealies), much more advanced than field crops round about, which would probably be harvested for silage. Their stems were topped with fine splaying tassels of male flowers and they bore spindle shaped corn cobs at the bottom, flaunting the glistening silken tassels, which must be the longest of all stigmas destined to waylay passing pollen grains.

In one of the other segments were other 'maize' plants, half the height, with ramrod stiff male inflorescences at the top, like bristly Typha bulrushes, but give-away spathes at the bottom, flaunting the shining corn silk down which the male cells would swim to make possible the crop of grain.

This was an unknown plant to me so I was delighted to see it again a few days later at the Caerphilly garden centre. There were two kinds there, both shorter than these and labelled. "Ornamental millet, purple baron" and "Ornamental millet, purple majesty". The 'majesty' was shorter, dominated by the more powerful 'barons'. Shades of Runnymede and the Magna Carta!

There were no corn cobs at the base, so I consulted a gardener. It seemed they had sown these plants late and they had not grown sufficiently to develop any of their usual cobs. The spikes of male flowers had the bristly consistency of a yard brush and were peppered with wispy yellow stamens.

According the books consulted when I reached home, Indian millet (Sorghum), is in the same sub-family as maize, Andropogonoides, but is said to have hermaphrodite (both sex) flowers - which rules out the possibility of basal containers for the grain. Or does it?

True millet (Panicum) is in a different sub-family (Panicoideae). Both millets are vastly taller than the South wales plants (I took photos of them in Nigeria, completely dwarfing the man alongside). Had the horticultural breeders been playing with their popular names again in calling the bristly brown 'poker plants' with basal corn cobs millet?

Another quarter of this bed was filled with Canna lilies, which I tend to associate with the Usumbara Mountains dividing Zimbabwe and Mozambique, where they are widely naturalised, although native to sub-tropical

America. These, too, featured at Caerphilly in the open, where they were doing well, adding weight to the global warming theory.

Trying to interpret their colourful red and orange flowers can present something of a problem. Sepals and petals are tiny. It is the petal-like staminodes or sterile stamens, as in members of the ginger family, that are so flamboyant. Although referred to as Canna Lilies, they are not true lilies but in a family of their own, the Cannaceae. Underground rhizomes of *Canna edulis* can be eaten, like potatoes. In Australia Queensland arrowroot is derived from this.

The remaining two segments of this flower bed contained two colour forms of another exotic. One set was all red, stems, leaves and flowers fused together, the other all yellow. I had seen some of their kind during childhood, bearing such names as cockscomb - a mantelpiece plant then. I was pleased, therefore, to see this, too, at Caerphilly, where it seemed the Taffs Well groundsmen had been shopping. They were labelled Celosia.

These and cockscomb proper, are members of the same genus in the Amaranth family, one which is so close to our saltbush family, the Chenopodiaceae, that the two have sometimes been coupled. This lateral joining of parts is known as fasciation and is a hereditary condition here. It crops up spasmodically in other plants such as Forsythia and the flattened flower stems of thistles and some of the cabbage family, such as cauliflowers.

The Caerphilly garden visit had been arranged for Brynteg residents on the mini bus used for our Brecon outing, by Jenni, one of our members. We were just north of the Graig-yr-Allt mountain ridge here, eastern counterpart of the Great Garth on the opposite side of the Taff Valley. These two were part of the southern rim of the Coal measure rocks dipping down below the South Wales Coalfield, to rise again around Merthyr Tydfil.

Astonishingly dark purple clouds with billowing summits and scudding grey counterparts stayed ominously atop the ridge throughout our stay, but sunshine continued to pour down on us, despite the forecast. For most the highlight was the hot lunch. Rita and I also partook of the proffered victuals, but we spent more time ogling over the plants together, coveting the most brilliant to lighten the Brynteg evergreens, but dubious as to how they would react to the move into our clods and pebbles mix which passed for soil. Also how were we going to make a hole big enough with no proper tools. My right palm still bore the scar of too prolonged pressure on the end of my trowel handle trying to manoeuvre great mats of periwinkle out of the front bed to make way for some little blue Ipomoea climbers, for which I had been out in the woods cutting pea sticks.

High on our list were Dahlias and other composites, including some giant relatives of ox-eye daisies. I was all for reds and yellows, she for pinks and blues. We drooled over multi-coloured Phlox, deep blue Delphiniums, some fine pink members of the Campanula family and elegant tall evening primroses with pink flowers instead of yellow - as I had seen growing wild in their native USA.

French lavender, plants to attract cats and plants to repel them, giant crimson relatives of the humble Montbretia and irresistible Violas, all at phenomenally high prices. Or was I too great an addict of propagating my own, at no cost? (The very small shoots broken from an untidy branch of my almost continuously flowering Pelargonium and stuck into borrowed soil with no rooting powder had all rooted, some bearing two or three inflorescences already.)

The spindly red campion on sale was not nearly as lush as the wild form that can be found flowering for ten or eleven months of the year in the hedgerows. Others set me thinking of where I had seen their wild counterparts. The blue half circles of fan flower (Scaevola) reminded me of the Scaevola bushes of Indian Ocean island seashores, the Cosmos of the environs of Harare, or Salisbury as it then was.

The all-over-purple ice plant seen now for the third time had a different name. This was Sedum purple emperor, not Sedum chocolate. There were cordon apples, John Downey crabapples, a cluster of Australian tree ferns, an outsize New Zealand flax and a lovely yellow-leaved Metasequoia tree, the supposedly extinct Chinese treasure seen, appropriately, on the day that the Olympic Games opened in the murky Chinese capital, with the magnificent flamboyancy and synchrony of some forty thousand actors and as many fireworks, portrayed on our TV screens.

At Caerphilly smaller numbers of bees and hover flies were doing their bit pollinating the flowers, but butterflies were few. No doubt their caterpillars were not encouraged. Bee larvae get their plant products without nibbling viable seedlings and their nurses pay in services rendered for the nectar and pollen on which they wax fat.

CHAPTER 33

Pisgodlyn Mawr, The Big Fish Pond, and Brynteg Home Front

On 8th August I set off to one of my old haunts in the rural heart of the Vale of Glamorgan. This was Pisgodlyn Mawr, the Big Fish Pond, the one of three or four soggy hollows in a lowland blanket bog that had not been allowed to silt up and sink, forgotten, into the peaty bosom of the earth.

It lies in the Northern Vale, north of the old Roman Fortway and the modern A48. The Hensol Forest, not huge, but much the largest forested tract in this region, closed in roundabout its shores, hiding it from the public gaze. The Forestry Commission managed the land, the Glamorgan Anglers' Club had the fishing rights and the nearest village was Welsh St. Donats.

The small roadside embayment where we parked back in the mid twentieth century when the Glamorgan Wildlife Trust was negotiating with the Forestry Commission about the nature reserve status of the site, was now an official, but small, forestry carpark. A series of boulders across the entrance excluded all but the smallest cars and these had to make their entry squareways on to avoid scratched panels.

Leading away into the forest and the apparent obvious reason for the facility, was a broad, surfaced walking track. Those 'in the know' knew where to find the little wooden stile on the hedgebank which led away in a different direction to another, more intriguing feature than a conifer plantation.

The narrow path which I took wound between fine forestry trees, mostly larches with tall straight boles, but also Scots pines, although this was no formal plantation. Most of the trees visible from ground level were deciduous, the oaks including sapling and mature Turkey oaks. There was birch, sycamore, holly, even beech and a few medium sized yews, which prefer limier soils to those.

Bracken and Blechnum hard fern characterised the ground flora, while surfacing tree roots provided stabilising footholds on the descent to lake level. And there, suddenly, it all was. The lake had always been beautiful, but from ten or fifteen years ago it had been more so because of the great spreads of water lilies which had appeared, whether by accident or design I knew not.

There were two main kinds, large white water lilies *(Nymphaea alba)* and yellow fringed water lilies *(Nymphoides peltata)* of the gentian family, with smaller, but prettily frilled petals and neater, but still round, floating leaves. One of the circular colonies of Nymphaea had pink flowers.

Some of the rafts of flowers bulged out from the shoreline, but only those shores inaccessible to fishermen. No-one could cast a line into that sort of tangle. Notoriously invasive, these plants were doing their best to conquer the whole and the anglers were fighting back. As I walked along the nearer, more open shore, I was passing soggy piles of their rubbery black rhizomes, like mini-hose pipes, fleshy and many feet long. These were a diagnostic character that flower identification books seldom mention - not that this aquatic beauty could be mistaken for anything else.

Apart from the floating rafts, the vegetation seemed to be much as I remembered, except that the carr at the opposite end had grown into mature woodland and sallows were infiltrating among the herbs and horsetails, moving relentlessly further and further out into the water.

Only the north and part of the east shores were now accessible. For botanists this was sad, as all the rare bog plants were now physically out of bounds, but it saved these treasures from trampling feet, if not from being shaded out by aggressive plant neighbours.

With the aid of binoculars I was able to identify many of the larger waterside species, but not the little treasures, the insectivorous sundew and butterwort, the lousewort and bog violet, that spoke of mountain peatlands rather than this remarkable island of upland plants in the lowlands.

The two herbs bordering the ungrazed, untrampled western shore were uncommon in lowland Glamorgan elsewhere. Forming a continuous bluegreen fringe at water level was marsh St. John's wort *(Hypericum elodes)*, topped with clusters of small yellow flowers. Water lay on their velvety leaves in shining globules, supported on a duvet of close-set hairs, leaving a blanket of air above the undampened epidermis. This was as remote as water on a duck's back but by a different mechanism.

Its faithful companion here was marsh cinquefoil *(Potentilla palustris)*, with stems looping along below water to rise erect and branch to bear the complicated red and brown flowers. Leaves were blue-green like the others but of more decorative shape with five radiating toothed leaflets.

A matrix of non-tussocky purple moor grass, rushes and sedges formed the main community stretching back to the forest edge. This was probably invading a community of Typha bulrushes with dark brown cats-tail tops, these now protruding evenly throughout. Tall Angelica and hemp agrimony topped what seemed a fairly uniform community, while little sallow bushes, only a few feet high, were popping up everywhere.

Relying only on memory, all my written records having 'gone with the wind of change', I expected to see a stand of unbranched water horsetail rising from the open water here. I could distinguish horsetail among the Typha, but this was profusely branched, more of a land form. The plant succession had moved on, silt building up in the water and land plants taking the opportunity to advance over the resulting shallows and overwhelm the pioneers.

This was carr woodland in the making. I could recall this community, where the little path reached the shore, as having been dredged out in years gone by to halt this process. Would this generation of foresters and fishers repeat the operation, sacrilege though it seems, with so many unusual plants at risk? Leave it alone, however, and this beautiful stretch of water would be reabsorbed into the surrounding peat, like the other woodland pools, and the fishermen would have to move on.

* * *

I moved on myself now, into the sunshine, to see what these good folk had left growing under the low but firm peat banks following the northern shore. The path led past a series of wooden fishing platforms. Here were depauperate outliers of the others, sometimes springing from a carpet of marsh pennywort's button leaves, sometimes with sprigs of bulbous rush and toad rush pushing from rather sorry looking Sphagnum moss or yellow flowers of tormentil and lesser spearwort.

The lake water was murky, not just dark with peat or limonite staining, but with silt in suspension, and I saw no water plants nor submerged animals, only expanding ripples where some creature had come up for air. Even the whirligig beetles were in short supply.

The piles of raked out fringed water lilies were quite fresh, but contained no other interesting flotsam or jetsam dragged with them from the depths. All over their soggy surfaces heart-shaped green leaves were pushing out among the black coils, the size and shape of lesser celandine leaves. This beauty was an aggressive invader and it was not giving up without a struggle. Like Himalayan balsam, it had no doubt been introduced by folk beguiled by its charms, without consideration of the possible consequences of an alien invasion. No matter, I, for one, was enjoying the spectacle of the lily laden waters as a great improvement on the fishable years when there were none.

Those were years when Idris Bowen, a fellow naturalist, conducted a study here, finding a wide range of insect life, but I saw little today. Although the sun was shining only a few blue and blue-tailed damselflies were on the wing and one beauty which must have been an emperor dragonfly came within my ken. There were green-veined white butterflies on the mint flowers and bumble bees on the Angelica.

Two couples were fishing from this shore and three from the one I visited later. I asked what they were catching. "Carp, roach, rudd, bream and tench", just about the usual range for coarse fishermen. I did not ask if these were introduced or well established populations. Toads used to throng here at mating time in March. Hopefully they still did.

In the past it had been impossible without gumboots and a steady nerve to cross the concrete dam over which water flowed from the lake into an outlet stream a few yards below. Now a concrete-topped, stone walled bridge had been constructed over the stream with a path leading down the face of the earth dam alongside.

Viewed from below, water flow over the first three steps was smooth as burnished brass, shining like Christmas tinsel in the direct rays of the sun. Below that, in the mini plunge pool, air and water mixed to give a bubbling cappuccino effect, the colour supplied by clay particles. From the bridge the lake surface stretched away at eye level, spread with the circular lily colonies, like platters on a giant's dining table.

The outlet stream gambolled away through young woodland over a bouldery bed about a yard wide, very soon to disappear into a tunnel of overarching birch, sallow and giant bracken fronds. A forestry ride led away in the same direction at a little distance.

I continued around the lake shore, disturbing the lady companion of one of the fishermen, immersed in a library book. What better place to be interrupted from a good read than the beautiful scene spread before her, enhancing contemplation of the goodies still left to us among the advancing concrete jungles? An emperor dragonfly sailed out over the lilies and the air was full of darting hirundines. The shoreline was firmer here, with gipsywort, devil's bit scabious and great willow herb. Could that be giant hogweed dwarfing the Angelica?

A single plant of greater water plantain *(Alisma plantago-aquatica)* grew just offshore and the fruiting spike of an orchid with faintly spotted leaved reared two feet high among a patch of wild raspberries. The firm track changed all too soon to a narrow, overgrown path, muddy and beset with puddles, following outside the invading edge of the carr woodland. Many years back there had been easy access along here.

Binoculars showed the level sward encroaching onto the fourth side to be much the same as that on the first, with the addition of a patch of single headed cotton grass shedding tassels of white fluff onto the gentle zephyrs seeping through the bordering scrub.

Fishermen this side had driven their cars into a nearby clearing, entering by the forester's house in a corner where the encircling lane turned sharply off to the south. A bar excluded other cars but allowed walkers and cyclists in - again with no indication that they were headed for more than a continuation of the forestry trail.

Approaching this exit, I passed a shady, plantless woodland pool on my left and a cluttered woodland, smelling of damp mould and rotting wood, on my right. Both sides yielded interesting fungi, although it was not yet the fungus season. On a sodden tree root beside the heavily shaded pool was an exquisite colony of tiny snow white fairy mushrooms, (*Marasmius ramealis*). These tiny fructifications from the invisible mycelium, bore the English name of twig parachute.

Larger, long-stalked, yellow-buff hemispheres with pale pink gills opposite, were *Mycena galericulata* or bonnet Mycenas. Here, again, there was quite a considerable colony, strung out along several feet of a woody tree root growing along the ground surface.

The forest rides here were broad, letting in full sunshine, which caressed a tall growth of wood St. John's wort, rosebay, devil's bit scabious, great willow herb and common figwort, leading back to a man-high bank topped by coppiced hazel and standard trees. Butterflies were out in force here, enjoying more meaningful sunshine, that I found difficult to cope with, having taken note of the dreary forecast and burdened myself with waterproofs.

Hedge browns were in the majority, favouring the fleabane, with meadow browns and ringlets in the wider clearings. Speckled woods sipped from mint flowers, red admirals and tortoiseshells from Buddleia. Hover flies and lesser beings favoured ragwort and the ground level flowers of silverweed and creeping cinquefoil.

There was more nectar for the taking - from meadowsweet and teasels, marsh thistles and spear thistles, red bartsia and centaury. Only the insignificant flowers of the enchanters nightshade romping among hard and broad buckler ferns in deep shade seemed to hold no charms for the insects, which had suffered so many rainy days of diluted nectar or none at all.

I tried to return along the path following the eastern margin of the wood but got turned back by a minor flood. Others had been diverted before me and a new path had been worn, winding through the woodland, round holly and yew, through ferns and even some uncommon wood millet (*Millium effusum*).

I lingered en route to study two honeysuckle branches that had climbed parallel willow stems, each making eleven tight, anticlockwise coils until their supports gave out. Nothing daunted, they continued to coil around each other, regular coils, each advancing three inches, for another four yards. This part of their journey was horizontal. They were getting no nearer the light by these prodigious efforts, nor to open space to attract pollinating moths. What is the green force that drives them on?

I found myself trying to recall the words of the Flanders and Swan song about a potential mating of the right handed honeysuckle and the left handed bindweed.

"Said a passing bee, they'll get no blessing from me
Consider their offshoots if offshoots there be.
The poor little sucker, which way should he go?
He'll twine the wrong way. Oh what a disgrace,
Or else he'll grow up and fall flat on his face."

* * *

Strangely, I was already involved with the twining of one of the bindweeds, the blue and white trumpeted *Ipomoea tricolor* which Rita and I were trying to grow from seeds which had germinated when thrown onto a patch of hard won compost. Their cotyledons consisted each of a double triangle, like the decorative sails erected on the Cardiff barrage. I grew six on in pots on my balcony, but the tips of four got broken after the production of a single heart-shaped leaf.

One of the two survivors went straight away into a spin, making several anti-clockwise twirls around its support only an inch apart, and continued to do so up to a total of eleven, after which it was transferred to Rita's south facing and almost windless balcony.

The other I retained and it started life lost and bewildered, the minute green sprout wandering all ways, however often I lodged it back on the right track. It could scarcely do otherwise, with the prevalent north-westerly gale constantly wafting it off course. By the fourteenth day it had reached almost to the height of the other, having made only two loose spirals to the other's eleven.

Then the gale diminished and it swung into action, pointing its tender tip in the right direction. Another half hour and it had completed a full circuit of the support, heading east, after which it grew vertically upwards, then round again anticlockwise. It had now achieved three revolutions in ten inches of stem above the epicotyl, where the ornate cotyledons were busy photosynthesising to supply the wherewithal, these helped now by four heart shaped leaves, the first and last quite small.

I saw the primordium of the fifth leaf appear on a bit of stem that wasn't there half an hour before. This little chap that grows in our temperate clime was certainly emulating its bigger, bolder, brighter, blue-flowered kin of the Tropics and Mediterranean that has earned itself the name of morning glory. I had been intrigued by the twisting honeysuckle at Pisgodlyn Mawr and here it was, all happening, before my eyes.

I don't often sit about watching plants grow. That could become tedious. Doing most of my activities, reading, writing, sketching and eating, in an armchair by the window onto the balcony, however, I could scarcely have missed this sequence. It was almost as enlightening as the speeded up photography of plant growth on the TV, and even more magical to see it in the real. My plant failed to make it to the height of Rita's, but hers had only a few undersized leaves to supply the power to produce that splendid spiral. It was likely that both were doomed.

Although too late for flowers, I planted two sets of six each under wigwams of 'pea sticks', cut in a Taffside woodland, six of elm and six of sycamore, six in the back garden and six in the front. Holes dug, compost applied, plants planted and tended as necessary with water and plant food, and every one of them disappeared after the first few days.

They didn't just wither, they vanished completely, no wisp of green remaining. There were no beetle or caterpillar holes, no snail or slug trails. Cats eat green plants medicinally, but prefer grass, and I have seen no rabbits in our grounds. Our garden birds, unlike water fowl, prefer seeds and fruits or animal matter to fresh greens, except for wood pigeons, two of which were regular visitors.

When in the Land Army I had shot wood pigeons, with a twelve bore shot gun or .22 rifle (they were said then to be the farmer's worst enemy). The targets went into the pot to help out with our war time rations, their crops always examined first to see what they had been eating. Corn appeared in autumn but fresh green leaves were common in spring and summer, young beech foliage, fresh watercress and snippets of cabbage leaves. These seedlings were more tender than any of those and could have been pulled from the soil with one tweak of those versatile beaks.

* * *

There were times when I left my favourite window seat. On 6th August I joined 23 other Brynteg residents in the lounge for a beetle drive. I hadn't played since I was a girl guide, but I got the highest score and came away with the prize. Not a matter of skill at drawing beetles - this genus having only four legs - but dependent on the throw of the dice.

On another evening I joined a threesome playing scrabble - a more sophisticated version of the lexicon that we used to play with cards, making up words. I failed dismally at this, only being allowed to use words that were in the scrabble dictionary and not being very clever at alighting on the red and blue spots that would have earned me extra points. My only experience of card games in my long life were family bouts of rummy at Christmas time and, very occasionally, making up a four at whist with the parents , but none at all since I left home at the age of 19. None of my contemporaries seemed to play so I didn't get involved. But it's never too late.

I had been down to the station in the morning to find out about train times and had wandered over the footbridge to see how the Taff was coping with the flood waters from the Brecon Beacons. The river was pounding down, brown with silt, submerging the rock cluster that usually provided turbulence, but with a turbulence of its own.

The reed canary grass of the grey wagtails' shingle bank was streaming along the surface and the accompanying osiers were up to their knees in the flood. Two days later and the canary grass was submerged, out of sight, like the streaming water crowfoot, and the osiers were up to their waist and bent over with the suppleness that makes them so useful for willow weaving.

Shore birds were dispossessed, but not the kingfishers. Two were hurtling upstream towards the bridge, appearing as orange dots. I stepped smartly across and watched them speeding on, sapphire gems from this angle, side by side and only a few feet apart. They might have lost their favourite fishing perches, but not their foraging grounds, as the wagtails had. I wondered how their tiny forms fared in that flood, or whether they crossed to the canal or country park pools, where we used to watch them fishing from the perches supplied.

Two more days and river level had topped the horizontal line of pendant branches determined by normal high water, so that leafy tips were being dragged under. Gil's rain gauge registered an inch in a single day, and agriculturalists were fearing for the cereal harvest. The corn had been ripe for days but it was too wet to get in and cut it. They feared it might have to go for animal feed if not right for our more fastidious tastes.

This unseasonally wet summer was not doing the bees any good, though bumble and solitary bees always seemed very busy as soon as the sun shone through. According to the media, one in three hives were seen to have failed at the midsummer harvest, this thought to be as much due to the wet weather as to the Veroa mites.

Honey bees do not fly in the rain and floral nectar becomes diluted and the pollen washed out except in those few species which have special adaptations, like the hooded dead nettle family and those that are able to close petals and sepals together, like globe flower and scarlet pimpernel, the 'poor man's weather glass'.

Nor do bees fly or flowers produce pollen when it is cold. Worker bees have to collect a cocktail of different kinds of pollen to supply their larvae with the full range of nutrients needed. British bee keepers fear the "colony collapse disorder", which is already prevalent in the USA and in two countries of Eastern Europe. Apparently Britain is currently importing honey from Australia, Argentine, Chile and Mexico.

And yet we are not making the most of our resources. Ever since Himalayan balsam or policeman's helmet (*Impatiens glandulifera*) arrived on the lower reaches of the River Taff in 1910, apiarists have stressed what a valuable source of nectar it is for their bees. It flowers from July on into October and beyond, and prolongs the nectaring season for hive bees for weeks. Yet conservationists are busy rooting it out or chopping it down, simply because it is invasive.

Certainly it is, and just as certainly it is one of the most colourful and beautiful of any in today's countryside, particularly near fresh water. As an annual, it can never be the menace which that other riverside invader, the Japanese knotweed, undoubtedly is - although even that sometimes serves a purpose in staying river bank erosion.

One of TV's excellent documentary films shown in August was about the hazardous collection, by men dangling on rope ladders, of honeycombs built by cliff nesting Himalayan bees in Nepal. Twice they showed shots of the bees foraging, pointing out how delicious the honey was compared with the norm. And what were they foraging on? Himalayan balsam, of course. Our honey bees, as well as the bumbles, which find so much room inside the capacious flowers, love it. Why don't we give them a chance?

CHAPTER 34

Porthkerry, Rhoose Point Quarries and Font-Y-Gary

"The Glorious twelfth" came the slightly sarcastic announcement from my bedside radio. "Not here it isn't" was the response from the reporter waiting for the 'shoot' to start on a northern grouse moor. A weather forecast followed. As every day for the past fortnight and the next week, the key word was "wet". Heavy showers, gales up to 60 mph, horrendous conditions on some roads but a few sunny intervals."

While we decided on the phone that we would venture out, the sun shone. While we made our sandwiches the rain tipped down from an all over shroud of grey. It would have been easy to cancel most of this summer's excursions if we had taken notice of the weather forecasts, so we pressed on. We got drenched at one point, but blew dry again in the sun and wind, and had no regrets.

I picked Madeleine up for an exploration of another of my old coastal haunts - the stretch of Liassic limestone coast formerly devoted to quarrying and cement production at Rhoose. The industrial phase, with its train of botanical interlopers was over now, but I was told the land had been used for a major housing development. I was apprehensive as to what I might find, but I needn't have worried.

On a sudden whim, after circling round Cardiff Airport, I turned down the narrow lane leading to Porthkerry. Madeleine, like many before her, thought Porthkerry was the westernmost section of the diverse Barry waterfront down at sea level, the Porthkerry Country park, where we enjoyed picnics and walks on the pebble beach and limestone clifftop.

That was only a part of it. The "village" was up on the western cliff, with only footpath access to the bay below. It consisted of little more than the church, a farm and two cottages clustered around the village green We strolled across the green under tall ash trees laden with fruiting 'keys', revelling in the old fashioned rural peace, only to be shaken to the core by a thunderous roar that seemed to come from under our very feet.

No. Not a plane taking off, though that might have been equally disruptive. We were right above the deep railway cutting that swallowed up the trains crossing the magnificent viaduct that provided the scenic backdrop to the country park.

The Bulwarks Cliffs where we stood, were higher than those further west and the tunnel continued for half a mile before the line surfaced at the level of the Rhoose Cliffs. We counted the coaches in a goods train seen later in the day: twenty four! No wonder the mechanical monster passing between those closely aligned banks had seemed like the passage of a bad tempered ogre. As if the roar of planes taking off was not enough. So much for rural tranquility in this modern age!

The church and churchyard looked peaceful enough, backed by tall woodland. The stone stile affording entry beside the gate consisted of two flat rocks protruding from the wall as steps. A more traditional style of stile in "The Vale" was a slab of rock, not as high as the wall, set vertically in a gap, sometimes with a basal step. The little cottage with a fine flowering Hydrangea by the door was labelled "The Old School House". It couldn't have accommodated many pupils, but its very presence suggested a pre-airport presence of other cottages, justifying the name on the OS map.

For three of my years in the Women's Land Army my address had been "The Old School House", where I boarded with the ninety year old retired schoolmaster and his spinster daughter. That, too, was alongside the village church - at Shurlock Row, in Berkshire, a happy place. The name conjured up visions of a very different countryside of sixty five years ago, where the loudest intrusive noise came from the new little Fordson tractor, Farmer Pyle's pride and joy.

On the other side of Porthkerry Green was a small whitewashed farmhouse with larger stone barn. The third house, "Elmshurst" had a little red post box on its garden wall, the fourth lay a short distance away behind tall wrought iron gates.

A rough metalled track led to a fifth dwelling set in the top of the woodland leading steeply down to the country park. To its left was a neatly mown sward, to its right a paddock, shaggy with a tall hay crop, mostly grass, but with yellow pea and pink Convolvulus weaving among the haulms and a few heads of bristly ox-tongue and ragwort pushing through.

Little trees planted along the drive included sweet and horse chestnut, laburnum and flowering currant. There was a fine view from here, back along the coast to Cold Knap Point, the most westerly of the three Carboniferous limestone headlands pushing out seawards beyond the newer Triassic and Liassic rocks of the varied Barry coastline. In the foreground was the long pebble storm beach connecting Cold Knap Point with the Bulwarks, backed by the shaly cliff face famous for the occurrence of the rare wild service trees.

We passed on to where a rough little path took walkers down to the bay. I had been that way before. It was steep and stony. Porthkerry Bay belonged to Barry and we were headed further west today.

* * *

A broad state of the art road swept left from a new roundabout interrupting the old highway, and we followed it, curving down towards the old floor of the immense quarry. That had been divided into two, the inland half full of streets of houses, the seaward half left as before, after removal of the cement making machinery and buildings.

Inland behind the tall quarried cliff backing the dwellings was another housing estate, built on farmland that had lain above, to seaward of the old coastal highway. Most of the houses were of the same red bricks used in all such recent developments.

Looked at in detail, they were a mixture of red, yellow and glistening black particles. These were the reconstituted bricks of the modern age, the mineral remains of old buildings (and slag heaps?) crushed and remoulded, just as so many modern "timber" constructions were made of pulverised wood fragments compressed into solid slabs to be tooled to shape. Ersatz, but laudable attempts at recycling.

We left the car in one of the low level residential cul de sacs and set off afoot, first along a tarmac path, then a metalled one, then a narrow foot track and then no track at all. Apart from low dry stone walls set out in patterns and circles of uneven boulders, the vacated land had been tidied up and left to its own devices, for residents to enjoy, a play place for youngsters and exercise tract for canines.

It was now green again, green in different degrees, depending on whether enough limestone dust had accumulated to form the basis of a soil and whether enough water had oozed from cracks in the rock, or got trapped where there were no cracks, to nurture a plant cover.

Happily the two lakes, in existence from at least the 1960s, were still intact, as were marshy areas that had nurtured orchids and other plant gems. The land had not been quarried away right to the cliff edge, a bastion of rock several yards thick having been left, broken through in places, as necessary to let out water accumulating on the quarry floor.

More water seeped out at this level between the horizontal layers of the

Lias, these appearing on the cliff face as aquifers -as they do outside the Font-y-Gary Quarry further west. From the seaward side they appear as lines of green vegetation following the lines of seepage on an otherwise almost bare rock face.

Mounded spoil heaps had been left or reconstituted, their more pulverised texture aiding plant establishment. Rabbits had helped to keep such swards neatly trimmed, leaving room for low-growing flowers that only they are so good at conserving - or rather, leaving room for when they have consumed the larger, competitive items of their choice.

This downland type of vegetation, with pink centaury, salad burnet, field forget-me-not and scarlet pimpernel, graded out into taller swards, more herbs than grass, where eyebright often dominated small plots, alongside clovers, common mallow, yellow wort, carline and other thistles.

Everywhere there were teasels, the horizontal bands of mauve flowers encircling their prickly oval heads a lure for bees. Others upstanding were bristly ox-tongue, red valerian, wild carrot, hogweed and the larger willow herbs.

The clumps of bushes were steadily enlarging, these almost entirely grey sallow - greyer in the past, when blown cement dust had often formed a crust over leaves moistened by rain. Goat sallow could have gone unnoticed, but I spotted a healthy clump of creeping willow where grassy swamp graded into open water. This is the hallmark of dune slacks in our sand dune country.

Buddleia was the main incomer on the broken cliff faces of loose boulders too well drained for most others apart from a little dogwood, sloe and hawthorn. Opportunistic vegetation had caught the mood of rehabilitation being practised by the house builders and was contributing its "two and fourpence worth" as my Irish friend would have put it. Resourcefulness and tolerance were to the fore here. New habitats were there to be exploited, if not permanently by the first comers, there would always be others cashing in on the ameliorated conditions - humans permitting.

* * *

The big deep lake under the west-facing quarry cliff at the east end formerly harboured fine growths of water crowfoot, but we did not approach closely enough this time to see more than the stretch of open water, extensive enough for the wind to have whipped up sizable wavelets, their colour changing from shimmering silver to formless black as the storm clouds scudded past.

It must contain fish, as the cormorant which had flown low over our heads earlier on had settled here, and we watched it diving later for these. Swans had formerly frequented it and there had been a pair nesting most years on the smaller pond on the quarry floor. That had no cliff backing but more marginal cover and I have slides of one pair which succeeded in raising seven cygnets. They were unlikely to do so again if the number of dogs being exercised here this morning was anything to go by, particularly as many were golden retrievers, which like nothing better than plunging into ponds.

Today there were just two coots. We saw neither mallard nor moorhen, but the scratchy songs of reed warblers indicated that there were more than one pair of these. It was difficult to approach open water here, the reed fringe being almost continuous, where before I remember the tentative march of regimented Typha bulrushes across bare shores. These were still present but willow thickets were closing in and I was delighted to see plenty of the tufty yellowish heads of sea rush *(Juncus maritimus)* here, as well as the hard rush of more open stretches and the articulated rush at the water's edge.

Another 'whiff of the briny' came from the sea club rush, which, as we have seen, is not averse to growing in fresh water. Stubby toads of false fox sedge *(Carex otrubae)* grew at the pool edges and the blue-green leaf rosettes of glaucous sedge on drier sand. Water milfoil was a former denizen here and might be still. When the water evaporated the wispy underwater stems and leaves were superceded by neat, shiny, fernlike fronds only an inch or so long. - a sub-aerial form of an underwater plant that is seldom seen. It pays to be resilient in such changeable habitats as this.

A plant of common sedge *(Carex nigra)* had the female fruiting spikes knitted into a silken web protecting a sphere of tiny white spider eggs. Drier patches yielded little heath snails *(Helicella itala)* clinging to rush stems, their flattened shells decorated with a neat black and white spiral. There were also conical shells of pointed snails *(Cochlicella acuta)*, bleached white by abrasive particles.

Brown jelly hemispheres of blue-green algae plastered rain sodden areas and pool margins. Low growths of self heal were everywhere, but succumbed to prolonged submergence in these spreading puddles, kept topped up so consistently in this remarkable summer.

We, too, suffered a thorough wetting in one of the promised thunder showers. Too hot to wear normal field kit waterproofs when out of the fierce wind, we were ill equipped. My three layers seemed to keep nothing out (despite being advertised as 'waterproof') and none of the sallow bushes were more than man high, so there was no cover. Splashing down to the central 'amphitheatre', we thought we might find shelter behind the flattened slab monument, but it was flattened in the wrong direction. A twist of ninety degrees would have given us at least lateral protection.

But the purple menace passed, as it always did, filling the north-eastern sky from horizon to horizon, while the billowing white cumulus scudded skittishly across the flawless blue overhead, chuckling at the sudden flurry of human discomfort. Sun and wind dried us out completely within half an hour and the next rain had the decency to fall when we were back in the car enjoying lunch.

I had seen the monument before. It was nothing to do with the housing development but had been erected by Blue Circle Cement, the firm at work here, to mark this particular spot, Rhoose Point, as the most southerly part of mainland Wales. Almost twice as tall as us, it had a Celtic cross carved in the summit. Not of the native rock, it was a dark grey mudstone, as was the circle of boulders set out around it in this natural arena. Most of these were decorated with white veins, probably of quartz. We were only a few yards from the sea here and the rock barrier protecting the quarry had been cut through, so that we could look down onto the beach and the churning pale fawn waves beyond.

We wended our way gently uphill and emerged, in error, not in the lower conurbation but in the upper one. Walking the immaculate streets of immaculate houses, we wondered how we were going to get down that great cliff to our lunch. There were obviously no roads.

There was, however, a flight of wooden steps, or series of many flights of steps zig-zagging down through a thick scrub which was mostly of prickly things like roses and brambles, which looped over the hand rails at eye level. We were pleased to find them, prickles or no, preventing a long detour. We paused to admire the robins pincushions on the rose shoots and the decorative green calyces sprouting from the fat red hips of *Rosa rugosa*. A trek along several residential roads and we were 'home and dry', or at least in contact with our victuals and suitably aired after the wetting.

* * *

There was more to investigate, so we threaded our way out of the suburban labyrinth into the comfortably familiar streets of Rhoose and down the next seaward turning. In the 70s, 80s and 90s this road had ended at the railway and the row of cottages along its landward side. We had crossed the level crossing on foot and walked to the coast a fair step away, either alongside the farmland to the right or through a motley of ill-remembered industrial paraphernalia to the left.

The two routes had been separated by a high hedge and a fast running brook. They still were but the approach was very different. We drove over the level crossing on a road continuing east into the housing complex, but stayed at its start. Surprisingly there was a capacious carpark here, with a bus stop on one side and the railway, and probably a station, on the other. The notice at the entrance read "Park and Ride".

Unlike the Radyr "park and ride", from which cars spilled up the adjacent roads, this one was less than a quarter full - on a weekday afternoon. Were children from the new settlement brought here for the school bus? Like other new settlements visited, we had seen no amenities, no shop or school or church, no meeting hall or pub, although more of the premises had lock-up garages than on the old Chunting Yards.

Madeleine had made an assessment of the opulence of the housing and decided that it would be mostly one of grandparent status here. Youngsters with school age children wouldn't be able to afford them! True or not, salary earners and food shoppers might appreciate contact with public transport. We walked to the coast by the western route, which was the same as in past years, and returned by the eastern one, which was not.

The ragged edge of the narrow concrete track followed above an undeviating, crystal clear stream bounding downhill over clear pebbles. Beyond was a dense bank of bushes - more than a hedge - mostly of blackthorn, but with some hawthorn. It must have looked wonderful in the early spring flowering season. Currently the chief waterside flowers were the less showy ones of woody nightshade with a few precocious shoots of fool's watercress covered with fluffy axillary umbels climbing up the hedge. An unexplained tip of pebbles blocking the gully at one point caused the water to flood across the path but it soon found its way back. Stretches of vertical earth banks bore a covering of slabby liverworts.

The big unfenced field opposite had held cereal crops on past visits and had given sanctuary to the very rare quail on one occasion. Now it was a thick grass crop, for hay or silage, full of clover, both red and white. Here, too, were other legumes, including yellow pea and a dense patch of dark flowered tufted vetch, as in the similar dense forage field under the Little garth.

Where the stream broadened out towards the coast was a thriving patch of golden flowered reed sweet grass *(Glyceria maxima)*. There was a gap in the cliffs here, presumably worn by the stream, so that the water spread out across the top of the pebble beach as a welcome supply of fresh drinking water for the shoreline gulls. We had intercepted the coastal path here and the track climbing up to the west led to the Fontygary Quarry, another prime botanising site in years gone by. What had happened there must remain a mystery at present, as our route led back east.

The wind off the sea was extremely powerful in this gap, with everything flapping as we surveyed the scene from the footbridge. We were literally blown up the wooden steps leading to the Rhoose clifftop. It was a south-westerly, so the strip of cliff preserved intact to seaward of the path afforded shelter to both us and the flora, leading to a rich collection of plants.

Outstanding species were the pink-flowered rest harrow *(Ononis repens)*, an undershrub, rooting at the nodes. Its English name stemmed from its propensity to arrest the old horse-drawn harrows, its latin name from its creeping habit. The spreading flower heads of greater knapweed *(Centaurea scabiosa)* emulated those of garden cornflowers, in shape if not colour, the deeply lobed leaves distinguishing them from the rayed version of common knapweed. Like the hedge bedstraw *(Galium mollugo)*, formerly used for human bedding, this was an obligate calcicole, needing lime.

At a windy gap in the barrier only a few yards wide, there was a fine crop of succulent rock samphire on the rock face receiving the full force of salty westerlies, but much less on that with a more sheltered aspect. The saved cliff barrier petered out a little to the east of here, the sheltered end of the horizontal rock strata thickly enwrapped in a tangle of ivy.

Just beyond here was the place where the old industrial railway line which we had been following got undermined. My 1970s photos show the ends of the wooden sleepers and the outer iron line suspended over thin air where the cliff had collapsed beneath them. The rock below was then a clean break, from the battering it had taken from the sea, with no colonising plants as yet.

It was vertical then, now it was bevelled back to the summit, bulging outwards below and signifying subsequent loss from the top, which couldn't be estimated because the railway track had been removed. The 'new' cliff face bore a crop of some of the finest cliff samphire I remember. Although this is a plant which I normally associate with wave-battered Atlantic cliffs, it seemed also to thrive on the much finer salty spume thrown at it this far up the Severn Estuary. With it were clumps of tall rock sea lavender. Most of this had finished flowering now, although at flowering prime on the Aberthaw strand twelve days earlier.

The foreshore below was a fine example of wave-smoothed limestone platforms, with dimpled surfaces. Each shelf represented the uppermost layer of one of the sandier white strata left exposed when the softer intervening black shale above washed away. The bedding plane was not quite horizontal, so beach walkers stepped up or down a few inches from each to the next - as on a broad staircase remaining on an overall level plane. Wave-strewn white pebbles scattered sparsely over the slabs were moved by every tide. There was no way down here, so no beach combing.

The zone inland, though still backed by a quarried rock face, had held a mature community of tall, marshy grassland for at least thirty years. In the 1970s groups of naturalists would come here to photograph the pyramidal and southern marsh orchids. Even rarer was the grass vetchling *(Lathyrus nissolii)*, an unusual pea, easily missed when not bearing its delicate pink pea flowers, because the leaves resemble those of grass instead of the more complex trefoils or frondose ones of most legumes.

Another speciality here was the ivy broomrape *(Orobanche hederae)*, and this we did see today, as a couple of spikes, the pale yellow flowers faded and the seed capsules brown. This is a complete parasite, with no green leaves, wholly dependent on the ivy, from which it sucks sustenance by clamping onto the below ground roots. It is known from a limited number of regions, all but one westerly.

The little used grassy path leading through this community was under water in places after so much August rain, but the community as a whole was drier than I remembered and it was easy to circumvent the submerged bits. The shorter height of the sward seemed to be due to rabbits, the smaller area due to overrunning by a thicket of grey sallow.

Looking onto the edge of this spinney was like looking onto a miniature version of hedgerow trees whose lower branches had been browsed off by cattle at a uniform height. All the lower twigs and any ground vegetation had been grazed off to a level ceiling - that to which a rabbit could comfortably reach, leaving only the main trunks. It was as if someone had been along with a neat hedgeing tool. The sward outside was littered with twice defecated rabbit pellets. This damp grassland was now their larder, all 'handy snacks' having been filched from the home patch.

Oxford ragwort *(Senecio squalidus)*, more elegant than the common ragwort and with more finely dissected leaves, had been a speciality in the early phases and was still here, guaranteed to brighten up any corner, however squalid. (The unfortunate specific name applied to the sites where they were found rather than the plants themselves.). Fleabane, yellow toadflax, the common perforated St. John's wort and uncommon creeping St. John's wort were incorporated in the sward.

Tall melilot reared turrets of short, two-seeded, down-turned pods high above the rest, among thistles, that rabbits dislike. Do they like onions? We found some intact stems of crow garlic but none with heads of bulbils. Black mustard *(Brassica nigra)*, formerly massed on newly dumped soil was still present to a lesser degree.

Shallow soils supported a sparse cover of wild strawberry plants and depauperate tufts of sea mayweed. These tolerated ground which fluctuated between very dry and very wet, rain unable to soak away into the rock base unless there were convenient cracks. As soil deepened plants heightened, downy willow herb grading into the more striking 'codlins and cream'. Among these I came across some tall graceful sprays of the uncommon tor grass or chalk false brome *(Brachypodium pinnatum)*.

Everything was too wet at present to see any of the fascinatingly symmetrical cracking of clay pans which simulated impermanent crazy paving. One of my most remarkable photographs taken here was of one such area, where every crack had become crammed with dark red and grey-blue seedlings of red goosefoot and hastate orache - a perfect outline for a patchwork quilt.

Both sun-loving and water loving insects emerged from hiding during bursts of sunshine. Hedge browns and meadow browns flipped everywhere while red admirals, sunning themselves with wings spread, were also easily spotted.

Blue damselflies and red Sympetrum dragonflies quartered some of the smaller pools and there were plenty of smaller fry to interest the little brown warblers (willow-chiffs?) popping in and out of Buddleia and sallow. The air was full of sand martins throughout and a few herring gulls had come in from the beach for a freshwater splash and a drink.

We returned by the other route, obliquely across the rising slope of reconstituted land, of which I had only the haziest recollections. It had been divested of all industrial relicts, smoothed, possible reseeded and meticulously drained. The several anastimosing water channels flowing between steep grassy banks were floored with flat stones which made the necessary crossings easier.

At the crest of the rise we crossed a broader section at the start of the more restricted but equally fast flowing stream of our way out. And so to the spacious new carpark, even emptier of cars now. The neatly manicured land just crossed, looked ripe for building development. I hoped I was wrong, but no doubt the residents of the new houses would appreciate a supermarket, a post office or a pub.

* * *

We drove a short distance west and dipped back under a railway bridge into the Fontygary Caravan Park. A short walk down a treelined gully in the cliff brought us to the series of steps down to the beach. More of the upper cliff face had fallen than the lower, leaving a convenient series of smooth limestone platforms at different levels, handy for picnics or sun bathing.

An elderly man, who obviously knew his way around, headed for an intermediate platform, edged his way along one of the narrower ledges and settled into a niche in the ledge above, that exactly fitted his not inconsiderable figure. Here were elbow rests both sides, head rest and adequate foot room, a prototype for some of those angular modern armchairs appearing in the shops.

On the pebbles below two youths were tumbling around in the not inconsiderable waves bowling across from Somerset, which loomed on the horizon. The storm beach had accumulated at the foot of the cliffs, each pebble a missile to be hurled at their base.

At low tide there were acres of wave-smoothed limestone platforms stretching out into the channel and making for more comfortable bathing than was available now, at high tide. We topped off our day with tea and toasted tea cakes in the little café.

CHAPTER 35

Forest Farm Wetlands and Chestnut Coppice From Tree Planting to Fungal Decay

By midday on 14th August the rain had let up sufficiently to entice me out on a short circuit of the country park. Local wildlife was responding similarly, the bench under a riverside Buddleia, was already occupied. A robin, fluffed up and flat out, as after a night on the tiles, was enjoying a sun bathe.

Like the garden blackbird before him, he faced away from the sun, both wings half spread this time, with little flips to let a current of air through beneath. I halted, about three yards off and he appeared not to notice. Not unduly perturbed when he did, he merely hopped onto a low branch a foot above the bench for a thorough preen, with his back to me. I was the one who tired first and moved on.

We wonder sometimes why robins are so comfortable in our presence, but their main mode of feeding is to follow large animals such as ourselves and pounce on the insects that we disturb in passing. We are allies, as cattle egrets are to big game and pest-guzzling gulls to the man on the plough. Aware of it or not, our life mode was fashioned to be in harmony with others on our planet. The only oddity in this case is that continental robins are not so closely in tune with European humans, and so not inclined to feed from their hands or wish them well on their Christmas cards.

After gathering a few seed pods of the purple goat's rue, with the idea of growing them on my balcony, I headed for the abandoned part of the Forest Farm carpark. Almost coming a cropper as I slid across the largely unvegetated surface, I realised that almost the entire ground was covered with a loose assemblage of slimy, hemispherical, olive-brown blobs of Nostoc, a blue-green alga.

While most of the mossy surface, cleared of all edible plants by the rabbits, bore loose colonies of this primitive organism, many of the puddles were free of it. In smaller ones, more recently flooded, the jelly spheres appeared to be partially dissolved. The shapeless communities consist of a mass of fine filaments encased in mucilage, which sticks them together in an amorphous, easily disrupted mass.

These growths appear as by magic, on tarmac and concrete, as well as ground in periods of summer rain. They were also under the picnic tables and benches where grass cover had been destroyed. Nature abhors a vacuum and with all this muggy warmth and bounteous water, her quickest growing troops seemed to have been mustered to fill the unoccupied breach.

The Nostoc was less enamoured with ground covered with shingle chippings. The jigsaw pattern of spaces between these had been colonised by anastimosing lines of minute, dew-spangled, mosses. The algae disappear when dry. Do they add their substance to the system or crumble to dust and blow away - to another?

I saw no rabbits today, although there were patches where they could have fed without getting their feet wet. Sunshine was continuous now and insects had emerged from hiding. Small winged creatures, particularly, needed to make the most of the hours when no rain was falling. A couple of emperor dragonflies *(Anax imperator)* zoomed close to my head in one of the lusher corners and there were both red male and yellow female common darter dragonflies *(Sympetrum striolatum)*.

The usual hedge browns, speckled woods and large whites were busy on the fleabane and hawkweed oxtongue Small moths and hover flies were visiting the round-leaved mint, which burgeoned so prolifically all around. The branched flower spikes above the wrinkled leaves were a rather dreary grey-white colour, which flower books are generous enough to describe as 'very pale mauve', but have not convinced the gardeners, although it was obviously such a prolific grower.

* * *

Next I visited the ailing farmhouse pond. There was no standing water there but the plants were not as expected. In spring most of the centre had been covered with shoots of greater spearwort. Had this produced its spectacular flowers and died back?

Currently the breeze rippled through an attractive stand of reed sweet grass in the centre, grading back to reeds, Iris and other expected marginals. Two specialities near the sitting out place were shoulder high flowering tansies and sweet gallingale *(Cyperus longus)*, the first very showy, the second very rare, but handsome and presumably introduced. An unusual sedge, the inflorescence consisted of a bunch of long, narrow tassels composed of neatly packed, double rows of bright ginger florets.

As I strolled through the farmhouse garden, seeking a gap in the fence to reach the new field pond, I heard a sepulchral voice from the rear: "Who goes there?". It was the warden Mike Wiley, pretending not to recognise me because I was in a flowery cotton frock instead of my usual field togs - not having expected the weather to let up sufficiently to lure me out.

Two days after this there were floods in Northern Ireland, with an underpass on one of their main road junctions under twenty feet of water! There had been plenty of rain nearer home. It looked as though the jet stream, said to be responsible, had settled on this more southerly course, bringing its train of cyclones with it. At least the 2007 floods in Yorkshire, Worcestershire and Gloucestershire, with such losses of crops and livestock, had not been repeated.

* * *

The new pond was in fine fettle, the water crystal clear, despite the bed of orange silt. The weedy hay crop round about, which had been through the ribwort-dominated phase to a disorderly one of docks, thistles and nettles, had been mown. Fenced off from future livestock was the pond enclosure and the young orchard at the far end - the little trees there rabbit-proofed individually with plastic sleeves.

The main aquatic plants were curly leaved Canadian pondweed (Lagarosiphon), almost free of clinging algae, thanks to the two floating straw bales. It had produced a surfeit of tiny flowers, something that seldom happened in this country until recently. The starry white florets appeared as three spreading, notched petals, borne on a fragile corolla tube of extendable length - up to twelve inches, although thin as a thread - this greatly outdoing the better known floral tubes of the early Crocus flowers springing from our lawns in February.

The Forest Farm flower tubes were three to four inches long, trailing obliquely under the surface, which was high now, after the rains. This was probably to no purpose, as seed could not be expected to follow. Male flowers break free and are wafted by wind and current to find and pollenate a female , but male flowers are seldom produced in Britain. Obviously the species is not dependent on seed production. It can fill a garden pool by vegetative spread in a few months - the original invaders of British waters having constituted an ecological disaster, blocking canals and the like when it first appeared. It is not such a menace now, having found a less domineering niche among the natives.

Its companion species here was an attractively delicate growth of water milfoil, with whorls of fine feathery leaves, but none of the protruding spikes of pink flowers at present. The only other true aquatic was a narrow-leaved pondweed, probably the lesser species (*Potamogeton berchtoldii*).

The embayment behind a log was covered by floating lesser duckweed, accompanied by lumps of Nostoc, which crept on around the shores. Pea-sized jelly spheres clinging to the water lily stems may have been more of the same. Marginal plants were few, but doing well, the bogbean bearing spherical green fruits and sending an exploratory shoot out over the water surface. Typha, Iris, brooklime and watercress shared the banks.

Upside down water boatmen (Notonectids) scudded among the water weed and some whirligigs were spinning on their chosen spot. An emperor dragonfly, with powder-blue abdomen and grass-green thorax, was hawking over the surface - this or another seen later over the little apple trees. A southern hawker dragonfly, unaccompanied by the male, was laying eggs on the water surface.

Blue damselflies were connected in copulating couples, flying as one but not laying eggs, while blue-tailed damselflies, much the commonest, were unconnected at present. Mike had seen a four-spotted chaser dragonfly laying eggs there in the morning. Later he and his fellow wardens had been called to deal with a big beech tree, blown over by the gales across the northern section of the canal, blocking the towpath at Tongwynlais.

Returning through the shadows of the damp railway bridge, I paused to examine a little cluster of spider hide-outs in crevices of the masonry. Webs of untidily woven silk over the surface, were pierced by neatly bordered round holes, entrances to the spider's lair within. Neat, like those of the funnel web spiders south of Castell Coch, these lacked the tapering funnel, cracks in the masonry affording sufficient protection. The builder was *Anauris similis* - a robust, brown patterned spider, which popped up to her front entrance to grab the prey, when she sensed the appropriate vibrations on the outer snare.

An odd plant caught my attention on the way up from this gloomy hollow. Half way between an oversized groundsel and an undersized ragwort, it turned out to be the Welsh groundsel (*Senecio cambrensis*). This was a hybrid between the common groundsel and the Oxford ragwort. Ray florets were present, although curling back as the flower head matured, and the leaves were attractively dissected, differing from base to apex. We used to call this the rayed groundsel (var. radiata). It was satisfying to know that the pundits have elevated it to full species rank.

Soon after I got back, I spotted a fine specimen of a short-winged conehead cricket (*Conocephalus dorsalis*) perched on the door near my newly discarded jacket. This is a bush cricket, with two wispy antennae almost twice as long as the body, splaying backwards or whiffling forwards to explore the scene ahead.

These, the body and limbs, were bright green, the short, folded wings, which extended half way down the abdomen, were brown, as was the underside of the tail. There was no sword-like ovipositor for egg laying at the nether end, so this was a male. Its normal habitat is beside water, particularly among taller vegetation, so this could have attached itself to my person at either of the Forest Farm ponds.

The hind legs were not as muscular as in many of the grasshoppers. When I transferred it to the balcony, expecting it to leap to freedom, it merely pottered around at a walking pace and made a short hop into the cover of a Geranium plant, probably because they are nocturnal and it was not yet waking up time.

It is mostly by night that they produce their high pitched 'song', by raising the wings and rubbing them together. The left wing carries the teeth or serrations and lies above the right.

Both this species and the long-winged conehead (*Conocephalum discolor*), which caused so much excitement when discovered at Coryton Roundabout in 1999, as a 'first' for Wales, were found only in Southern England until recent years, since when they have been steadily moving west and north, so this was one of the exploring pioneers.

Only a few days before I had discovered a scorpion fly in my bathroom, also probably imported on my person. This was a male, with the swollen end of his tail curved up over his back - not an ovipositor, but a quite harmless anomaly. Active by day, this one accepted his freedom with greater enthusiasm, but only after a considerable time perched on a flower pot nibbling his front left foot, which appeared undamaged.

* * *

Sunday afternoon, the 17th of August, and the air as invigorating as if filtered through damp felt, but it was no good waiting for the sun. The world and his wife were out - awheel, with their families, on the Taff Trail. The leg-powered vehicles that passed me were like a circus parade.

Most fascinating was "the bicycle built for one and a half" instead of two. A tandem, yes, but the back wheel was half the size of the front one and the back saddle three quarters the height. First there was Dad, with his little boy pedalling away behind, then a Mum, her little girl doing likewise although seemingly scarcely big enough to toddle.

Next came a bicycle and sidecar, or covered waggon, a smaller replica of the motor bike and sidecar that had introduced me to the countryside back in the 1920s. The little lad in the sidecar didn't look as though he had enough push power to pedal. The next two couples were Mum on the bike and nipper in a box on wheels trailing behind.

This must have been a cycling club on the move, to get so many innovative methods of propulsion in such close proximity. They left me plodding round the puddles, far behind. My own parents had met as members of the same cycling club - and formed a union that lasted into their mid eighties. They had got mechanised earlier in the family history than these. Petrol cost less in those days.

There were plenty of lone cyclist awheel and joggers afoot. Much as I prefer solitude on my strolls abroad, it was good to see so many folk taking healthy exercise instead of pounding up and down on a mechanised treadmill in a stuffy gym - which you have to pay to get to and pay to go in. I was headed north, past the rabbit field, but no rabbits were seen out in the wet grass, only horses, stirring up more puddles in the muddy patch where they gathered to beg from passers by.

Radyr weir was in spate. Any salmon trying to make an early passage upstream to the spawning grounds, would have a hard job making it through the racing water in the fish pass today. Two beach balls were bobbing at the foot of the main torrent, pushed back by the recoil of the white turbulence at its base. They were still bobbing when I returned three hours later.

I had already passed a torrent downstream of the weir, seldom seen before. This was the one passing under the Taff trail in the excavated channel leading from the feeder canal to empty out into the Taff. Moving into the mounded ground under the beeches, I found the two falls by which the water stepped down into this normally dry channel.

History has it that this was the route used by boats following on down the Taff to by-pass the weir, with some sort of a lock to accommodate the changing levels. The old tub boats bringing iron down from the Gwaelod foundry to the Melin Griffith tin works, followed on down the feeder canal.

Circuiting the lily pools, I was impressed by the way rhizomes from the marginal Typha bulrushes were penetrating out under the lawn, as well as into the water, pushing up robust shoots. Some of these had grown a foot or more above mown grass so short that they could only have had a few days since the passing of the mower, which hadn't swerved to avoid them.

White-flowered hemp agrimony was unusual and the Siberian dogwoods were full of clustered green berries. Those undersized purple and white ones seen earlier in the year must have been abortive. Moorhens make their nests in the silliest places. There was one here, neatly woven with broad bulrush leaves, so close inshore in a dense patch of water lilies, that few dogs could have resisted it - nor winged egg thieves either.

* * *

Following the road past the grounds of Amersham International, I ducked back into the wood, following the path parallel to Longwood Drive. During the construction of the M4 motorway alongside and the Coryton Roundabout in the early 1970s, this had been a site of excavation and tipping. The route of the motorway was finally agreed in 1974 and heavy machinery was withdrawn in 1977. A pool appeared amidships and the whole tract between the roundabout and the river was levelled and ploughed up at least three times. I had followed the fortunes of the plant and animal succession during the first two decades, recording progress, from ephemeral pioneers, through annuals to perennials and so to trees, some spontaneous and some planted, under the management of the Parks Department as a conservation site. Seed mixtures were sown and the first trees planted in 1978, when eighty two different herbs were recorded.

The rare Nottingham catchfly, field woundwort and gallant soldier arrived with the poppies and fumitories - the last having been arable weeds since Neolithic times. A broad path was bulldozed through the centre in 1979 and is there still, with well established woodland to the south and tall herbs, dominated by Himalayan balsam towards the M4 embankment to the north. This followed an initial sward of perforated St. John's wort, with other tall herbs and undershrubs growing up through to make the community nigh impenetrable by late summer.

It was the coppiced woodland that interested me particularly now, thirty years after the original tree planting. The sweet chestnuts seemed to have overtopped the rest, those on the margins as tall as the line of pylons following along the more open strip, where some had to be lopped off. The unmolested ones held a good crop of spiny chestnut burs now in late August. It was salutary to learn how much these had grown in that thirty years.

I tried hugging some to my bosom, but failed by a considerable margin to touch finger tips around the far side. A nearby beech, I could only get my arms about half way around at shoulder height, where the trunk had already branched into three - and the middle one into three again at a height of about nine feet. Yet I had seen these being planted. No wonder I had got lost among the newly burgeoned trees on Coryton Roundabout a few weeks earlier. There were numerous, mysterious, marble-sized warts on the lowest four feet of that beech trunk. Sheer witchery. Trees seem so solid and immovable. It must have been easy for our forest dwelling forebears to call upon extraterrestrial forces to explain their capabilities and portents.

By the end of the 1980s this machine-tortured strip of bare fallow had become woodland. Meadow pipits and stonechats had moved in and then moved out, making way for noisy jays and over-wintering woodcock.

Small mammal trapping yielded wood mice and field voles in the grassland, with the rabbits, wood mice, bank voles and common shrews in the tree plantations. Moles were tunnelling and grey squirrels were using a sawn off stump as a dining table, strewn with split hazel nut shells.

By 1982 poplars had reached to fifteen feet, willows not far behind, and by 1987 the woodland was mostly impenetrable, the central path the only throughway. By 1989 the chestnut, beech and field maple wood was beginning to open out, as lower branches died for lack of light and snapped off.

In 1991 self sown birches appeared marginally and precocious ashes were springing up in the interior. Poplars felled in that year had trunks seven inches across but revealed only twelve annual rings - a phenomenal rate of growth outside the Tropics. These and the abundant, related willows were notoriously fast growers and were popular at the time for wood burning stoves, and since for bio-fuels as an energy source.

By 2002 the spreading canopy of a now substantial yew tree had reached down almost to ground level, the innermost twigs choked by their siblings. Now, in 2008, there was easy entry to this part of the wood and I located that same tree, with its leafy skirts still reaching to the ground. The smooth red bark was deeply furrowed below its division into four main branches, these largely hidden among the mass of smaller growth to which they had given rise.

We tend to associate yews with enduring longevity and great age. Such speed of growth in their youth engendered quite new thoughts - until I remembered all those yew hedges in the gardens of stately homes and how much the massed new shoots managed to grow between the routine hedge clipping sessions.

Fern spores took their time drifting across from the Long Wood and canal side. My records show the first male ferns in 1986 and the first broad buckler ferns in 2000. Now, in 2008, there were not only more ground ferns among the spindly, etiolated enchanter's nightshade , but epiphytes as well. I saw fine clusters of the larger, Welsh polypody ferns growing on the moss-clad branches of elder and willow at head height and a few higher up in the canopy.

* * *

Although open-floored and easily penetrated now, there was little ground flora apart from moss and a few tall nettles where a little light filtered in. Even the ground cover of ivy, which is the hallmark of gloomy mature woods, was not very widespread. Irrepressible ash saplings were questing hopefully upwards, some alongside spindly dogwood bushes which had produced extra large leaves to compensate for the low light intensity.

It was evident that the wood had been coppiced for some years, notably the hazel and sallow, the cut wood being left in piles to rot. The low branching of some of the standard trees suggested early cuts which were not repeated and most of the rotting piles looked well settled in. Swathes of *Trentipohlia aurea,* a green alga, had painted some of the tree trunks orange, and much of the rest looked ripe for fungus growth.

Fungi had started moving in by the year 2000 - and no doubt earlier. Variegated stump fungus and common brackets were appearing on old wood by then, and tiny fawn elf cups (Peziza) among cut hazel stumps. I had not expected my Sunday afternoon stroll in 2008 to turn into a fungus foray, so early in the year, but this was, in effect, what happened. It seemed the muggy dampness had simulated autumnal conditions and hastened things along.

I sat on a low log to do up my shoe lace and found that I was not only sitting beside an aggregation of rabbit pellets - an apparent meeting place for the exchange of pheromones - but that the ground about my feet was strewn with very recognisable small fungi.

These were jelly babies *(Leotia lubrica)*, one of the jelly fungi which appear from August to October in damp woods. Just a few inches high, they consisted of shapeless, lobed heads on bulging, sometimes grooved stalks. Firm and rubbery rather than slimy, they were described as being an 'olivaceous ochre' - transparent brownish-yellow to you and me. Once I got my eye in, I saw that many scores had pushed up out of the otherwise bare, black humic soil.

Two others, colourful but small and easily overlooked, occurred on the surface of barkless, blackened logs, like sequins on an evening gown. Soft pink pea-sized balls were young specimens of a stump Lycogola, one of the slime moulds. This is a group distinct from normal fungi, with a mobile, animal-like phase in the life history. Lycogola hardens into little red balls, not unlike fallen holly berries, but attached to their substrate, and are quite common later in the year. The other miniature was probably Calycella, a bright orange growth, no larger but more shapely, somewhat discoid with a sunken centre, like a malformed elf cup.

Much the most conspicuous of the ground dwelling fungi were earth balls, not the common species which romps across woodland floors in sites such as the Great Garth, but *Scleroderma verrucosa*. The English names of these two have got somewhat muddled. Today's finds were called scaly earthballs, although their tough yellow surfaces were covered with dark brown pinprick dots, slightly raised in older specimens. Common earthballs *(Scleroderma vulgare)* actually ARE scaly, being covered throughout with darker beige scales about a quarter of an inch across.

Those irregular spheres are attached to the ground by white mycelial fungal threads. The Longwood Drive ones tapered below into a tough, complicated system of solid white branches, penetrating two inches or so into the soil under the larger fructifications, which were two inches or more across but slightly flattened, so less high. Smaller ones were about an inch in diameter with smaller, but still complex attachments.

Mature balls were full of dark brown spores, these released through irregular rents up to an inch long in the outer fabric, not through neat apical pores as in the true puffballs. I squeezed one and a jet of black rain water erupted from the rift. The second one discharged part of its legitimate load of spores in a sooty cloud. I saw only one colony of these striking fungi, but it was many yards across. Was it coincidental that a ring of nine was arranged symmetrically around the bole of a living tree, or was there a mutually advantageous mycorhizal association underground between the tree roots and the fungal threads, as so often?

A small conical toadstool with slaty black cap, white gills and stipe (or stalk), was probably moss bonnet *(Mycena bryophyllum)*. It was growing among moss on the rotting side of a waterlogged trunk the texture of humus. The milking bonnet *(Mycena galopus)* was a more delicate white throughout, with a slightly frilled margin to the spreading head and a little central peak, as on a gnome's cap. Both were quite small, about an inch across.

Bracket fungi were common, not yet on the living tree boles but on the discarded felled logs, many of which were riddled with the little round holes of boring beetles. Fluted, overlapping flanges of bright orange hairy Stereum *(Stereum hirsutum)*, sometimes row upon row, were common, as often. So too, was the velvety turkey tail *(Coriolus zonatus or Trametes versicolor)*, similar of form but banded in different colours. Both of these have thin, leathery, overlapping flanges, with the porous, spore-producing surface facing downwards.

Bleeding oak crust *(Stereum gausapatum)* manifested itself as spreading white crusts on the surface of dead wood, the flanges sometimes growing outwards as rudimentary brackets. Usually white, sometimes pale buff, this only 'bleeds' if injured when fresh.

Seen only once but larger, woodier and more striking, was the black hemispherical willow bracket *(Phellinus igniarus)*, formerly used as fuel, hence the specific name. It can live for many years, enlarging from a central point, each year's growth clearly demarcated from the next. The current outermost one bearing the spores is of soft white tissue, and makes a conspicuous margin to the whole. This species is not always on willow and is quite uncommon.

I moved into a clearing and discovered it was raining. Time to go home. Walking back alongside the Taff from the M4 bridge I was going at the same pace as a herring gull, which was drifting downstream with the current, tail first, towards the weir. The mallard, headed upstream, was getting nowhere, but was probably paddling hard to stay put on that lively flood.

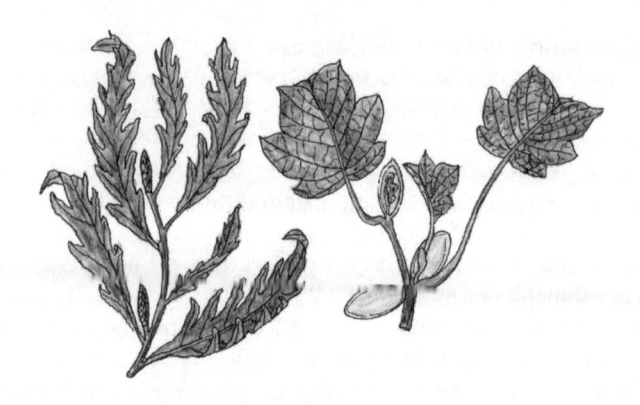

CHAPTER 36

St. Fagans Folk Museum, Tongwynlais Fallen Tree and Pollination of Himalayan Balsam

Tuesday 19th August and two of us sipping morning coffee in my parlour, gazing out at the rain. The aroma from my newly created blackberry purée came wafting in from the kitchen bearing 'come hither' or 'go thither' messages from the great out of doors. A midsummer day. How could we, in all conscience, stay indoors?

Local paths would be muddy and beset with puddles. Was there anywhere non-urban where there were made-up paths suitable for elderly ladies to take the air? A penny dropped. St. Fagan's Museum of Welsh Life, catering for the public with ample grounds and plenty of show cottages offering sanctuary if the rain got too troublesome.

We took the lesser road above the dripping Plymouth Woods strung along the valley below. Down past St. Fagan's Castle, a late Sixteenth Century Manor House, and we turned off alongside the River Ely just short of the level crossing over the London to South Wales main railway line.

The Ely was as full as I had seen it, with water swirling up towards the approach road, lapping round the bases of the big willows alongside and flattening grasses and herbs. So lively a source of water could have been useful for 'mopping up' after the Battle of St. Fagans, believed to have been fought here in 1648, during the Civil War.

Rain or no rain, the carpark was full, but a new area had been floored with 'egg box' paving to take the overflow when the sloping grassy parking lots on the adjacent hillside were too slippery. "But we'll have to open them on bank holiday", this from the amiable parking attendant

Past tall hedges speckled with orange Berberis flowers, we found ourselves admiring the simple efficiency of a slate fence, probably peculiar to the slate quarrying country of North Wales. The narrow, waist high slivers of stone were joined near their tops by two twists of wire, woven in and out of the sequence.

My mind drifted back to when I had been fascinated by the magic of a craftsman splitting elegant roofing slates from a chunky slab of blue-grey rock in one of the quarries. Such was the alignment of the mud particles that had gone to its formation over aeons of time, that a few taps along the edge of the block caused two planes to pull apart - as easily as though cleaving wood along the grain. Another old craft was manifested in the basket work bee skeps on show in stone recesses.

The maypole from past frolics still stood, with a cohort of swallows circling its base only just above ground level. Rain had evidently beaten their potential prey almost down into the grass. We lingered awhile by the pile of individually numbered stones where an ancient chapel was being reconstructed. The site of the original had been pointed out to us when we passed through West Glamorgan on our way to Stackpole in Pembrokeshire.

Our digestive juices stimulated by the aroma wafting from the Bakery, we climbed the wooden staircase into the barn above the tin baths and buckets of the Old Iron Store, to partake of mushroom soup, served with rolls and butter. Outside the window crowds continued to pass, family parties and visiting foreigners, many under bright coloured brollies. At least it was mild, and conditions improved as the afternoon progressed.

Casting envious eyes on the fine rhubarb crops in the gardens of the "Merthyr Miners' Cottages from over the years", we headed past Downland sheep which were trying to avoid the mud around the newly vacated site of a marquee alongside a spinney of tall beeches.

A uniform stand with fine straight trunks, this was obviously a plantation, the foliage borne high up among ripening beechmast. A few initials and heart symbols carved on trunks decades ago were only just discernible.

Unmoved by the expectations of the sweethearts, the so much longer lived trees had been soldiering on in their own quiet but inevitable way, gradually obliterating trace of the human passing. Each year's new increment of timber added as an annual ring stretched the bark and distorted the signature.

Another growth zone, the cork cambium, was producing new cork cells, replacing the old ones as these sloughed away, dust to dust. In today's fast moving world the young romantics had probably forgotten this episode. The trees which had satisfied their whim to put their feelings on record, provided decent interment as the message became irrelevant. The smooth, unfissured bark of beeches commends these above all other trees with cracked or furrowed bark, for this traditional practice of leaving harmless graffiti.

Elsewhere in this more spacious part of the grounds, sweet chestnut trees produced their crop of nuts in October - eagerly gathered from the ground below, as the spiky green husks opened to reveal their shining contents. The more difficult operation of extricating beech nuts from their triangular wrappings could safely be left to the squirrels and tits.

* * *

Heading down the slope after passing through the tunnel to the more formal gardens, I paused to admire a fine example of the primitive tulip tree (Liriodendron). The polished, dark green leaves, indented at the tips instead of pointed, appeared as anomalous as always, but what caught my attention this time was the abundance of paired, almost white ovals, the size of small plums.

These sprang from the base of the leaf stalks, as greatly enlarged stipules, making little pockets protecting the next young leaf with its accompanying bud. So transparent were they that the folded leaf inside could be distinguished when seen against the light. As the new shoot pushed out, the envelope was shed, to litter the ground, a cross between confetti and paper chase markers.

A rectangular, two partite lake occupied the valley under the ornate stone terracing of the old castle. Fifteen mallards rested on the bank, all looking like females, as the young drakes had shed their juvenile down in favour of camouflage adolescent feathers and the adult males were in eclipse. One bona fide duck was in charge of two half grown ducklings.

Much smaller was the brown-sided tufted duck, with tip tilted bill, or snub nose, making her look very young, but she too, had two ducklings, these considerably smaller. A moorhen, too, was still in the family way with a youngster trotting in her wake. It is likely that all these were second broods. A thickly wooded island would have provided a safe nesting site.

A young pied wagtail was foraging in the mown grass alongside the water, making rapid little runs of a few feet to pounce on some hapless, edible morsel. Sunlight had pierced the clouds now and the swallows were flying higher than those seen earlier in the rain, while a few large white butterflies had ventured out.

Most striking of the waterside plants were a big clump of Gunnera with upstanding spiky leaves. Less usual wildlings clustered along the lower side of the dam, which functioned also as a path between the two halves of the lake, were water bistort and water figwort.

Zig zagging up the terraces on the further side, we were within touching distance of the lower branches of the same cut-leaved beech tree on two different levels. Magnificent was the appropriate epithet for this, as well as for those forming the cathedral like knave in the other garden. Those had grown tall. This one had grown sideways, shading two terrace levels at once.

The slender twigs and pointed buds were an exact replica of those of the normal beech. The leaves, apart from a few small throw-backs, were four to five inches long but only an inch wide at most and deeply toothed.

These terraces bore a wealth of flowering shrubs, but the most flamboyant blossoms were those of *Magnolia grandis*, which saves its floral exuberance for August when most others of its genus are producing their bizarre red fruits. Like the tulip trees, Magnolias are regarded as primitive in evolutionary terms, their symmetrical flowers an embellishment of the cones of coniferous forebears.

Most primitive of all here, and sometimes not regarded as a plant at all, but grouped with bacteria, was more of the blue-green Nostoc. Larger aggregations preferred damp stone slabs to the numerous puddles and there was a neat row of pea sized colonies ranged along the angle of a wall base.

In the upper garden we were greeted by a colourful spread of Asters in neat flower beds. Other displays were of more sombre lavender and attractive red-purple Penstemons which were proving very popular with the bumble bees. Santolina made up for the absence of yellow bobble flower heads with the extravagant fragrance of its grey foliage.

Most showy in the herbaceous borders were the five foot high globe artichokes *(Cynara scolymus)*, which are frequently grown as ornamentals for the beauty of the pale blue flower heads, like those of giant thistles. These may be sacrificed for culinary use from late June onwards. The artichoke hearts are the combined young flowers in the involucral cup, but extra flavour can be got by sucking the bases of the fleshy scales of that decorative surround.

Showiest in the vegetable beds of the walled garden were the spherical yellow pumpkins standing out among the green marrows. The rose garden was a joy with its borders of colourful annuals and central island surrounded by a narrow circular pool, the evergreen shrub in the middle clipped into a living igloo. This is where we saw song thrush and robin, the only other birds being the ever present magpies and passing clouds of jackdaws.

* * *

The piece de resistance for me, however, was what must in the past have been termed the mulberry orchard, this having the added bonus of flowering Colchicums at this season. No less than seven of the ancient mulberry trees were lying down, propped on elbows of branches and looking incredibly ancient, with their knobbly deformed trunks. These appeared to have fallen naturally, their upended root ball having been covered with a mound of soil, now grassed over, but two old stumps had been sawn off.

One of the reclining veterans had a Cotoneaster rooted on its trunk. However gnarled and twisted the boles and wildly divergent the branches, the leafy twigs at what should have been their tops were in pristine condition and bearing a heavy crop of reddening fruits, the ripest turning black. These were the black mulberry *(Morus nigra)*, producing clusters of fruitlets which become fused together around a core, into multiple fruits resembling a plump loganberry. They are edible when ripe but quite acid at the red phase, which I sampled.

One veteran had given up, its root mound overgrown with creepers, but a few staked saplings showed that the tradition of mulberries was being perpetuated. Cuttings taken in June are said to root very easily, almost any severed portion clinging relentlessly to life. It is the white mulberry *(Morus alba)* on which silk worms (the caterpillars of silk worm moths) are reared. The black is the species usually planted in Britain, with several thriving at Llandaff.

The delightful colony of meadow saffron *(Colchicum autumnale)* was clustered about the base of one of the mulberry trees. As in the Canadian pondweed, but on a grander scale, the apparent four to five inch stem supporting the Crocus-like flower, is actually an extension of the petals, the corolla tube, springing directly from the fleshy corm.

The pinkish mauve petals appear above ground about September on their own, hence the popular name of naked ladies. The leaves, resembling those of tulips, emerge from the corm later. Seeds and corms may be collected for the extraction of colchicene, which is a narcotic drug said to cure gout.

Colchicum is a British native and is a sight to behold where the flowers spring haphazardly from grass and bracken in a few of the rough grazings on the English-South Wales border. We used to make annual pilgrimages to admire them, as we did to the fields of snake's head fritillaries in flatter country further east in spring. Sadly Colchicum is poisonous to livestock, so few farmers will tolerate it on their land.

There is an autumn Crocus *(Crocus nudiflorus)* which flowers at the same time, before the leaves, but this is easily distinguished. It has deeper mauve flowers, closer to the ground and usually with the petals tipped inwards, like mini tulips. Also it has three stamens to Colchicum's six. The orange saffron used in cooking is extracted from the three branched stigmas of *Crocus sativus*, despite the popular name of saffron for Colchicum.

* * *

On Thursday 23rd August I visited Tongwynlais on the other side of the River Taff to look at the big beech tree that had blown down in the gale of a few days before. This was not the only one, another having fallen at Roath

Lake in East Cardiff, fortunately into the water and not over the busy encircling path where another fall had caused a serious accident a while back.

The Tongwynlais beech was almost as big as they come, and rooted only just above the canal. Falling obliquely, it had blocked a considerable section, the leafy canopy intruding into the spinney on the further side of the towpath, damaging some of the marginal shrubs. Tangled roots, defying gravity, protruded gauntly into empty air, non-functional now but sustained by their siblings still ensconced in Mother Earth.

When I had met the wardens at Forest farm they had just returned from clearing a passage to let walkers and cyclists past. Hand manipulated chain saws were sufficient to sever the upper branches, to be thrown into the spinney as future fungus fodder. Heavier tackle would be needed for the rest, which looked like a lot of valuable timber, to add to the stacks from the municipal parks gently weathering near Forest farmhouse.

Beeches are notoriously shallow rooted and this one had been growing on a slope exceeding forty five degrees - and not one of bedrock having crevices into which it might have insinuated stabilising roots. The parent rock, of Old Red Sandstone Marl, was way below this level, carved into a great gully by the ancient river and glacier following this line of weakness along the geological fault passing through the Taff Gorge.

The rift was filled during the course of time by glacial deposits of relatively unstable sand, gravel and boulder clay. A change in sea level caused the ancestral river to cut down into this, subsequent meanders gouging the sides of the new valley back to form the bordering scarps.

The foot of the eastern boulder clay scarp here at Tongwynlais is followed by the Glamorgan Canal. The foot of that on the western side below Radyr is followed by the Valleys Railway Line. Between the two Old Man River flows on, moving his meanders progressively downstream.

Currently pressure is on the Radyr side at Radyr Station, from where the river swings east and then back again to strike the cliff under Radyr Comprehensive School - below where the canal and feeder empty back into Father Taff. Some of the unstable glacial deposits from this east bank now clung to the upended root platform of the beech, which was tilted skywards, while loosened material slid down into the water alongside.

A grey wagtail arrived to bob up and down on the tilted base of the trunk, as though in a frenzy of perplexity as to what had happened to its former peaceful little world. Wagtails always behave like this, of course, and no-one quite knows why. The moorhen cruising downstream had to flutter up and over where the trunk was uncluttered by lesser growths. The meshed branches, twigs and leaves across the towpath created a thicket that might have perplexed a woodland bird, let alone one of open water. Was the shriek of a passing jay one of consternation? I peered long and hard into the closely piled branches, but saw no signs of nests.

The trunk had forked quite low down, so it was the equivalent of two trees which lay at this long angle across the canal. Water was still flowing through, quite gently beneath, crystal clear, although the rippled canal bed was of soft silt, this having had time to settle since the disruption. When the lumber jacks come to clear the remains, it will be interesting to count the number of annual rings on the cross section of those two trunks.

The trees were so closely aggregated on the slope of the Long Wood which flanked the valley here, that the fallen monarch had scarcely left a gap in the leafy border. This was no doubt because most of the boughs had reached out over the open canal to get a better share of sunlight - this making them more vulnerable to falling towards the greater weight of timber.

This over arching beech canopy intercepting more than its share of the sunlight had been responsible for drawing up the bank vegetation below to more than its appointed stature - hemp agrimony, meadowsweet and gipsywort spiked with purple loosestrife. The Long Wood is a living entity, just as its component parts are. One part of the skin sloughs away and another part grows to heal the breach.

The great naturalist, the late Ronald Lockley of Skokholm Island fame, spent much of his boyhood here, building a hide-away on this east bank a little further down the canal. Here he became at one with the wild - a fitting introduction to his later life dealing with nature in the raw on that remarkable sea bird sanctuary, until forced off by World War II. From these experiences sprang his many delightful natural history books.

Water mint in the 2008 shallows, currently in full flower, was two to three times its normal height. The main blocker of the channel here, however, as during at least the last forty years, was the lesser or unbranched bur-reed *(Sparganium simplex or Sparganium emersum)*. This is not a common plant and is held in high esteem, but it is too invasive here for its own good, causing hours of work clearing the waterway.

The greater or branched bur-reed *(Sparganium erectum)* is far more widespread but occurs here more spasmodically along the banks, sometimes with marsh woundwort. The smaller species, as the 'emersum' suggests is more likely to grow in rather than beside the water, with many of its leaves floating - like those of the much smaller, much rarer species of mountain lakes which thrives at the head of the Rhondda Valleys. The flowering spike, with its proximal, spherical bur fruits and terminal, smaller, pollen-bearing flower balls which fall off after their pollen has been shed, are more simply branched than the other, as the 'simplex' suggests.

* * *

Passage south down this portion of the canal is blocked by the motorway embankment, through which the water flows in a long dark tunnel. To meet it again one has to follow the embankment, with its narrow basal water course, to the capacious bridge where it crosses the Taff and back along the other flank.

The noise filtering down through the flimsy screen of trees from that moving lava flow of traffic was horrendous. I had always hated following that stretch with the constant pounding of the ear drums and it was worse than usual today. Some invisible irregularities in the slip road leading down to the A470 at junction 32 caused the heavy pantechnicons to shudder, producing a noise like a fusillade of artillery.

Amazingly a small flock of hirundines was coursing back and forth over the traffic, like sparks thrown from the lava-producing volcano - presumably scooping up winged insects thrust aloft by the slipstream from the speeding vehicles.

As soon as practicable after negotiating the severed end of the old railway embankment, now a ridge of mature woodland, I stepped over a low stile and slithered across a grassy quagmire into the adjacent sports field.

Conservationists, with the unrelenting cacophony of sound in mind, had planted a linear woodland to try and muffle the impact. Not very mature yet and closer to the river of sound than the chestnut coppice on the other side, where I had been able to ignore most of the racket among the close set maturing trees, it helped.

First I wandered alongside the old railway, where today's oaks, beeches and sweet chestnuts would have quenched the noise from past rolling stock and the less obtrusive canal boats carrying freight from the coalfield before the railway materialised. Man changes the environment to suit his immediate needs. Trees work on a longer cycle mitigating his ecological footprints over the course of time. No doubt they will be here still when we have moved on or moved out, as a result of climate change, adapting their life form to current conditions.

At present common blue butterflies and speckled woods were enjoying the reflected light as the sun moved round to the west. Nourished by the rain, which had already neared the known upper limits for August rainfall, the lush grass of the playing field was an unbelievable green, except where churned to mud on the football pitch.

How my Australian farming friends would love to see a sward of that calibre on their drought stricken grazings! We complain, but how lucky we are. Water is the staff of life and may well be the cause of wars that finally throw the human race into a state of confusion if climatic trends proceed as predicted.

I crept into the young woodland strip through the few points of access still available. Remembering the sallow bushes and dogwoods of the initial plantings, it was good to see how much else had infiltrated. Trees were taller now but still of smaller girth than those in the southern chestnut copse.

Among the largest was a field maple, coppiced early in life to produce ten to twelve trunks from two feet above the base. Sallows still formed the main canopy but there were well established oaks, hawthorns and hazels and the inevitable juvenile ashes. Dogwood was regenerating from stolons or seeds. Guelder rose tended to be more marginal, poking through enveloping Clematis and wild raspberry where the pioneering ferns were invading marginally.

The floor was fairly open in parts, easy to walk through without too much stooping, but where light filtered in the fragmentary moss cover was overwhelmed by straggly herbs, nettles, hemp agrimony, docks, ivy and even leggy self heal. Mounds of soil were reminiscent of mole workings, but could well have been man-made in a habitat such as this. There were tunnel entrance to mice and vole lairs and snatches of bird song, but few signs of coppicing or woodland flowers. The only fungus seen was a lonely earth ball.

It was quite startling to move from the gloom within that embryonic spinney to the sunny field. The only clouds on the background of peerless blue that we had seen so little of lately, were sharp-edged snowy mounds of pristine beauty.

Topography such as ours in this corner of Glamorgan guarantees a variety of views. Looking west across the river here the five hundred foot high beechwood of the Little Garth continued as sloping farmland, stretching away into a distance crowned by a lonely farm barn. The brackeny sweep of the Great Garth peeped over the top. Just visible above the trees of the defunct railway embankment in the other direction were those around Castell Coch, while swinging south brought the trees along the summit of Long Wood onto the skyline. Southwards the M4 blocked everything, visible as well as audible.

But I was concerned with more immediate matters. A broad strip of rough grassland had been left between the sports field and the new wood at the riverward end, this a riot of tall herbs buzzing with insects. A golden drift of perforated St. John's wort graded into white milfoil, rising to wild carrot and hogweed among the spent heads of seeding knapweed, these with a backing of bramble and briar. Yellow pea and tufted vetch rambled throughout, knitting the others into a cosy shield for the wildlife behind.

* * *

Most ebullient were the shoulder high yellow tansies and head high Himalayan balsam, the first so tall that some had been felled to the ground by the recent bad weather. Bees large and small, blue bottles and green bottles, flesh flies and hover flies took their turn at the spherical honey pots.

It was fascinating watching them probe the tiny florets of the tansy buttons, the tight buds in the centre of the discs as well as the open ones around the margin. Individual stems were waving in the breeze but the tiny actors continued to perform on hand held flower heads. The small dark bees carried no pollen away here as they did from the more dramatic balsam flowers.

A fine stand of balsam provided viewing at a more convenient height. I lingered long at these. Fortunately there was no-one else in the field to wonder at such strange immobility. I had understood that bumble bees found room to turn round inside these capacious flowers, in order to come out head first, but most of the Tongwynlais bumbles were backing out, as from smaller flowers.

As they entered white pollen from the double ranked anthers fixed on the ceiling of the entrance hall brushed off on their backs. Their target was the nectary, this apparently sited in the hooked tip at the far end of the commodious body of the flower.

Honey bees and solitary bees came out head first from the open rift around the sides of the flower, above the rigid receptacle containing the means of fertilisation and the prize awarded for services rendered. There was ample space between this receptacle containing these vital parts and the loosely attached, flamboyantly fringed petals above and below the entrance. Whatever route they left by the bees' pollen baskets were seen to be loaded with white pollen grains.

Extra floral nectaries were visible as little red glands on the short leaf stalks and around their points of attachment to the angular red stem. These are thought to attract ants, to visit and protect the plants from aphids or other unwelcome visitors.

That fertilisation had been effected was evident in the number of green capsules bulging with their load of shiny black seeds. The slightest touch with a finger tip and these containers, turgid with hygroscopic pressure, shot their vital cargo of seeds out to a distance of as much as six feet. These would germinate in spring to give a complete ground cover of the paired, tiddlywink sized cotyledons.

Many, but not this particular stand, are beside rivers, water distribution of seeds presupposing that those shiny black coats are water repellent and will not germinate until washed ashore and dried out in suitable terrain. Immense wastage is allowed for during the long, productive flowering season that keeps both bees and bee keepers satisfied for so long during the evening of the year.

Their growth, from March seedlings to August plants two yards high with no support from climbing organs, is phenomenal, savouring of the Tropics. Rigidity of the hollow stems is achieved by their breadth of well over an inch. In addition there are whorls of 'guylines' radiating from the lower nodes. That the purpose of these is the same as that of the rick props that were used to steady lop-sided hay ricks in my farming days, is amply demonstrated by the extra length of those supporting the leaning side of any stems that have sagged sideways. The resultant height attainable gives extra throw for the little black missiles that have taken over so much land in so short a time.

We have few or no native flowers with this particularly complex shape. The fact that bees of different species have learned to manipulate them to earn their reward of nectar since its arrival not quite a hundred years ago - just as they learn to exploit our garden introductions - is a miracle in itself.

Out through a metal kissing gate, past flowering rosebay willow herb, I was on the Taff Trail, at its junction with the Iron Bridge leading to Gelynis Fruit Farm. I crossed over briefly. The plants in the maize maze had increased in height and put out their tassels of male flowers, but tall children could still look over the top - and cheat.

Back and on up the river I paused twice, once to watch three young willow warblers (or were they chiff chaffs?) flipping back and forth across the path, and again to admire three new born calves playing round the base of one of the great old trees fringing the resown riverside pasture.

My return was up the narrow lane from the footbridge where I always expect to see the first lesser celandines of the year in February. Strangely I saw a single plant of the rarer greater celandine today. The banks had been shaved, leaving mostly just the ferns with some of their fronds severed, and low growing herbs. Without this rather drastic looking management, the lesser celandines might well get shaded out in the resulting tangle. They, too, must reach out to the light of day to attract their pollinators. Also the lane would gradually narrow. This is all part of the partnership that we enjoy with the natural world.

CHAPTER 37

South Devon. Torquay, Paignton and Berry Head

Sunday 31st August was earmarked for our annual family party, to be held this year at Paignton in South Devon. None of my considerable collection of road maps showed the new motorways and, there being no other family members in Wales to act as navigators, I had ceased driving to these celebrations a few years back. My cousin, Stella Anderson, now widowed, was this year's hostess and had offered me a bed for a stay of several nights. So it was that I boarded a train at Bristol for Paignton on the afternoon of Saturday the 30th.

My first posting after graduation at the start of the 1950s had been at Exeter University and I was all eyes as we trundled through this noble city looking for known landmarks. The only building that I managed to recognise was the mellowed cathedral, its twin towers unusually set half way along its length, one on either side.

At the beginning of every term the university staff used to parade in all their glory of coloured gowns and mortar boards, from college to cathedral for an 'inauguration service'. This might seem facetious in these casual modern times and just a big joke for some of today's students, but not then.

We felt it added dignity to the noble pursuit of knowledge, appreciated particularly by freshers, who felt they had come to something rather special. That was a time when lecturers wore black gowns at lectures. When I got to Melbourne University 'Down Under', students wore these as well, and in Hall for dinner at night, customs of the Mother Country lingering longer there. (I still have my gown, at the bottom of a chest. Welsh Science was crimson and gold and rather splendid. Sadly it will never be worn again).

The banks of the River Exe around Countess Wear and Topsham were more recognisable than the modern city, these the scene of plant studies on the gradation of plants from fresh to salt water. This stretch and the next, where the estuary, full of little boats straining at their moorings, broadened towards Exmouth where it emptied into the English Channel, I viewed in perfect sunshine. Then the sea mist closed in.

I saw nothing of the sand dune system of Dawlish Warren, scene of much field work, nor of Dawlish except for the river flowing through the town centre. The view seaward along the coastal stretch to Teignmouth was a grey blank, but the New Red Sandstone cliffs seemed as bright as ever by contrast. No longer naked rock, these were draped with 'safety first' netting in case of falls. Some stretches seemed to have receded from the railway line and were more thickly vegetated and I failed to notice the outlying stack. Soon we were speeding up the estuary of the River Teign to Newton Abbott - far enough from the sea frett to be in sunshine again - and so across country to Torquay and Paignton.

My taxi driver had little idea as to the whereabouts of Broadsands Avenue, to seaward of the main conurbation, but fortunately I had a map, which helped. Stella's son Graham, was already installed. His wife, Mary, was driving down later from Oxfordshire after closing the bookshop which they ran together.

Stella, two years younger than me, and her sister Marjorie, two years older, had, with their parents, been my family's constant companions on all major holidays at home and abroad during our childhood and teens. All this came to an end with the outbreak of war in September 1939, when we got back from our car tour of Switzerland just in time.

We split up then, to go our separate ways and had seen very little of each other since, except at these annual gatherings, where, with anything up to forty folk present, mostly strangers, we had little time to get to know any of them. All were on my mother's side of the family, with no Gillhams apart from brother John and myself. With nearly four days at our disposal now, we could make up for lost time.

On the early jaunts the two sisters were adept at finding likely young lads to join the party, while I was addicted to poking into rock pools and other unsavoury corners, while John was investigating the local transport. They both married and brought up families. We did not. It was good to reminisce on times long past and learn of happenings since.

Next day scudding clouds let go their rain until 11.00 pm. Guests started to arrive at noon, when the sun had had time to dry the stones of the patio though not the grass beyond the steps. It cast its benevolence upon us for the rest of the day so, with buffet food and lots of cushioned garden chairs and tables, this was a garden party as well as an indoor one.

Folk had come from all over: London and the Home Counties, Norfolk, Middle England, Winchester and some from as close as North Devon and South Cornwall. They started dispersing in mid evening, leaving just the four of us - all very experienced at dish washing by bedtime.

* * *

On Monday September first the sun shone until late afternoon, despite scudding rain clouds and a chilly breeze. We enjoyed a walk along this section of the South Devon coast path, which commanded fine views up and down the shoreline.

A leafy footpath led between houses and under the fine stone viaduct currently used by trains of the Dart Valley Railway Company on the Tor Bay and Dartmouth Line. The trains were pulled by noisy steam engines puffing columns of steam and/or smoke all the way to Kingswear to the delight of railway buffs.

Our path skirted the side of the hill which blocked the view of the sea from the house, leading through an impenetrable thicket of bramble, nettles and traveller's joy, completely overrun by matted hedge bindweed, covered with handsome white trumpet flowers.

The inland side of the hill was grassed and occupied by a herd of cattle. The seaward side had borne a cereal crop, this recently harvested, leaving cylindrical wrapped straw bales over the slope. The gradient looked horrendously steep for tractor work, but was marked with the up and down furrows of the harvester's wheels.

We emerged onto a concrete promenade, backed by a neat row of white-painted old style beach huts (hired out at £35 a week). One row behind the prom faced onto a flat grass field used for picnics and ball games, with two huge carparks beyond. Despite the sunshine, the latter were almost empty and we were practically the only walkers. The tide was high, the beach only a few yards wide, but a vast area had been uncovered, nicely washed, at our return. This part of the coast backed the four mile stretch of Tor Bay running from Torquay in the north to Brixham and Berry Head in the south.

Low cliffs of horizontally bedded New Red Sandstone rose from the sands to the north, this stretch continuing with the erodible face unvegetated for some distance. A sizable collapse near its centre was marked by a pile of newly fallen boulders, ammunition for the sea to use to scour away more of the soft rock. The beach terminated in the south as a mass of seaweedy rocks exposed by the falling tide at the foot of the rising cliff. The only plant life on the promenade was a line of rock samphire clinging desperately along a crack in the masonry.

A cheerful little stream gurgled out under the walkway before we started the ascent to the south. Water full of bloated gutweed (Enteromorpha) within its mouth suggested inward seepage from the sea. The two plant dominants were reeds and brookweed, both of which tolerate a fair degree of salinity. The watercress was slightly removed upstream.

As we climbed higher we could piece together the geography of the ever widening scene. Tor Bay, four miles across, had been eroded back into the soft Devon sandstone. The hard grey headlands to north and south were mostly of hard grey Devonian slates and sandstones to the north and Devonian limestone to the south.

Torquay, the English Riviera, occupied the northern promontory, terminating in the Lead Stone off Hopes Nose, that, like London Bridge further into the bay, being of limestone. Between the two jutting headlands facing into Tor Bay, off the islanded Thatcher's Rock was Millionaire's Row, set luxuriously among sheltering trees.

The conurbation of Torquay seemed huge from this angle. Hills reached to the north and west completely built up for two miles. Houses were, however, decently surrounded by gardens and trees, but considerable heights had to be scaled after the morning sea bathe. At least the inmates could enjoy expansive views.

The immensity of the urban spread was mind boggling. Naively I had imagined this South Devon coast still to be as pleasantly rural as it had been on childhood holiday visits - countryside and seaside all in one. But that was seventy to eighty years ago. Britain is not like that any more, particularly such desirable parts.

Near the attractive thatched village of Cockington open country still swept quite near the sea before the urban sprawl of Paignton broadened out again, with more houses climbing the successive lines of hills rising towards Dartmoor. A photo in one of our family albums shows my brother and me as toddlers watching the smithy magically shaping a gobbet or red hot iron in the Cockington Forge, in a wholly village setting.

As we moved on the view broadened. We were looking towards Goodrington Sands and those to the north of its humpy wooded headland. The coast road and the Tor Bay Steam Railway were far enough inland here to leave a naturally vegetated clifftop. Inland from where we stood we could see and hear the trains trundling over the viaduct.

A few strategically placed benches invited sea viewing of the sparse offshore shipping - a tanker, a tug and a two sailed yacht similar to the one formerly kept and sailed on the River Dart by Stella and her husband when they lived at Totnes.

The immediate sward was of tufty grassland containing a few pleasant wild flowers. These included blue flax, purple betony, mauve storksbill, pink centaury, yellow agrimony and white hedge bedstraw. Further inland we spotted yellow and fawn waxcap mushrooms, the prize Hygrophorids that characterise natural grassland untainted by agricultural practices other than mowing.

Brixham was out of sight just around the corner, the lines of floats off the intervening headland thought to indicate a shellfish farm, possibly for oysters. A sycamore wood occupied the brow of the hill which hid the town as we followed up the edge of a nine hole golf course. Swallows and house martins were sweeping low around the base of an isolated, many trunked sycamore, the fierce wind evidently keeping their prey down within the local shelter.

Over a stile and back round the now exposed intertidal zone, we watched a carrion crow scavenging for marine life and barefooted children playing among the seaweeds. Every member of a loose flock of herring and lesser black-backed gulls scattered over the now enlarged sands was headed upshore into the land wind, that was stretching the beach flags to the ends of their tethers. Powerful south-westerlies such as these struck most of the coast head on, but these were cutting across the base of the promontory leading out to Berry Head. No birds like cold winds sneaking in under their feathers from behind. Best to head into it. The juvenile gulls, in their brown camouflage plumage had no such scruples about personal comfort and were playing in the shallows, like the young of humankind.

* * *

Next morning Graham drove me into Paignton on a few errands and a drive along the sea front. This was a traditional old style seaside town - and difficult to make it into anything else with all those steep inclines, sharp turnings and houses seemingly stacked in lines one behind the other, with connecting roads as steep as those of the Welsh mining valleys. Both here and at Brixham, explored later in the day, I was put in mind of the steep winding seaside towns of North Pembrokeshire.

Other memories from further back in time crept stealthily into my consciousness - memories of a journey with my immediate family to contact more distant relatives on my mother's side. The key figure was big, burly Uncle Alf, a senior agricultural chemist living in Canada until war broke out in 1939. He was first cousin to my mother and Stella's father.

He had hired a seaside holiday house in Paignton in the hope of meeting up with long lost family. After joining the Canadian Mounties and serving for a short while in Europe during World War II, he was taken prisoner and spent most of the war labouring in the salt mines of Eastern Europe.

On release he set up home with his very Scottish little wife, Maggie, in Southern Rhodesia as it then was - back in his own world of succouring agriculturalists and their crops. The couple moved to Capetown for their retirement and I had the good fortune to visit them both in Salisbury, now Harare, and in South Africa, on a memorable jaunt around the scenic margin of Table Mountain.

My memories of his two daughters and one son in Paignton are slight, aroused only by perusal of the family photographs taken there, but I visited all three later on in Rhodesia before it became Zimbabwe. Valentine, the oldest girl, was a doctor in the main city hospital, Catherine, her sibling, a matron. Dudley had taken up dentistry and I stayed with him and his wife in Bulawayo. How well I remember our trips around the astonishing Umtali Mountains, with their rounded tumps and placid lakes.

The beheaded, barkless trunk of a strategically placed geriatric Paignton tree had been adorned with some intricate carving - an attractive feature, like some seen recently in Caerphilly, nearer home. There were monkey puzzle trees, one loaded with cones, and rank upon rank of flowering Mexican fleabane, a very successful newcomer to Britain's stone walls and rockeries, plus, of course, the palms and cabbage trees that impart the prized sub-tropical look.

With so much prosperous suburbia and a harbour full of holiday craft, it was hard to imagine Paignton as the quiet little fishing village that it had once been. I was reminded that Jan, a lively member of one of my natural history groups visiting the South-West, had taken us around the highly esteemed Paignton Zoo and 75 acre botanical garden where she worked as a zoologist.

* * *

It was on that visit that we had been able to see the rare white rock rose (*Helianthemum apenninum*) at Berry Head, one of its only two native sites in Britain, so I was more than delighted to get a second chance to see it here on our tuesday excursion. I had been lucky also to come upon the other site at Brean Down in North Somerset, opposite Steepholm Island - and also at a third, where it had been introduced on Pennard Cliffs on the Gower Peninsula in my own county. All three of these sites are on ancient Devonian or Carboniferous limestone.

With its flowering time from May to July, would I be able to recognise it? I needn't have worried. There wasn't much in the colony we happened upon, right out on the point, but the vegetative parts were very distinctive, the leaves white with woolly hairs on creeping stems. These were co-habiting with a prostrate form of hedge bedstraw - a plant well able to climb high among the wind-stunted blackthorn of the headland if the opportunity arose.

The tip of Berry Head is both Country Park and National Nature Reserve, but there was only one quite small location where I came upon this plant gem and others with it. This was an enchanted herbaceous thicket of flowering greater knapweed and a smaller than average version of Alexanders, consisting now of umbels of black seeds and new, ground level, yellow-green leaves.

Most charming at this season was the flowering autumn squill *(Scilla autumnalis)*. We have wonderful swards of spring squill on our coastal cliffs and islands in South Wales, these essentially western, northern and coastal, but not the autumn squill with its longer flower spikes. That is essentially southern, mostly around the edge of Devon and Cornwall and probably nowhere north of Gloucester, though there is an old record for Glamorgan.

Another rarity, unexpected here as I have only ever seen it on English chalk hills away from the sea - and once on the Lizard in Cornwall - was dropwort, the downland meadowsweet *(Filipendula vulgaris)*. This flowers from May to August and was represented here by twelve inch high splaying, downy fruit heads rising from dense leaf rosettes with crowded, finely dissected leaflets. It grew in my Gwaelod garden, where I tried to spread the oval tubers around, but that is cheating, with so selectively local a wildling.

Others in this remarkable community were lady's bedstraw with a few yellow flowers, the cucumber smelling lesser salad burnet and thyme, smelling of tranquil days on sunny sand dunes. Also, unexpectedly, some bristly wild madder *(Rubia peregrina)* was insinuating stiff shoots among the grass, although it is more likely to be straggling up among the wind crippled sloe bushes, hiding their arthritic joints. Related to the bedstraws and clinging cleavers, it is woodier and bears small black fruits.

To complete the magic of this little community, we spotted a lizard basking on a sun-warmed slab of limestone. There were plenty of grasshoppers and black ground beetles about should it feel like a snack when it awoke, but it was much too exposed on this windy point for butterflies.

Between the patches of spiny scrub, tangled into unbroachable hedges by the gales, and the turf worn down by tourists' feet, the plant community was rough grassland threaded with bird's-foot trefoil and overtopped by wild carrot, bristly ox-tongue and lesser knapweed.

The whole was permeated by the strawy heads of yellow rattle - this now beyond the 'hay rattle' stage, with the seeds shed from the dry transparent capsules. This species is a help rather than a hindrance to the non-competitive rarities fighting their corner among the more pushy commoners. Partial parasites, the plants weaken the usually dominant grasses by clamping onto their roots and stealing mineral nutrients.

The main tourist feature of this headland was the fort erected to repel Napoleon, which we passed through twice. This had its own special flora, featuring bristly spikes of blue flowered vipers' bugloss *(Echium vulgare)* on the ramparts and small scabious *(Scabiosa columbaria)* at their foot. Flowering from June to October, this last was still at prime. Found mostly on chalk and limestone hills inland, it occurs also on dunes.

Pellitory of the wall *(Parietaria diffusa)* clustered round the base of the masonry and insinuated itself into cracks, above yarrow and wild fennel smelling of aniseed. Some of the bracken fronds in this windy site had suffered severe wind-scorching in the salty gales of the past two months when they should have been enjoying high summer.

We had reached the tip of the head via the northern road past Shoalstone Beach, a narrow lane involving Stella, at the wheel, in some awkward manoeuvres to allow inconsiderate drivers past. We left by the southern lane, with only marginally more passing places, looking down on St. Mary's Bay, which was traditionally Mudstone Bay, until the local authorities decided that such a name was not tourist friendly.

Brixham was the home of the famous, trend-setting Brixham Trawler, which became the prototype for North Sea trawlers working out of Lowestoft, Grimsby and Hull, when our eastern fishing grounds were discovered in the nineteenth century. As in Paignton, the streets of suburban houses had had to accommodate themselves to the undulating landscape, leading to a picturesque but complicated street layout.

All too soon, luxuriously fed and watered, I was on my way back to South Wales. Graham dropped me off at the station on his drive to Oxfordshire and I saw more from the coastal line to Dawlish than on the way out. Just in time! Three days later storm waves were breaking against the trains on this section of the railway - as depicted in an action photo in the public press, taken on Friday, 5th September. That was caused by wind and tide, but exceptional rainfall in Wales through that week caused at least one death by drowning and hillside dwellings with water running in at the back and out at the front.

True to expectation, Welsh rain started falling as we emerged from the Severn Tunnel and I got drenched walking up the hill from Radyr Station in the gathering dark. We had been incredibly lucky weatherwise. Current statistics filtering from the media about this dreary month recorded a total of seventy hours of sunshine during August 2008 as against an average of a hundred and seventy hours. Perhaps all those clouds picking up moisture from the Atlantic Approaches would lessen the risk of sea level rise. Or is that short term thinking?

* * *

I brought back a memory of my visit in the form of a pot plant, quite new to me and with intriguing sleep habits - or nyctinastic movements as they are known in the world of botany. This splendid, purple-leaved specimen proved to be *Oxalis triangularis ssp. palilionacea*, which says it all, with the possible addition of var. *purpurea*. By night light the equilateral triangles adopted by the large sleeping, three-partite leaves resembled neat pyramids or resting butterflies. By daylight they spread into horizontally held trefoils of silky texture and sufficiently translucent to reflect more of the red light rays.

When clovers fold their three leaflets closed at night they turn them upwards. When Oxalids (including our familiar wood sorrel) do so, they fold them downwards. It is still uncertain which of these two groups is favoured as the model for the Irish Shamrock.

Hoping to leave the pot behind, I had investigated its contents only to find a mass of roots and two to three inch long tubers, like gnarled fingers of an elderly gnome, completely filling it, so back into the pot they had to go. Despite their delicate long stalks, the leaves arrived undamaged, to enliven the months to come.

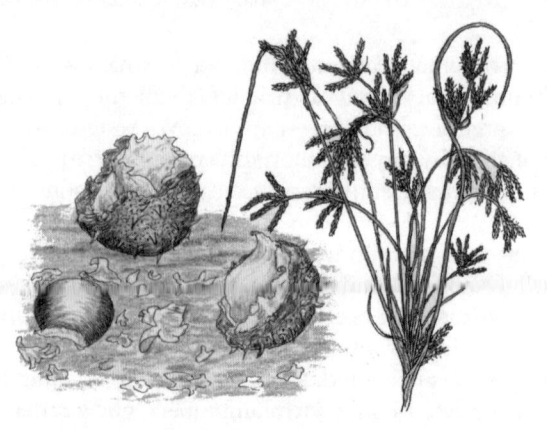

CHAPTER 38

Radyr Woods and Shunting Yard. Forest Farm Floods, Fruit And Fungi

What started as a brief amble along suburban roads, changed to something slightly more ambitious as I turned into the top of Radyr Woods on the 28th of August. Curving down to river level, I wandered over the Iron Age Encampment towards the Duck Pond to see if anything was afoot in the intervening quagmire.

Was that marsh horsetail or water horsetail bordering the lively trickle winding through the naked tree roots of the backing slope? It was neither, proving to be a hybrid with ten very fine branches in each whorl and the main stems so weak that they flopped onto the piled debris below. There is more to these 'living fossils' than the giants of Morganstown and the much reviled weeds of allotments and gardens.

This was a weird forgotten corner, where ancient alders, from which the water had receded long since, eked out senescent lives, getting progressively more gnarled and knotted with the passing of the years. Those in better fettle shared the pond waters with upstanding tufts of the unusual tussock sedge (*Carex elata*), a plant more appropriate to the East Anglian Fens than here in the west. I had always likened those to mangroves, with almost as many woody appendages growing downwards as upwards. These moss-grown relics, however, were nearer their end than those.

Here were advanced examples of deformed timber resembling that which we had encountered in the St. Fagan's mulberry trees, and just as tenacious of life. One thick trunk had snapped off on a long, oblique plane just above head height, the crown lying alongside the standing, warted axis. That had a single short twig bearing half a dozen green leaves sprouting from the main bole, a last indication that it was not completely dead.

The grey trunk was covered with bloated mounds of bark the size of cricket balls, with a round hole the size of a ping pong ball in the centre of each. In one of these holes was a bright orange ball of rubbery material surrounded by transparent mucilage.

There was just room to get a couple of fingers in behind the ball, but it refused to budge. So neatly did it fill the pocket which it occupied, that I felt it must be the cause of the growth and hence of many dozens before it, and not a haphazard infection. Slimy enough for a slime fungus (which group is not included in the standard fungus books) I failed to find any reference to it on my return.

Another puzzle observed on the way into this crypt for the dying was the hard, elongated white fungal growth occupying part of a vertical fold in the trunk of one of the mighty beeches on the slope above. This resembled the hoof or tinder fungus *(Fomes fomentarius)*, but that was always depicted as dark and this was a pristine white.

The third example of this non green plant group was no trouble to identify. It was an attractive cluster of white porcelain mushrooms *(Oudmansiella mucida)*, these also covered in transparent mucilage except for the curvaceous stipe. Entirely white, the two to three inch wide cap was delicately thin, the striated edges down-curved and the gills few and far between and of three different lengths, dipping in towards the stipe.

My next encounter was an avian one, Three special woodland species in a single spinney of dense young saplings and all unusually visible in the leafy tangle. The cheeping of nuthatches brought me to a halt and there they were, two of them running up and down quite slender vertical saplings in quick succession instead of more circumspectly on larger trees where they are normally seen feeding.

Another bird doing just that, in one direction only, was a tree creeper, moving at a more measured pace probing into crevices. The third was a cock bullfinch, plumply ebullient as cock bullfinches usually are. Then came a robin and three blackbirds, while the anxious cawing of carrion crows wafted in from the treetops throughout.

Germander speedwell bordering a clearing had been used as a creche for a generation of *Jaapiella veronicae* gall midges. A woolly pubescence had developed on the backs of paired young leaves at the shoot tips which had swollen, their serrated margins interlocking to form a snug haven between for the parasites. About twelve to twenty midge eggs had been laid in the terminal bud between. These had hatched, the little pouch containing a crowd of actively squirming, bright orange larvae. They would pupate inside and emerge as adult midges.

Kingfisher Pool was even more overgrown with bulrushes than when I last visited, the moorhens heard but not seen. I noticed as much of the tiny American duckweed as the ordinary lesser British one. It may be small, but it is certainly getting around since its recent arrival in this country.

The grassy patch fenced in around the north end of the pond and planted now with young birches alongside the osiers and dogwood, provided sanctuary for a different wild flower community, with bird's-foot trefoil and tormentil among the rayed form of common knapweed and water mint.

* * *

My quest among the new houses in the Old Shunting Yards was mainly for another plant group, the arable weeds - fugitives from too well tended farmland finding refuge on building sites. These are botanical freebooters, aggressive, opportunists, ready to take up residence wherever they found a vacant niche. This is usually on the unnatural habitats created by man. The house developers and the railway engineers before them drove Nature out, but how readily she forgives, returns and repopulates!

First I came upon some delicate little fungi pushing up through a lush lawn alongside a new tarmac pavement. This was a colony of milky cone cap toadstools *(Conocybe lactea)*, quite charming, with their creamy white, conical or bell shaped caps, just topping the lush grass on four inch long white stipes. The spores on the gills within the cone were a bright ginger-cinnamon colour. The favoured habitat of this quite uncommon fungus is "roadsides and lawns". This was both.

I walked to where the new houses had reached to the river bridge at the end of the site - where the sand martins had nested. None were seen, but quite a lot of house martins were swooping round the eaves of the new dwellings, planning, perhaps, on whose walls to plaster their mud nests next summer.

There was no shortage of muddy building material at present on the cleared but still vacant lots. Rain water had collected on the circular path of the new public garden and on the lawn of the adjacent open shrubbery. Just as major floods in valleys map the geography of the landscape for all to see, these mini-floods showed where the house builders had defaulted in their estimation of levels.

The third plot in this sequence, apparently destined to be open space, had been sown to grass and clover. Alsike *(Trifolium hybridum)* was abundant among the red and white clovers, and there were other legumes, melilot and vetches, with copiously fruiting black medick around the margins.

Elsewhere, on the true wasteland, the plants fell into two categories - the new, short-lived, fly-by-night weeds and choicer plants taking longer to establish, these being tail-overs from the fine collection that had evolved on the old sidings before the bulldozers moved in.

They included evening primrose and great mullein *(Oenothera cambrica* and *Verbascum thapsus)*, both sometimes regarded as fit for the herbaceous border by gardeners. Celery-leaved buttercup and wild carrot were others. Scentless mayweed, bristly ox-tongue and weld were the most distinguished in the 'weed' category.

Many of the other pioneers had little to commend them visually, only their persistence, but the clustered, curled and broad-leaved docks are a good source of food for seed eaters, as are the thistles. The water pepper and lesser water pepper, pale and common persicaria, had recently been moved from the genus Polygonum to Persicaria. The last, formerly known by the vernacular of persicaria or redshanks, had to change its specific name too - from *Polygonum persicaria* to *Persicaria maculosa*. Not only that, but the English has changed to 'redleg'. We don't have 'shanks' any longer, begging Shakespeare's pardon.

Black bindweed, whose flowers resemble a small cornfield version of the highly invasive Russian vine, has been moved, with that, from Polygonum to Fallopia, these now *Fallopia convolvulus* and *F. baldschuanica*. This brings them into the same genus as the dreaded Japanese knotweed, which has changed from *Polygonum cuspidatum* to *Fallopia japonica* as the pest officers working on methods of eradication have got to know it better. Only the knotgrasses of the plants we are concerned with here are still called Polygonum, often grouped as the aggregate *P. aviculare agg.*

All six of these are in the dock:sorrel family. Another family here, shared between salt marshes and such sites as this, where the concentration of salts in the soil may be boosted, is the Chenopodiaceae or saltbush family. Common orache and goosefoot or fathen *(Atriplex patula* and *Chenopodium album)* are the chief members sprouting here among the builders' cement and rubble.

Here also were thale cress and hairy bitter cress and a touch of colour with dovesfoot and cut-leaved cranesbills. Almost all were annuals, some able to achieve several generations in a season and with copious seed to fall into the breach when another plot was cleared - a living thread of continuity.

I was investigating the new estate's rather dreary flora in a thin, spirit-sapping drizzle wafting in over the backdrop of hills, which were no more than blurs on the horizon. Maybe that affected my assessment of their worthiness. Sadly the industrially induced weed flora included none of our ancient farmland's best - the field poppy, cornflower, corn marigold and corn cockle.

Suburban ruderals pushing through cracks in Radyr pavements have had longer to adapt. Petty spurge and broad-leaved willow herb, two of the commonest, can produce more than one crop of seeds in a season. *Helixine solerolerei*, not in the wild flower books, but which I have heard referred to as hundreds and thousands, commonly forms mats of tiny round leaves along wall bases and steps. Flowers, if produced, are nigh invisible.

Boldest and most decorative of Radyr's urban weeds is the red valerian and there are, of course, members of the Compositae, sow thistles, dandelions, groundsels and field daisies. In Devon and at Llandaff, the more attractive Mexican fleabane has joined forces with these adaptable, uninvited components of our flora.

Most acceptable in this category are the little wall ferns, maidenhair spleenwort, wall rue, polypody and the occasional rusty-back fern. And, of course, the attractive ivy-leaved toadflax romping over walls everywhere.

* * *

Continuous rain all day on Friday 5th September spurred Cardiff's main river to roar down in spate, swirling over the Taff Trail in parts of Sophia gardens downstream. BBC's Today Programme reported a death by drowning in floods at Tregaron and a house at Machen with water from a swollen culvert flowing in at the back and out at the front.

I ventured out on the 6th to see how our local patch had fared. Instead of the usually translucent water, a brown flood, heavily charged with silt, was roaring under the Radyr footbridge. It looked threatening, but the flattened Japanese knotweed on the bank showed that the level had recently been five or six feet higher. Two of the wardens intercepted later, as we converged on a barn during another downpour, reported that the bridge had been shaking on its foundations the previous day, the supports having to fend off waterborne tree trunks torn from their anchorage.

The more than man-high osier tree on the grey wagtails' shingle bank was completely under water and the general level well up among the lower branches of the bordering woodland upstream. Trees there leaned over the water from both sides, reaching out to the greater light intensity, making the river appear narrower now, with its margins hidden.

Turning downstream along the elevated river defences, I observed flattened grass and herbs between this and the riverside fringe of bushes and brambles augmented with nettles. The excess water had drained off since combing the vegetation flat. Tumbling down from nearly three thousand feet in twenty five miles or so from the Brecon beacons, the Taff is a flash flood river. Water rises quickly but rolls on just as quickly to be dealt with by the "Docks and Harbours" personnel when it reaches the now enclosed "Cardiff bay".

No water fowl were about, just swallows and house martins well above the river and the usual jackdaws and magpies. Water was surging up out of the drain by the cricket field - the drain that was supposed to conduct water in the other direction - but not much cricket had been played lately!

There was little change in the Forest Farm carpark except that the puddles were more extensive and the Nostoc less so, except where sheltered by the benches and picnic tables. I moved on to what I call the Dexter cattle field, to view the plot planted to attract seed-eating birds. And attract birds it had.

A flock of at least thirty greenfinches rose in a cloud from among the dripping seed heads at intervals to take cover in tall trees alongside, filtering back a few at a time until something triggered another mass exodus. They moved very fast but the ones I saw clearly all had the diagnostic yellow flashes on the wings and were larger than the house sparrows that flock around the barn and adjacent hedge nearby. Once on the flower plot they sank into invisibility among the tall grasses, cresses and other tangled herbs, completely out of sight.

Remaining wholly visible on the tall bordering thistles were goldfinches, in all their colourful glory. On the even taller giant sunflower heads I saw only great tits. And then the rains came, gently at first. I put on a head scarf and continued watching, having come equipped with raincoat. Suddenly it became a downpour. Up went my umbrella.

The finches and tits seemed not to notice. They had to make up for lost time after yesterday's continuous deluge, so I continued watching. Elbows steadied on the five barred gate, umbrella in one hand and binoculars in the other, I held out for a while, but the wind had dropped and the rain was sheeting down vertically. I could not maintain my hold on both indefinitely.

The two rabbits that had been munching steadily through newly plucked dock leaves between me and the birds when it was only a drizzle, had given up long since. I did likewise, saw a warden disappearing into the nearby barn and followed him in. Another warden arrived a few minutes later and the two compared notes on their respective monitoring of the water situation.

The second arrival had been battling with the penstock at the sluice just above Radyr Weir, through which water flowed into the Melin Griffith Feeder. Unsuccessfully. "It's all rusted up. Can't budge it. Needs renewing." My popularity didn't increase with this thwarted young man when I said it had already been renewed. I knew it had, because I had included colour plates in my tome on the Taff Valley, of the old penstock in 1974 and the new one in 1990.

The latter, I then realised, was taken eighteen years ago when this now competent amateur water engineer was little more than a schoolboy. Time passes so quickly while moth and rust doth corrupt. I kept quiet from then on.

My reward was to be shown the photos he had just taken on his mobile phone. Is there anything one can't do on those useful little bits of apparatus which everyone except me seems able to produce at will? He had a shot of an attractive river which shouldn't have been a river at all, but the usually almost dry middle reaches of the feeder and the bridleway alongside. (The path along the other bank was still above water.) The bridleway bordered the allotments, where some of the garden plots had gone under.

Instead of returning over the footbridge as intended, I walked up river to the weir to investigate. The two exits of the canal from the river had coalesced at one point and water was pouring over the iron girder into the newly excavated channel through the beech coppice alongside, roaring into the tunnel which penetrated under the Taff trail downstream, to empty back into the river below the weir.

Just a month before, in early August, I had registered the river in flood. I had done so again on 17th August when this circuit around the weir had been almost as full as it was now. The two beach balls bouncing endlessly on the circulating foam under the weir on that occasion had moved on. It was empty paint tins and small oil drums doing their endless St. Vitus dance there now. A washing up bowl, full to the brim but still afloat, was bobbing off downstream at the same pace as the muscular jogger alongside. At only one stretch between the footbridge and the weir, however, did I have to detour through the bordering scrub to avoid an extensive puddle.

An enormously long goods train, all the covered coaches labelled EWS, was trundling very slowly down the railway line along the foot of the Radyr scarp. Water was swirling past the six foot high embankment holding up the track. Knowing the colossal weight following in his train, the engine driver was apparently proceeding gently. The two carriage and four carriage "Valley Sprinters" were travelling at their usual pace, others of their size having been along before and discovered no hazards.

* * *

Far from awaiting the long delayed summer, Forest Farm fauna, flora and fungi seemed to be advancing into an early autumn. Every log I looked at in the undergrowth approaching Forest farmhouse was strewn with the chewed remains of horse chestnut husks, left by what could only have been squirrels, but unexpectedly early in the season.

Two new diseases were currently affecting horse chestnut trees in Britain. I vaguely remembered hearing somewhere that one was caused by a leaf miner and the other a bark canker, but, as newcomers, they had not yet made their way into the literature. Leaves of the tree supplying the ingredients for these feasts had been gradually yellowing for weeks. More leaf surface area now was judged to be brown or yellow rather than green, but there was obviously a prolific crop of conkers.

Those were much in demand, but it was hard work getting into the prize. First the still green and very spiny burs had to be gnawed through, then the thick, fleshy white lining. Inside was one, occasionally two nuts, grading from white to a rich chestnut brown as they ripened. Most of the remains were of chewed scraps of rind and pith up to an inch across. Most was white, but some had already oxidised to pale brown, like a peeled apple.

In only one area did I come across more than half a rind intact - several dozen of them - with the nut cleanly removed. Only one conker was found, white grading to brown, and with a layer of husk still firmly fixed to the base. This had been abandoned, unblemished, beside the shell remains on a prominent stone topping the farmhouse garden wall, where the perpetrator might well have been disturbed.

I saw no fallen nuts, although the tree grew by the road, where any such would have been clearly visible. It seemed the squirrels were climbing aloft and carrying them as much as thirty yards away from the mother tree to eat in comfort on the many ranked logs set out as for a banquet. The personnel at Forest Farm had always been ones to let sleeping logs lie!

As so often with hazel nuts, the little animals could not wait for them to ripen. This could be a matter of taste rather than greed or necessity, if these nuts are anything like coconuts in developing palatability. Those are delicious picked from among the palm leaves, when the green hull is still full of coconut milk and soft white jelly. By the time they reach Britain most of these have been solidified to the stringy, dry coconut flesh which is so difficult to chew. As after the big cats of Africa, scavengers came to feed on the remains, small flat snails, yellow slugs and long slender golden centipedes, which I thought were carnivores.

I could find no reference in the literature to squirrels eating conkers, only chestnuts, which I took to be sweet chestnuts. The more prickly husks of the latter might prove quite as difficult as the more ferocious but more widely spaced spines of the other - which is quite unrelated. Hazel nuts, walnuts and seeds enclosed securely within the cones of coniferous trees seem to present these highly intelligent mammals with few problems, so why not conkers?

I had, in fact, watched one in the carpark that very morning, prising open the closely packed cone scales of the deodar cedar. The ground was littered with the scales of scores of dismembered cones, so smoothly integrated as to seem impregnable. When disturbed the squirrel bi-passed the deodar trunk and scuttled up the adjacent giant Sequoia.

More easily opened larch cones were present here, and berries of dogwood, guelder rose and rowan, along with hips and haws for fruit eaters in general.

* * *

A few weeks after writing this, I came across an article by Louise Gray in the Daily Telegraph stating that larvae of a species of leaf mining moth (name unstated) were causing horse chestnut leaves to turn brown and fall prematurely. This was first observed in a Wimbledon Garden in 2002, since when they have been spotted as far south as Bournemouth and as far north as Norfolk. (But leaves of this species are always among the first to yellow and fall in autumn.)

The author avers that the conkers of infected trees were smaller. That certainly was not true of the robust 2008 burs at Forest Farm. Maybe those are far enough from London not to be infected yet. Whether they are fewer, as predicted, is impossible to judge, but the prevalence of the remains on the feasting sites, suggests that our squirrels were having no problem finding them.

The second disease of the hard-pressed London conkers in 2008 was referred to as 'bleeding canker' caused by bacteria, which had thrived in the recent spate of mild winters and wet springs. The article suggests up to 50,000 trees or one in ten of the national stock had been infected.

* * *

Just as every log was seen to have been the site of a conker feast, so was every log home to some fort of fungus. Best known and most colourful were the firm but contorted jelly masses of yellow brain fungus *(Tremella mesenterica)*. This had traditionally been called witch's butter, with such an appropriate butter colour, but that popular name has now been transferred to the dull brownish black *Exidia glandulosa,* suitable for a more reprehensible breed of witches.

Common jelly spot *(Dacrymyces stillatus),* one of the colourful antler group of fungi, starts the same bright colour, but had turned crimson here. It occurred as small discs adpressed to the wood. (All these logs had lost most of their bark long since). Well shaped orange discs about the same size were a Calycella as in the chestnut copse, this one very likely *Calycella citrina,* formerly *Helotium or Bisporella citrinum.*

A humpy, carbonaceous black crust occupying furrows on a beech log was *Hypoxylon nummularium,* a close relative of the more shapely beech wart. Several logs supported the two common bracket fungi, turkey tail and hairy Stereum, some in good condition, others long past their prime.

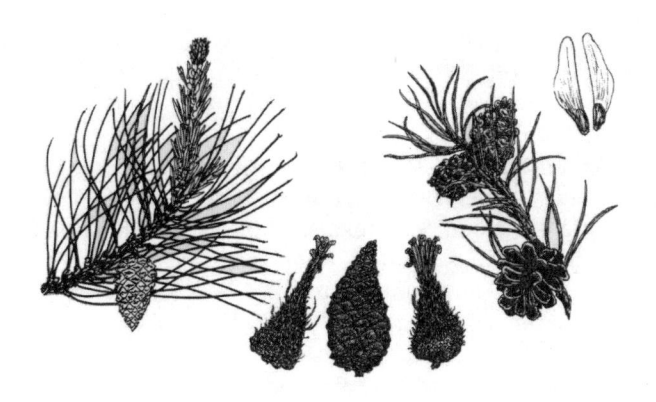

CHAPTER 39

The South Wales Coalfield, Forestry and Hill Farms

A new Monday morning, 8th September, and the BBC Weatherman welcoming it as "The only day this week when it won't be raining". I rose pronto, to head into the Coalfield while the going was good. Matters did not go according to plan, but I achieved a few hours rambling through an entirely different type of country from that of the Coastal Plain and Border Ridges.

With three valleys converging at Pontypridd, there may be a valid reason for the complicated roundabout that had been constructed below the old Brown Lennox Marine Chain Works since my last visit. And did I really need to cross the united Rhondda Rivers twice and thread back through the multi-arched railway viaduct to reach the town centre?

I got through the maze, more by luck than judgement, and headed up Graig Wen alongside church and library from the High Street. The steep climb was round three right angle bends in suburbs peopled, I assumed, by folk with strong leg muscles, but failed to find where I wanted to go. This was the Gelli Wion back alley entrance to Schoni's Pond. No matter. I'd carry on up the mountain and go there on my way back.

Once over the cattle grid at the upper edge of Hopkinstown, I was launched on five to six miles of one track road along the ridge, with few passing places and even fewer draw offs. This scarcely mattered as in two to three hours. I saw only two heavy farm vehicles and three cars.

Not far along I stopped to admire the panoramic view dropping abruptly down to the hub of the area at Porth - the confluence where the larger and lesser Rhondda Rivers join. There used to be an overhead coal bucket railway here, rolling endlessly round and round on its cables. The coal mines were down in the valley, close to the seam, these now incorporated in the Trehafod Museum. The cliff railway had brought mine waste up to pile on the ever growing hillside spoil heap.

This was now rounded off and grassed over, showing little evidence that it had been added to the natural contours of the hillside. East towards Pontypridd were Trehafod and Hopkinstown, west up Rhondda Fawr were Dinas and Tonypandy. North up Rhondda Fach were Ynys hir and Wattstown. Both valleys were quite narrow. This was hill country with deeply incised valleys cut down into it rather than a rolling amalgam of the two.

I stopped briefly by a mature forestry plantation, but a fearsome tree lopper, man and machine, occupied the approach and the black peaty track leading beyond had been churned to mud. Trees were of telegraph pole calibre, some cut, some fallen, with the shallow root plate on edge. A forester met later said that no trees had been blown down in recent gales, so those may have been pushed over to get a bit of extra length.

Two stops after this I found myself by a gated forestry ride labelled by the Forestry commission as Llanwonno Forest. On the OS Map this whole, discontinuous forestry block was labelled St. Gwynno's Forest. The name Llanwonno seemed to apply only to the church where the runner, Guto Nith Bran was buried when he died of exhaustion after a long, message-carrying run. Beyond is a pub and a car park, from which many a wild flower walk or fungus foray had been launched in past years. A wonderful low, ferny cliff beside a nearby lane was home to the beautifully crisped and rare parsley fern *(Cryptogramma crispa)*, more likely to be found in North Wales.

After my walk here I enjoyed a fine viewpoint just short of Blaen Llechau where this mountain ridge road finally wound down into the valley and across the lesser river to Ferndale. En route I had passed the smooth dome of Tylorstown Tip.

Formerly that was the "Burning Tip", with so much small coal among the slag that it had ignited spontaneously and was burning quietly below the surface. A good place to be, that, on a winter's day, when we had sometimes got busy with the cameras photographing grotesque tree bases moulded by the lesser pulses of smouldering heat. There was another burning tip with even more bizarre growths alongside the Cynon Valley on the other side of the ridge. It was said by the locals that vagrants who dossed down here to make the most of the warmth would "wake up dead" because of the fumes.

But those days were past. The unloading track which we used to drive up to collect bizarre shapes of furnace slag, was now fenced off. At one time when the smooth dome had cooled down, it was suggested as a practice ski slope, but nothing came of that. I had seen the little trees being planted all around and now they constituted an almost mature forest.

* * *

But what of the landscape that was here now? Before the Forestry Commission took over most of this country would have been unproductive, tussocky purple moor grass, part of the Welsh Upland's "Molinia desert". Largely the product of overgrazing, there was evidence that at least some of this country had once carried heather. Land reclaimed now from the unproductive Molinia was mostly ploughed and seeded to finer grasses with fertiliser input, making the sward more palatable to sheep, and sometimes to hardy Welsh Black cattle.

I pulled up at one point to watch a quite romantic mustering of a huge flock of sheep from the open hill grazing. A hundred or so were crowded together at a lower gateway and a great river of fleecy white bodies was snaking down from the tussocky summit at a gentle walking pace to join them.

Packed close together, as least twenty deep, and stretching for a hundred yards or so, the mob moved like clockwork, as in a child's picture book. I could not see the end of the column to witness men and dogs at work, as there must have been.

This was pure drama, the re-enactment of the Welsh way of life for centuries. Sheep were the mainstay of these hills long before coal was mined or iron smelted. The industry had come and gone. Nature had healed the scars and the land was green again, thanks to help from shepherds and foresters. The industries that kept the people in work today were mostly tucked discretely away in the valley bottoms, but, as most of the roads are in the valleys, the visitor can come away with the impression that this Eastern Coalfield is still an urban landscape. Not so.

These were not the native Welsh Mountain sheep, lean with fawn tufts on the neck fleece, but downland animals from the Lowlands, many with the Oxford or Sussex Down black faces, some white faced. I wondered if, in view of the atrociously wet weeks recently suffered in the hills, they were being brought down from the mountain already to overwinter in the lowlands and produce early lambs. All were neatly shorn. I was denied a closer look as a muddy farm car was hustling me from behind. Finding a break in the undermined craggy edge of the tarmac, I drew off to let it pass, but the vision was lost, leaving me musing on mobs of Australian Merinos.

On past the neat round tump of Trwyn-y-Glog where a lane slipped off northwards to Ynysybwl in the Clyach Vale, which was insinuated between the Rhondda and the Cynon, and I was soon into the Forestry. This had swallowed up a lot of land but some blocks had been felled, so the country was opening up again. Some fine views had been exposed as a result but rumbustious natural regeneration precluded entry.

All the conifers seen were Sitka Spruce, the branches of marginal trees exposed to daylight thickly clad with stiff, silvery needles and dipping right to the ground, excluding all light within. No plants grew inside and lower branches of the trees themselves scarcely got beyond the twiggy stage before they became starved of light and snapped off. This left the long straight boles growing ever upwards, just what the timbermen wanted. Biodiversity was not a relevant word here.

Even the birds were scarce. I saw only one flock of tits, including cole tits and a few even smaller goldcrests. Fox tracks entered in places and there were signs of marginal rabbits. Fallen spruce cones, their soft scales nibbled, showed where squirrels had been busy extracting the seeds.

On my second walk I had a brief encounter with a forester, who said the trees were mostly felled at twenty to twenty five years old, unless they had a specially fine stand, when they allowed it to grow on. Sitka was the species planted on all the exposed high tops such as this. Others, Norway spruce, Corsican pine and western hemlock, were unable to withstand the fierce winters so well.

Mature plantations had been planted so close to the lane that some of the outer branches had had to be lopped to allow traffic past, though mostly there was a narrow strip of bordering herbs. New plantations ceased well back from the tarmac, leaving a broad strip for natural regeneration, modern foresters being more in tune with the word biodiversity than were their predecessors.

These borders burgeoned with a matrix of Molinia and tall soft rushes, interspersed with leggy heather, neater bilberry bushes and rank upon rank of rosebay willow herb - the Americans' 'fireweed' for its ability to move in on areas denuded by fire - or felling. These were just as impenetrable to humans as the plantations, at least at summer's end, and made the perfect seed bed for native trees and cover for small animals.

Downy birches were particularly abundant, along with durmast or upland oak, also rowan and a little hawthorn. The forester referred to the birches as weeds, which may be why I saw a number of six footers with their leader still present, but killed, while leafy twigs burgeoned from the denuded bases. Or was this due to ring-barking by squirrels?

This regenerating underscrub benefited here at around 1,250 feet from the shelter provided by the adjacent conifers as well as the absence of grazing sheep, so was more diverse than the average Molinia desert that may have preceded tree planting. Here were small thickets of wild raspberries and low looping stems of bramble, also a few clumps of western gorse. The latter is an August-September flowerer, leaving the other ten months for the common European gorse - hence the well known- "When the gorse is not in flower, kissing's not in season."

The immediate roadside strip was neater than unforested stretches further back, and must have been mown. Scottish heather or ling was in full flower as low mats here, in contrast to the straggly specimens with dead flowers further back. Also the purple moor grass tended to be more even, the characteristic tussocks with hidden gullies between only apparent in damper areas.

That is all too often the prevalent growth form arising from the annual burning of the mountains practised so persistently in the past. Burning destroyed the coarse, inedible trash to make way for new spring shoots, but it destroyed all the more palatable competitors as well and those were not capable of regenerating as the Molinia was, from its fire-proof stools. Hence the resulting Molinia deserts, offering forage only in early spring, with species diversity almost nil.

On steeper sections the laneside ditch plants had been flattened in recent downpours. Ditch banks were plastered with creeping mosses and a few clumps of more upstanding Polytrichum, while a few hard ferns occurred with the prevalent male and lady ferns. Spires of dead foxgloves and flowering heads of hemp agrimony overtopped most others.

This shorter border allowed entry of smaller plants such as tormentil and lesser stitchwort, rough hawkbit and milfoil or yarrow. Where a broader strip had been left unplanted, these were squeezed out - the predominant plants being closely packed soft rush and Molinia and tall, loppy rosebay, the long seed capsules split to release their fluffy seeds onto the wind.

I followed a forestry ride across tousled, open country, from which the trees had been removed. Dense herb flora predominated, but small marginal areas were kept clear for others. One was where there had been a dump of limestone chippings, brought in to surface the track and a welcome source of calcium in a predominantly acid landscape.

This was enough to change the dominant wayside herbs to even more of the prevalent flowering eyebright, along with seeding fairy flax and fine-leaved grasses. Creeping cinquefoil grew alongside the acid-loving tormentil, giving rise to hybrids between the two. There was perforated St. John's wort, fleabane, ragwort and even red bartsia. Big leaves of coltsfoot, speckled with orange rust pustules, as so often, indicated where the lovely golden flower heads would burst forth in February. A vibrant aroma drew my attention to a colony of one of the several hybrids of corn mint surrounding a soggy hollow.

Even the yellow field ants *(Lasius flavus)* had responded to the change in soil type and had erected one large and two rudimentary anthills, these of soft black earth such as we associate with molehills. They had sponsored a whole new community of barren strawberry, bird's-foot trefoil and heath violet, with a little centaury and sandwort.

A small swarm of long narrow flies was systematically poking their heads into the eyebright flowers, busy pollinating. With black and white transversely striped bodies they looked like hover flies but were not hovering. A

Vanessid butterfly came winging across the expanse of spent flower heads to feast on the yellow fleabane, despite the heavily overcast weather.

As I considered a somewhat deflated front tyre on return to the car, a vehicle cruised gently alongside. A helpful young man assessed the situation and produced a foot pump to harden it up. He explained the location of a garage in Pontypridd which could help, but I decided to try and make it back to Radyr.

A sleek bird of prey - a sparrow hawk swooped into the lane ahead of me and flapped along between the hedges, close above the road. I cruised gently along behind, admiring its dexterity and speed. It perched briefly on a stone wall while I 'hovered', then took off and perched again on a gate post - finally taking off and shooting away down the slope.

Soon after that I saw a police car approaching, two bends ahead and drew into a passing place to let it by. What could such a vehicle be doing on such a remote road - the third in as many hours? Everyone these days seems to have a mobile phone. Had the forester who left me wandering off the highway, or the young man who came to my aid apprised the local bobby that an elderly female was at large in the wilderness? Or was I imagining they had as little to occupy them as the two in TV's "Last of the Summer Wine?" I drew away with an exchange of salutes as they passed, so I shall never know.

Two hours after delivering the vehicle to Steve Sugarman in the Radyr Station Garage, it was returned, a new tyre fitted.

* * *

Two days later, on 10th September, I tried once more to find Shoni's Pond, but again failed. I feared that this unusual valley woodland and adjacent rehabilitated coaltip must now be concealed behind new surburban housing. This time I found myself on an even lesser road, going in the same direction but at a lower elevation. From a back road in Hopkinstown this followed the contours for a while before ascending and petering out into a track, which I followed on foot above Trehafod and Porth.

Where the lane deteriorated, I turned into an open space opposite Hafod Ganol Farm run by the Woodward Brothers. That fact was stated outside by an image of horses' heads. It seemed I was in the mustering yard of fell ponies or other mounts. A white leghorn stepped regally across the farmyard and a white goose with drooping paunch regarded me suspiciously. A grown lamb strolled across, looking as though he owned the place. No doubt hand reared and part of the family. No other sheep were in sight.

The farmer came out, grandson at heel. Not a lot of strangers would be passing on such a narrow way. He had not heard of Gelli Wion or Shoni's Pond but was happy for me to leave my car where it was and proceed afoot.

"Nice views, but a lot of steep bits mind!"

This hillside, worn down over the years by wind and weather, consisted of a series of corrugations where each run-off stream had found its own way down the slope, wearing individual valleys with mounded ridges between. I set off on the switchback over the ridges, past several water outlets from the farmyard above, where an extensive plot of Himalayan balsam came as something of a surprise. Through pipe or over angled sheet of corrugated iron, water tumbled into stone-built troughs inserted in the roadside ditch to be piped under the road into the next wooded cwm.

The sunken lane was banked on either side, the banks topped by one of the most fabulous collection of ancient trees that I had seen for a long time. These had obviously been pleached in their youth, along with lesser hedge components and then left to do their own thing, sending as many trunks upwards as woody roots downwards, the latter now exposed on the ferny banks.

Ash trees were the most massive, some having huge 'elephant foot' bases developed over centuries. Curiously two ashes of similar upper growth might have two different sorts of bark, one vertically furrowed but the other with horizontally aligned splits or cankers all the way up. A lone ash in mid field had half its substance dead on the ground alongside, but the lower living branches bushed out into a neat dome.

Some of the oaks were almost as large. These were mountain or durmast oaks, with bunches of green acorns held fast against the twigs and not on individual stalks as in lowland oaks. Beeches, too, were huge, one with three trunks being twelve feet across the flattened base above the splaying, naked roots. The oak on the other side of the lane had produced a similar wooden wall parallel, restricting the passage between of any vehicle broader than average.

Sycamores were in the same size category. Stretches of holly between had to be trimmed back of necessity and haws planted as quickthorns for a neat hedge atop the bank were now excessively leggy.

Despite their age, trees were almost fungus-free. Just a few delicate white Mycena or bonnet fungi on a mossy beech base and larger, buff-tinged *Pluteus depauperata* or deer shield fungi on oak. A sycamore had a pink, white-edged crust of *Peniophora lycii* on the lower trunk, while some trees were covered with moss as far up as I could see.

* * *

I was sketching a delicate toadstool, which I knew would not look so good when it came out of my polythene bag, when he came trudging up from the next hollow. We greeted each other as one always does when meeting a stranger where none is expected. A wizened little man, his frame paired down by a life of toil. He indicated his shopping bag.

"Just walked up from the valley. Going to Ponty to get a loaf of bread."

He could have got a bus back, even a train along the valley floor, but was going to return afoot.

"I love this walk. Fine views. I'm sixty seven now." he continued to add weight to this achievement. He was the prototype of an overworked hill farmer. The source of local information, I thought.

I asked him about the sheep muster I had witnessed two days before, but he didn't know there were two types of sheep, mountain and downland. I had just seen some extraordinary birds, but no, he didn't know anything about birds either. I should have known better. No hill farmer plodding sheep walks in the course of duty would have walked that far for pleasure. He would have hopped into his 'ute'. And herein lies the enigma of 'The Valleys'. He lived in the serried ranks of terraced houses in the valley bottom and was the essential townsman. A few hundred feet up lived a different breed of citizen, the true countryman.

I mentioned the Women's Land Army in passing. An inept introduction(?)

"How old are you then?" "Twenty years older than you."

"My. You're no spring chicken then." He beamed admiringly and asked how old my family had lived to.

"Ah. It's all in the genes." and went on to discuss the displacement of the jet stream in relation to the 'two awful summers we've just had'.

I did glean some local knowledge, however.

"Farmers not keeping sheep any longer. Its all horses on tack. They get twenty pounds a week for looking after a horse. Sometimes folk default in paying. Then there's trouble." He pointed across the valley where little bushes were pushing up in the old corridors of herbage between allotment huts and pigeon lofts

"Sheep used to eat all those down. Now they're coming up everywhere."

Those slopes, squeezed between the crowded houses below and the even more crowded spruce trees above, were not used for horses, which were doing the land clearance job on this side of the valley. There seemed to be four to six to each field, some wearing blankets against the bitter wind, which made me glad I had worn a thick anorak despite the few glimmers of sunshine when I started out.

"There's rich farmers here. Sold a lot of their land for building development. Another chap. Thousands of sheep he's got. Says his wool cheque keeps him in funds for the rest of the year." It seemed "pure wool" was back in favour after a spell in the doldrums while non-shrinkable synthetics captured the market.

I had noticed a field full of grassed anthills, a sure sign that it had not been ploughed up for many years, and asked if the grazings were ever ploughed and resown. It seemed not - for at least thirty years - or thirty years before that. We went our various ways and I met him on the way back as I drove out along the smoother part of the lane. He proudly showed me his shopping bag. Not too heavy. Perhaps his Missus got the milk and the spuds.

* * *

Lane maintenance involved pushing piles of soft black sediment off the centre into corners large enough to receive it. Deep shade from the monster trees and the verticality of the banks left little room for flowers. Most of the verdure was from male, lady and hard ferns, with a few patches of yellow pimpernel *(Lysimachia nemorum)* or woodland loosestrife, with tormentil and the ubiquitous herb Robert, also a little marsh cudweed *(Gnaphalium uliginosum)*.

For one short stretch the field above was open to the road, with a flock of fifteen or so chaffinches busy tweaking seeds from a patch of knotgrass just inside the fence. A contingent of swallows was wafting round the sky and above them the "birds of the day".

Raptors, big ones, were cruising lazily round over the grassy slope. Broad blunt wings, reminiscent of a buzzard's but with a more distinct backward curve and primaries sometimes separating in a splay tip. If they had had forked tails they could have been red kites - which are no longer the rarities that they used to be. But the tails narrowed as they left the body, broadening into modest fans above unusually long, dangling legs.

Nor were they soaring in thermals, buzzard fashion, but cruising effortlessly back and forth with scarcely a movement of the wings, just a few languid flaps and another long glide. Sometimes they were not much higher than the horses and low enough to disappear behind the lone sycamore up the hill. Mostly one to five were visible at a time, but for a brief period seven, possibly even eight, swept low overhead, disappearing beyond the trees on the downhill side so that I had no chance to see their backs to check if any wore a white rump. They seemed uniformly dark.

I am not familiar with harriers, but these would surely have to be either marsh or hen harriers. I watched for a long spell on my way out and again on my way back when they were still loitering over the same grassy slope, until I could hold the binoculars no longer. A kestrel flew into the scene at one point - a useful scale object, dwarfed by the larger raptors.

Mountain birds, hen harriers nest in North Wales on the moors and sometimes the coast, although there are very few in England. My ornithological friends tell me they could have been migrating south at this season. Wheatears have been leaving early on their autumn migration and it is quite a while since I have seen a swift.

Dragging myself away I continued past a neat little cottage and outhouses among the trees below, with "Nyth Bran House" on the gate. At my second meeting with the man from the Valley, he told me that the runner, who was buried in Llanwonno Church, had been born there. Apparently there were other cottages in the wood, a snug little settlement, but there was no mains water and they were allowed to fall into disuse.

Those were by Cwm George, the major stream hereabouts, and it would have been a goodly hike to get out of there to work or play. Having recognised the pithead wheels of the Rhondda Heritage Museum down below, I had been looking out for this particular stream. Many years back I had helped Jenny Tann, a local naturalist of repute, in leading wildlife walks up Cwm George from the museum, across the railway by the waterfall on the clifflet above the river.

I thought I'd identified it, but that was the lesser, southern fork. When I came to the next foot crossing there was a footpath sign up pointing down the valley. A necessary shoring up of the lane across the top, however, had resulted in a cascade of rubble and stones pouring steeply down the path into the declivity - easier to slide down than to scramble back up at the end of an ascent. But the path looked little used. I had fond memories of primroses, wood sorrel and golden saxifrage under the trees there and of bilberry and heather on a rock bluff alongside.

Immediately beyond I came to a big farm with a surfaced lane leading directly down to the valley below - so the one I'd come by was not the main road out. There were two houses here with walled gardens, a range of huge modern barns, with grass growing along their roof gutters and swallows swooping through the open doors. Another Dutch barn was piled full of squared hay bales for the horses.

Six state of the art horse boxes were ranged along the brink of the outer yard. I followed the beer coloured dribbles up the final slope to a huge pile of horse manure. The smell made me want to keep my distance. Not so the red admiral butterfly, drinking deeply from the juices and flying past in pristine condition without if not within. Their taste in apples was not the same as mine either. They used to come regularly to sip the alcoholic juices from the Bramley windfalls disintegrating on my lawn at Gwaelod.

There was a fine view from here, up both valleys from Porth, with the unmissable, unbeautiful village of Penrhys on the skyline above all the rest - on the flank of Mynydd Ty'n-tyle between the two Rhondda Rivers, I lingered only to watch two angrily swearing robins doing battle on the entrance drive before returning.

CHAPTER 40
Ebbw Vale Owl Sanctuary and More Conker-Eating Squirrels

The weather cleared up for our minibus Brynteg visit to the owl sanctuary at the Ebbw Vale Heritage Park on Friday 12th September. I had hoped we might go up the Rhymney Valley for a change as we were going east, but it was not to be. We branched off eastwards at Troedyrhiw just south of Merthyr to join the Heads of the valleys Road.

Dowlais Top must be one of the few places left in Glamorgan where there are still raw, unvegetated slag tips Although no active machinery could be seen from the incline out of the valley, I suspect that open cast coal mining might still be in progress there.

Attempts had been made to revegetate the lower parts of the symmetrical black slopes rising south of the road - this evidenced by just the sparsest sprinkling of grass blades no more than a couple of inches high. And likely to stay that way, while so many free range mountain sheep were gathered to nip off the tender blades as they pushed from the powdery matrix. Sheep, like the rest of us, know that "the grass is always greener on other side of the fence" and here there was no fence, so problem solved.

Barren grassy moorland stretched away on the north side of the "Heads of the Valleys", across the empty acres of Llangynidr Mountain. Much of that lay within the Brecon Beacons National Park, the boundary dipping northwards to exclude the valley leading up to the Trevil Quarries and the track over the Duke's Table to Dyffryn Crawnon - one of our favourites during the happy years of mountain walking with the Merthyr Naturalists' Society.

To the south we passed the head of the Rhymney Valley and Tredegar at the head of the Sirhowy Valley before turning into Ebbw Vale. We seemed to travel a long way down this before reaching our destination. I had visited at the time of the 1982 Festival celebrating rehabilitation of the area after removal of the great steelworks, but I remember only vaguely walking in the conservation area, new gardens and prettified lake up the slopes to the west

Post festival development was still on this side of the valley, but seemed to be further down. On our short visit I got the impression of four levels. The scenic flank of the mountain lay above the big new shopping arcade and carpark. Below this were attractive new dwellings of many designs and set in private gardens, with an area given over to a spacious lake set in public gardens. Clinging to the woodland alongside was the owl sanctuary, the high spot of our visit.

Embayed land here felt like the valley floor, but there was more land below, occupied by the old industrial dwellings and spacious playing fields. The whole area seemed to have been planned with tourism in mind. Flights of wooden steps and signposted footpaths led away into the woods from the roads connecting the chief attractions. Planners had aimed high in transforming the huge, towering eyesore of the steelworks, whose furnaces had blazed orange through the restive nights, and they had certainly succeeded.

The most attractive feature overshadowing the whole, was the one closest to the old industrial scene. Two towering knolls of gleaming black rock, attractively draped with grass and ferns, overshadowing the whole complex, were composed entirely of slag, dumped in layers to simulate the horizontal bedding planes of a native rock. They reminded me of the great vertical rock pillars rising from formerly little known waterways in China, and were so like some of the world's most attractive scenery, that it was only the unconformity with the Coalfield rocks that gave them away as man-made artefacts. In fact they were part of a much larger slag dump, the southern section of which had been removed.

Some boulders of this same black, iron-hard material decorated the lake gardens which we visited first, alongside others of local Pennant Sandstone. There was a little café here on a tongue of land where the long lake narrowed, to be crossed by an ornate, red Japanese bridge. This was the obligatory coffee and comfort stop for most and gave some of us time to explore the lake shore, though not enough to circumnavigate the whole.

Leaning over the bridge rail, we spied huge grey fish moving languidly among feathery water weed, that looked like hornwort (*Ceratophyllum*), the shoots too thickly beset with leaflets to be water milfoil. They seemed not to rise for flies and create circular ripples, like trout. Instead they generated smooth, satinny swirls as they suddenly changed direction. I learned later that these were carp of various sorts, including coy carp and mirror carp.

Such ornamental fish are valuable, but my local informant commented that the Hungarians tried to catch and eat them and a Chinaman had wanted to buy some. Fishing was allowed, but fish caught had to be thrown back. A chap on the far bank was using a long pole rod, reaching far out into the depths, while the big fish were nosing into the bank where I stood, creating wavelets as they twisted away. The café sold bags of tiny pellets to attract the fish, but there were no leaflets or information of any sort describing what had been achieved during renovations.

An expectorated crop pellet had been left on the bridge rail by a bird feeding on a mixture of seeds and tiny flat-shelled snails. A black-tailed skimmer dragonfly patrolling over the silky purple heads of neat marginal reed clumps, was harried briefly by a speckled wood butterfly. Fifteen or so mallard had gathered where largesse was being distributed at the lake end opposite to the Cleopatra's needle type monument at the narrower end.

Fringed water lilies were flowering across the surface, while marginal flowers included bright spikes of purple loosestrife, yellow greater spearwort, water figwort, yellow Mimulus and 'gardeners' garters' grass, probably a variegated form of reed canary grass.

The lakeside was planted with trees and clumps of a cultivar of bistort with red flower spikes. One bank was covered with huge butterbur leaves, another with the smaller, rounder ones of the related winter heliotrope, which was actually flowering

This normally blooms in January and February, when the powerful honey scent is wasted on a chilly atmosphere devoid of pollinating insects. It seems some may get pollinated after all, although the area occupied by these effective ground cover plants is proof enough that vegetative spread is more than adequate without the services of insects.

* * *

Back into the minibus and up a couple of zig zags to a higher level and we disembarked for the highlight of the day, the Owl Sanctuary. The owner, who had guided us down from the carpark, ran this establishment as a private enterprise, unsponsored by official grants, in order to maintain his independence, unfettered by red tape.

Enclosures for far more birds than we had expected, were distributed through a steepish section of woodland, so all were overshadowed by the tree canopy, protecting these birds of the night from the glare of the day. We approached along a railed board walk, erected high above the ground, at least on one side, the ends of the sturdy timbers liberally covered with moss and algae.

An enormous beech tree below was girdled with a wooden platform bearing a large enclosure. I mounted the steps and spied a headless bird with its back to me and wings spread - to a wingspan greater than my own arm span. A sinewy neck appeared above the spread of mottled feathers, and a head much too small for a frame that size, to peer back at me over the hunched shoulders. A griffon vulture, with velvety fawn down over the head and neck that is so often naked in these carrion feeders, to prevent the feathers getting fouled with blood and guts.

He would want some feeding - like the free range red kites of other sanctuaries in Central Wales. Hopefully there was liaison with the local abattoir, for all the birds here were meat eaters, whether owls or raptors. All, that is, except the tiny quails. I couldn't believe how small they were, although having witnessed them among a gift of their numerous eggs in pens kept by some of Merthyr town's countrymen. Little owls, too, were an exception, so tiny as to be mistaken by most for chicks, these able to get by on a diet of beetles and worms.

It is a long time since I saw any little owls in the wild, though apparently there are still quite a lot about if we know where to look. It was probably the great size range of birds having this same basic pattern that impressed us most.

Truly majestic were the European eagle owls and the great grey owls - cat sized, flat faced, bright eyed and tufty eared, or what passed for ears. These would compare favourably with the finest pedigree puss, and would certainly get the better of any feline in conflict - being masters of the air as well as the land.

One of these giants was known as Houdini, having got away nine times, but she was not the only one with a yen for flying free over the local mountains. One was said to be at large on the eastern skyline of the valley at present. This was a hand-reared bird, imprinted on the human race as a chick and likely to choose one such as a mate. The two mountain walkers who had had this bird alight on their backs were not flattered.

Houdini was on heat today, as she announced to the world at large with her constant booming cries and flaps up to the roof of her pen.

"Put her in with that owl over the way and she'd kill him."

Imprinted on the man who had brought her up nine years before, all others of her kind were rivals. (We had recently been shown on TV the lengths to which ornithologists have to go when bringing up baby European cranes hatched in incubators to repopulate British habitats from which they were exterminated years ago, to prevent them from becoming imprinted on humankind.)

Owls escaped from distant emporia were sometimes attracted to others of their kind, and turned up here in the surrounding woods. All are said to be micro-chipped, so can be returned to the rightful owner, if that is the right word for those who serve the needs of these majestic creatures?

Ebbw Vale's Owl Man told us of a time when the RSPB called him in to help capture an escaped alien likely to harry the natives, for which they were responsible.

"Going about it quite the wrong way. One glimpse of that net and he'll be off."

He produced some meaty food, held it out in the right hand, made an appropriate noise and grabbed the birds 'ankles' with the left, for attachment of the 'lead'.

A leather gauntlet glove was a must. Those claws are sharp. He spoke of a 'properly brought up bird' which only encircled the wrist of the handler, but cut off the circulation so that the hand went white. The remedy Just press the leg against a hard surface and it will relax its grip. There is much to learn at this game.

There was no such problem with the tawny owl, which was flown for our benefit, between its owner and one of our own number - furnished with the appropriate gauntlet. A kestrel was also released to show its paces - the proffered food being ample incentive to return to its source. Most of the birds, both owls and raptors, were in moult at this season, with downy 'baby feathers' fluffing out on their flanks, these not fit for flying.

Some were loosely tethered on long leads to knee high perches, free to move around their pens. Others were spared this standard impediment. The native tawny owls had a larger, more wooded enclosure with a nest box that looked more like home - a wooden artefact like those that so many wild barn owls choose for themselves when the right sorts of barn are on the housing market.

The feature of these birds of the night that appealed to me most strongly was their big, beautiful, brown eyes - like the glass ones that I used when making teddy bears for Oxfam. Some gazed into mine, unblinking, seemingly assessing my worth and leaving me somewhat embarrassed. Others were constantly blinking their heavy eyelids against the muted light under the trees.

The proverbial all-seeing 'hawks' eyes' of the raptors and the quite numerous large ginger and black Harris hawks were less compelling. Despite having seen so many buzzards perched on roadside posts when driving along lanes, I was still impressed by the size of those easy going raptors when viewed at close quarters.

This emporium was also the site of some fine wood carvings, viewed only through glass doors. These were large, the artist guided by the shape of the contorted log chosen for the masterpiece.

We adjourned to a higher contour for a restaurant lunch and employed the rest of our time enjoying the extensive, state of the art shopping precincts, with everything from garden centre, garments, equipment and, the best patronised, I fear, Thornton's Chocolates.

* * *

By 15th September the Taff had settled back to its fair weather level. Water was once more crystal clear, revealing the delicate wafting water crowfoot colonies as firmly attached to the stony bed as before the tumult. A fisherman was casting his line hopefully downstream, standing thigh deep in the flow.

The grey wagtails' shingle bank had emerged from the water intact - but no wagtails. Had all the small fry in the gravel been washed away? The more than man-high osier had retained its roothold, but was leaning drunkenly downstream. Its mid level branches were festooned with unsightly polythene, washed down from the Coalfield Valleys.

Upper ones were free, very likely because these were headed downstream in the lee of the lower parts which were sieving out the debris. A lot of bric-a-brac must be washed away in floods, but there are always more drifted branches caught up on the piers of the bridges after a spate than after a spell of calm, during which some must get dislodged. Most osiers and sallows, the genuine native riverside species, had sprung back to near vertical, but the bordering Buddleia and Japanese knotweed remained nearer the horizontal.

Drawing level with the sports field downstream on the east bank, I came upon a major gash in the flood defence. A big sycamore had fallen, taking much of the path with it, some clinging to the upended root ball, some slid away from beneath, although a narrow ridge of ground still separated the rift from the river brink.

The fall was oblique, pointing downstream. The trunk divided into two a few feet from the base and had crashed over the elm which still held the adjacent bank. The branch canopy was intricately mixed with that of an osier downstream, the unfamiliar tangle being investigated by a jay.

The displaced path material, exposed to a depth of four feet or so, was of black clinkery shale, a bi-product of industry. Similar erosion of the 'natural' river bank in past years often showed a distinct layering of black and yellow horizons an inch or more thick. Yellow was sand, black was coal dust swilling down from coal washeries upstream, but all that sort of deposition had stopped, now that the salmon and otters were back.

* * *

The conker-devouring squirrel population had changed location, having presumably exhausted the product of the roadside horse chestnut near the farmhouse garden. Practically all the logs previously used as dining tables were now completely devoid of the former detritus of chewed husks. Just a few very stale bits remained on the bench opposite the still fine stand of sweet gallingale by the pond.

Feeding activity was now much greater and was concentrated in the carpark. A more generous source of provender was provided here by the line of mature horse chestnuts separating the area from the playing fields. The main sites to which the prizes were taken to be enjoyed at leisure, were at the base of trees in the picnic area, but plenty of left-overs remained at the source of supply.

Open areas of grass between were almost devoid of meal debris, suggesting that the banqueters preferred to have a trunk handy as an escape route. Except that a couple of ground level stumps in the open had been much used, suggesting that another important asset was a level dining table.

Below the cedar, Sequoia, walnut and birch trees a number of small holes had been excavated in the ground, descending obliquely for three to four inches and an inch across, but no buried conkers were seen at the ends, and the squirrels would scarcely have been digging titbits from old stores in the midst of such plenty.

The burs were more cleanly opened than those seen previously. Instead of the laboriously chewed fragments of the various wrapping layers lying around before, there were now neatly split burs with the conkers falling free, and not all carried off, so great was the bonanza. Presumably these nuts were riper and easier to dismember. Either that or the takers were becoming more expert.

I watched two squirrels busy on the ground under the supply trees. When I approached too close, they scampered up the tree and started dropping half husks and whole conkers down from the branches. Three fragments actually hit me, so fast and furiously were they - and possibly others - working up in the branches. At least one of the harvesters came down for the spoils as I moved on.

Another grabbed its prize and carried it the entire length of the carpark, following the edge of the central plant barrier. While gathering the spoil, the bushy tails flicked in complete circles at every hop, these agile sprinters acquainting the whole world with their movements, instead of pursuing the stealthy approach and prolonged 'freezes' of most of our wild mammals, aware that movement can advertise the whereabouts of even the best camouflaged forms.

The donor trees had greener leaves than the roadside one and scores of burs could still be seen on the branches from below. I found no half opened cedar cones, only hundreds of severed scales, and but a handful of nibbled Sequoia ones. Nor did the large amount of soft fibrous bark at the foot of the latter's trunk look like the work of squirrels. These ring bark trees to get at the sweet juices travelling down from the leaves through the phloem, but that conduit was way back inside the fibrous, fire-proof bark here.

I returned to the logs to find a handsome clump of sulphur tuft toadstools

(Hypholoma fasciculare) with their somewhat plumbeous gills beneath the colourful caps, a species which seemed to be popping up everywhere at the time. Another bore several large, bulgy white brackets in pristine condition and hard as the wood itself, along their flanks. These must have been 'lumpy brackets' *(Trametes gibbosa)*. Obviously present before, they had been hidden behind a clump of cocksfoot now flattened by the rain. Small lobes of white off the end grain may have been more of the same.

Pausing to admire the red rather than pink fruits on the lanky spindle bushes behind the logs, I found myself watching a little possie of long-tailed tits, tumbling around in the hawthorn thicket six feet away. They were not attacking the haws, being evidently after smaller, invisible prey.

Returning via the bird seed plot, I looked in vain for seed eaters, but saw only another jay, the usual rabbits and a somnolent group of cattle chewing the cud.

CHAPTER 41

Ogmore-By-Sea and Southerndown

It was 17th September, the third dry but overcast day in a row, when Madeleine and I visited the western end of Glamorgan's Heritage Coast. We took the northern route out, through Talbot Green, Pencoed and Ewenny and the southern route back, through Wick, Cowbridge and Pontyclun.

The usual (winter) flood lay in the valley where the River Alun joined the Ewenny, a short way above their confluence with the River Ogmore. In between lay the motte and bailey ruins of Ogmore Castle, erected on the site of the earth and timber castle built at the river crossing in 1116.

We turned off at the Pelican Inn for another peep at this historic landmark, parking on river-washed shingle by the ford leading across to the thatched village of Merthyr Mawr. Floods had not yet subsided sufficiently to expose all the limestone blocks of the stepping stones. When they did, foot traffic would be able to cross dry shod alongside the ford used by horse riders. Currently water gushed over most in a smooth silvery flow, leaving only a few breaking surface.

Just upstream were tall clumps of the uncommon, brackish water grey clubrush. Downstream the river flowed deep and clear and almost plant-free. A heron flapped majestically across the river flats over peacefully grazing horses and house martins swooped around the grey castle walls.

The adjacent cottage, its garden walled against river floods with one-way, flap-protected drainage holes, wore a brand new thatch above spotless whitewashed walls. When last seen this had been roofless and blackened by fire. We strolled a short way along the bank, where ponies grazed the lush, much rained upon swards, before driving across the attractive, brackenny commonland between river and hillside to Ogmore Mouth.

* * *

The tide was on the way out, exposing a broad belt of pristine sand. Tusker Rock offshore was rearing above the water, the marker buoy beyond warning mariners of its presence when it disappeared below the waves. The mouth of the three united rivers was broader than often, dividing and uniting again around a gravelly island. By the time we returned from our walk, the sea had withdrawn further, revealing a lower bifurcation with the water dispersing via two separate routes. In the days when I was seldom parted from my camera, I used to record the position of this versatile river mouth on each visit and it was never the same as the last time.

Some of the gravel down there would be from the ancient raised beach, the remains of which were plastered against the low rocky headland where we parked - and later lunched, watching boys sailing a home made toy boat.

We set off afoot along the shoreline, to the east, on short rabbit grazed turf clothing a superficial layer of sand. Rocks immediately below were a conglomerate or breccia - a natural concrete on a massive scale. This had been deposited in late Triassic times on the slabby horizontal strata of ancient Carboniferous limestone that now stretched away seawards to meet the pristine sands or piled grey beach pebbles.

This junction is a classic unconformity of two rock layers, now juxtaposed, one upon the other, but separated, so the geologists tell us, by 80 million years in time and a 4,600 metre depth of rock. These were laid down and eroded away again during the whole of the Permean and part of the Triassic eras, with the underlying Carboniferous limestone sticking up through as hills further inland - precursors of today's Ogmore and Ewenny Downs.

The 'puddingstone' breccias over which we walked consisted of chunks of the older limestone embedded in a matrix of sand from the semi-arid desert of late Triassic times. There would have been alluvial fans of rocky material washed down with the desert sands by intermittent floods, sometimes along wadis or gullies carved out by the rush of water, the debris solidifying into the natural coarse 'concrete'.

Current wave action was wearing this down gradually to release the grey boulders and hurl them around on the beach, wearing off the corners to form the beautifully rounded beach pebbles present today. The matrix, released as sand grains, was shared now between the tide-washed beach and the sward clothing the low shoreline. There were mini sand blows here, breaks in the turf revealing loose sand, and the intermittent clumps of marram grass helping to restabilise it, although no real dunes had developed this side of the Ogmore River.

* * *

Bare sand faces about a foot high were the ideal places for rabbits to excavate their burrows and we saw a number of the excavators, large and small, busy nibbling the grass down to a smooth sward, particularly in the vicinity of a low gorse thicket providing cover on the slope above.

The resulting sward was just right for foraging choughs or red-legged daws, and I was more than delighted to be able to watch a flock of these prodding the short turf for invertebrates. Recently extinct in England and Wales, it was thrilling when they started returning to the sea-bird islands and mainland cliffs of West and North Wales. More unexpected was the advent of the Ogmore population, which I had heard about but not seen. Only latterly had the first pair returned to England - to one of their old haunts on the Cornish coast.

The Ogmore birds were remarkably tame, working their way towards me and feeding unconcernedly within twenty feet - a few steps on the elegant red legs between each probe with the slightly curved crimson bill. A walker with two white Scottie dogs finally put them up, enabling them to show off the characteristically splayed primaries of the wings as they took to the air. They continued with us for the rest of our time on this stretch of the coast.

All I needed now on the ornithological front was a sighting of the Dartford warblers that had also recently moved in here. I searched the rabbits' gorse clump with binoculars for the characteristic outline of this colourful little warbler, known chiefly on the RSPB reserve at the mouth of Poole Harbour in Dorset, but no such luck. Not even a stonechat!

There was, however, an intriguingly large group of pied wagtails, some with black backs, some with grey, feeding over turf and shoreline rocks. Usually seen in ones and twos, I wondered if autumn movements had started. The paler plumaged ones could have been white wagtails from the continent or home bred youngsters. Other birds were hirundines and gulls, the latter including black-headed gulls among the larger shoreline species. Flocks of Corvids on the beach off the Merthyr Mawr dunes across the river could have been carrion crows or jackdaws. I spotted none of the usual oyster catchers there, nor other waders newly arrived from overseas.

An outstanding feature of the sandy grassland was the many scores of fairy rings - whole or partial circles of lusher, darker green grass from which sprouted fawn mushrooms an inch or two across the caps. These were fairy ring champignons (*Marasmius oreades*) which are also a feature of the spray-tickled grassland of cliffs nearer Cardiff. Mycelial fungal threads beavering away below ground were responsible for releasing nutrients leading to the richer grass growth.

Another notable feature was the presence of many thousands of little flat, humbug striped Hellicella snail shells, scattered thickly over sandier parts.

Up to half an inch across, some living, some dead, shells might be highly polished, as when new, or abraded by sand-blow. Such a presence was a sure indicator of a favourable lime content of the medium.

Salt spray had a minimal effect on vegetation, apart from boosting the buck's-horn plantain, thrift and sea storksbill on the barer parts, including the footpath. Patches of thyme were present and a few small swards of the mauve flowers of common storksbill. Common orache and rock samphire occurred sparsely among the shoreline rocks. Sadly we did not get as far as the Pant-y-slade section, where parts of the cliff face can be yellow with the late flowers of golden samphire *(Inula crithmoides)*.

* * *

From Ogmore we moved back east to Southerndown, taking note of the roadside exposures of Sutton Stone in Ogmore village. This is a much valued freestone, with no natural lines of cleavage, and was taken by horse and cart to be sawn at Merthyr Mawr Mill for ecclesiastical carvings.

The new connecting road from Southerndown village to the bay below Dunraven Castle had been in the early stages of construction, well back from the crumbling cliff edge, when we were here in February. Now it was of spanking new blue tarmac with double yellow lines along both sides, these bordered by ridges of limestone chunks. Part of the newly contoured hill slope above was still bare, awaiting a plant cover, but we were told at the Heritage Coast Centre below, that it had been completed in good time for the summer season, and that the cost had been borne by the Dunraven Estate, whose owner lived in Ireland.

Another fact gleaned here was that there are known to be ten choughs on the Ogmore coast. We paid our respects to the very forthcoming ginger cat and strolled off afoot to catch up with topographical changes. These were a serious cliff fall where an earlier path had led out to the Witch's Nose (Trwyn-y-witch), and a blocking of the concrete road leading to the extensive sands beyond the uncomfortably large rocks which made the crossing of the upper beach difficult.

A wall had been constructed at the end of the yellow Liassic limestone cliff on the east flank of the bay and this remained intact, but the neighbouring cliff section had fallen away, leaving a cavity behind it and the stretch beyond was dangerously undercut. At the other side of the bay the concrete walkway had been interrupted twice. We encountered first the newest of the pebble storm beaches, which stretched the whole width of the bay, neatly triangular in section, the crest dipping down on its landward side to the old beach level, the moving pebbles unphased by the change of substrate on which they were being stranded.

The second interruption further downshore was the lifting and displacement of two sections of the path itself. The great slabs of concrete had been thrown off to the eastern side, the longshore currents responsible for undermining them flowing from the west. This region does not suffer the great Atlantic swells which batter much of the Welsh coastline, but it has to deal with the second biggest tides in the world, bringing pressure to bear twice a day on anything movable.

From the lower margin of the wide stretch of upshore boulders, rock slabs and piled pebbles, the level sands stretched a hundred yards and more to the sea. The eastern beach was littered with rectangular blocks of limestone from recent and earlier falls. There were always some present, but in summer they nestled cosily into pockets in the sand, Now most of that upshore deposit had washed away in recent gales, as it always did in winter, the transition to permanent sands retreating downshore.

Today's waves were minimal and no flotsam or jetsam had been brought in, so there was no beach combing to be had. Rocks here were more recent than the two kinds at Ogmore. We followed westward around the seaward edge of the almost horizontal Liassic limestone platform, which stepped down gradually from the base of the tall cliffs. Those were as unstable as the others, composed of Southerndown beds of alternating yellow sandy rock and blacker shales between - those softer, and the weak lines where falls occurred, leaving piles of angular fragments at the cliff base.

To the west these sea level upshore limestone platforms replaced the great deposits of boulders piled in the bay. Their extensive surfaces weathered too evenly to form many rock pools, but they showed fine examples of potholing, where pebbles had been rolled endlessly around in small hollows to gouge out mini pools, often circular with the basal circumference greater than that at the top as the rotating missiles worked their way down. In places adjacent potholes coalesced.

These were much easier to walk about on than the mobile pebbles and we were able to explore this mid shore tableland which was not much higher than the great spread of sandy shore below. Except, that is, where erosion had progressed to the stage where the surface ridges of rock occupied less area than the anastimosing crevices between.

This dissected platform, sometimes continuous and sometimes a series of dissected blocks surrounded by tide-smoothed sand, was full of fossils. These were harder than the matrix in which they were embedded and so stood proud on the wave-scoured surfaces. Particularly recognisable here were the Devil's toenails (Gryphea), bivalve molluscs where one of the two shells was larger and incurved, like a rather ugly ingrowing toenail.

* * *

Erosion was happening on a smaller scale to individual pebbles and softer shaly rock layers - this caused not by waves but by marine animals. Quarter inch tunnels in white limestone pebbles were likely to be the work of a mollusc, the rosy-nosed rock borer *(Hiatella arctica)*. Similar holes in black shale layers often still held the white molluscan shells of the boring piddocks *(Pholas dactylus)* which had caused them. The meshwork of tiny holes seen in smaller rocks were likely to be the work of boring worms *(Polydora ciliata)*. Another common borer had been at work here on oyster shells rather than rocks and is actually a sponge *(Clione cellata)*. Most of the oyster shells, which were immovably transfixed in crevices, seemed to have more tunnels than matrix.

Shell fragments were tightly wedged and few brown wracks were able to cling to the wave swept surfaces. The only seaweeds seen were coralweed *(Corallina officinalis)*, deep in cracks, and a few fronds of *Porphyra umbilicalis*, from which Welsh laverbread is made, these on the sandy approach. A few of the larger pools were home to a little green gutweed (Enteromorpha).

Living animals visible above the sand were mostly shining purple tops *(Gibbula umbilicalis)*, black shelled common periwinkles *(Littorina littorea)* and white or yellow-shelled dog whelks *(Nucella lapillus)*. These last are carnivores, feeding on the barnacles, as mussels, another favourite of theirs, are in short supply here. Slimy algal coatings or other sediments flooring the mini pools sometimes showed the feeding trails of winkles browsing on the microscopic algae. It was possible to follow their ramifications, criss crossing each other and with the maker tucked under a ledge at one end.

There were plenty of rather flat shelled limpets on the rock slabs, but we saw none of their distinctive zigzag grazing trails. The barnacles were tiny. Some rocks were liberally spattered with the white shells, like confetti, but there must have been a recent spat fall of young ones, because they are usually much larger. I saw none of the maroon coloured beadlet anemones or red algae eaten by the Irish as carragheen, though both are common on other wave washed limestone pavements hereabouts.

Much the most interesting and obvious of the wildlife here were the sand reefs, built up on rock surfaces by countless honeycomb worms *(Sabellaria alveolata)*. As we moved westwards these became increasingly common, spread unevenly over an acre or so and building up to more than a foot deep in places.

Nationally rare, these Sabellaria reefs are another of the geologically unique coast's claim to fame. They are fragile and not to be walked on, consisting as they do of piled tubes, each inhabited by and being continuously built by a marine worm at the advancing end. These intercept waterborne particles wafting over the rocks and glue them into a shelter with mucous. Each worm needs only to build half a tube, slotting this into the furrow between the two below. A tube fifty centimetres long will have been built by a single worm of two centimetres, adding sand grains at the growing mouth, the finished product like a huge mineral honeycomb.

These reefs provide an essential oasis in a desert of bare, wave-swept rock, and supply habitat for mussels, winkles and tops, as well as being highly decorative in their symmetry at the top, though often damaged at the bottom. Beach walkers such as ourselves never see them in all their beauty, when they reach out from the mouths of their tubes to feed on the incoming tide. They become commoner to the east of the Witch's Nose on Traeth Mawr and Traeth Bach.

Driving home along the road to Wick, where banners welcomed their returned gold medallist from the Olympic games, we saw a large dispersed flock of Corvids flying to roost.

CHAPTER 42

From Weir To Canal, Gwaelod-Y-Garth and Fforest Fawr

I was lured out afoot by unaccustomed sunshine on 17th September and set off upstream on the Taff Trail. A good force of water was still tumbling over the weir, sufficient to defeat the two fish making ineffectual leaps from the maelstrom at the base. These were probably too small to make the grade at any time. It was early days yet for the late summer run upstream for spawning.

A heron gazed expectantly into the shallows on the lookout for smaller fry, but the only passing titbits seen were dragonflies and craneflies. Scarcely a ripple ruffled the surface of the feeder canal as I passed on into the bridle track. I feared that might be overgrown at this end of the summer, but it was still passable, and with fresh hoof prints in the muddy patches.

The springtime bracken near the M4 bridge that had reached above my shoulders when still with unfurled croziers, had continued growing, but was now overtopped by a flowering stand of Himalayan balsam, simply buzzing with bees - some turning around within the welcoming pink cul-de-sacs to emerge head first.

The sweet chestnut coppice proved disappointing from the fungus point of view. Apart, that is, from hundreds, nay thousands, of bright yellow and orange sulphur tuft toadstools. These certainly brightened the gloom, growing everywhere, at tree bases or on and alongside old logs. Individual clusters might be of a dozen or a score and dozens or scores of clusters might grow together. The caps averaged one to two inches in diameter and the gills had a characteristic plumbeous tinge.

Fungus forays are aimed at finding many different species rather than many individuals of the same, however decorative, but there were few others. Most colourful was the amethyst deceiver *(Laccaria amethystea)*, with lilac cap, gills and hollow stipe, three to four inches tall and an inch across. There were large, pale bonnet Mycenas *(Mycena galericulata)* and more distinctive, flat-topped *Psathyrella obtusata*, with pink gills and a tough, buff cap, the stipe rising from a basal ball of mycelia. I realised I was walking through the earth ball colony when I noticed smoky clouds of dark brown spores rising around my feet.

A multi-stemmed dogwood, taller than me, had produced hundreds of green twigs about twelve inches high, sent up by the web of roots in a desperate quest for a bigger share of the life-giving light. Sadly few bore leaves as yet, to absorb the radiance and 'fix' a little more of the carbon dioxide - so necessary to all life but threatening to overwhelm us with its abundance if the media are to be believed.

Sweet chestnut burs had started to fall, thickly beset with prickles and more painful to handle than those of the horse chestnuts, some of which from the playing field trees had dispensed with the usual hard spines altogether. Husks of the edible nuts here had opened into three to four pointed stars, with up to three chestnuts nestled within, these flattened together and peaky topped, unlike the beguilingly smooth conkers. Nuts were smaller than imports from Spain and other countries of Southern Europe, the native home of our chestnut trees, said to have been introduced by the Romans

In my schooldays, we used to gather these, preferably in gloves, score the brown shells with vertical penknife cuts and roast them around the fire grate. How many households have open fire grates now? We also liked them boiled, when the soft contents could be squeezed from the shell through the nicked tip, like tooth paste from a tube. Our only modern contact is likely to be imported chestnuts to stuff the Christmas turkey.

I turned back when nearing the Coryton Roundabout and returned along the Glamorgan Canal. This was transformed, and not for the better, the flow impregnated with clay from some soil disturbance in the catchment, and flowing the colour of milky tea. Muddy streams came simultaneously from the stone tunnel under the motorway and a broad diameter pipe spewing quantities from its outlet at the base of the Long Wood.

Clear water was cascading down over the steep woodland floor a few yards away in a series of waterfalls, some three to four feet wide, and other lesser runnels were draining from the wood but had no diluting effect. Water plants, even in the long section filled bank to bank with bur reed and water mint, failed to filter out any of the solids and the brown seepage became a brown torrent through the lock, but was accepted as a suitable swimming medium by the dozen or so mallard on the downstream side - the drakes now back in the shining glory of their breeding plumage after their ignominious spell in eclipse.

A worrying feature was the presence of the same clayey water on the further side of the elevated towpath, suggesting leakage through the bank beneath, as there was no indication that the coloured spate had overtopped it. The foreign material was particularly apparent in the extensive hollow where we sometimes watched water rails foraging in winter.

An unexpected flower was common calamint *(Clinopodium ascendens)*, which is more usually a plant of South-east Britain. A row of six inch tall cereal seedlings occupied a crack in the massive timber of the lock gate, where grain was put out as bird food. Two great tits were doing their best to see that more seed did not fall in to join the mini garden.

* * *

It was with mixed feelings that I drove to my old Gwaelod-y-Garth cottage two days later to acquire more contributions to the Brynteg garden. My primary quest was for columbine seeds, these plants running riot everywhere in midsummer, but all had been overgrown by other plants - largely untended. Out of sight was out of mind, but I didn't return empty handed.

The red kaffir lilies, pink Japanese Anemones and St. John's wort bushes were in full flower, as were Cyclamen, while the passion flower vine had covered the entire kitchen roof and still bore some of its exotic flowers. Everlasting peas that had formerly grown vertically up a trellis had instead grown vertically down the wall into the pub yard - from where I collected a jar full of ripe seed pods.

Barbara came to help and show me where the vulnerable toad still sought shelter in a dark corner. A gardener at heart, but too busy by far with other commitments at present, she had, at least, erected a couple of tripods for runner beans, which had provided instead handy climbing frames for hedge bindweed. Most was a veritable jungle

I scooped up tangles of two of the most rampant ground cover plants, a pink Sedum and creeping Jenny, more yellow loosestrife and the knobbly rhizomes of spring-flowering leopards bane Doronicum, plus a few others that might benefit from thinning. A big tree from the end of the upper garden had been blown down in a summer gale, smashing the fence, and the invading ash in the old shop-cum-bonfire site had been sawn off.

Raspberry canes were sprouting right across the unmown lawn from far travelling rhizomes, but I was told that the soft fruit harvest had been excellent, particularly black currants and gooseberries. Not so the rhubarb nor bramley apples. That noble tree, that had kept me supplied with apples over nearly half a century, was on the way out.

Branches had been badly cankered for years. They were now practically leafless, many lichen-covered and the apple crop poor. A few had been used for chutney and I gathered up the remaining windfalls - their flavour as good as ever, despite the blemished skins. The life span of an apple tree is said to be around fifty years. This one had another few years to go, so must be mourning my departure.

Not to worry. The next day I would be visiting Madeleine Lewis in Llandaff, who had two prolifically bearing apple trees and had promised me some of the crop. It was a new and wholly satisfying experience to be reaching up and twisting that ripe fruit from its hold, having been unable to reach any but the runts on my own tree. Fortunately the windfalls had fallen softly on the lawn below.

The feral cats had stopped jumping in through the shed windows for their food. It was thought that someone else must be feeding them. Great strides had been made inside. All the walls had their final coat, some new carpets were down and new furniture incorporated with the old. Everywhere, indoors and out, were the three year old grandson's toys - not just in the two rooms allocated solely for his use. Not having ever lived in a house with children younger than myself, I had never seen so many playthings before. Quite an eye-opener.

Richard took me down to the pub after my tour to partake of cappuccinos and I managed fleeting meetings with two of my old neighbours before he sent me on my way with a container of hot food for lunch. I had no regrets. Would I have coped with the chaos any better, or the tangle of cars as I turned out onto the mountain road from the pub yard?

More folk patronised the premises for meals since the smoking ban, including families with children. As at Brynteg, there was far too little parking space, with the gradients too steep at both to produce more, yet the number of vehicles seemed to increase on every visit. Time had moved on. Gwaelod - a designated conservation area and still a little village, belonged to another phase of my life - the longest and busiest. It was time now for my more leisurely second retirement.

* * *

I returned to the village a few days later to renew my acquaintance with the Coed-y-Bedw Nature Reserve run by the county Wildlife Trust. This occupied the valley between the Coal Measure rocks of the Great garth and the Carboniferous, Dolomitic Limestone of the Little garth, with tributaries joining the central stream from both.

Walking up through Georgetown from Heol-y-Beri, I entered the valley where it abutted onto the river plain. This first part was forestry land, covered with regiments of Norway Spruce trees like telegraph poles only much taller. These lowland spruces, like the Sitkas of the Uplands, excluded all else but, at this stage of growth, instead of being impenetrable, they were more open-floored than deciduous woodlands. Light was excluded by a high reaching canopy, resulting in the death of all lower branches, so that a vehicle could have been driven through if the ground had been less steep.

In fact it had, quite recently, as thinning was in progress' The piles of sawn logs awaiting transport were pit prop length, as in the old mining days. I wondered why and what they were used for. Almost the only ground plants grew where a little light had sneaked in alongside the path. These were mostly mosses and liverworts, with a few ferns, hart's tongue, polypody and hard fern, and some wispy saplings struggling upwards.

The massive beech that had fallen across the track some thirty five years before, necessitating a detour, had succoured a succession of wood sorrel, moss, fungi and wood boring beetles, until exhausted of nutrients. It had been cut through amidships and the crumbling remains lay disintegrating, black and sodden, to either side. A source of life to others during its heyday, its senility and its decay, it was now adding its final fragments to the peaty soil to help nourish new generations. Earth to earth - over a longer term than ours.

The sombre but commercially productive spruce plantation occupied the ground between the gate from the row of cottages in Georgetown to the gate into the Nature Reserve. Once through that I was at the confluence of two loops of the sparkling stream tumbling down through the valley alder wood, between mossy rocks to flow through Lower Gwaelod and empty into the River Taff.

In times long past it had been dammed back into a reservoir on what is now the grassy spread of Heol Beri Green. The resulting head of water had been used to power the old Pentyrch Iron Furnace, with the tail race driving the Forge.

In hastening down the gully worn in the soft band of Millstone Grit between the two Garths, the flow had led to silting of the reservoir. Rather than dig it out, the Portobello Weir had been constructed obliquely across the River Taff in 1790, and a canal led off to supply necessary power for the heavy industry. But that was two centuries ago. As I first knew it this waterway was the nesting site of kingfishers and grey wagtails.

Now, in the twenty first century stream power had scoured out rocks and pebbles from the deposit of Boulder Clay upstream. The low bridge by which we had formerly crossed was now blocked by stones with the stream, flowing as wide as before, gambolling around its end. An easy crossing in gumboots (which were safely in the car boot), I chose to remain on the near side, where another rather indeterminate path followed upstream.

It was sad to see the bared face of the shaped boulder that had held the iron plaque designating the area as a County Nature Reserve - one of the first, from back in the 1960s. That had been vandalised long since. A typical woodland mountain stream, following the line of least resistance, and augmented by a lateral flow from the overgrown entrance to an old coal mine, it had a particularly elemental feel for me. Brought up in lowland England, the sight of rocks this size and this mossy, meant that I was in holiday country.

Among the riot of ferns, violet plants and persistent leaves of dog's mercury was a fine stand of uncommon wood sanicle, the bobble seed heads borne two to three times as high as the usual springtime flower heads. The tall earth bank carrying the path between river brink and wire fence, narrowed progressively, and I opted out at the next stile and moved into the adjacent meadow to make the most of the welcome sunshine, none of which penetrated the leafy canopy.

The field had been badly poached by cattle, the deep hoofprints masked by subsequent grass growth in the generous summer rains. Walking was difficult and I was glad of the makeshift walking stick that I had pulled from a pile of thinnings on entry, to use as a third leg.

I made for a large hollow occupied by a dense sallow-alder spinney surrounded by quagmire. Where this abutted onto the woodland edge a pool had been dug out for livestock to drink, this currently the haunt of a restless emperor dragonfly which took no siestas. On the opposite flank a brown female common darter dragonfly quartered its little plot, taking numerous long rests.

Brooklime and lesser spearwort encroached onto the water by a clump of meadowsweet and ancient hazels coppiced many years back. Where standing water diminished but the land was too wet to plough and reseed, the sward was of purple moor grass with rushes, the latter pushing through stubbornly even on "improved" sections of the sward.

I use the adjective in the agricultural sense, not as a conservationist. The main turf, as intended, was almost entirely of nutritious farm grasses, without even a companion sowing of clover and with scarcely a weed. The only invaders I noticed were a few common sorrel plants, the odd dandelion and nettle and an army of three to four inch high bracken fronds in the lee of the upper part of the wood. No doubt the bracken would take over if not checked periodically.

The fabulous views as I stumbled up the rolling contours was reward enough, and were viewed in windless sunshine for a change. The silence was absolute. It was mid afternoon, when most birds take a nap except in the short days of winter, when necessity drives, and some might still be in the post nuptial moult. I saw nary a one apart from a buzzard sailing unconcernedly far overhead.

I had seen no-one since leaving the village street. No rabbit was allowed to encroach on that lush sward and even the magpies and jackdaws stayed under cover. This is not a complaint. The stillness was noticeable because it is so seldom experienced in our modern world. The M4 was on the further side of the Little Garth beechwood and the A470 was cutting through the Taff Gorge with wooded hills rising all round. How fortunate I was to experience it, so close to the Principality's capital city.

* * *

On 25th September balmy weather enticed me out once more - to Fforest Fawr on the opposite side of the Taff Gorge, beyond the fanciful Castell Coch. It was the afternoon siesta hour again and, once within the mature beechwood silence reigned supreme for most of the time. So much so that it came as something of a shock when a green woodpecker rose chortling loudly from the adjacent rough grazing to plunge in among the blanket of trees.

From the top carpark I avoided the main track, as was my wont, but made an initial tour of a fragment of the adjacent golf course. The putting green in the lowest corner, below several steep grassy slopes and out of sight of the driving tee, was amusing for its unpredictability. Presumably golfers aimed for the top of the uppermost slope and let the ball travel the rest under its own volition. Otherwise that corner of the wood must be the gathering ground for many golf balls.

I threw several back onto the neighbouring fairway as I progressed. The 'barrier' between, once a laid hedge, was fragmentary, but with some of the magnificent old trees so characteristic of these ancient hedgerows, their bases malformed by woodsmen in their far off youth.

Fungi were few, the most decorative being a group of stump puffballs *(Lycoperdon pyriforme)*, the only puffball to grow on wood rather than soil. The balls of spores were elevated on narrower sterile bases. In pristine condition, these contrasted sharply with the small black, white-tipped candle snuff fungi *(Xylaria hypoxylon)* on old stumps, tough and twiggy, long-lived and generally widespread. The only others seen were a few birch brackets or razor strop fungi *(Piptoporus betulinus)* on a fallen birch trunk and some large white toadstools too far gone for identification.

The woodland sculptures had changed at the "Arena", where parties of children were brought for woodcraft experience. The metal cutouts of fox and crows, that had adorned the woodland perimeter over a number of years, had gone, their place taken by a massive timber 'throne'.

Firmly attached to a big stump, the seat, big enough to hold half a class of infants, and the back rest, were carved and polished in the shape of massive oak leaves, to match the contours of the contorted trunk from which they were hewn.

This spot, on the upper brink of the woodland, was a favourite viewpoint, the land falling sharply away into what had once been an ancient glacial lake, backed up against the bottleneck of the Taff Gorge until the plug was finally broken through and the water escaped. The old lake bed now held the village of Taffs Well, but the wider panorama was mainly a comely mix of deciduous woodland and pastureland dissected by old hedgelines.

The upper flank of Graig-yr-Allt was clad in the deep bronze of dead bracken, capped by a small yellow patch of mountain grasses, while the foliage of round-topped beeches was adopting a richer coppery sheen. Across the valley, on the opposing slope of the Great garth, also topped with bronzed bracken, was a tiny whitish splodge among the trees - "The Cottage" that had protected me from the elements for forty five years and was now entering another lease of life as it approached its third century. The entire vista was bathed in sunshine, the one purple raincloud settled over Caerphilly Mountain away to the right.

The only livestock in the nearby fields were horses, but a colourful flock of goldfinches was busy among the seeding heads of ragwort bordering the wood, while a mistle thrush and magpies foraged at ground level where the woodpecker had been busy. Soon after this the woodland extended north, up valley and the path veered south through a less sombre mixed woodland of younger deciduous trees.

More light penetrated here, to nourish tablecloths of wood sorrel on old stumps and carpets of wild strawberry plants on the verges. This path finally joined up with the main track from the carpark. Broad verges had been mown alongside, leaving space for herbs, tall yellow spikes of agrimony and pink heads of hemp agrimony with noble Angelica plants. Here, too, were several colonies of columbine plants in pristine condition, but no flowers or fruits. This species, better known in gardens than in the wild, is a feature of these woodlands along Cardiff's backing ridge of hills, particularly those of Draethen further east.

Butterflies were mainly speckled woods and bees were busy on the flowers of hedge woundwort, but not those whose upper stems were infested with black aphids. Those were sucking out the sugary juices before they could replenish the floral nectaries.

Robins, blackbirds and wrens were more visible in this open section. At one spot I came upon a couple of large clearings, one furnished with benches, picnic tables and two iron barbecues, with grill tops, the other available for mass activities by visiting schools. Peering from the trees behind was a life-sized lynx, carved from another stump.

Then came the greatest puzzle on what had been a very ordinary woodland stroll - an anomalously large number of bumble dor beetles *(Geotrupes stercorarius)*, known also as lousy watchmen, because of the tiny mites which sometimes infest them. The name of dor comes from the droning sound of their wings when attracted to lights at night.

Not uncommon, these shiny black dung beetles are often encountered singly or in couples. On this occasion, after realising how many were strewn across the broad gravel track, I started counting and got up to forty seven before their numbers thinned. As always, I picked one up to admire the lustrous blue sheen of its undercarriage, although it was always difficult to overturn them because they clung so effectively to the fingers and fought to right themselves when dislodged.

Some were moribund, scarcely bothering to right themselves after toppling over an extra large stone. Almost two thirds of those seen were dead, some partially dismembered and some squashed by passing human feet or mountain bikes. The puzzle was, why did they walk out onto this stony desert in the first place, when their mission in life is to make burrows in soft soil, stuff them full of dung and lay their eggs on top - one per tunnel?

They work at this as a mating pair, so why so many together? And where would they find the necessary dung in such a forested habitat? Preferring cow dung, they will use horse dung, but the only source of that within a very long way was offerings left by the odd horse and rider - of which I saw none.

Adult beetles do not emerge from their food-stuffed natal burrows until three years after the egg is laid. If these were newly emerged, why all at once and why would they be so lethargic? Had they given up in the absence of dung to nurture the next generation? The high mortality rate precluded a mass migration in search of the elixir of life. The natural world is full of unsolved puzzles - or maybe there is a good explanation.

The next day I tried following up on that other puzzle of the rubbery orange 'ping pong' balls in one of the many coconut sized 'eggcups' of the moribund alder in Radyr Woods. The 'egg' had vanished, the woody container was just one of the many massed around the trunk.

The slabby white fungus occupying a groove of the nearby beech, had started to develop a series of shelves with thick white rims, white below and a rich cinnamon colour above. This brought it into line with a young colony of 'artists' fungi' *(Gannoderma applanatum)* , the cinnamon layer a dusting of spores from the bracket next in line above.

CHAPTER 43

Cefn On Gardens, Walterston, Font-Y-Gary Bay and Merthyr Mawr Dunes

During that last week of September we thought the laggard summer had arrived at last, chilly, yes, but with sunshine and blue skies. That is until Irene Payne arrived here from Pembrokeshire for her second visit, from midday on the 29th. Weather forecasters had warned that a weather front with gale force winds was approaching from the west. She brought it with her, the heavens letting fall their burden just as she carried her luggage into the guest apartment.

It was February when last she came. We had hoped for better conditions this time and had planned visits to the coast and the Brecon Beacons, which now seemed less alluring. We opted currently for the thickly wooded gardens on the south facing flank of Cardiff's backdrop of hills. These had been constructed around one of the lesser streams feeding into the River Rhymney via the Nant Fawr and Roath Brook, through the city's playground of Roath Lake.

Entry afoot from the carpark was under the broad bridge of the M4, which spans the gorge occupied by a now defunct railway line. That had led north from Lisvane station into the long tunnel through the ridge of hills, to emerge into the Coalfield Basin beyond. Domestic pigeons chortled contentedly from the lateral supports. That was a good place to be in this sort of weather - and not the only one where they seemed content to put up with the roar of overhead traffic.

The lower half of the gardens was gloomy at this time of year, whatever the weather, with darkly evergreen Rhododendrons dominant under the trees - only one bearing two misplaced crimson flower heads at present.

Black logs coated with emerald moss blended with the dark peaty soil beneath. This scene would brighten up with bluebells and Wood Anemones when the bushes, and their smaller brethren, the Azaleas - were in their full flush of spring flowering.

Nothing, however, could take away from the tall straight trunks of the specimen oak trees, so unlike the angular dwarfs of sheep grazed oakwoods throughout the hill country. Nor of the other specimen trees, both deciduous and coniferous, which those old time gardeners had planted for future generations to enjoy and for which Cofn On gardeners had been awarded special accolades. Oaks, like so many others, came in various shapes and sizes. The leaves of one were ornamented with the little brown discs of spangle galls, caused by the oak Cynipid wasp *(Neurotus quercus-baccarum)*.

One of the brightest touches was a drift of yellow russule toadstools *(Russula ochroleuca)*, recently given another popular name of ochre brittlegill, for the fragility of their chunky, white-gilled crowns. Pale circlets of Hydrangea heads and the dangling red fruits and orange arils of broad-leaved spindle also brightened dark corners.

By the time we got to the Dragonfly Pool, the rain had really set in. No dragonflies! Just a grey squirrel busily digging holes in which he neither buried provender nor removed it - this at the base of a monster evergreen near our inadequate haven from the rain.

Of interest on the further margin were the stalked bobble fruits of a flowering dogwood, which flaunted four big pink bracts around each cluster of tiny florets in spring. Those were now shed, the fused fruitlets forming a plethora of spiky green balls. Long stalked leaves of a waterside plant resembling those of horse chestnuts (Aesculus) were *Rodgersia aesculifolia*. This is an oversized member of the Saxifrage family, the plumes of pink flowers now transformed to untidy appendages like ill treated pampas heads.

As our path wound up the craggy Old Red Sandstone slope, we enjoyed a feast of colour supplied by the many different kinds of maples, always bright, but at their best prior to autumn leaf fall. A last glimpse of the rich green, well watered golf course, and we turned back to cross an undisciplined little stream tumbling over rocky outcrops into a rain-pocked pool, to commence the descent.

The leafy flanks of the gully closed in around us, the now light drizzle emphasising the feeling that we were in a mountain cloud forest - an emotion which I always felt when here. Delicate *Hypnum andoi* feather moss wrapped the twigs almost to their growing tips, while bigger boughs were lichen caked and crumbly.

Back in the lower section, we circled west, past a remarkable horizontal variety of the giant Sequoia *(Sequoiadendron giganteum pendulum)*. When last seen this had escaped from its stabilising stake on reaching to about five feet and had headed off sideways, supported on a line of Y shaped props. Either the tree or the installers of the props had given up and the wandering section of trunk had been sawn off. Not to be outdone, the leading shoot had set off at a right angle, but still parallel to the ground.

The lower pool held other examples of these ancient cone bearing trees. On a little island was a fine specimen of the rare pond cypress *(Taxodium ascendens or T. distichum)* and on the bank a dawn redwood *(Metasequoia glyptostroboides)* of the same family, two deciduous conifers whose leaves take on bright hues before falling.

Clustered in the shade of the island specimen tree was another remarkable member of the Saxifrage family, Peltiphyllum *(Darmeria peltata)*, called the umbrella plant for the shape of its circular, long 'handled' leaves. Water lilies, skunk cabbage and bogbean added lustre to this bizarre collection, shaded by a tulip tree. A fitting finale. It was time to give up, dry out and enjoy a hot meal in a warm room.

* * *

The following day, as forecast, the rain was almost unremitting. Fortunately we had planned a morning visit to my good friends Joan and Jeffery Raum in the little village of Walterston in the Vale of Glamorgan. They had been leading lights in the County Wildlife Trust during the early and middle years, just as Irene was at present. Also they were regular visitors to the Scilly Isles, which Irene was hoping to visit shortly, so they had much in common.

Rain or no rain, we enjoyed a visit after our coffee to the outer precincts, where chaffinches and tits were commuting continuously to and from the bird feeders. Sarah, the donkey, was enticed from her shed beyond the vegetable plot into the streamside paddock, to say "Hallo" over the garden fence. Not only she, but Bracken, the spaniel, enjoyed eating the windfall apples, many of which were succumbing to brown rot while still on the tree. Was this yet another depressing feature of this wet summer? One of Sarah's dislikes was fleabane, which had to be pulled up to make way for tastier fare.

Evocative farmyard smells drifted over the trees from the barn in the field behind. Across the lane, the only other dwelling in sight was being re-thatched, the work currently in abeyance. The newly applied straw was soaked to a deep orange hue by the rain - like so many of the still unharvested wheat crops that languished in the fields round about, awaiting a few rainless days in a row to dry them out and let the heavy equipment onto the sodden ground

Harvests other than of cereals could sometimes not be lifted from the sticky medium. The only crop which was responding joyously to the weather was grass - but this had to be eaten in the field. Haymaking was often a non starter and silage taking almost as difficult. A farmer's life is not an easy one.

Before leaving we were treated to a tour of Joan's delightful water colours and acrylics, not all landscapes. She, like Irene and me, was also an incurable picker-up of unconsidered trifles, so we found plenty of interest in the way of fossils, skulls, shells and natural driftwood gems sculpted by wind and water.

* * *

We headed towards the coast to find a suitable place to eat our picnic lunch in the shelter of the car. I was assessing one place after another according to its merits in a veritable gale from the west, not to mention the sometimes sheeting rain, when Irene spotted a signpost leading to Font-y-Gary Bay.

"My father used to speak fondly of Font-y-Gary bay. He was stationed at nearby St. Athan with the RAF during the war. I was shown it once when I was small but can't remember much. Can we go there?"

She was a post war baby, born in 1949, so scarcely remembered the rationing, that went on well into the 1950s, but had a lively interest in family history, as in almost everything else.

The nearest we could get to the point in the car was the now almost empty caravan park. We found an appropriate spot to eat, gazing across an expanse of green and were entertained throughout by a lively flock of starlings, trying to balance on a high wire and obviously revelling in the wind.

Instead of heading into it, like the frequent flocks of gulls, so that it didn't ruffle their feathers and chill the skin below, they usually headed away from it. Most were preening, the wind lifting their feathers so that the beaks found no hindrance getting in under. As in a bird bath, the rain seemed to be all part of the fun. They came down in relays to splash in one of the big puddles on the tarmac roadway.

I was reminded of blackbirds that I had watched breaking the ice on a puddle at Merthyr Mawr one winter, for a good douching. The expert consulted later informed me that it is most vital to preen thoroughly in cold, wet weather when a pristine plumage is essential to retain body heat. (Welsh miners used to swill down in the water butt outside in all weathers in the bad old days.) Maybe we have got too soft. A "little trotty wagtail" shared the carpark with us and there were the usual Corvids, carrion crows, jackdaws and magpies. Strangely, also, two buzzards were hanging on the gale, headed into it instead of spiralling gently on a thermal.

Donning extra rain gear over our anoraks, we made our way to the wooded gulch leading seaward, pushed along at more than our normal speed by the following wind. It was much deeper than I had realised on my recent visit with Madeleine, the bank dropping almost vertically into the shadowed depths alongside the path and rising almost as steeply through the trees on the other side.

Clearly this was a fault or joint in the Liassic Limestone and responsible for the right angle bend at this point in the general east to west alignment of the cliffs. The tide was lower than on our earlier visit, exposing the gleaming foreshore, stretching way out into the Bristol Channel. All visible from this access point consisted of a wave-polished limestone platform, terminating in a scalloped edge, where a flock of oyster-catchers sent distracted cries into the gale as they foraged along the water's edge.

We did not see the composition of the shore beyond the western headland until we had climbed the steps taking the coastal path up to the caravan site. It was quite different - a broad, level spread of small boulders and pebbles stretching right along the coast to the complex of multiple storm beaches, creek-dissected saltmarsh, old and new sand deposits and the lagoon now replacing the old estuary at Aberthaw. This is Watch-House Beach, leading on to the Leys Beach and Breaksea Point.

The Thaw River-mouth interrupts the line of Liassic cliffs that stretches west from Barry to the caravan site and starts again west of Aberthaw and Gilstone Beach, to continue to the mouth of the River Ogmore, with the Merthyr Mawr Dunes beyond. (Gilestone is known, not only for its power station, but for the stranding of a large humpback whale in October, 1982.)

The Glamorgan Coast from Ogmore Mouth to Summerhouse Point at the western end of Gilestone Beach, was granted Heritage Coast status because of the famous Liassic cliffs. This accolade was denied the eastern section encompassing Font-y-Gary on grounds of the industry and quarrying that had moved in to exploit its geological riches for building stone and cement.

While not the thickest sequence of Liassic rocks in Britain, these cliffs reveal the longest continuous exposure of this geological succession. There is considerable fossil interest here and the great spread of wave-cut limestone platforms is recognised as some of the finest in Britain. Their downshore extent at low water is, of course, dependent on the great tidal range, that finally peters out as the Severn Bore.

Gazing seawards now, it was mind boggling to realise that the great swath of wave-smoothed rock, stretching away to the murky waters of the Severn Estuary, was actually the basal layer of the cliff which we had just descended, all the overlying layers having been nibbled away over the millennia.

Changes in conformation of the shoreline have been easy for me to record photographically at Aberthaw and, to a lesser extent, at Ogmore Mouth over the past forty years or so. Not so obviously, change is also proceeding here, as Nature tackles the harder substrates at a steadier pace, with more permanent results.

The pebbles, sands and muds of the others move from season to season at the whim of tides and longshore drift. Time scale for cliff change is vastly greater but just as inevitable, and subject to radical modification over a geological time scale beyond our human comprehension.

* * *

The stream bounding down the gully we had descended disappeared underground before escaping from the cliff face. It was hard to judge where the water was finally released, because in this sort of rain there was water seeping, oozing, trickling and finding its level on the rocky shelves here, there and everywhere. The more permanent seepages were marked with slabs of green algae and a few mosses, blown awry by the wind - although that was mercifully much mitigated here in the lee of the jutting cliff. Deeper pools afforded haven for true and fool's watercress.

The thicker, pale yellow, sandy strata forming the shelf that was so much broader than the rest, was obviously composed of harder rock. The weaker stratum that had worn back on top, letting all the layers above collapse, was of softer black shale. Its exposed edge simulated a smoothly rounded layer of tar, sealing the gap below the recessed yellow bed above.

A large notice warned of the liklihood of cliff falls, one of which had happened during the seven weeks since I was here on the 12th of August. The pile of rock, clay and gravel, equivalent to a good lorry load, heaped against the back wall of the wide shelf, had been spawned by slumping of softer, more earthy material nearer the surface, loosened, perhaps by the persistent rain.

Curious, as always, Irene had a rummage through the newly exposed debris for fossils, keeping a weather eye open for further movement. She returned with some Crinoids or sea lilies, in transverse and longitudinal section, and some bivalve shells, possibly oysters. These she added to down on the beach platform, which offered comfortable walking - unlike piled cobble beaches elsewhere - but received the full force of the gale once beyond the protection of the jutting cliff.

After beach exploration, we walked along the edge of the site, where the seaward caravans, with their elevated balconies affording sea views, gave us a little shelter. A sturdy hedge outside the wire mesh fence stabilised the cliff brink. Clipped on the inland flank and top by groundsmen and the seaward side by the wind, it provided a dense barrier along the crumbly brink, which could be distinguished only a few feet away through its base.

Tightly tangled branches were woven together by ivy, covered with the yellow pimples of unopened flower buds. Here, too, was wild Clematis, fluffy with old man's beard seed heads, and the much less cosmopolitan wild madder (*Rubia peregrina*). This is a bristly member of the bedstraw family, as is cleavers or goose-grass, but is much stiffer. It bore little clusters of starry, cream-coloured flowers and hard black fruits, and is characteristic of this coast, but uncommon elsewhere.

More edible bird fodder was supplied by rose hips and haws, fat juicy sloes and blackberries, black dogwood fruits and squishy oval berries of black bryony. Birds spurned the orange seeds in the splitting, boat-shaped capsules of foetid Iris which brightened the hedge base, along with seeding Alexanders, bristly ox-tongue, see beet, yarrow, hedge bedstraw and creeping cinquefoil.

The neatly mown lawns around some of the caravans imparted an incongruously summery look to a cliffop world that was far from summery. When the rain started pelting down in earnest, we turned tail and headed for shelter from the chilling drops, but had gone far enough along to have the wind behind again for this last lap. It was the main road and short cut over St. Fagan's level crossing for home and a hot meal at his stage, with no dallying around the lanes.

* * *

The first of October dawned with another dire forecast of bitter wind and squally showers but there were, in fact, considerable spells of sunshine. We were glad, however, of pullover, anorak, waterproof and woolly hat, and got very wet at one stage, but blew dry again in wind and sun.

Our destination was the Merthyr Mawr Dunes, the great expanse of shifting sand between the mouth of the River Ogmore and the holiday resort of Porthcawl to the west. First I wanted to introduce Irene to the famous Dipping Bridge over the River Ogmore, about two miles upstream from the start of the Burrows or dunes.

On the map this is marked as New Inn Bridge, haunt of Cap Coch, the nefarious smuggler and murderer, immortalised in Alun Morgan's novel, "The Inn of Fear" (1977). I first saw it as a child when on a family holiday in South Wales. One of my father's London colleagues was visiting her family nearby and took us to see this as a local landmark.

It was an architectural delight in grey stone, with triangular buttresses facing both up and downstream, and so narrow that we had to squeeze against the wall when a car came by - always slowly, as it was a humped bridge with no view of any vehicle coming the other way.

The remarkable feature was the holes in the balustrade on the downstream side, through which sheep were pushed into the deep water below, to wash their fleeces before shearing. They found their own way out onto the bank, now cut back into an earthy cliff bordering a spot where a few cars could be parked.

Irene photographed it from all angles, while I handed tufts of greener grass to a willing equine recipient in the adjacent field. Later, when gazing into the depths from the bridge, I was approached by a man in a soiled yellow roadman's anorak, carrying a rubbish tweaker and bulging plastic bag. He addressed me by name, before I recognised him as the local land owner and former lieutenant of Mid Glamorgan.

"Murray McLaggan. I thought you were a workman.!"

"I am!"

Nuff said. His self appointed task was to patrol in turn different lengths of road and other parts of his estate to which the public had access, in order to gather up the rubbish that visitors had left by way of thanks!

He and his wife Jenny had moved out of Merthyr Mawr House and the farm, leaving his son in residence, and they were now living in one of the cottages in his picture-book village, almost all of which were thatched. He no longer farmed himself, the land being in the hands of tenants, but he could not relinquish physical tasks altogether.

I have a colour slide I took of him slashing gorse on the brink of South Cornelly Quarry, to let sunlight in to a colony of the rare wall germander *(Teucrium chamaedrys)*. This species is native only on chalk downs near Cuckmere Haven in Sussex, and is much prized where it turns up, on limestone, as there, or old walls, as in the Bishop's Palace at Llandaff. In those days he was active as chairman of the Mid Glamorgan Group of the County Wildlife Trust.

He told me he had celebrated his eightieth birthday a few days before. I had been greatly honoured when he had attended the eightieth birthday party put on for me by the Trust, seven years before. It seemed that neither of us thought we had yet reached retiring age.

During the next twenty minutes or so we learned much about the sheep dipping, which apparently continued until about twenty years ago. A hurdle had been placed across the road and the sheep driven towards it, so that the only exit was through the jump holes into the river. In the resulting press some would scramble up onto the seething mass of bodies and go over the wall.

He told us of changes in the dunes, with which I used to be a great deal more familiar than I was now. At that time there were great blow-outs, shifting dunes and watery slacks silting up with blown sand. After decades of no grazing and the spread of sea buckthorn *(Hippophaea rhamnoides)* bushes, vegetation cover had progressed beyond the marram grass and herb stage. There were now considerable areas covered by buckthorn between the linear strips of birch-dominated woodland occupying valleys between the old lines of dunes. This was in spite of prodigious efforts to get rid of it by the Countryside Council for Wales, this being one of the country's prize National Nature Reserves.

Back and across the lower bridge over the Ogmore, we made a detour to the little footbridge near the village church. Crossing afoot, we briefly explored the riverside commonland, home to swathes of Himalayan balsam. Horses had free access to this, but seemed scarcely to have touched it. A fine view opened out over the traditional stone stile to the downland rising beyond the River Ewenny across the horse grazed river flats between.

We failed to spot the old water-wheel, the hares or the even commoner pheasants on the grassy expanse rising to the limestone outcrop backing the inland edge of the dunes. Considerable time was spent exploring the various cul-de-sacs and perimeter walls of the Candleston Castle ruins in the woods above the dune carpark. The central section was newly fenced off, Murray having told us that he had the go-ahead to get the sometimes crumbling masonry stabilised.

A special wildlife feature here was the spreading ramifications of dozens of yards of mole runs, constructed close to the ground surface, throwing the fine, rabbit-grazed turf up on either side in criss-crossing ridges. This is the sort of thing we used to see in snowy winters when small mammals had been tunnelling under the snow, but I cannot remember seeing such extensive workings as here in turf. Molehills only occurred in peripheral, deeper, woodland soil, these dark and crumbly, like Christmas puddings.

* * *

We made our way back through holm, turkey and common oaks and old stems of giant bellflower to lunch in the car. The trunk of the poplar or aspen just in front of the bonnet was swaying so alarmingly in the gale, that we moved the car away in mid sandwich, lest it should fall on us!. Then it was on with the woolly hats and away over the dunes.

From the tree-bordered, stream-bordered car-park, we emerged onto a rising slope of completely bare sand. Along the crest of the rise a series of sand humps was topped by individual trees, each holding a mound in place. The sand under the holm oak at the windward end of the line had blown completely away on the downhill side, exposing bark-covered woody roots, two as wide as mini trunks. Remarkably, the strutting roots behind still held the considerable canopy in place, like contorted rick props but pulling rather than pushing. We wondered how - and for how long.

Many years back I had emerged onto the great plantless expanse below to find it littered with black Berber tents and palm trees, with not a British plant in sight! Film making was in progress! It may be kept open at present by joggers and aspiring athletes, developing muscle power on the yielding, unsupportive sands. We had to step back from the reedy watercourse under the bounding trees to allow a Welsh cob and rider to splash through.

Paths had been kept open through the sea buckthorn thickets from the beginning, the bushes towering above our heads as we walked through the quite impenetrable, thorny tangle. Most twigs were laden with rows of bright orange berries, formerly an attraction for hosts of fieldfares and redwings flocking in from Northern Europe in winter, but with far fewer recently, as the climate has warmed up. Murray said some fieldfares had already arrived, but no redwings as yet.

Like legumes and alders, sea buckthorn harbours organisms in nodules on the roots that fix atmospheric nitrogen and boost the nitrate content of the soil. Even the complete removal of bushes leaves this added fertility behind in the formerly highly infertile sand that is so necessary for the persistence of native dune plants. In their stead come nettles, thistles and elder bushes, which signal death to native dune plants unable to compete with these aggressive ground-covering interlopers.

While Irene was busy with her digital camera, I excavated a six foot long woody sea buckthorn root from the sand, with silvery-leaved shoots of diminishing height sprouting along its length. With such powers of vegetative spread, coupled with the millions of seeds, either shed naturally or coughed up as crop pellets by birds taking the berries, it is almost impossible to eradicate this species, which was once more or less confined to the East Coast in Britain. (Increasingly now it is turning up in civic plantings on dicey soils around new developments in our towns.)

Partially vegetated sand away from this menace was a riot of flowers in spring and summer, but few were left now. Most attractive were the little purple and yellow dune pansies, most abundant the ground-hugging autumnal hawkbit. There were yellow evening primroses, feathery tufts of wild mignonette and the last mauve flowers of storksbill and calamint.

Two shrubby ground cover species were fruiting burnet rose with fat black hips and dewberry with pruinose black berries among the deep red leaves. Some spikes of vipers bugloss were still flowering, but the related common gromwell stems were beset with white alabaster-like nutlets , paired instead of in fours as with most of its family.

We followed tiny paths up and down successive dunes, pausing to admire the splendid views east across the two rivers to the distant downland, or to huddle under the low-dipping boughs of the Corsican pines to shelter from scudding rainstorms. Climbing another broad expanse of bare sand, we noticed marginal footprints of fox, rabbits and small rodents, as well as dogs. Massed sand-abraded shells of little Helicella snails and larger brown-lipped and white-lipped hedge snails were abundant.

We watched tightly coiled tips of dry dune moss *(Tortula ruraliformis)* unfurl into golden-green stars as big splashy raindrops fell on them. Scarlet berries of wayfaring trees were changing to black, along sharp perimeters, with no intermediate purple phase.

Murray had told us that the rare, much prized birthwort *(Aristolochia clematitis)* had increased apace, but we failed to find it in the wilderness of sandhills. The name? An extract was used in medieval times to save peccant (erring) nuns from misbehaving with peccant monks.

With more than a mile of spreading sands reaching to the sea and a mile and a half from end to end, plus a sandy beach half a mile wide at low water, it would take the proverbial "month of Sundays" to do the Burrows justice - but this was the wrong time of year to savour the botanical riches. Irene, who was not familiar with any of Britain's great dune systems, had got the general picture. Next time, perhaps, weather and season would be more propitious.

CHAPTER 44
Home Front, Radyr Farm, Pant-Tawel and Peterston-Super-Ely

The second of October produced a few breaks in the cloud cover as another 'wet front' moved in from the west. Irene did not have to leave until the afternoon, so we wandered along the river bank and around the country park. The formerly ever-present grey wagtails had not returned since their old haunts were scoured by the floods and the only water birds seen were cormorant and mallard.

The late flowers of goat's rue had finished, as had those of round-leaved mint, but the air was still redolent with the all-pervading scent of the latter. Intensely blue alkanet flowers were the only ones offering the still busy bees a respite from the long-lasting beverage supplied by the Himalayan balsam nectar.

The conker frenzy among the squirrels was over, finished as decisively as it had started. Looking up into the horse chestnut canopies we spotted not a single green fruit, where boughs had been laden only seventeen days before. Husks below had opened cleanly, with none of the chewed remains that had heralded in this seasonal bonanza.

Scarcely any of the polished nuts remained and it is unlikely that the squirrels had been competing with small boys for these in this age of addiction to computer games. Had the harvest all been consumed or had it gone into store for even rainier days? There were plenty of holes newly opened in the peaty soil, but none sealed over, unless done too skilfully for us to detect.

The white 'lumpy brackets' had increased on the logs and there was a new colony of toffee-brown, very sticky 'scaly caps' *(Pholiota adiposa)*. White frills separated their hemispherical or bilobed caps from the even scalier creamy-yellow stipes. Irene drew my attention to the fossils in the accompanying boulders, which I had failed to notice before. Carboniferous rocks, veined with streaks of shining calcite, these contained the shells of small, coiled Goniatites, Brachiopods and Corals. Long-tailed tits were still fussing around the spindle fruits.

Irene was intrigued by the various country crafts pursued in the farmhouse garden, from slate fencing to hurdle making, wood carving and willow weaving. Always with an eye for detail, she was particularly drawn to the feathery green patterns achieved by algae growing up inside the protective coating of the various display boards, and she acquired a small collection of photographs of these 'accidental designs'. Many modern artists produce worse.

How often is that old adage "Nature abhors a vacuum" vindicated. All that those tiny plants needed was moisture and daylight - the frame and the glass were a bonus - supplied unwittingly and unwillingly by those who put these useful screeds of information on display.

More substantial patterns which intrigued the photographer were those of the old farmhouse outbuildings, their walls as skilfully constructed of river-rounded cobbles as if made of neatly fitting blocks.

We were surprised to see red and yellow common darter dragonflies still haunting the new pond, one pair coupled and laying eggs in the water, despite the late date. Corixid water boatmen were more active than usual beneath the whirligigs and pond skaters.

It seemed quiet after lunch when Irene had left to visit her old aunt in Sussex. I sat watching the relays of jackdaws that had been coming fairly constantly throughout September to tweak off the ripe lime fruits, allowing the denuded wings to flutter to the ground below. On quiet days such as this they fell vertically, spiralling down quite slowly, the single wing acting as a propellor. These were not taking the disseminules to pastures new, as intended. That only happened on windy days, but few would survive predation and other hazards. It is the winged seeds of ash and sycamore that give rise to the most prolific of our garden weed-trees.

Full sized lime fruits had been on the tree for a prodigiously long time - since the end of May. By August they were beginning to fall and litter the lawn, but not until September had the jackdaws and wood pigeons been so busy feeding on them, along with a few great tits. Squirrels, too, were taking their toll, principally two undersized youngsters, which often brought them down on the lawn to eat, elegantly hand-held. They presented fewer problems than unripe conkers and hazel nuts, which last had been on the squirrels' menu since before the pale green shells had become flushed with brown.

Another taker was a scrawny young magpie with a small, white-splotched head on scraggy neck that made me think of a bald ibis. Central tail feathers were glossy green, others the usual iridescent blue. Two juvenile wood pigeons also joined the feast, smaller than their plump, self satisfied parents and without the white neck patches.

The red twigs of winter and spring, by which I had first recognised this tree back in February, labelled it as a large-leaved lime *(Tilia platyphyllos forma rubra)*, the only species which does not produce masses of twiggy shoots around the base of the trunk each spring. It had seven trunks, but only a modicum of basal twiggery.

* * *

It was 7th October before I found myself once again among the Radyr Farm cornfields, discovering that these crops were neither wheat nor barley but millet. Of the three fields which I explored, the most northerly on the higher ground had given the best crop. Here the combine harvester had managed to cut most of it, despite the almost impossible weather, and neat rows of widely spaced golden stubble stretched away from the boggy mush by the gateway.

In the others the millet, none of which grew much more than knee-high, had been laid in parts, before the broad corrugated wheels of the mighty machine had pushed them into the mud. In the lowest, wettest part of one of these, against the Llantrisant Road no crop had been sown and no attempt had been made to reap the adjoining strip. Standing water was distressingly common, and not only in the deeply sunk wheel tracks.

Binoculars showed other fields to have been sown to the same crop and a week later, on 15th October, I saw yet another against Clos Parc Radyr Road, where a fine crop was still standing, the haulms at least two feet high, and the ground better drained.

By then I had made contact with the Povey farmers at Ty Gwyn Farm and learned that they had put all their fields down to millet apart from the two "setasides" by the new houses. They regarded their harvest as good, despite the unpropitious weather . The big firm that bought the grain for poultry feed, bird seed and related uses, had assured them that they would take as much as they could grow. "All eggs in one basket" had paid off this time. They had planted in May for an expected harvest in September, and not suffered unduly by having to wait until October. The previous evening I had attended a lecture by Dr. Peter Randerson on "Bio-fuels. Are they as green as they seem?" Perhaps this was another possible candidate for this up-and-coming use.

The Ty Gwyn folk worked the Povey Farm that had taken over from Radyr Farm and the daughter kept ponies in loose boxes alongside their white cottage and ran a pony club on Saturdays. I enjoyed my short visit to these real country folk, living, as I now do, in a wholly urban community - although town and country are sometimes quite closely linked in these spacious suburbs - as they are in the "Valleys". From them I learned of new footpaths and bluebell woods.

It seems that when the four hundred-year-old Radyr Farmhouse was being renovated, a forty foot deep well containing clear water was discovered under a flagstone on the kitchen floor. Handy indeed! I learned, too, of land girls working on these farms during the war, some 'living in' and some in hostels. They had asked to see my WLA medal, having had their curiosity aroused by snippets on TV of their issue. Naturally horses featured in our conversation.

The man of the house capped my story of the seventeen-hand 'Mahogany' who I always had difficulty in persuading to walk past a pub. The hero of his tale emerged nightly from the pub, completely sozzled, climbed into his trap and dozed off while the pony took him home. One night his contemporaries released the motif power from the shafts and replaced him, back to front. I didn't learn which was the more startled when the two came face to face!

Apart from field speedwell the autumnal millet field weeds were not the same as the springtime ones. I saw none of the formerly common sun spurge, but was delighted with the little yellow field pansies. American speedwell *(Veronica peregrina)* with four narrow calyx lobes extending far beyond the flattened, heart-shaped seed capsule, was new to me. Redleg, with water pepper and toad rush dominated the soggier patches.

I was greatly puzzled by the fact that, with so many standing haulms and small discarded piles of threshed grain on the headlands, there was not a single seed-eating bird taking advantage of the bounty. I learned later that wood pigeons and crows had been shot to prevent predation, but where were all the finches, starlings and sparrows? A jay commuted from tree to tree and a buzzard sailed overhead, mewing petulantly, hoping, probably, to drop on mouse, vole or rabbit.

A red admiral butterfly in mint condition was sunning itself, its wings tilted at right angles to the sun's rays, and large whites were on the wing. Still colourful in the hedgerows were bush vetch, tufted vetch and red campion.

I learned that poachers came down from the "Valleys" by car or train, to shoot anything and everything, foxes, rabbits, buzzards and even house cats. They had infra-red lights on their guns for shooting after dark and also used ferrets. Folk walking their dogs could be at risk.

* * *

On 10th October I sneaked out from the north-west corner of Old Radyr along Pant Tawel Lane - half a mile of single track road where two lady dog-walkers had to squeeze back into the hedge to let me pass - as I had three days earlier, when a large van was easing its way down the Radyr Farm bridleway.

This lane led out past the golf course and was the surviving lap of an old farm lane and mule track which crossed the Old Red Sandstone of the southern Border Ridge and continued up over the Carboniferous Limestone of the Little Garth, to emerge near the "King's Arms" in Pentyrch. I followed it on foot today to where the puddled branch track led off westwards past the surfaced lane to the Pent-twyn Garden Centre and on to Craig-y-Parc.

Paths had formerly led in from the Ty Nant Inn opposite Pugh's Garden Centre, along the southern flank of the Little Garth and the grassy track of the Old Barry Railway. Then the motorway came and, later, the great sprawling Radyr Gardens Housing Estate, eating up more of the precious green belt. The Pant Tawel Woods were fenced off from the track, which gave access now only to Coed Cae Fach between motorway and railway and Coed Cae Fawr to the north. (Coed = wood). The now somewhat misnamed Pant Tawel Lane crossed the M4 on a narrow bridge, the tarmac ceasing when it reached the lofty bridge over the abandoned railway, to continue as a deeply rutted track between woodland and hedgerow. The railway had been in a deep cutting here, this part now a linear pond, whose bordering trees, now fully mature, only just reached up to the bridge.

Goods trains had trundled along here from Barry Docks, the lane surfacing eastwards and used as a footpath to where it curved round to tunnel through the Little Garth and cross the Taff Gorge on the lofty viaduct. That remarkable edifice was demolished during the 1970s. I had watched the track being lifted off by helicopter. One of the tall brick piers remains, as a monument to the industrial era.

In 1976 Wimpeys had sought planning permission to dump waste from the new motorway here in the wood - that being the future route for the freight traffic. This was refused, in view of their high amenity value as well as their biodiversity. They are now protected, hopefully in perpetuity. One of the first to have been filled would have been this deep railway cutting, so rich in ferns, mosses and creepers, where I had scrambled around with Dr. June Chatfield of the National Museum, looking for no less than nineteen different species of land molluscs for the museum records.

Red squirrels were seen here right up to 1950, while stoats, weasels, grass snakes, great crested newts, woodcock, woodpeckers and a great wealth of fungi persisted among the swards of wild flowers. Kingcup pools and primrose glades had already been fenced off as a potential dumping site.

When exploring here prior to publishing "The Garth Countryside" in 1999, it was springtime, when the woods were blossoming with bluebells and Anemones, bugle, sanicle and marsh valerian. They seemed very barren now, with little but the leaves of violets and woodland loosestrife on show - but this was mid October and not a fair comparison.

It was many years since any woodland management had been carried out. Open and ivy-floored, it was easy to get around, the impression gained being mainly of moribund, coppiced hazel, the overgrown sprouts rotting in situ and breaking off to lie among fallen birch and ash and nurture common bracket fungi cashing in on the dead and dying. Here were beech blackspot *(Diatrype disciformis)* and one of the mottlegills, *(Panaeolus rickenii)*. Frequent mossy stumps showed where big trees had been felled long since. Some of these were undermined by the burrows of mice or voles, and strewn with empty nut shells and partly chewed berries. Moles were present, throwing up mounds of reddish clay soil from the Glacial Drift and Lower Old Red Sandstone Marls which underlay the soggy black leaf mould.

A few fine beeches remained on the triangular moss-clad island where streams converged at the divergence of the two tracks. Other arboreal specialities were deformed specimens in the bordering hedgerow, rather than thriving timber trees. Hollies in the understorey bore white flower buds contemporary with berries left over from 2007.

I heard not a single bird and the nearest I got to green or spotted woodpeckers, was the sight of odd hazel nuts wedged in crevices for ease of hammering. It was not until I got back to the spreading yards and gardens of the house near the motorway bridge, that I encountered a robin and a busy flock of long-tailed tits.

This was a slack season in the bird world away from the shores and estuaries where waders and wildfowl were flocking in from the north. Skies that had been full of swifts and hirundines were now empty apart from the odd circling buzzard and the inevitable crows and pigeons. First the swifts had left, then the swallows, after gathering on telegraph wires waiting for a propitious spell of weather in which to set out on their great twice yearly adventure. Now the last of the house martins would be on their way south, trekking back down the Taff flyway, that they had used so optimistically in the spring - hoping for a better summer than the one they had been served.

I was waylaid on the last lap by the house owner, who was out with his slasher clearing brambles There followed an interesting chat, as so often in out-of-the-way places where every person is an individual instead of an anonymous member of a crowd. He was the sixth generation of his family who had lived here, so his ancestors in this apparently remote corner of overgrown countryside had suffered the rumbling of the railway, as he was now suffering the rumbling of the motorway. This, sadly, is an all too common aggravation in poor, overcrowded little Britain.

I commented on an adjoining field, as neglected as the wood, and two thirds overgrown with bracken and brambles. Apparently that was a bog - probably harbouring interesting plants - as was some of the low-lying land now occupied by a stretch of the M4. He used to collect pheasants' eggs there, taking six and leaving six. He also gathered mushrooms, but not this year, which was a poor one for fungi generally. They mostly prefer a warmer summer in which to sporulate than the one which they had endured.

Foxes he shot, although he no longer kept poultry, regarding most as mangy. He maintained, rightly or wrongly, that the hunts only caught the sick and mangy ones, the others being spry enough to get away. I had heard the same in Gwaelod, where locals were aware that the two Garth hills were riddled with holes and that the foxes knew them all!

Returning from my random stroll by the path (an improvised one above the original sunken lane which was partially under water) I saw notices "Shooting in Progress". Fortunately it wasn't, but it might explain the ten foot high fine-mesh, black net stretched between trunks, which I had only spotted because fugitive rays of sunshine penetrating the canopy, had glinted on the meshes, making it look like a giant spider's web, Amazon-Forest style.

I assumed this was to catch birds, but it was certainly not a bird ringer's pocketed mist net. Mammals would be likely to run along the base to the open ends and escape. Not so. I learned that the wood was used for rival gangs to shoot coloured paint balls at each other, something I had seen depicted on TV, so quite credible. The lady at Ty Gwyn Farm told me subsequently that one of her pony trekking girls had won the prize ticket for thirty to join a paint balling session. Girls and parents complied, emerging, apparently, covered with bruises as well as paint where balls had found their mark.

Ron of Pant Tawel, a retired engineer, ran his vehicles solely on bio-fuel and used oil, which he filtered, these obtained from West Wales and stored in tanks on the premises, where he parked his boats and grew exotic plants - Cordylines, monkey puzzles, oranges, pomegranates olives and conifers obtained from Ireland. He was just off to Spain to collect more, to furnish a monster glass-house which was to rise in the woods behind the house. A landing field for a private aircraft was also on his agenda......!

Not far from Pant Tawel Lane on the way out, I followed another, almost as long, the Golf Club lane, fortunately meeting the car coming in the opposite direction at one of the few passing places. This brought me onto the Llantrisant Road at Ty Gwyn Farm, which I had been trying to locate, to ask about the recently discovered millet crops.

* * *

By midday on 11th of October, I was in Walterston again, with a number of others, helping Joan Raum to celebrate her eightieth birthday and meet old friends from a past life. On such a day of peerless sunshine, it was inevitable that we should drift outside after the repast and the cutting of the cake. So powerful was the unaccustomed sunshine, that we actually sought the shade.

Sarah chortled her approval. Why do we always laugh when a donkey brays? It is their main way of expressing themselves, particularly for a herd animal deprived of company of its own kind. No advance had been made in the thatching of the house across the road, which had been started back in May, when there was more weather such as this.

On the way home I stopped at Peterstone-super-Ely to imbibe some of the unaccustomed warmth, embellished with the warm tints of autumn. The first lap between foot bridge and road bridge brought me past a fisherman casting his line from the shallows and catching nothing, but able to enjoy the general ambience of the sparkling waters of the Ely. This was ample compensation, and maybe what he had come for. I saw no fish in the knee-deep water below during a long lean over the footbridge railings.

Mayflies, also known as dayflies, were still on the wing here, wafting to and fro immediately below. No doubt the fisherman was trying to delude the trout or grayling into thinking there were more, the choicest of these on the end of his line. Despite the name, these elegant flies, with three tail prongs as long as themselves, can be found in all but the coldest months - different species maturing in sequence.

Sunlight scintillated on their obliquely held wings, which cannot be folded, but close together over their backs when at rest. Their lives as adults are brief and involve no feeding. The underwater sojourn as well camouflaged nymphs, can last anything from two months to two years, the shorter-lived species having two generations a year.

After as many as twenty seven instars or skin changes as they grow, the nymphs surface, to split open and allow the winged insect to emerge. Opaque wings expand immediately and the dull brown insect, known to anglers as the dun, flies off to skulk under leaves on the bank. Unique among insects, there are two 'emergences'. The dun is the sub-imago, not yet the perfect insect. With scant delay, it undergoes another moult to a second flying stage, the sexually mature imago, brighter bodied than the dun and with translucent wings.

These live but a few days, the reason why the group is called the Ephemeroptera. They are ephemeral indeed, at least at this stage. It is as well for the fish that rise to feed on them and the anglers who cast their lines to lure them, that there are so many 'hatches' throughout the warmer months. When the real McCoy is not present, the men fashion inedible 'flies' to resemble them and hopefully delude their prey.

Instinctively I felt that the hurrying river was heading the wrong way here, until realising that its ultimate destination on the coast in Cardiff bay was east rather than south. Its wiggly upstream passage across the Peterstone Moors past Pendoylan, swung sharply around hereabouts to head north-east to St. Georges, then swoop south and north again to St. Fagans. From here it set off east and south towards the now canalised stretch which replaced its former meanderings over the Penarth Moors, to release it more tidily into Cardiff Bay.

Lingering to identify a singing bird, just a robin, in an oak, I noticed that the leaves of the tree were either green or brown with fewer of the usual intermediate phases of withdrawal of pigments prior to leaf fall. The brown ones proved to be heavily infested with attractive silk bobbin galls or silk button spangles. These millimetre wide discs with apical dents were caused by Cynipid gall wasps *(Neuroterus numisalis),* related to those causing the flattened, centrally attached spangle galls with apical peak. Seldom had I seen such a heavy infection.

Past the road bridge I turned right, peering through the undergrowth at the neglected pond alongside. The old riverside path had been blocked by tall iron gates. Walkers were now directed through a kissing gate to a well trodden path across fields owned by the National Trust.

It was not until the third or fourth field that this path returned to the riverside and the monkshood *(Aconitum anglicum)* that is the Ely's main claim to botanical fame. Its eye-catching dark blue flowers are at odds with its internal poisons, which could prove lethal to livestock. I remembered them here as being usually out of reach of the cattle beyond a substantial fringe of Himalayan balsam. This species is specific to Britain, flowering several months earlier than the ones commonly grown in gardens.

An information board informed walkers that they were entering the Lanlay Rhos Pastures - wet, lowland grassland, which nurtured wild orchids and devil's bit scabious, the food plant of caterpillars of the rare marsh fritillary butterflies that lepidopterists were trying diligently to sponsor in such habitats.

The only butterflies seen today, both here and at Walterston, were red admirals in pristine condition, although so late in the season. Would they stay to pass the winter here? Their usual counterparts, the painted ladies had been exceptionally rare this year. Bees were as busy as ever in the Himalayan balsam flowers and smaller fry mingled with the mayflies. Was this "the last of the summer wine" for them or would the subsequent flowering of ivy delay their ultimate decease?

Rough grass in the meadows had thickened up since the summer grazing by ponies, some of the sprouting grasses 'presenting pollen' long after the hay fever season which TV weathermen warned us about during the summer months.

An antediluvian pedunculate oak was some eight feet across the bole where it forked into two massive trunks and one lesser one. Lumpy brackets, probably *Trametes gibbosa*, were bursting from deep furrows in the bark. The long-stalked acorns were brown and small, but held in green acorn cups still on the twigs, and ready to topple out at a touch.

Far more numerous on the ground under the canopy were bud galls (*Andricus fecundator*). These formed spherical leafy cones, the size of a finger tip, the overlapping scales dry and chaffy but the cones intact. A few of the hard, better-known brown marble galls were attached to low twigs, these caused by *Andricus kollari*. Some had been ripped open by birds extricating the grub from the central chamber. Others showed tiny round holes through which the inmates had left as adult wasps. Tits can be seen tapping at those. If the sound indicates hollowness, they do not bother to excavate

A mixed flock of tits, including long-taileds, was busy in the tall hedgerows, which harboured wrens as well as jackdaws, magpies and wood pigeons. Bushes bore bumper crops of haws, hanging on whether the leaves had fallen or not. Dog rose hips appeared at one place at least fifteen feet up in a supporting tree and there were red holly berries, spurned throughout the summer season and soon to be joined by the new crop. Sloes were few, blackberries abundant but the elderberries all gone.

Two fields, one cut for hay, were separated by a burbling stream crossed by stepping stones. Hemp agrimony was still flowering among meadowsweet laden with pale green fruitlets and supporting meshes of tufted vetch. Creeping Jenny trailed down a grassy tump to be caught in the flow and brooklime was advancing into the crystal shallows.

Loath to leave the unaccustomed sunshine, I returned along the further side of the Ely from the road bridge and strolled up the magnificent avenue of horse chestnuts behind which the 'desirable residences' had been built. The trees must have been here long before the houses. A notice announced imminent closure of the road for tree felling, so it seemed some of their alloted spans must be coming to an end. There was no shortage of conkers beneath, but I saw no signs of squirrel nibbling.

CHAPTER 45

The Salmon Run, Llandaff Weir, Roath Gardens and Lake

During the second week of October news filtered through that the salmon had begun their annual run up the Taff to spawn, so I hied me to Radyr Weir on sunday the twelfth to see what was afoot. I was not the only one. The sun was shining and families were out in force on the Taff Trail, afoot or awheel.

The fish were there alright, and pitting their muscles against the frothing flood, but none were seen to make it to the top. Many were too small, others larger, up to eighteen inches, but not as big as those appearing on fishmomgers' slabs

Most had chosen a section of the weir with a slightly easier gradient, offset a little from the west bank. The biggest often got about half way up before sliding back or being washed over the edge of the ramp into the main stream. Some jumped from too far back and missed the ramp altogether. Most had a few moments of stillness on landing, as they gathered themselves before weaving frantically from side to side to breast the current. It was evident that the water was too shallow on this particular slope for them to get any purchase on it, at least half their muscular contortions being wasted on thin air.

Some tackled the main fall where the water was deeper but did no better. None were seen to enter the narrow maelstrom under the eastern bank or the salmon pass, where water raced through below the grating under our feet. These opened out at river level, so there was no need to jump and there was so much froth and bubble that we wouldn't have seen any going in anyway. This watery passage was not always an open throughway. At certain times fish migrating up to the gravel redds for spawning were waylaid at the top for tagging, but probably not on a Sunday afternoon.

It was fascinating to watch the energy expended, but sad to see no successful passages. The little people watching today with their Mums and Dads were not getting the thrill that my brother and I had when we first watched salmon running the smaller but more turbulent Pot of Gartness on a Scottish holiday. A photographer acquaintance turned up with a telephoto lens at least two feet long and four inches across - a weight almost impossible to hold at the ready without the elbow rest provided by the safety railings. I hope he got some results.

Almost throughout my vigil a patient heron was tucked in against the junction of weir and wall opposite undergoing his own. Headed downstream, statuesque in his tense concentration, his gaze was on what was coming up, but the only fish we saw were much too big to slide down that slender neck. None of the resident young fish of suitable heron fodder size were seen to have joined the hopefuls surging up from their long sojourn at sea. Finally the sentinel heron tired and took off to perch on the fence alongside the railway line, to relax and stretch his wings before being put up by an oncoming "Valley Sprinter" train.

At that point four single-man kayaks appeared on the still water ponded back above the weir, their occupants in crash helmets and life jackets and 'buttoned in' with a waterproof joint. A cursory look over the brink and they backed off, to come shooting the rapids, one at a time. It looked tame compared with white water rafting, but they whooped as they tilted over the edge and disappeared briefly in a flurry of spray at the bottom. Fortunately, unlike the debris travelling downstream during the floods, they were not caught up to bob around permanently in the undertow.

On the walk back a whim took me down one of the narrow tracks to the river's edge. Two brilliant flashes of orange and blue shot by, quite close, to speed up river to perch. This was possibly my best view of kingfishers to date. How lucky can one get?

* * *

Any fish reaching Radyr Weir had already succeeded in negotiating Blackweir and Llandaff Weir downstream. Perhaps they had achieved this during the floods, when water was at more suitable depth. Further investigation into this exciting annual phenomenon was called for. I made two subsequent visits to Llandaff, a longer weir, not only on a wider stretch of the Taff but crossing it obliquely. I saw no jumping fish.

Ask those who know about these things when the annual salmon run is due and the answer was usually something like "Any time from August to December, or even later." It depended on the level and force of the water rather than the calendar. No riverside walk, however, is without interest. I kept to the eastern bank both times, being more familiar with the other. Both had good paths alongside. The Taff Trail and the Three Castles Cycleway followed the eastern, Gabalfa, flank of the river. This took cyclists from Cardiff Castle, past Castell Coch to Caerphilly Castle, with its famous leaning tower, or on up to the Brecon Beacons.

For the upper stretch I started from Danescourt, crossed the Llandaff North Bridge and followed the river from the playing fields of Glyntaff High School. As on the Home Stretch, there were fine black poplars here, but seven of them had recently been beheaded, at three to four times higher than the normal pollard. Six had responded by producing great mopheads of new branches from the truncated summit. The seventh had managed to achieve only side sprouts from the lower trunk.

The mighty lopped trunks lay along both sides of the path, most swallowed from sight by subsequent growths of Japanese knotweed. One, kept clear of undergrowth as a seat, supported a colony of a hundred or so tiny elf-cap fungi, fawn above, with white gills changing to black. These were fairies' bonnets or trooping crumble *(Coprinus disseminatus)*. Although belonging to the Inkcap group of toadstools, they do not deliquesce into black, ink-like fluid after maturity as most of those do.

Just downstream of the bridge is a considerable spread of tall, broad-leaved bamboo by the river. Colonies of such plants tend to mature and flower simultaneously and then die, endangering the World Wildlife logo of the giant panda, if these happen to be dependent on it. I have seen this happen (not the pandas) in the Tongwynlais Woods, but not here. A smaller clump of narrower-leaved bamboos persists closer to the weir alongside purple-stemmed dogwood.

The plant speciality here is the Himalayan knotweed *(Persicaria wallichii,* formerly *Polygonum polystachium)*. Unlike its relative, the Japanese knotweed, and its compatriot, the Himlayan balsam, this is not a pernicious weed, but the most flambuoyant of these 'strangers-on-the-shore'. It is an attractive, shoulder-high shrub, producing a veritable counterpane of feathery white flower sprays - from July to October. It was at prime here, along a considerable stretch of bank, excluding all else, including its much maligned relative, which can hold its own against almost anything.

On a part of this stretch the shrubs also lined the other side of the path, but I have seldom seen it elsewhere. The red-veined leaves are long and soft, like those of the unrelated balsam or the docks of its own family. The white flowers grow on terminal sprays, not on short, individual stems by each heart-shaped leaf, as in the related Japweed. Most of those had now fallen, leaving a ragged collection of dangling, triangular, three-winged fruitlets. Said to be a shy flowerer, it is certainly not that here, and can be relied on year by year to brighten the October riverside.

One saving grace of the much reviled Japanese knotweed is its autumn colouration - much of the foliage currently a bright yellow. Nevertheless, it is an undoubted problem plant. Scientists have been testing a species of Psyllid from Japan for several years and have not found the insects to attack any other plant species, so they may have the answer to keeping it in check by biological control.

* * *

Llandaff Weir is fenced off from the path by iron railings around two alcoves furnished with sitting-out benches, where the falling water is concealed from view by trees, but the din makes conversation impossible. The first is a safety measure, the second not a little odd, as there are no benches from which the fine spectacle of falling water can be seen.

Approach is allowed below the weir beside a wooded gully, to view the flat, water-smoothed slabs of red Triassic Breccia or Radyr Stone. This is the rock responsible for the siting of the weir during the initial gathering together of the flood waters that had formerly spilled willy nilly over the river flats downstream.

It projects from the steep, river-cut escarpment which rises on the opposite bank from the cathedral at river level to the Cathedral Green and residences high above. The leat taking water from that (western) end of the weir to a mill which formerly stood where Western (Eastern) Avenue now runs, flowed along the base of this old, river-cut bluff. The east bank of the river upstream, from Llandaff North Bridge, the oblique weir and the old leat form a straight line, while the river bank swings briefly northwards before resuming its general west to east trend.

At the weir the rock is only a few feet thick and appears as shallow shelves protruding from the bank, the softer, marlier layers eroded from beneath and between. Silt and clay gets washed away, leaving beaches of pebbles loosened from the disintegrating breccia (the 'raisins' from the 'pudding-stone'). Some are stained red with ferric iron. Their corners are smoothed off, but they have not been there long enough to have become rounded river cobbles. A few fossil corals occur.

Water is diverted from a small central section of the river by a low wall, leaving a short stretch of turbulence on my side, where a small fish pass covered with an iron grating had been installed. This rose at a low angle and carried only a small amount of water at present - obviously too little for mature salmon.

* * *

The wall above the dry stretch was being used by a heron and a cormorant, both headed upstream to see if anything of interest was being washed down. A few gulls were also on the lookout from the watery brink further along, until displaced by a low-flying cormorant. Mallard dabbled below my feet on a patch of water crowfoot clinging grimly to a rock slab in the fierce current.

That this had been a deal faster recently was shown by the osiers on the spreading gravel islands below the falls. All the larger bushes leaned downstream at an angle of more than forty five degrees and had flood debris caught in branches that would have been eight or nine feet up if they had been erect. Eroded faces of the brink on which I stood were of vulnerable river silt and pebbles, these stabilised in most parts by low bramble and alder, with flowering evening primroses wild turnip and a little dovesfoot cranesbill.

No salmon put in an appearance on either visit and the wind was too chilly on both to hang about, awaiting their pleasure. From here down, the river is separated from Gabalfa's roads and houses by a broad grassy strip, with the flood embankment on the side further from the water. A narrow footpath along the brink supplemented the tarmac of the Taff Trail.

This was a pleasant stretch, with several little spinneys and some giant trees. A lime with a great fuzz of twigs as big as a house formed a spinney in its own right, with others availing themselves of its shade. Additional veterans were oak, sycamore and Norway maple, leaves of the last two turning a glowing autumnal red.

A sweet chestnut tree had been lopped at a considerable height above the ground. All that was left, the bare trunk and a few branches, were soldiering on, with tufts of leaves on two upper boughs and a big bunch sprouting from the lower trunk. A line of small poplars had been planted as replacements.

The chestnut was host to a colony of sulphur tuft toadstools, but the prize fungus was found by peering between two logs lying parallel in the lee of a bramble clump. This was oyster fungus or oyster-of-the-woods (*Pleurotus ostreatus*). Excentric, shell-shaped toadstools, with wavy edges, these were up to four inches across the blue-grey caps and with snowy white gills below. Stipes emerging from vertical surfaces curved around to orientate the sporing bodies horizontally.

Most of those cosily hidden between the two logs had been seriously nibbled, whereas clumps on the outer face of the further log were in mint condition. This suggested small mammals as the culprits, the space too confined for most birds other than wrens, and with no slime trails of slugs or snails which, as night feeders, would not be so selective as to their dining site. Oyster fungi are prized as human food, but I do not ventuure far from the mundane in this gastronomic field.

A blackbird was tucking into the blackberries in the adjacent thicket and I was able to watch a couple of uncommon coal tits finding minutiae among the boughs of a crack willow. A jay flapped across the path, flaunting his diagnostic white rump and attractive pink and blue plumage.

I dallied awhile watching a lone mute swan and bevy of ducks just under the bank, headed upstream and dipping their necks to reach provender below. Birds have no teeth and I was intrigued to see the swan opening and closing his beak two or three times after each emergence, as though chewing, but presumably gulping each find down into his crop. He drifted with the current while the long neck was below water, but paddled back to his chosen spot each time, so there must have been something good there - and out of reach of the upending mallard.

I watched the same sort of behaviour a week later on Roath Lake. The bird was a young coot, close enough for me to see that, with each gulp, he was progressively hauling a long strand of filamentous algae up from the depths - to which he was able to dive, unlike the dabbling ducks and swan.

Something, probably a dog, had partially excavated a series of burrows constructed just under the turf quite close to the river bank. Their diameter suggested that the builder was a rat - animals which abound in our modern, throw-away world, particularly alongside such an efficient delivery system as the water swirling those bags and bundles, not all of them empty, down from the "Valleys".

The Taff Trail continues downstream under the Western Avenue Road bridge with steps leading up to nearby houses. On my first visit I turned back here, into the eye-watering gale, which belied the beauty of the billowing satinny-white clouds piled in a flawless azure sky. When still a quarter of a mile from the car, I saw the deluge approaching, but was drenched by the time I gained its shelter, and I was steamed up all the way back.

* * *

The forecast and the brilliant dawn on 18th October were a delusion. Rolling purple mounds of liquid were being chased round the sky by gusting winds. Coats off, coats on, umbrellas up or not, or left in the car after believing too trustingly in those holiday postcard skies.

It was the Roath Corridor in Carfdiff's northern heart that drew me out today, the brook-bordered Playing Fields, Pleasure Gardens, Ornamental Gardens and Boating Lake. I parked in Alder Road near the southern end next to a mobile kitchen selling "Mediterranean snacks" and smelling of vinegar and exotic herbs.

Roath Brook threads through the whole complex and is the best known tributary of the River Rhymney which flows into the Severn Estuary three to four miles up-channel from Cardiff's other two rivers. Entering the playing fields from the north-west corner, it struggles across their end, choked almost to death by advancing great bur-reed, hemlock water dropwort and nettles.

The bridge where it bends to flow along the eastern margin as an open, sequestered waterway under tall trees, was being renovated. Some half dozen sinister notices warned the public -and the workmen- of the dreadful things that might happen if they ventured within that tiny plot of bricks and wet concrete and six inch deep water. The 'Nanny State' was taking no chances, despite the unscalable barriers barring trespassers.

Around the corner the double avenue of bordering trees quelled the riotous plant invaders, leaving the sparkling waters as the dominion of flowing water-weeds, whose delicate leaves belied the tensile strength in the sinuous stems that would not let them go.

This side of Alder Road was bordered by clustered horse chestnut trees, great of stature, with largely green instead of autumn-browned leaves like most others, but to all intents and purposes quite devoid of fruit. Gazing upwards until the crick in my neck put a stop to it, I could see not a single chestnut bur. Nor were there any burs or nuts on the grass beneath.

The trees flowered prolifically each spring and the mightiest among them, which had been sawn off just above ground level, had continued to thrust out chunky twigs topped by the sticky buds beloved by children, long after they should have succumbed to the hard shelves of black and white fungi embracing their trunks. The fungi remained, but the stumps had given up at last.

* * *

Crossing the road into the Pleasure Gardens, I was impressed by the extensive bed of bright orange Chinese lanterns or Cape gooseberries. Mother used to grow these seventy or eighty years ago, maintaining that they were aggressive weeds, although enjoying them as dried winter decorations, but they seemed to have gone out of fashion now. When I asked for gooseberries in West Australian green grocers' shops I was more likely to be offered the little orange balls from the interiors of the airy lanterns than gooseberries as we Pommies know them.

Other colours defying the onset of winter here were supplied by head-high sunflowers, branching mullein, purple Verbena, pink yarrow and crimson Fuchsia, which has a prodigiously long flowering season. A few dry, bell-shaped flower husks clung to the great spikes of Yucca. These may have contained fruit, but viable seeds were unlikely. Yucca has a unique type of pollination. The female Yucca moth *(Pronuba yuccasella)* collects pollen grains, rolls them into a ball, stuffs the ball into the end of the hollow stigma and then lays her eggs in the ovary. The transported pollen fertilises the eggs, some of which are eaten by the larvae and others produce seeds, to the mutual benefit of both. This, of course, is in its native America. It is doubtful if the moth exists here.

This garden lies just south of the overhead crossing of Eastern Avenue - the old A 48 to West Wales which becomes Western Avenue beyond its half way point. It embraces tennis courts, two bowling greens and a netball court, in addition to well stocked flower beds and a wondrous cohort of exotic trees.

Here are giant tulip trees, giant Sequoias, American oaks with giant leaves, dawn redwoods and furry-budded Magnolias. Liquidamber and the maples, including the ginger-trunked paper bark maple, were taking on their brilliant autumn colours. A few of the veterans I had known in the past had been given the chop, replacement trees, such as a perky young monkey puzzle, many years away as yet from filling the gaps.

I followed the brook for a while, spotting a few fat carp, almost as big as herrings. These were allowing themselves to be drifted downstream, unlike trout, which like to head upstream, not only to maintain their position but to snap up any goodies that might drift their way.

On my return I followed the western side, where the large summer 'show beds' carved from the lawns under planes and other big trees had been freshly dug and raked. Where planting had begun, Primulas and button daisies loomed large, although some of this season's Primulas were still in full bloom

The rain began as I crossed the main road to visit Roath Gardens proper. I hurried under the Eastern Avenue bridge and into the handy main entrance, with a view to taking shelter in the Conservatory. But no. The bridge over the brook here was also fenced off for repairs, and there was not another until a long way upstream. Fortunately it was only a shower.

As always, I had to stop and admire the great grandfather specimen of giant Sequoia variety pendula, leaning on its supports alongside and across the path. A new bridge had been constructed to carry it across. The frame was of metal this time, with a height warning on it and a padlock which could be released to allow the barrier to be lifted for tall park vehicles to pass. I did not linger by the famous osage orange tree or other attractions, as I intended circum-navigating the lake upstream, adding an extra mile to my amble.

* * *

The bedding-plant troughs set along the promenade occupying the dam which holds the water back were empty, stripped and raked over between the autumn and spring displays. Activity was centred around the water fowl. This was saturday morning and a high proportion of the duck feeders were fathers with toddlers. I could picture the Mums, at work all week, either out buying victuals or cleaning and cooking at home. Sunday afternoons saw bevies of strolling pensioners. Young couples made free of the facilities at any time.

It is said that too much white bread is bad for water fowl but they don't know this. Some dads had brought whole sliced loaves for their offspring to distribute to the feathered throng. Three slices, aligned along the brink of the dam, had excluded all but pigeons, which averaged about ten per slice, bumping heads in the middle as they dipped into the proferred bounty. Gulls might have joined in, but were less confident in such a confined space.

The mob below consisted largely of mute swans, mallard and coot. There were white geese, grey geese, Brent geese and Canada geese, but none of the knob-billed Chinese geese that used to feature here. An Australian black swan stood aloof, preening and displaying the large white patch that normally shows only in flight. The only legitimate duck species seen apart from the plebs were tufted and muscovy, but there were plenty of unofficial patterns arising from illegitimate matings.

So many webbed feet had puddled stretches of lawn into liquid mud like oxtail soup. Swans and snow geese, after long and careful preening of pristine white feathers, would snuggle down into this and tuck heads under wings in sleep, instead of tip-toeing out to a nice clean bed on the smooth, rain-washed turf alongside! I compared unwebbed feet, wondering how moorhens managed to swim as competently as they do, although lacking the useful lobes along the spreading toes of the coot. I was able to compare these organs of locomotion on two birds perching on the half submerged trunk of a mature white poplar fallen into the water - new furnishings much favoured by preening mallard.

A coot had built itself a nest as blatantly conspicuous as those of moorhens so often are. This was balanced on under-water branches dipping down from an island evergreen. Two herons were hunched together, dozing, on a low tree bough and another flew into the treetops on the main island to join the cormorants.

Rounding the head of the lake by the Wild Garden, I was watching the antics of a jay, when two tiny birds left the island sanctuary and settled in the larch under which I stood. Smaller than tits, they were goldcrests, and as confiding as always. Maybe they think they are so small that humans fail to notice them. This is true of most humans anyway. They are always delightful with their red and gold crowns and yellow wing bars.

Almost every one of the blue and white floats supporting the barrier delimiting the nesting area was occupied by black-headed gulls. The larger gulls seemed not to be attracted, being more likely to join the scrum where largess was being distributed. Coarse fishing is permitted and I was interested to see a new style in fishermen's bivouacs. This was a tent and yet not a tent, rather an oversized, camouflaged umbrella lodged obliquely, with curtains of similar material pegged out from both sides to combat wind and rain.

A beheaded weeping willow on the west shore had produced a new crop of branches, as incapable of supporting themselves as the ones that had been lost, the elegant new dangles as attractive as before. Two-inch long pollen-bearing catkins stood erect on an adjacent, tapering cedar tree with all the branch tips directed skywards. This simulated a giant Christmas tree adorned with yellow candles, each rising from a neat rosette of needle leaves. It would not have found favour as indoor decoration, however, every slightest puff of wind broadcasting clouds of bright yellow pollen.

It was gratifying to see this, because the finest cedar of them all, alongside the 'Smokebush Garden' by Lake Road West, had been brutally felled, its massive, unadorned trunk rising like a naked, overgrown statue east of the main path. This mighty tree had been a fast-growing Atlas cedar, bigger than the three hundred-year-old oak nearby. It had been puffing out similar pollen clouds in November 2004 from among a bumper crop of cones, which were models of symmetry. How had so noble a tree lost favour with those who tended it? Only one specimen of the lush Fatsia bushes that had grown gratefully in its shade remained on the wilderness of scraped peat around its denuded trunk.

Returning down the western side of the gardens, the prize exhibit was one of the clumps of butchers broom, the flattened leaf-like evergreen stems covered with fat scarlet berries. Most colourful were the beds of tall Michaelmas daisies and there were still plenty of blooms in the rose garden.

Glowering purple storm clouds were travelling across the eastern horizon on the last lap, but I made it in the dry. A session with fellow resident, Pansy, planting tulip and narcissus bulbs after late lunch was also achieved in the dry.

* * *

I came to Roath Gardens again with Madeleine a few days later, on 30th October, after our first serious frost. All colour had gone from the Michaelmas daisies, but a similar hue was manifested in the clusters of pill-like mauve fruits of the beauty-berry bush *(Callicarpa bodinieri)* among the last of its pink and yellow leaves. An uncommon beauty, aptly named, I saw this again a week later at Slimbridge, but recalled meeting it only once elsewhere, at Westonbirt Arboretum.

All the blooms had been snuffed out in the Rose Garden, but the first lone Magnolia flower had opened to make amends. The fine display of New Zealand and other exotic shrubs had been removed from the little side garden and replaced with an oval lawn, but the autumn colours in the Acer Garden, which we had come especially to see, were fully up to expectations. The plant troughs along the dam had been set out with fat, purple-tinged

Hyacinth bulbs and button daisy plants to greet the Spring.

We left this time to the North, calling in at Lisvane Reservoir to see if any migratory wildfowl had arrived on the wings of the gale. None had, the tufted ducks still countable on the fingers of one hand. Fifteen cormorants were sleepily drying themselves out on a variety of perches.

The chief entertainer was a busily fishing little grebe, ridiculously small in comparision with that Mephistophelian mob. It was good to see the Mexican fleabane lining of the upper reservoir walls flowering as exuberantly as it had been during most of the summer - in flagrant defiance of its tropical desert origin.

Ascending a lane to Caerphilly Mountain, we observed the ponies snugly wrapped in their horse blankets. The mountain had adopted the bleak aspect to be expected during the next few months and the tortuous lane winding down past Castell Coch was awash with water, as the bordering stream swished from side to side. It was good to get in out of the cold to our strawberry tea.

CHAPTER 46

Lavernock Point Nature Reserve and Gun Emplacement

I had missed the official 'open day' at the County Trust's Nature Reserve on Lavernock Point earlier in the year, so set off to make amends on 17th October. Quite unknowingly, I had chosen a day when one of the quite frequent work parties of volunteers was helping with tree felling, scrub clearing, path making and other maintenance tasks.

Although in at the beginning of this reserve in the 1960s and 70s, I had been visiting more spasmodically in recent years. There was always something new to see. Run-down farmland at first, it had become scrub, with the backing woodland advancing and gobbling up that all too rare asset of flower-rich cliff grassland. It was a constant battle to keep the advancing ash trees at bay and open out clearings to accommodate the fine collection of wild flowers fighting a losing battle for Lebensraum.

Quite early on, following a period when the reserve was grazed by cattle, John Zehetmeyr, former Forestry Commission Chief in South Wales, had taken on the responsibilities of voluntary warden. His special study, maintained over the years, was of the butterfly populations, and butterflies need flowers. Geoff Curtis, who had recently shown me the floral treasures at Cosmeston, was his faithful henchman and had been with him from the start. He was here today.

John spotted me as I drew the car to a halt, surprised by all the vehicles parked in the approach field. He came out to shepherd me into the least muddy of the laneside slots. One of the two men setting slabs of turf along-

403

side the newly surfaced gateway and track proved to be an ex-student of mine. "A long time ago." It must have been. I had been retired twenty years.

Excusing himself from wielding the hay rake which he carried, on grounds of age (he had clocked up as many years as I had), John became my guide for the morning, delighted to expound on the achievements of years of work, his initial enthusiasm undiminished. As he pointed out what had been removed from where and what the results had been, his dedication was infectious. No wonder he had gathered such a willing band of volunteer helpers. I felt I should take up my old billhook and join in.

Currently half the considerable area of clifftop had become mellowed meadowland, with individual trees and small spinneys trimmed back at regular intervals. The goal was two thirds open land and one third woodland, with paths and stiles. While encouraging the grass to grow under his feet literally, he certainly did not let it do so figuratively.

Although only recently returned from his regular ski-ing trip to the Alps, he was soon off to Egypt. For many years he had been a ski instructor on Cardiff's two practice ski slopes as well as on real snow, but he was thinking of retiring from that 'in view of the steepness of slope involved.' Awarded an OBE for his services to conservation, he was still too young to retire. In his spare time he was writing a history of the early years of the Forestry Commission - in addition to daily attending his sick wife in hospital when not away. In mid December I learned that he had broken a leg. Where but on that practice ski slope? Nine months later he died of natural causes. A life well spent, if ever there was one.

We went first to see the new pond, which was a great success. "The water was flowing in as we were digging it out and it hasn't dried up since." Suspended clay had made it the colour of mulligatawny soup when I had seen it the previous year, but it was now crystal clear with a neat backdrop of bulrushes and Angelica and an open rushy front. The stump of a neighbouring ash had been sawn off at seat level, the edge bevelled for comfort. A fat yellow frog hopped out of the long grass to welcome us.

The reserve's most striking plants were dyers greenweed *(Genista tinctoria)*, non-spiny sub-shrubs which blossomed with sheets of yellow pea flowers in early summer. My only memory of another such colourful display is from the Ynyslas sand dunes in old Cardiganshire (now Ceredigion). Described as "A plant of coastal cliffs in the South-West" this was formerly used as a dye.

Most colourful now, in October, was the devil's-bit scabious *(Succisa pratensis)*, the round blue flower-heads overtopping the sward over much of the area - but with none of the rare marsh fritillary butterfies present to lay their eggs on it.

Others of special merit were the primitive adder's tongue ferns and white butterfly orchids. Relatives such as pyramidal orchids had spread surprising distances. Both primroses and cowslips had benefited greatly from the opening up of the canopy and false oxlip had turned up - a long way from where the two grew together. The pollinator must have been a far-travelled bee.

Delicate flowers of pale flax, a species found especially near the sea, appeared among its own strawey seed heads and the bearded umbels of wild carrot were still flowering, as were leggy spikes of agrimony and the two ox-tongue species. Self heal and meadow buttercups, old die-hards, were still attracting bees, as was the rare saw-wort, a spineless relative of the thistles.

The last were present in abundance, the yellow heads of carline thistles, deep purple florets of marsh thistles and the two specialities. These were nodding or musk thistles, the globose heads tilted to face the ground, and woolly thistle, the largest of them all, the spiny part of the handsome heads spider-webbed, like cobweb-bed houseleeks. All were in the feathered fruiting phase.

The rich seed harvest, contributed to by knapweeds and various yellow Composites, had attracted about fifty greenfinches and a dozen goldfinches. Restless feeders, these kept whirring up and away en masse, circling briefly and then re-settling to tweak out more seed, releasing the thistle down to float off into the balmy air of this perfect, though delayed, summer day.

For other birds there were hips, haws, sloes, dogwood and wild privet berries. A visiting team from the Trust had erected nesting boxes, but these faced into the sun and only one had been occupied, this receiving the unwanted attentions of a marauding green woodpecker.

Crossing a stile, we were in a wood developed from a former hawthorn spinney, both haws and dogwood unduly tall and leggy. Dimly lighted, this was a different world, with polypody and hard ferns. This is where the early purple orchids burgeoned in spring, with well over a hundred spikes in some years, though sometimes fickle in their flowering. These lovely flowers had been an integral part of the Home Counties bluebell woods which I associate with childhood weekends, but it is a high privilege now to see such beauties in our depleted countryside.

Twayblades, less flamboyant orchids, also preferred the deep shade here. This was so deep that the wild madder, that stiff bristly component of the cliff brinks, produced stems and leaves as softly pliable as the related hedge bedstraw and sweet woodruff. Tutsan fruits were subtly changing colour, from yellow, through crimson to black, each neatly cupped in a starry calyx.

* * *

Plant-covered mounds, thrown up by countless colonies of yellow field ants *(Lasius flavus),* had arisen when this ground was permanent pasture. A sure sign, these, that the ground had not been ploughed for decades. They had persisted through the woodland phase and did so still, but there was little sign that they were still inhabited. Some, up to two feet high, had vertical, eroding sides of sticky yellow clay, a product of the Blue Lias rock below and quite unlike the usual dark, powdery soil of occupied anthills with their multiplicity of aerating tunnels.

Decades back, when there was a thriving rabbit population here, the rabbits used to gather on selected mounds to pass the time and exchange pheromones, as is their wont. They left collections of their twice-defecated dung pellets on top, altering the nature of the immediate vegetation, just as the ants themselves were doing. That was a time when the walking-stick-shaped, white-flecked dung pellets of green woodpeckers were common here, discarded by these ground-feeding, tree-dwellers, which had left their calling cards when probing for ants.

We caught up with the work gang at coffee time, when tools could be laid down for a spell. Geoff could abandon his noisy brash-cutter, discard his protective visor - and ear plugs if he wore them. The chain saw was not in use today. When it was John followed up to paint the stumps with a poison that would prevent them from re-sprouting.

The sun smiled down, as on a summer picnic, and I found myself discarding my outer layers of clothing for almost the first time this 'summer'. On along sinuous little paths through different communities, we two came to St. Mary's Well Bay, where a fine view opened out to Sully Island beyond the red rock promontary at Swanbridge. Further along were the three headlands projecting from the Barry complex. Away at sea was the familiar outline of Flatholm Island, which I had not managed to visit even once this year.(There are many long-term Cardiff residents who have never visited it at all!)

Swanbridge Point beyond the bay was thickly wooded with the evergreen holm oaks from the Mediterranean that do so well on the South Wales coast, these fringed with Alexanders around the low cliffs. We both wondered why the big house in their midst, in such a desirable locality, had been allowed to crumble into ruins. We would have expected a long waiting list to buy.

The way down to the beach at the further end displayed a small cliff exposure of black paper shales - Rhaetic rocks between the Red Trias below and the Blue Lias above; but this was not for us. It was quite a scramble down to beach level on our (Lavernock) side of the bay, more difficult now due to sundry crumbling of the rocks than when we were young.

At present that was the only way through for coast walkers because a cliff fall further along had taken away the cliff path outside the fence of the adjacent caravan park. Perhaps someone would move the fence back in due course and re-open it. The yellow sandstone layers were very crumbly here, but I was delighted to spot some of my almost favourite cliff plants (after thrift) on the face. These were rock samphire, bedecked with the reddish purple seed heads which sometimes persist far into the winter and remind me of those of the Sedum ice-plant of gardens. These were dangling rather than erect, due to their instability of tenure, but others such as sea beet and thrift were hanging on alongside.

The tide had retreated far enough to expose the overlapping but almost horizontal wave-smoothed platforms of blue-grey rock. The edges of individual strata, only a few inches high, faced west. A beach walker would step up these in transit while remaining on the level.

Where the soft cliffs had been worn furthest away in the bay centre, there were lines of boulders and pebbles on the shore, sufficiently stable to support colonies of brown seaweeds. Only wracks (Fuci) grew here in abundance, the oarweeds (Laminarians) fading out down channel on the tip of the Witch's Nose at Dunraven. Those deep water species thrive only in saltier waters than these. John remembered the St. Mary's Well Bay beach as sandier than this when he used to come here to bathe with his grandsons. Only gulls were there today, with a raven onshore and none of the expected oyster-catchers.

We took the coast path back through the reserve, where the cliff line slanted north-eastwards, the grassy path separated from the edge by a line of salt-hardy shrubs. This corner, that I remember as a thicket of ash saplings, was now coastal grassland, blue with scabious flowers and a little flax. Ground cover included plenteous salad burnet, the delicate pinnate leaves simulating those of maidenhair ferns and co-habiting with almost equally soft bird's-foot trefoil, meadow vetchling, several vetch species, cinquefoil and rock-rose. I missed the spurge laurel *(Daphne laureola)* that characterises this limey site, but it is still there, flowering in winter.

So, too, were butterflies, attracted first by hemp agrimony but now by ivy. There were several red admirals and a lot of large whites. Two speckled woods came fluttering out into the sunshine, their natal spinney too shady to hold them on such a beautiful autumn day. I spotted a single small tortoise-shell. These were uncommon this year. Apparently many were suffering from a disease. John, more butterfly-minded than most of us, had spotted only one painted lady. A major disaster on their spring migration here from North Africa and the Mediterranean was blamed for their scarcity. More remarkable is that these fragile creatures, or the new generations that they produce en route, ever make that colossal journey at all.

Every cloud has a silver lining, that of the Vanessids being that there had been an abundance of commas this year. Ony a few decades ago these were rare, but there is something in our modern landscapes that suits them. The oakwood across the approach lane is a classic site for purple hairstreaks. As haunters of the treetops, these are probably not as rare as they seem.

A variety of small moths flitted round at grass level and there were still common darter dragonflies around. We saw a red-bodied male and yellow-bodied female flying rings round each other. It was not too late yet. Earlier in October Irene and I had watched a couple laying eggs.

The only fungi seen today, apart from thin brackets, were some delicate, almost evanescent hare's-foot inkcaps *(Coprinus lagopus)*. The ash-grey caps on brittle white stipes were tissue-thin, with the gills showing through. Brittle, and with the remnants of fibrillose rings, they were not deliquescing in true inkcap style.

* * *

Lavernock Point was not only of special wildlife interest and as a once much-used site for bird migration watches. The tangible relics of World War II gunposts were also of national significance. These came under the care of Cadw, which body had a say in how much scrub should or should not be cut to reveal them.

John was knowledgable about this side of the reserve too, having been in the navy during the war, manning and cleaning such guns. A long term resident of Penarth, he had been thrilled when his ship, the "Ulster Queen" put into Penarth for a refit. She had been built to travel back and forth across the Irish Sea, but successfully achieved several voyages to the Far East when called upon to do so in the country's hour of need. Her ex-crewman explained proudly that she was in the forefront of naval radar at that time - something that I, quite coincidentally, caught up with in a small way a few days later in the Sea-Watch Centre, further along the coast. Each relic was explained as we moved back from the western bay.

The building overlooking Sully Bay and the Western Approaches had housed the searchlight, the apparent floor of solid concrete well above ground level. Circular in plan, iron screens, now rusted into immobility, had formerly swivelled around to direct or shade the beam as required.

The main central, circular bunkers, cleared of their masking bramble cover, had housed the low-firing guns, aimed at the enemy ships which never came - as were those of the supplementary gun batteries on Flatholm and Steepholm - all protecting citizens from invaders coming up the Bristol Channel.

All showed narrow gullies that I had assumed were to drain away water. Only now did I learn that these were to house the electric cables that gave life to the equipment. Most of the encrusting yellow stonecrop had been scraped from the bricks and concrete, along with much else, but the huge, red-flowered rambling rose still rambled over the eastern part.

Next along was the anti-aircraft gun emplacement, aiming higher and with targets in plenty. This was in a worse state of preservation. John pointed out a dangerously leaning wall, half hidden in nettles. We can't let students in there now." The platoon was billeted on site and the next large building, walls and roof still intact, seemed to be some sort of a mess hut or billet. John had left me by this time, returning for sandwiches with his work team, so I had to guess.

A certain amount of return fire was suffered and the reserve boasted two extant bomb craters, one dry and pleasantly vegetated, the other a pond. These had been made mostly by the sort of missiles I had met in my land army days - unused bombs jettisoned at random by departing enemy aircraft rather than take them home. Looking back over the years from a United Europe, it all seemed so pointless!

My path out led me along a wall of trees separating the reserve from the Lavernock Holiday Village, a collection of wooden dwellings with little gardens ranged along the cliff edge at the end adjacent to the approach lane. Garden birds commuted back and forth over the barrier, these a mixture of tits, house sparrows and a handsome pair of bullfinches. More significant was the flock of about thirty house martins, twisting and turning overhead as they stocked up with midges to sustain them on their long journey south.

House martins had nested on these cliffs in the 1960s, but probably did so no longer. These would be part of the great autumn migration. The cliff describes a right angle bend here, running due south from Penarth and Cardiff Bay and turning west to Sully Island. Some continued past Barry and Aberthaw to West Wales, others headed straight on to the Somerset Coast, so clearly visible across the Channel on a day such as this. Migrating flocks taking off across the water sometimes plumped down on the Holms for extra sustenance en route.

During the 1960s and 70s migration watches were carried out regularly here. A late September count clocked up nearly four thousand birds flying out from Lavernock Point during an eleven hour watch. Warblers, swifts and others had gone long since. Those were thrushes, finches, larks, pipits and countless others. We were more than half way through October now and these were likely to be among the last batches to leave.

* * *

Rather than return straight away, I walked on down the lane to the sea. One of the paddocks opposite accommodated a herd of Welsh cobs. Five were piebald, including a small foal, and with them a bay and a black. 'Lucky' black and white horses are not common, but I came on another group of five a few days later at Miskin.

Beyond the farm at the lane's end was a little grey church. A plaque in the wall commemorated Marconi's first successful transmission of radio waves over water - to Flatholm Island. Three large residences had been built recently, Church House, Church Side House and Lavernock House, two protected by electronically manipulated iron gates.

Four sea anglers were assembling their equipment and donning their gear by the boot of their parked vehicle. I asked what they hoped to catch. "Whiting, probably. Cod if we're lucky." A narrow track led steeply down to the beach here, where the cliff dipped almost to sea level, although there seemed to be no stream to have formed the valley. Maybe its waters had been swallowed up further back.

A brief visit to the shore and then I followed the cliff path a little way to the north. The cliff-line was unbroken here, right to Penarth. On a little knob was another war-time relic. This, a neatly rounded stone turret, had the door missing, but looked as though it had only recently been abandoned, with electric wires and bits of apparatus dangling from the walls and in a small fixed cabinet.

Clouds had swallowed up the sun by now and it was quite chilly. Much of the view to the islands was blocked by the line of bushes along the brink, so I did not go far. Long past my usual lunch time, I called into Cosmeston Country park for fish and chips and a spell of fraternising with the big herd of at least sixty swans and other water fowl, possibly as many as at Roath lake and no more backward in pushing forward for victuals. There were almost as many coot and mallard, but only Canada geese and few tufted ducks.

One family of five grown cygnets dabbled in the embayments by the board walk. Another was on its own among adults near the seat where I sat watching the feeding scrum. This loner was always too late to win a prize. When one of his elders flung a whole slice of bread into my lap with a flick of the bill, I was able to apportion this out so that the learner got his fair share.

I was kept entertained by three elderly gentlemen sailing their model yacht, by electronic control. It was carefully carried down in a small crate like a mini ironing board, tall enough to accommodate the deep keel. The remote control reached it afar off. When I couldn't see the vessel for trees, I knew where it was by the orientation of the three grey heads. Some of us oldies never grow up.

A day or so later I had a phone call from John inviting me to dinner to view the local coastline from his new eyrie in Upper Penarth. My last visit was about forty years back when his delightful garden in Augusta Road, Lower Penarth, was open to the public for charity. That was in daffodil time. I remember it still.

CHAPTER 47

Boverton, Summerhouse Point Iron Age Fort, Limperts Bay and Sea Watch Centre

On 22nd of October another such summer day dawned and I sped off early to enjoy it on the coast. I was headed for Summerhouse Point at Boverton, following lesser roads through Miskin, Pontyclun, Ystrad Owen and Cowbridge. Slightly phased by the big new main road slashing across the Southern Vale, I extricated myself from the intricacies of Llantwit Major and reached the ivy-clad ruins of Boverton Manor - the subject of one of my early monochrome sketches. The great pall of sea mist rolling lazily over the Channel, lifted in minutes, absorbed by the sun-warmed air.

Two miles of narrow lane led obliquely south-east to Summerhouse Point, a point now in no more than name, because of loss of part of the erodible cliffs to the sea. In this it resembles Stout Point and Pigeon Point to the west, but Col Hugh Point, reached from Llantwit Major, involves no cliffs, being the broad, stony delta of the partially infilled Col Huw Valley, extending out into the channel.

Half way along the lane is Boverton Mill Farm, formerly one of the Prince of Wales model farms, which he had sold about nine years before. Building works were in progress at present, the final touches of a roof going on to a neatly pointed grey stone building with extensive glass walls, suggesting more than a normal residence.

I remembered going round the Boverton Farmyard and Greenhouses in past years, when this embraced a major market garden enterprise run by the Duchy of Cornwall, growing tomatoes and a wide range of vegetables as well as field crops.

Now all the flat land extending seawards was devoted to cereals, big fields bearing crops of wheat and barley and all harvested successfully if the neatly severed rows of stubble were anything to go by. Oil seed rape had been incorporated in the rotation in the 1980s. I saw a photo later of fields burgeoning with its acid yellow flowers. Currently the only crops left standing were maize, the Americans' corn and Africans' mealies. Some stands were more than head high, the marginal ones that I could examine bearing fat corn cobs in their nether regions. Would any of these be used for sweet corn, I wondered, or would the whole go for silage?

The complete absence of livestock dispensed with the need for fences. Instead the broad lane verges had been planted with little holm oaks in 1992. I remember seeing them peeping expectantly from their protective plastic sheaths. Now they formed neat, unbroken rows of spherical evergreens, as broad as long and at least twice as tall as me. Quickthorn whips had been planted in the backing hedges by the Duchy at the same time, closing some of the gaps. Not that this mattered now and the the old stone-walled drinking pool for livestock nearer the sea had fallen into decay.

I had plenty of time to view the terrain as I eased the car around and through the water-filled potholes at a snail pace. I learned later that the holes had been filled with ballast recently but this had washed out again because of the heavy farm vehicles using it through harvest and the ploughing and harrowing of some of the stubbles. A tiny carpark had been cleared for visitors in 1983 and a glass-plated display board installed, elucidating the history of the site. Sadly that had been vandalised by 1984 and nothing was in place now but a mossy slab inscribed with the name of the site and a more modern label pointing to the Sea Watch Centre.

I missed the unobtrusive entrance and found myself at a new house, where I was told that the carpark was still there but somewhat obscured and puddly. Also that the paths beyond were muddy and dangerously slippery after the recent rains. No matter. I found the track in through the trees and my trusty gumboots lived in the car boot, there being no room indoors for such vital equipment these days.

* * *

I started off well, spotting a peregrine falcon flying over the maize field opposite. There were several pairs of these noble raptors nesting along the cliff here by 2008. I remember the excitement among ornithologists when the first pair moved in after their practical extermination by the use of DDT chemicals on the land. That particular nest was right alongside a patch of maidenhair fern. Common enough in greenhouses, as a denizen of the Tropics, it is extremely rare in the wild in Britain and the Glamorgan Heritage

Coast is one of its special locations. The larger, female peregrines have been seen to take wood pigeons. Later on I spotted a hovering kestrel, neatly proportioned and less streamlined, also a jay at close quarters.

The little path led first to the Celtic Fort, known to have been in occupation from around 700 BC to 78 AD. The establishment protected the inmates from sea-borne invaders, who could come ashore where the cliffs dipped down to Limperts Bay at the eastern corner - and also to ward off harassment by the Romans.

This is much the most complete and complex of the multi-vallate Iron Age forts along this coast. It is the only one having four concentric earth walls - plus another thrown up on the inland flank from past excavations. As with all the others, much of the seaward side of the old encampment had been washed away over the centuries by waves undermining the cliffs, but it still covered about three acres. Also it was the only one that was still completely wooded, the full-canopy woodland lessening atmospheric erosion and the inroads of farming.

Open-floored, the ground covered with ivy, it was easier to get about in than the greasy, puddled path, with handy boughs to steady passage over the still sharply demarcated embankments. An ash wood, with sycamore, elder and thorns, there were plenty of ground-dwelling ferns and tree-dwelling lichens reaching almost to the branch tips, but little else at this time of year.

We had always regarded these shady banks as one of the best primrose sites in Glamorgan. There was no indication that they were still, although leaves can persist through the summer. The accompanying bluebells, wood Anemones and lesser celandines, which had added to the spring exuberance, were all underground at present. Arum and ground ivy remained, and I learned later that there were still cowslips, even false oxlips.

Few ways in existed, because of tangles of old-man -beard Clematis that crawled over everything else around the lighted margins, this decorated with fine trails of scarlet berries borne on equally adventurous black bryony vines. The deep shade kept bracken, grass and even brambles at bay within, where splendid hart -tongue ferns flourished.

In the 1980s this had accommodated a thriving badger sett, with scores of burrows. Badgers occurred in the other forts along the coast and in the river-cut valleys as at Monknash and Nash point, but they were subjected to molestation by badger diggers then and I have no information as to their present status. I saw no signs of current occupation.

* * *

I headed next down the little path to the eighteenth century stone summerhouse that gives this part of the coast its name. This was erected for the Seys family of Boverton Manor in 1730, to enable the gentry to come and picnic. The main structure is octagonal, surrounded by a low but massive stone curtain wall surmounted by two turrets.

Its lofty chimney stack is illustrated in the fifth book of my Heritage Coast series (colour plates nos. 64-66). I took these photos in 1976, but it was demolished soon after, being regarded as unsafe. The photos show the glory of the tall, flowering great mullein which romped along the top of the curtain wall and the ground outside to make a golden border to the backcloth of the sea view. Trees had grown up to obscure that view now and I saw only one flowering mullein spike, this in the grassy interior, which was kept open by mowing.

Lush leaf rosettes of primroses grew along the base of the curtain wall, where Alexanders sprouted new shoots after removal of the old. Rooted in the Summerhouse walls and around their base were upstanding plants of red valerian, still in full flower. The most notable species however was the wild sea cabbage - always a predominant feature along these cliffs. Its leaves are indistinguishable from those of kale and other loose-leaved cultivars, the flower spikes dead now, but having larger blooms than the other Weedy Crucifers of the coast. Ragwort, ribwort and a single foxglove pushed through the lush grass.

The central building had more than two storeys. Current ground level was half way up the lower doorway and the one I peered through opened into an upper storey with the windows blocked by stonework. An iron barbecue was set in one wall and there was a separate stone bothy within the enclosure, roofed only by wooden rafters now. Presumably this was where the servants prepared the victuals

There might have been a coachman to feed, too, because an entrance for carriages had been cut through the embankments of the old fort, this the basis of today's muddy footpath. I wondered if the potholey approach lane was any smoother then for carriages without pneumatic tyres.

The Summerhouse was famous in ornithological circles for the thriving colony of rare tree sparrows, which had set up home there in the 1970s and 80s. I remember seeing newly fledged young in 1976 and they were well established by 1985. I learned later that they were still seen hereabouts occasionally. In past summers there had been common and lesser whitethroats, pied and spotted flycatchers, grasshopper warblers and blackcaps - riches indeed by today impoverished standards.

I didn't see the green hairstreaks, large and grizzled skippers and ringlets of other years, but I counted at least twelve red admiral butterflies sipping the sweets of the ivy flowers, where the sun was striking the growth covering the inner face of the landward wall. One came and perched on my shoulder, to make sure I knew they were still about, despite the lateness of the season. With them were bees, wasps and hover flies imbibing the last of the summer wine before their impending decease - the last meal before execution.

During my several hours on this fascinating section of coast, I saw no-one, but the remains of a sizable wood fire near the stone mess hut showed that others came for modern barbecues. On the half-burnt ash boughs were some of the charcoal-like fungal balls known, very appropriately in this instance, as burnt potatoes or King Alfred cakes *(Daldinia concentrica)*.

A small cherry tree, its trunk as thick as my arm, had been planted but its trunk was broken off at chest height - apparently vandalised. Forty or so yard-long leafy sprouts radiated from the truncated stump and two attractive vases stood at its base, one full of sprays of garden ice-plants. This apparently, was a memorial to the mother of a local resident. It seemed particularly appropriate in a spot with so much history, though seeing little of today citizens.

* * *

I back-tracked from the Summerhouse, east along the coastal path, following the crumbling cliffs down to beach level in Limperts Bay. The tangle of wind-trimmed shrubs along the cliff edge had encroached gradually inland as the sea chiselled away the rocks from their roots on the other side.

A new cliff path had been cut through the woodland edge in 1975, when the former one, edging inwards ahead of the shrubs, seemed perilously near the brink. By 1991 that, also, had got too close for comfort and was fenced off, with yet another path being opened.

Anglers still cast their lines into the sea from the more stable western rampart of the fort, at high water, to pull in whiting, bass, dogfish and conger eels. It was easy to appreciate how the line of coastal forts had been reduced from full circles to semi circles over the course of more than two thousand years. They had been built to defend that land against human invaders from the sea, but the long-term enemy was the sea itself!

The 1991 path left a scrap of grassland to seaward where the shrubs had collapsed overboard. Here was a whole new mini-community, with salad burnet, rest harrow, hedge bedstraw, cinquefoil, red clover, yarrow and delicate seed-heads of hedge parsley.

The wind barrier to landward of such stretches of open path was a tangle of contorted trees supporting polypody ferns and shaggy lichens, wind-bowed hawthorns and sloes. Leaves of some of the latter were bordered with pale pimples, with more amidships, these the work of blackthorn gall mites *(Eriophyes similis)*. Dense aggregations coalesced, causing inrolling.

Huddled alongside were orange seed-heads of gladdon Iris and fluff-crowned ones of woolly thistles. The handsome, three-dimensional leaves of the latter were up to two feet long, with alternate spine-tipped lobes directed upwards. I flushed a little flock of finches from their upstanding, globose heads, and a mistle thrush and a wood pigeon from the path. One stretch bordered a little paddock with a pony shelter in a corner, and such a rich sward of grass that no pony could have been kept there for a long time.

The summit of the final incline down to the beach afforded a fine coastal panorama of the Gilestone Power Station. A great plume of white belched skywards from the imposing concrete edifice, hopefully only of steam, but still a waste of heat energy. This burgeoned into an attractive white cumulus cloud as it reacted with the cold but clear rain-washed air round about.

The low cliff petered out rather ignominiously here. Instead of neat layers of pale limestone and dark shale, elbows of shattered sandstone strata protruded from unstable slabs of rain-pitted, putty-textured clay. Viewed from the chunks already fallen, it was apparent that a competent job of summertime stabilisation had been undertaken by upstanding rosettes of buck's-horn plantain and wispy tassels of ungrazed red fescue among fragrant salad burnet. Come winter these might die back, allowing the creeping carnage to continue. Here, too, are great mounds of sea cabbage, some as big as the white-flowered domes of sea kale that used to grow at Aberthaw and still do on parts of the Anglesey coast.

Between the cessation of the cliff line and the start of the industrial sea wall lay the long strand of Limperts Bay, an amalgam of limestone platforms and jumbled boulders. This swept seawards to form Breaksea Point. On the map this lies as far south as the furthest south Rhoose Point, but this one is intertidal. At high water Rhoose justly claims this honour.

The Summerhouse Point corner of this great beach was where I had come across a little colony of flowering deadly nighshade - a plant seldom found nowadays outside rabbit warrens on England's chalk hills. So poisonous that even the rabbits won't eat it, hence its local survival, it tends to get pulled up elsewhere before some child is tempted to swallow its beguiling black berries.

`There were no such finds today. Instead, weaving among the pebbles was its relative the woody nightshade, still with its purple flowers and crimson berries. Slender-bodied black spiders scuttled among bird's-foot trefoil round about. A remnant of the Liassic strata remained visible as a two foot wide yellow shelf extending out from the base of the landward blackthorn thicket, whose intertwined branches seemed firm enough to walk on.

Beach cobbles, bleached from yellow to grey, had been thrown up onto this shelf, which I remember photographing decades before, so there might have been little change here unless the whole system was retreating landwards. Few tides reached this high. This was the basal layer of the cliffs on which I had just been walking, with nothing left to fall off, and likely to remain thus unless and until sea level changed.

Built against the foot of the cliff where my path emerged was a fragment of wall - all that was left of a post-medieval jetty, destroyed in the 1930s by a ship which got out of control. Mooring posts persisted for some years but these had gone now.

A circular stone structure looked like a World War II relic, the base of a gun, perhaps. Beyond was a ruinous twentieth century building on the site of the old Hafod Camp. This had been the Summerhouse Point Miners' Rehabilitation Centre, built in the 1930s. Resident miners had befriended Hector, an old boar from the badger sett in the banks of the Celtic camp. The bribes, of course, were food. When they left the National Coal Board sold the premises to the Christian Outreach Trust, which used it as a conference centre, but it was a sorry remnant now. Generations of mankind come and go, while the fragile land continues its long drawn out battle with the sea.

* * *

Man still has a foot in the camp, or just outside it here, in the form of the Sea Watch Centre. This was manned by the Coastguard Service until the Heritage Coast took over management in 1984, as a public amenity and educational centre. I retraced my route and continued along a new path cut in 1987, up and down over the two major embankments of the multi-vallate fort. Flights of stone steps had been installed to deal with the steep slopes. I remembered a fine show of cowslips here where the scrub had been cleared and was told later that they were here still.

In a grassy clearing fenced off from the great cornfield beyond, stood the little four-square, two-storey lookout point. I tried the door and, to my surprise, it opened. By good luck I had come during one of the few spells when the building was manned, or womanned for one of the three weekly three hour spells.

A voice came from above. "Is someone there? Come on up." Where were the stairs? Of course, I remembered. An iron ladder was fixed to the wall, as vertical as those on the side of ships that I had boarded so often from a bobbing dinghy in the course of my island researches. That was a long time ago. I felt a little unsure. Can I? Can't I? I found I could, and was greeted as I emerged through a hole in the floor of the upper deck by Louise, the officer on duty.

This was the "Bridge" affording wide views up and down Channel, with cut-outs of every kind of shipping using this busy sea lane to Avonmouth and Bristol on the window, so that passing vessels could be identified in the flesh as well as on the radar screen. We were a hundred and twenty feet above the sea, on a clear sunny day, when the duty officer could point out the many landmarks on the Somerset coast, across the gleaming waters. Binoculars inside and a telescope outside on the railed balcony aided recognition.

Louise explained how to use the computerised weather forecasting and how to listen in to the VHF radio exchanges. This post had been functional since 1992 as a coastguard reporting position linked with the coastal rescue service manned by the sixth form students at Atlantic College, a few miles along the coast at St. Donats.

I learned that dredging for sand in the Channel off Nash Bank was still proceeding, despite the worry that it was not being replaced and that beaches along the fourteen mile stretch of the Heritage Coast could be seriously depleted.

Sightings of porpoises and other sea mammals were recorded in the log, but not in the numbers inhabiting the waters of Cardigan Bay on the West Coast. Apparently a loggerhead turtle had been found at Ogmore - only a little one, ten inches long - not the wandering monster leather-backs that follow jellyfish plagues inshore on that more distant strand.

Louise also noted the birds, of the land as well as at sea. Apparently red-legged partridges were much commoner than the native grey ones. Yellowhammers and tree sparrows were still seen occasionally and peregrines were often spotted, one seen taking prey as large as a wood pigeon. The birds I was seeing through the windows today, rollicking in and out of the cliff brink bushes, were common house sparrows, unexpected so far from habitation in view of their dwindling numbers nation-wide.

Black drums, which Louise thought might contain seed for game birds, had been erected at shoulder height along the field boundary leading inland, but no birds were attending them. The sparrows were more interested in a considerable patch of cabbages occupying the nearest corner of the field, apparently a little plot of setaside. Indistinguishable from the wild sea cabbage of the cliffs and with few old flower heads, I assumed the plants to be that. They may, however, have been oil-seed rape, left over from a former crop or specially sown in this corner for the birds, as that too, although grown for its oily seeds, has fleshy, frilled lower leaves like a cabbage.

Beyond the picnic benches and tables in the grassy enclosure, a narrow wooden stile connected with the cliff path, which threaded its way between the bushed cliff brink and the denuded stubble of the great wheat or barley field. (I examined some of the scanty leavings of the thresher on the next headland. Those were the awned ears of a barley crop.)

* * *

Well past my lunchtime again, I bumped back inland over the potholes and hied me to the little beach café at Llantwit Major. This still produced its tasty lamb stews, as in former years, but I opted for something lighter and sat outside in the sun where others were drinking coffee.

A spruce, creamy-breasted meadow pipit came and perched on the rail quite close. Pipits had been as rare for me this summer as skylarks and this bird gave me more pleasure than the sight of the buzzard coursing back and forth over the broad infilled valley above commuting wood pigeons. Decades ago it would have been the other way. Buzzards are no less majestic than they were. It is just that they are now of everyday occurrence since the use of DTT had been stopped. Jackdaws and magpies have scarcely received a mention in this 2008 chronicle, simply because they are everythwere, even in places innocent of all other birds, and it would be tedious to keep mentioning a presence that is taken for granted - as sparrows and starlings used to be in older, more urban times.

Pensioners were enjoying the spell of calm weather, one couple carrying armfuls of driftwood up the rocky beach to their car. For the surfers it was a different kettle of fish. Only one was in the water, wading waist-deep with his board off the Castle Ditches Iron Age Camp on the eastern cliff, flinging himself onto embryonic waves before these petered out without taking him anywhere. The rest were standing round in disconsolate groups, most not even bothering to don their wet suits.

Some students of Atlantic College were faring better. A flotilla of canoes had taken off from the launching pad under their castle home just along the coast. These bobbed easily over the gentle waves, the services of the man in the inflatable on their seaward side unlikely to be required.

I strolled to both edges of the flat-floored infilled valley, looking at paths I had formerly used to scale the cliffs on long distance walks. Both were now partially collapsed over the brink, or too perilously near the edge to be used and were fenced off. The stack I had known had dissolved into the nagging tides long since. I climbed neither of the replacement paths today but took a short jaunt through the lush grass alongside the briskly flowing little Col Huw River. Was it just coincidence that the fine watercress beds were all on the other, inaccessible, side?

CHAPTER 48

The Onset Of Winter, Cold Front, Bewick Swans, Autumn Fungi, Howardian Dormice

It seems that those two days spent on the coast in the penultimate week of October were the last trumpet serenade of summer. - in recompense for the pathetic show of sunshine during the months when we expected more of those 'lazy, hazy days' than we were granted.

BBC weathermen warned us on 26th and 27th of October of a bitter blast of cold air sweeping down from the Arctic, bringing severe snowstorms to Scotland and the Welsh Hills, with freezing night temperatures. It arrived just after midday on Tuesday, 28th and, because this was half term and the Tuesday "Food for Thought Meeting" was having a day off, I was able to witness it.

There was no creeping stealthily up on us, like most cloud systems. It bore down on us as a black wall, through the Taff Gorge, to eat up the balmy sunshine that had been with us all morning. I had waited, coatless, in the suntrap outside our front door, for the messenger who was calling at 11.30 to pick up books.

Business achieved, I had wandered into the garden, where Pansy and I had been planting out winter-flowering heathers and pansies the previous day. A flawless, second brood, red admiral butterfly was busy on nearby ivy flowers. Strolling to the shops along the back lane, I assessed the state of the orchard apple crop and admired the lavish display of pink Schizostylis lilies in a Heol Isaf garden. Some errant purple clouds sailed into the picture as I returned, heralding in the drama of the approaching storm.

Back in my north-facing apartment, I witnessed the splendid spectacle created by the unseen sun lighting up the entire foreground with an ethereal glow. Colours were intense, the bronze of beech and bracken, yellow of birch and larch and the changing shades of the distant hills where the pale turf had been gnawed down to the bone by sheep and the sharper angles sandpapered by the wind.

And behind it was the advancing weather front, creeping up on the sun-drenched panorama and swallowing the backdrop behind the gorge. Every landscape artist must dream of reproducing such a scene of contrast, but only the camera, not the brush, can capture a scene so fleeting. The turreted walls of Castell Coch reflected the rays, as when floodlighted at night, and was over-arched by the western arc of a rainbow, broad of base and with a second ranking of the red-purple bands. How I wished for my camera.

The wall of cloud, from floor to ceiling, rolled through the gap in the hills, its flanks seeping down over the bright faces of Garth Hill and Fforest Fawr, to either side, as though a celestial blind cord had been pulled. No zephyr swayed the branches of the garden lime tree, from which the last few winged fruits were floating gently earthwards. This was the calm before the storm!

As the advancing mass, black as a roof of wet Welsh slate, closed in, there was a great flurry of wind. Branches were clashing together, dislodging a whirlwind of leaves. The squirrel hipperty-hopping on the lawn dashed into the cover of the hedge, tail waving, and five magpies went rollicking past, tails and wing primaries askew.

I was so impressed by the sudden change of mood, that I later consulted Gavin Pretor-Pinney's "Cloudspotters' Guide". The chilly air of a cold front, in collision with warmer and hence lighter air, pushes the less dense mass up over the top, the sudden upward swirl of the sun-kissed mass producing fierce, but often short-lived winds.

Then came the rain, not much and not heavy, but some of it in the frozen state. Small hailstones bounced off the balcony rail, hit the tiles and bounced again, to tinkle on the glass doors, so lately closed. The squall passed, the drizzle continued and the menacing cloud dissolved into an all-over pall of grey.

I thought of that peerless red, white and black butterfly of an hour before. Was this 'Goodbye' to summer and 'hallo' to winter? Half an hour later sun rays were sneaking round the corner of the building to light up the Agave and Photinea leaves. A questing nose followed by a bushy tail had emerged from the hedge bottom. Then a flock of fieldfares (or were they redwings) passed overhead, in from Europe on the wings of the same weather perhaps, to seek a cushier existence here.

The evening TV weather news, raked from the ether in glorious techno-color, showed pictures of much of South-east England under a blanket of snow. It was not all their side. Next morning, the slopes of Mynydd Meio, seen through the gorge, wore a blanket of white, but this melted soon after ten am. "Not since 1934 has Southern Britain been snow-covered in October." Roll on, global warming.

We saw also, pictures of citizens of Ottery-St.Mary digging paths through knee-deep accumulations of frozen sleet and slush. Cars and houses were flooded there when a local storm delivered the whole month's ration of precipitation in one go. BBC News on 13th September stated "The coldest start to winter for thirty years" and later, in February, "The coldest winter for eighteen years."

* * *

Bewick swans were late arriving on British waters this year. Because of a mild spell in the Russian Tundra where they nested, they had had no incentive to leave. They came with the Arctic blast of air, having left on the 28th October, to ride the winds, like a troupe of Valkyries. In Holland by the 29th, where some would stay to over-winter, others were moving on to Slimbridge and the Martinsmere Wildfowl Reserves by 1st and 2nd of November.

Our "Food For Thought" group had arranged a coach trip to Slimbridge Wildfowl and Wetlands Trust (and the Jenner Museum by Berkeley Castle) on Tuesday 4th November, so the wild Bewicks, which are one of the highlights of those busy waters, should be arriving by then. They were. The first had made land on the morning of Sunday the 2nd, this an old friend, a named bird, recognisable by the black and yellow pattern on its bill - these diagnostic features recorded for all members of the flock when they arrived. More followed, so we saw some of these stalwart travellers joining the few that were in residence among the mutes and trumpeters that were resident all year.

The guide who showed us round confirmed that birds don't migrate according to the calendar, but when conditions get too uncomfortable to stay put - or, in spring, when the urge to breed gets too strong. "Hector" or whatever his name was (I didn't catch it) had been here before. He knew the way and led the posse. And who could blame him when we saw the great barrows loaded with wheat grains, protein pellets and other provender being delivered to all and sundry during the main feed just before our 4.30 departure? The indignity of being grabbed to have a leg ring put on was small price to pay for such generous largesse.

A nice touch was the resident pair of Australian black swans, who had produced four white cygnets a week or so before. These were still small and fluffy, having arrived earlier than a more usual hatching time here of late November-December. When their kind had first come to Roath Lake in Cardiff, they had adhered more closely to their usual laying time "Down

Under", but had adapted to fit our seasons more closely.

* * *

Winter came in with a bang, quite literally, for the residents of South Radyr. The explosion happened just after midnight on Saturday, 1st November, when many yards of mains water pipe split assunder. One of several four foot deep holes produced was in the middle of the main thoroughfare, the others in adjacent gardens. From one resident: "It was like a bomb exploding!"

I knew nothing of this until the Tuesday morning. On boarding the coach to Slimbridge, I learned of long detours awheel or afoot, for folk coming from Llandaff. The only way in from the south was to continue on the Llantrisant Road and curve back through Creigiau, Pentyrch, Lower Gwaelod and Morganstown. In restricting the new connurbation behind church and tennis courts to a single road outlet onto that north to south highway (which had been a winding lane before the Mint was built), officialdom had eased the traffic problem when all was hunkey-dory but not in emergencies. The only alternative route to neighbouring Danescourt was along a woodland footpath.

Next day I investigated on foot, taking the path along the top of Radyr and Hermitage Woods to the start of the Danescourt housing complex and turning along a hedged footway under a line of pylons, to emerge at the junction of the Radyr and Llantrisant Roads.

A workman eased himself backwards from a manhole in which he was upended. Dusting himself down, he put me in the picture. He indicated two manholes, newly excavated from under the turf.

"Didn't know these were here. This is where we should've shut off the mains on Sunday but we couldn't find them. Had to go way over there."

He pointed across the stubble fields to the west.

"Meant that three villages got cut off that should'nt'of". He named them.

"All the valves used to be greased regularly. Easy to adjust. But not for years. Made of plastic too, 'stead of iron, like car steering wheels. Sealed solid. Try and budge 'em with a crowbar and the whole lot cracks."

The flow had been staunched, but the holes now extended right across the road along the front of the Comprehensive School, with big machines lifting the four inch thick tarmac off in great slabs when I got there. This was the week after half term. Pupils were enjoying a generous extension of that holiday while another means was found of supplying them with water.

My informant insisted that the burst was due to the thawing of the frozen subsoil around the mains conduit, but that I could not accept. Temperatures had dropped only a few degrees below freezing, providing little more than a sparkling hoar frost on the long grass and quite incapable of producing a permafrost zone. I never did find out the cause of the catastrophe.

A notice announced that the path as well as the road was closed when I got to the main scene of action, but I was allowed through. Holes were being excavated in the road, a line of skips being filled with subsoil and channels being cut for branch pipes down nearby garage drives.

The disruption lasted all week, but the breach was finally resealed the following Monday, after eight days. This was just in time for me to drive to my evening meeting of the Cardiff Naturalists' Society - in a torrential downpour - in lieu of my usual Monday evening commitment making up a foursome for scrabble with Frank, Mary and Margaret at Brynteg.

The Sunday morning Armistice Parade on 9th November (90 years after the first Armistice day) was necessarily curtailed. During the next upheaval - gas mains this time - we were told that a single traffic lane would be left open, as it had been on the last long upheaval during early summer. Why could the various corporate bodies with big trenching "toys" not cooperate and use the same holes?

*　*　*

I enjoyed two sojourns on the other side of the Taff from Radyr during that last week of October, the first after a night-long deluge. Heading downstream I made a circuit of the three sports fields between Forest Farm and Velindre. The big cricket field, its boundary marked with a low fence of white palings, was bounded on two sides by a dense border of Himalayan balsam. There was scarcely a flower left open, though these had been attracting bees in plenty until now.

Not all the hygroscopically pressurised seed capsules had reached maturity, though many exploded at the lightest touch, as they are designed to do. It seemed that the entire population had been cut off by a colder snap than they could tolerate. Flowers surviving were blue alkanet, the deep purple of the tallest of the toadflaxes and a few cresses and Composites. Warmth had returned and a few comma butterflies, as well as red admirals were sun-basking alongside busy long-tailed tits.

New fungal brackets were sprouting from the Forest Farm logs and there were others. A dozen or so eight-inch-high common inkcaps (*Coprinus atramentarius*) had sprouted in the lee of one, the upstanding conical caps beginning to deliquesce into the fluid for which they are named. Smaller but more numerous were the clusters of fairies' bonnets (*Coprinus disseminatus*) on the giant log where the canal emerges from under the motorway.

The other two were smaller but more distinct, both related to the commoner candle-snuff fungus of stumps and sticks. One was dead mens' fingers (*Xylaria polymorpha*), firmly solid replicas of a man's thumb, black on the outside but smoothly white within. The other was beechmast candle snuff (*Xylaria carpophila*), as tall as the other but wispily narrow and wavy, the lower third black, the rest white.

Most decorative was the big colony of pale oysters (*Pleurotus pulmonarius*) on logs by the landward riverside path. Smaller than the better known oyster-of-the-woods, the shell-shaped brackets with radiating gills were three to four inches across and a pearly cream colour deepening to fawn. They are edible, like their 'big brother' and hundreds of smaller flanges were bursting from side grain and end grain to replenish supplies, should anyone choose to harvest them.

More exciting was a fine view of a water rail below the canal towpath near Forest Lock. As always when in open terrain, this rarely seen little bird was scuttling from cover to cover as fast as its long legs could carry it. Visits to the weir produced no more sightings of jumping salmon. Rain storms in the Brecon Beacons changed the force of water on a daily basis and it was a matter of luck whether I coincided with periods when it was just right for the ascending breeders to be tackling this hazard.

The black-headed gulls being bowled down the river, tail first, were more safety conscious during these spates, taking off well above the weir to fly back upstream. The local heron's favoured lookout station was a cauldron of seething water. The one I spotted took off from a leaning branch, unfurling vast wings from the folded umbrella of its body. A buzzard spread galleon sails to lift itself over the Gelynis Iron Bridge, followed by a low-flying cormorant, shooting underneath, straight as an arrow and black as a witch.

And what of that hopefully twining miniature morning glory (*Ipomoea tricolor*) that had embarked on its tortuous course in early August? It had soon reached the level of my balcony rail. More infrastructure was needed. I visited the lady in the apartment above to ask if I could drop a lifeline from her property to mine. She acquiesced.

Several awkward joints between the two supports were negotiated by the game little creeper with two to three-inch-long loose twists. Once it had reached the length of smooth new rope, the coils tightened to one per inch and continued thus to a height of just seven feet. It finally gave up in mid October. The leaves that fueled it withered and the three flower buds produced remained tightly coiled, but the stem held firm. Released and the flowering lengths brought inside, the warmth failed to stimulate opening, the blue petals remaining tightly twisted. It was a good try after so belated a start.

* * *

My final sortie in October was to the Howardian Nature Reserve in East Cardiff on the 29th, after a lengthy session scraping congealed ice from the car windows. Full circle back to those days of February. The waxing sun gave promise of better things, but soon defaulted in favour of a raw, grey morning. I circled the reserve anti-clockwise from the south-east, following alongside reeds a deal taller than myself, these sending exploratory underground stems out through the grassy path to push up lines of new culms.

Pools and puddles coated with a thin layer of ice were not too difficult to avoid. Rising air became trapped beneath their shimmering surface, as blobs of white. The waning rays of sunshine sparkled from the rime of frost on bordering herbs, and brought out the best from the belt of trees planted many years back, when the Docks Link Road alongside was pushed through from the motorway.

Most elusive were the colours of the field maples, predominantly yellow but fading back from green and on to red. A poor imitation, perhaps, of those Japanese maples in Roath Gardens, but of infinitely more value as natives, widespread throughout copses and hedgerows in the Vale and suburbs.

Dogwood leaves were a deep crimson, as were those of guelder rose. Both bore berries, like the spindle, whose leaves were not to be outdone by the orange and pink of their unique fructifications. I was surprised to see so many stalked red fruits dangling from the branches of wild cherry or gean. These are supposed to appear in June so this must have been 'a second bite at the cherry?'

Another surprise was the seasonal colour change shown by the five inch long needles of the Monterey pine - which are borne in threes instead of the usual pairs. Leaf-fall occurs in all evergreens, but usually a few at a time so that there is no bare phase. Here it was synchronised, but delayed for a full season in a two year cycle.

The branched apical twigs produced in 2008 were clad in normal, dark green leaves. Branches behind, produced in 2007, were enwrapped in bright yellow needles, ready to be shed. The next back, formed in 2006 or earlier, were leafless. Little light penetrated the thick external canopy, so any leaves inside would have been starved of nutrients and non-functional. This concentrated leaf-fall was not seen in the scots or pitch pines.

There were other fruits to supply the birds, though most of the berries had gone from the monster brambles - so large that they must have been Himalayan giants. Hips, haws and sloes would provide sustenance in the hungry months to come, as would the little green crabapples. Many of those were still on the trees. Others, fallen to the ground, had been sampled by various means, some ragged from gnawing by small incisors, others pitted with the triangular marks of stabbing beaks.

All these, ripe unto harvest, have their poignant aspect. What is ripe must fall or be gathered and disappear. In the past we helped with our crab-apple jelly, blackberry pies and (in the war) rose hip syrup, and may yet do so again in the current credit crunch.

The annual mowing of the central sedge field, with its Irises, orchids and loosestrife, inevitably reduces the amount of seed available to canopy feeders as winter fodder, but much had been left marginally - teasels, knapweed, docks, umbellifers and vetches. Late-flowering Michaelmas daisies, golden rod and Spanish broom spoke of more to come - if there were enough pollinating insects around for them to set seeds. While birds may prefer to collect their provender in situ, a percentage must fall to supply the mice and voles. Rabbits have had no problems in this year of maxi grass growth, and grey squirrels are much too canny to go hungry.

White mould on the oak leaves had not affected the acorn crop, but I saw no chestnuts and the hazel nuts had been eaten or collected and stored long since, leaving only split or nibbled shells. Little catkins had already formed on hazel, birch and alder in preparation for the 2009 crop. Alder cones continued to hang aloft to tempt in siskins, linnets and tits.

Of predators higher up the food chain, both fox and hedgehog had been spotted by the man walking his two spaniels - the only other person abroad in the reserve on this chilly morn. There were plenty of molehills, so worms were at risk. Kestrels would no doubt move in from the motorways sometimes to join the resident sparrow hawks.

Birds seen on this occasion were mostly in passing migrant flocks. One was of winter thrushes, fieldfares or redwings (our native thrushes do not flock) and several others were of finches, with their characteristic looping flight. There were unusually many blackbirds about, all of them cocks, and in little groups that would not be tolerated in summer when most would be territory-holders. These must have been incomers from the continent, seeking an easier living on our little island. For more than a week the jackdaws had been gathering in great flocks which sometimes split into two, each half of forty to fifty birds, and then drift together again to ride the winds in untidy confusion.

All was quiet around the willow-girt pond with its marginal kingcups and brooklime, the lone carp thought to have consumed most of what it once contained. Formerly mallard and moorhens nested here and kingfishers came for sticklebacks, while the air buzzed with dragonflies. Bulrushes, spike-rushes and others seemed to have almost swallowed up the lesser pond in the open.

The tumbling stream, which had cut its mini-gorge into one of Cardiff's few exposures of soft yellow Silurian Wenlock stone, our oldest rock, was in gentle mood today. It is subject to flash floods and in 1992 I had watched it grow from a trickle to a torrent in a matter of minutes during a sudden rain storm sweeping down from a non-absorbtive surface in the urban landscape above.

Trees planted in 1973 by Martin Doe and colleagues were fast catching up with those in the ancient woodland alongside and coming to support their burden of epiphytes. One of the smallest and most attractive , on a birch trunk, was a dark red colony of the little liverwort, *Frullania dilatata*, with tiny, pitcher-shaped underleaves. It is easier to plant trees than to create a woodland, but some of the lesser woodland components were creeping in, including a few late flowers of red campion. Newcomers, I learned later, were rare white lesser butterfly orchids and not-so-rare twayblade orchids.

A puzzle, throughout my circuit alongside impenetrable thickets were small oblong boxes, of dimensions suitable for storing thirty five millimetre colour slides, these fixed in tree branches at head height. Their open ends faced inwards, each furnished with a mouse-sized entry platform

Obviously traps or feeders for small mammals, I had seen nothing like them before but, set so high, they must be a means of discovering if dormice were present. Abroad only at night, these winsome little mammals are difficult to track down, although their presence was suspected by the way some of the discarded hazel nut shells were scarred, more neatly than by mice or voles. Those others leave untidier patterns of tooth marks around the hole through which the nut is extracted.

Baited traps had been put in place by conservation agents (Michael Woods Associates) for the County Council and a team was coming a few days hence to check them. Installed in June, they had been examined monthly, in an attempt to gather dormouse hairs, to verify their presence. The boxes were open-ended, the sliding inner floor projecting as the entry platform turned up at the further end to make a cosy niche. A push on the platform and that is exposed, to reveal any signs of curious visitors.

Finds this time were better than that. Twelve nests had been built in the hundred and twenty ready-made hide-outs and one contained a sleeping dormouse. This was in a characteristic nest of neatly woven strips, some torn from honeysuckle bark. More dishevelled nests of jumbled leaves and debris, along with winter stores of nuts, berries and seeds, were attributed to wood mice, these known to be in residence. The mice were in need of winter sustenance, as they did not indulge in the long hibernation opted for by their lesser, more arboreal neighbours. Dormouse presence had also been proved in other sites round about by similar live-trapping surveys.

In the early 1970s, just forty years earlier, the main part of the Howardian Nature Reserve had consisted of a newly covered landfill site on part of the lower Rhymney River flood plain. Dormice are believed to shun open ground and to need an overhead tree canopy to cross even small roads. The reserve is almost entirely encircled by broad trunk roads and industrial yards, so they must have been living, undetected, in the three marginal plots of mature woodland that were incorporated. They have had no trouble in radiating out through the newly created habitat - on which over twenty five thousand trees have been planted.

Their presence is a vindication of the audacity of those pioneering environmentalists who believed that such unpromising territory could be made eventually into a valuable wildlife sanctuary. Hopefully the new area of woodland and scrub is sufficiently large to sustain a viable breeding population of these little-known elfin creatures, to which most of us were introduced as the sleeping partner at "Alice in Wonderland's" tea party.

In the reserve's early years colonising rabbits sometimes ejected remarkable objects from their burrows, but few visitors could now detect, or imagine, what lies beneath the colour symphony of the wildflower meadow where members of "The Friends of Howardian" converge each summer to make hay. This is one of many success stories of site recovery where man and nature have worked together in the restoration process.

* * *

Now, at the onset of winter, I propose to emulate the dormice by lying low for the next few months, but, unlike them, I shall sally forth when sunshine tempts me out. The nine month 'digging in' period in my new retreat has been accomplished. That move, seemingly so disruptive at its onset, was right for me. I have made new friends and found new wild corners where formerly exploited plots have metamorphosed into pleasing green diversity.

The young will still stride across our wind-shorn, sheep-denuded Welsh Mountains and enjoy splendid views, but are likely to see fewer of the small wild things that can afford pleasure to those who linger more often to stand and stare.

There is time in retirement to disentangle ourselves from the stresses of this manic, man-made world and savour matters that we had little time for when on the everyday treadmill. Those "primroses by the river's brim", "the lark ascending" and the wonder of mature trees are still there for those with eyes to see. Perhaps the foregoing view of unremarkable wanderings will encourage other 'oldies' to stroll forth and enjoy what the countryside has to offer while there is still the time, the ability and the will.

* * *

A further exploit for me, necessarily booked months before, was to the Isles of Scilly, during the stormy, wind-tossed end of April in 2009. Thankfully the sun burst through on four days to illuminate the ethereal land and seascapes.

This was by no means my first visit to these alluring isles where stone walls are ablaze with the flowers of succulents and stonechats play hide-and-seek with wheatears among great granite boulders., but the magic had not diminished.

Great waves still swooshed onto the headlands in Bryher's Hell Bay; whimbrel flocked across the sodden heather moor of Wingletang Down on St. Agnes and the blaze of gorse trailing down from St. Martin's red and white sea mark was as aromatic as ever. Another generation of a hundred shags was silhouetted against the cloudless blue vault over Annet, 'London' sparrows were now expert at exploiting the exotic flowers in Tresco's enchanted garden, a cuckoo called through the rain at Old Town bay on St. Marys and inquisitive seals and puffins hovered around our boat off the Eastern Rocks.

Was this my last venture into another world? Hopefully not. While the spirit is willing and the limbs sound there is always something to look forward to in the landscapes that mankind has treated so thoughtlessly over the millennia.

List of illustrations

Chapter 1:   Early Mauve Crocus
Chapter 2:   Long-tailed Tits
Chapter 3:   Buzzards
Chapter 4:   BankVoles
Chapter 5   Tree Creepers
Chapter 6   Mallard
Chapter 7   Wood Anemone
Chapter 8   Daffodil
Chapter 9   Sea Radish
Chapter 10   Goosanders
Chapter 11   Song Thrush
Chapter 12   Skylarks
Chapter 13   Fox
Chapter 14   Rabbits and House Martins
Chapter 15   Moorhen
Chapter 16   Wild Arum and Toothwort
Chapter 17   Dippers
Chapter 18   Great Spotted Woodpeckers
Chapter 19   Scurvy-grass and Sea Purslane
Chapter 20   Spotted Flycatchers
Chapter 21   Damsel and Dragonflies and Water Crowfoot
Chapter 22   Jays
Chapter 23   Foxglove and Broad Helleborine
Chapter 24   Rosebay and Evening Primrose
Chapter 25   Reed Warbler and Flowering Rush
Chapter 26   Mexican Fleabane and Mulberry
Chapter 27   Bats, Wood Sorrel and Violet
Chapter 28   Herons, Branched Bur-reed and Crack Willow
Chapter 29   Lousewort, Bog Pimpernel and Ivy-leaved Bellflower
Chapter 30   Sunbathing Blackbird
Chapter 31   Little Egret and Sea Heath
Chapter 32   Goatsbeard, Millet and Field Pansy
Chapter 33   Kingfishers and Grey Wagtail
Chapter 34   Cormorants

Chapter 35 *Scaly Earthballs*
Chapter 36 *Cut-leaved Beech and Tulip Tree*
Chapter 37 *Lizard, Autumn Squill and White Rock-rose*
Chapter 38 *Conkers opened by Grey Squirrels and Gallingale*
Chapter 39 *Pine Cones*
Chapter 40 *Tawny Owl*
Chapter 41 *Choughs*
Chapter 42 *Toad, Sweet Chestnut, Stump Puffball and Sulphur Tuft*
Chapter 43 *Oyster-Catchers and Dune Pansies*
Chapter 44 *Grey Squirrel and Lime Fruits*
Chapter 45 *Salmon*
Chapter 46 *Dyer's Greenweed, Tutsan, Pale Flax and Frog*
Chapter 47 *Peregrine Falcon, Wood Pigeon and Black Bryony*
Chapter 48 *Hazel Dormice, Guelder Rose and Spindle*